Contemporary Policy Analysis

Contemporary Policy Analysis

MICHAEL MINTROM
University of Auckland

New York   Oxford
OXFORD UNIVERSITY PRESS

Oxford University Press, Inc., publishes works that further Oxford University's
objective of excellence in research, scholarship, and education.

Oxford   New York
Auckland   Cape Town   Dar es Salaam   Hong Kong   Karachi
Kuala Lumpur   Madrid   Melbourne   Mexico City   Nairobi
New Delhi   Shanghai   Taipei   Toronto

With offices in
Argentina   Austria   Brazil   Chile   Czech Republic   France   Greece
Guatemala   Hungary   Italy   Japan   Poland   Portugal   Singapore
South Korea   Switzerland   Thailand   Turkey   Ukraine   Vietnam

For titles covered by Section 112 of the US Higher Education Opportunity
Act, please visit www.oup.com/us/he for the latest information about
pricing and alternate formats.

Published by Oxford University Press, Inc.
198 Madison Avenue, New York, New York 10016
http://www.oup.com

Library of Congress Cataloging-in-Publication Data
Mintrom, Michael, 1963–
Contemporary policy analysis / Michael Mintrom.
  p. cm.
Includes bibliographical references and index.
ISBN 978-0-19-973096-4
1. Policy sciences. 2. Political planning. I. Title.
JF1525.P6M68 2012
320.6—dc22 2011010639

With unending love to my sons,
Seamus and Hugo—
brilliant, gorgeous, talented, fabulous

BRIEF CONTENTS

CONTENTS

ix

PREFACE

There is another world, and it is this one.

—PAUL ÉLUARD

Human history contains much that is messy, bloody, and mysterious. Yet it also tells an astonishing story of imagination, ingenuity, and innovation. Through the centuries, societies have developed ways of living and working that have allowed for continual renegotiation of human relations with the physical world. Rarely do people strike on excellent solutions to problems individually and without struggle. It is when people engage in collective efforts and find productive ways to build on the previous efforts of others that great things happen. Stable systems of government have played increasingly important roles in allowing this progress to occur. They will continue to do so. As human knowledge expands and technologies evolve, the roles governments are required to play in society also change. The challenges for governments, and hence for policy analysts, are forever shifting. For instance, new frontiers of scientific discovery soon reveal new economic opportunities, and the resulting activities highlight information problems, property rights issues, and ethical dilemmas. Citizens and businesses look to governments to address these matters. Government decision makers look to policy analysts to clarify the nature of new problems, analyze alternative courses of action, and recommend effective policy solutions.

For many years, I have been fascinated by government and eager to study governmental processes. This fascination has stemmed not so much from an interest in systems of power and control, as from an interest in how governments can create opportunities for people to channel their creativity in a myriad of meaningful ways. That is my starting place for caring deeply about policy analysis. It is why I view policy analysis as an activity with huge potential to have positive, transformative effects. Through their efforts to generate sound analysis and advice, policy analysts can improve the lives of those around them. As a collective project, policy analysis can contribute to human progress.

To say "there is another world, and it is this one" is to acknowledge our transformative power. It also suggests the importance of perceptual shifts as precursors to leading change. Policy analysis as a discipline is based on a simple imperative: Think first; then act. Impulsive actions that take too much for granted can lead us in very unhelpful directions, both at the individual level and the collective level. The ability to break impulsive action is vital for individual development and for the collective development of societies and humanity. How do we catch a glimpse of the possibilities for improvement? When we quiet things down, when we take the time to think deeply, and when we create spaces for respectful conversations, that is when we can see new possibilities—many of which will have been lying here among us all along.

This book is written for people who want to change the world, people prepared to wrestle for a better future. Sure, our shared existence comes with its quota of difficulties, drudgery, and broken dreams. Many efforts to see a better future will take decades. As in the past, we should expect that the lengthy toils of many dedicated people will not produce their largest harvests until long after those people have passed on. Meanwhile, there is work to do. A great sense of accomplishment can come from working with others for better outcomes, even if the outcomes we attain today are no match for our ambitions. As Max Ehrmann once noted, it is still a beautiful world. We can enjoy it—indeed, we must take joy in it—even as we acknowledge those things that trouble and challenge us.

I wish to make several points about the structure of this book and the specific audiences for whom it is intended. The book highlights project work and the development of creative ways to engage with the intended audiences of the project reports. That is because I strongly believe that we learn best through working on projects that force us to confront the limitations of our current capabilities and extend them. The project orientation has led me to structure the book in a fashion that is quite distinctive from previous books on policy analysis. I also appreciate that the structure can appear disconcerting to people who have acquired their training through engagement with those previous texts. The book has two main sections, an overview of policy analysis (six chapters) followed by a set of analytical strategies (eight chapters preceded by a briefer introductory chapter).

The opening three chapters of the overview section consider what policy analysts do, what governments do, and why governments engage in specific actions. Such chapters would be expected to open any book on policy analysis. However, the placement of the three chapters that immediately follow them may seem premature. These chapters cover the management of policy projects, the presentation of policy advice, and doing ethical policy analysis. What is unusual is that all of this material is presented before any of the analytical strategies. When we know where we are going, the more difficult parts of a journey seem easier to negotiate. With a sound overview of policy analysis and guidance on how to organize their work, readers of this text will understand the point of the analytical strategies that come next. To do otherwise would be to suggest that policy analysis is essentially an exercise in application of techniques. It is much more, and the overview chapters clarify that up front.

The analytical strategies section introduces a set of common approaches to analyzing public policy problems and assessing feasible solutions. Most policy projects that contain policy analysis do not incorporate the use of every potential analytical strategy. The analytical strategies chapters all follow a common format and contain an applied example. When conducting policy projects, I expect that readers using this book will make intensive use of approaches suggested in just two or three of these chapters. But it is vital for policy analysts to understand what analytical strategies they could use and to appreciate the circumstances where some strategies are more useful than others.

This book is designed to work as the primary required reading for policy analysis courses where students have had no previous exposure to the topic. I teach both an upper division undergraduate course on policy analysis and a first-year graduate level course on policy analysis. I have designed the book to work effectively in both courses. For the undergraduate course, I assume that students will do little other reading, except as it relates directly to the policy projects that they will produce in the course. For the graduate-level course, I expect students to read this book as the core required reading and to augment their reading of each chapter with some of the suggested additional readings.

The book can also serve as the core reading in an advanced graduate-level course. The expectation here is that students in such a course would have attained familiarity with research design and quantitative methods. With that background, students could be encouraged to carefully read the original articles referred to in the applied examples and discuss them at length in our group meetings. This would create conditions under which students could discuss designs for the production of master's degree thesis work or doctoral dissertation work incorporating original research inspired by the best contemporary applications of quantitative and qualitative research methods.

I further expect this book to be of considerable use to practitioners who need a good grounding in policy analysis, but who have not taken university courses in the topic.

My understanding of how to conduct policy analysis and engage in policy development has been strongly informed by the work of many scholars, too numerous to name individually. But I do wish to express my deep gratitude to writers of earlier books on policy analysis. Those authors include Eugene Bardach, Kenneth Bickers, Michael Munger, Edith Stokey, Aidan Vining, David Weimer, Aaron Wildavsky, John Williams, and Richard Zeckhauser. Their ideas have deeply influenced my own thinking. For the encouragement they have given me at different times in my career, I also wish to thank Michael Howlett, Jack Knott, Elinor Ostrom, Barry Rabe, Timothy Sinclair, Paul Teske, and John Witte. The material in this book has been developed through my years of teaching policy analysis, both inside and outside of the academy. During those years, I have had the privilege of meeting and mentoring many highly dedicated people. A lot of them have produced excellent policy reports in the context of their university studies and gone on to have incredible careers inside and outside government. Others I met when they were already in professional settings and deeply involved in transformational efforts. I am grateful to many course participants (undergraduate, graduate, and professional alike) whose questions and comments led me to think hard about the material I was presenting, and how to make it more accessible and coherent.

I am especially indebted to Jacqui True, my wife and colleague. Jacqui has encouraged me at every stage in the development of this book. Our conversations and disagreements often force me to think again about matters I thought settled. I also wish to offer special thanks to Claire Williams, who provided excellent research assistance through much of the writing process. Thanks are also due to Jennifer Carpenter, my editor at Oxford University Press. Jennifer showed great enthusiasm for the project from the outset and even greater patience as the book came to fruition. I wish to thank the group of reviewers who provided excellent suggestions for improvement at several stages: when I first floated the idea for the book, when we were moving to contract development, and when the first full draft was completed. I could not have hoped for a more committed, helpful and encouraging set of readers: Dana Lee Baker, Washington State University; Deborah Brock, Virginia Commonwealth University; Brian Collins, University of North Texas; Michael Collins, University of Memphis; Megan Mullin, Temple University; Liliokanaio Peaslee, James Madison University; Derek Reiners, University of Florida; David Rochefort, Northeastern University; Daniel Scheller, Florida State University; Bill Tankersley, University of West Florida; Robert Wassmer, California State University, Sacramento. Of course, I accept full responsibility for any unchecked mistakes or omissions.

In January 2010, when the final structure of the book was established and all the chapters were near completion, I had the good fortune to spend three days presenting the content to participants in a seminar I conducted at the Fairview Hotel in Nairobi, Kenya. I am indebted to Eric Momanyi, the program director at Policy House, for setting up that event. We engaged with the material in the book in exactly the order it is presented here. It was a very special moment in my life and my career—a chance to premier this work as a live performance and to contribute to an important capacity-building effort.

I hope others gain as much from reading this book as I have gained through writing it. Robert E. Quinn has observed that the world creates us and we create the world. Policy analysts are uniquely placed to work with others to make the world a better place for more of its people. My wish is that this book will be a powerful resource for those pursuing that goal. I welcome feedback on its content and suggestions for making improvements. An associated website contains a range of resources intended to be of use to readers, be they students, professors, or policy practitioners.

Michael Mintrom
Auckland, New Zealand

1

⚮

Introduction

The Story Begins... Contemporary policy analysis makes use of a range of analytical strategies that have been developed over time. People training to be policy analysts can benefit from having a sense of the emergence of policy analysis as a practice and as an academic discipline. This chapter introduces key steps involved in producing policy analysis, it reviews the rise of policy analysis, and it previews the book's structure.

THIS CHAPTER REVIEWS
- The point of policy analysis
- Key aspects of policy analysis
- The rise of policy analysis
- The purpose and organization of this book

What makes life good? One response is the possibilities life offers, how—through our interactions with others—we can accomplish many things. The results of our collective actions often appear miraculous. Humans are always doing things, making new things happen. We act as individuals, families, organizations, communities, and governments. Often, a lot of what we do seems spontaneous. Indeed, sometimes our actions are spontaneous, or driven by instinct. But humans are also very good at breaking their instinctual responses. A lot of deliberate control and ordered thinking informs our actions. Usually, we think first, then act. The importance of thinking before acting is acute when what we do has implications for the quality of our lives and the lives of those around us.

Public policies are the choices that governments make on behalf of citizens living in their jurisdictions. These choices are codified in the rules, plans, principles, and strategies that guide government actions. As individuals, we can and do make policies for ourselves. These are personal commitments we make to act in specific ways when particular sets of conditions arise. Given a moment to reflect, we can probably think of quite a few policies or rules that we have adopted and that guide us in our daily lives. Consider the Golden Rule: "Treat others as you would like to be treated." We follow such rules—we make them our policy—in the belief that, by doing so, we will enhance the quality of our lives and, hopefully, the lives of those around us. Governments adopt public policies for the same reasons. That is, they are intended to promote control and order, to help structure our environment in ways that lead to overall improvements in the quality of the lives of citizens. The control and order rendered by public policies create stable, structured contexts in which we engage in a vast range of activities. At their best, public policies enrich our lives and open up many possibilities for positive, productive interactions.

This book offers an introduction to policy analysis. Viewed broadly, policy analysis consists of all efforts to examine the actions or proposed actions of governments, determine the impacts of those actions, and weigh the merits of those actions against alternatives. Early representations tended to cast policy analysis as a subset of policy advising (Lindblom 1968; Wildavsky 1979). As such, policy analysis was seen primarily as an activity conducted inside government agencies with the purpose of informing the choices of a few key people, principally elected decision makers. Today, the potential purposes of policy analysis are understood to be more diverse (Radin 2000). Many audiences beyond actual decision makers are seen as holding interests in policy and as being open to—indeed demanding of—appropriately presented analytical work.

Beyond people in government, people in business, members of nonprofit organizations, and informed citizens all constitute audiences for policy analysis. While policy analysts were once thought to be mainly located within government agencies, today policy analysts also can be found in most organizations that have direct dealings with governments, and in many organizations where government actions significantly influence the operating environment. In addition, many university-based researchers, who tend to treat their peers and their students as their primary audience, conduct studies that ask questions about government policies and then answer them using forms of policy analysis. Given this, an appropriately encompassing definition of contemporary policy analysis needs to recognize the range of topics and issue areas policy analysts work on, the range of analytical and research strategies they employ, and the range of audiences they seek to address.

THE NATURE OF POLICY ANALYSIS

Policy analysis can be conducted for a variety of purposes and can make use of a range of analytical techniques. Throughout this book, I tend to treat policy analysis as an enterprise primarily motivated by the desire to generate high-quality

1. Engage in problem definition.

2. Propose alternative responses to the problem.

3. Choose criteria for evaluating each alternative policy response.

4. Project the outcomes of pursuing each policy alternative.

5. Identify and analyze trade-offs among alternatives.

6. Report findings and make an argument for the most appropriate response.

Figure 1.1 Key Steps in Policy Analysis

information to support high-quality decisions on the part of policy makers. That said, I am aware that not all policy analysis is motivated by such utilitarian goals. But underlying the diversity of policy analysis as a practice, a basic structure can be deduced that guides the work of all who do it. For the purpose of explanation, rather than as a prescription for action, I here portray this basic structure of policy analysis as having six key steps.[1] These steps are summarized in Figure 1.1.

First comes *problem definition*. Policy analysis starts with actual, existing problems. Usually, discussion of those problems has advanced to a point where those who care about them have started to raise the possibility of government action being taken to address them. Importantly, many problems we face in society do not immediately present themselves as problems for government to sort out. So an important part of early discussions of problems involves interpreting the context and defining the nature of the problem (Eyestone 1978; Rochefort and Cobb 1994; Stone 2002). In general, we can expect to find different groups of stakeholders characterizing and talking about problems in distinctive ways. A crucial role for people engaging in policy analysis involves carefully documenting the nature of the problem at hand and relevant contextual factors. The approach taken in this initial work will usually have ongoing implications for how the problem is discussed and the kinds of policy solutions that might be explored as ways to effectively address it.

The second step in policy analysis involves *proposing responses* to the problem. Knowledge matters greatly in determining the set of possible responses that may be proposed. For example, if people know of particular government actions that have worked well in addressing problems of this kind elsewhere, then they are likely to mention them. The more knowledge that can be brought to these early discussions of approaches to dealing with problems, the greater the likelihood that a sound solution will be found.

Two additional points are worth making here. First, it is not always the case that government actions are necessary or desirable. Sometimes knowledge of how to solve a problem may be insufficient, or a problem might be viewed as

---

[1]Stokey and Zeckhauser (1978) proposed five steps; Bardach (2008) proposed eight steps, but both approaches are similar.

too insignificant to warrant public action, or the view might be taken that the problem could be rectified without government action. It is common to hear people mention that the decision to adopt no policy is a form of public policy. This is the "no-policy" policy. Indeed, there might be times when some form of voluntary solution to a problem makes sense (Friedman 1962; Ostrom 1990). There are also many instances where professional associations take actions to structure and regulate the actions of their members (Gunningham and Rees 1997). These can be quite effective. Sometimes the prospect that professionals will have to relinquish some of their freedoms to the government if self-regulation is not upheld represents a sufficient threat to ensure that professional associations work hard to uphold good, ethical business practice among their members. Second, several public policy scholars have noted that problems and solutions come intertwined (Kingdon 1984; Wildavsky 1979). The claim here is that we often are not really aware that a problem is a problem until we see a possible solution. It is quite reasonable to anticipate that policy solutions chase policy problems. This is a useful point to bear in mind for several reasons, perhaps the most important being that it leads us to challenge the notion that the key steps in policy analysis being laid out here are necessarily applied in a logical sequence. Policy analysis is often messy; discussions circle around, and conflicts arise among people with different points of view (Sabatier 1993). But the good news is that—even so—policy analysis can do a lot to help decision makers and others increase their understanding of problems and issues and effective ways to address them.

The third step in policy analysis involves *choosing criteria* for evaluating alternative proposals for policy responses to the problem at hand. There are no hard-and-fast rules concerning what criteria should be invoked. Usually, the most salient criteria will emerge out of discussions concerning the problem, how it has arisen, and what should be done about it (Forester 1999; Schön and Rein 1994). However, policy analysts can do a lot to help people think carefully about the criteria that would make most sense to use to evaluate policy responses. That is why it is good for policy analysts to have a comprehensive knowledge of common objectives of government and more specific goals that relate to each of them. Chapter 4 of this book contains a discussion of objectives of government and how to develop criteria for evaluating alternative policy proposals.

The fourth step in policy analysis involves *projecting or estimating the outcomes* of pursuing each of the policy alternatives that have been put forward as possible solutions to the problem. Suppose, as we usually do, that we care about the costs associated with adopting particular policy options. Then as part of this fourth step, we would do cost estimates for each of the policy alternatives being given serious consideration. These cost estimates would need to take into account both the costs of putting the policy response in place and the ongoing costs of the relevant government actions. These cost estimates could be offset by estimates of the savings to society that would be associated with effective solution of the problem. If we care about how fairly different groups of people are treated under different policy options, then we might make that a criterion too. We would then have to develop a means of assessing the comparative fairness of different policy approaches. The work associated with projecting or estimating the outcomes of particular policy approaches can require a lot of effort to gather appropriate evidence and analyze it. Many approaches that can be used to do this are reviewed in this book.

The fifth step in policy analysis concerns *identifying and discussing trade-offs* among the policy alternatives that have been considered as solutions to the problem. Each policy alternative will have its unique strengths and weaknesses. It is quite possible that one policy will look like the best in terms of one criterion but not stack up so well when evaluated against other criteria. With all the information in front of us concerning the estimated or projected performance of each policy alternative, we can discuss the pros and cons of each. Most importantly, we can make explicit what comparative strengths we would gain and weaknesses we would have to live with if we chose one policy option over others. Work of this kind can greatly advance discussions of alternative policy solutions to particular problems. Often, decision makers will be prompted by a discussion of trade-offs to ask "what if" questions about the development of policy options that blend characteristics of current options. This can mean that policy analysts are required to do more work in terms of policy design and the projection of outcomes. But if this leads to improved policy design and better social outcomes then the effort is worthwhile. As we proceed through this book, advice will be given on how to present analytical results so that they are as useful as possible to your audience.

The sixth step in policy analysis involves *making arguments* concerning the most appropriate response to the problem, given the evidence that has been gathered and the analysis that has been undertaken. This is the point where policy analysts change their hats and become policy advisors. Of course, the better able you are to anticipate the needs of those that you are advising, then the more likely you will be to inform all steps of your policy analysis with insights into audience needs (Mintrom 2003). This is important to bear in mind. There is no point in engaging in highly sophisticated comparative assessments of policy options when two or three of those options are deemed unacceptable to decision makers from the outset. Then again, if you are conducting policy analysis in a more academic setting, you might seek to deliberately pay close attention to policy options that have not been given attention in policy-making debates, simply because you think that what you have to say matters. As we will see shortly, efforts like this on the part of people who cared deeply about the gendered impacts of policies or the effects of policies on the environment have led to the development of distinctive methods for policy analysis.

THE RISE OF POLICY ANALYSIS

Since the mid-1960s, an increasingly large number of people have come to devote their professional lives to producing policy analysis. This global phenomenon has served to transform the advice-giving systems of governments, and it has challenged informal yet long-established advising practices through which power and influence flow. Demand for policy analysis has been driven mostly by the emergence of problems and by political conditions that have made those problems salient. It is worth noting here that people who do policy analysis are not always given the title of "policy analyst." Possible titles include "advisor," "project manager," "investigating officer," "researcher," and "business analyst." I have heard others. Early in the development of policy analysis techniques, the people who identified the problems that needed to be addressed tended to be government officials. They turned to academics for help. Frequently, those academics deemed to be most useful, given the problems at hand, were economists with strong technical skills who had the ability to estimate the magnitude of problems, undertake statistical analyses, and determine the costs of various government actions.

During the twentieth century, as transportation, electrification, and telecommunications opened up new opportunities for market exchange, problems associated with decentralized decision making became more apparent (McCraw 1984). Meanwhile, as awareness grew of the causes of many natural and social phenomena, calls emerged for governments to establish mechanisms that might effectively manage various natural and social processes. Many matters once treated as social conditions, or facts of life to be suffered, were transformed into policy problems (Cobb and Elder 1983). Together, the increasing scope of the marketplace, the increasing complexity of social interactions, and expanding knowledge of social conditions created pressures from a variety of quarters for governments to take the lead in structuring and regulating individual and collective action. Tools of policy analysis were developed to guide this expanding scope of government. Yet as the reach of policy analysis grew, questions were raised about the biases inherent in some of the analytical tools being applied. In response, new efforts were made to account for the effects of policy changes, and new voices began to contribute in significant ways to policy development (Smith 1991).

Early discussions of the role of policy analysts in society often portrayed them as "whiz kids" or "econocrats" on a quest to imbue public decision making with high degrees of rigor and rationality (Self 1977; Stevens 1993). Certainly, proponents of cost-benefit analysis considered themselves to have a technique for assessing the relative merits of alternative policy proposals that, on theoretical grounds, trumped any others on offer. Likewise, proponents of program evaluation employing quasi-experimental research designs considered their approach to be superior to other approaches that might be used to determine program effectiveness (Cook and Campbell 1979). That the application of both cost-benefit analysis and quantitative evaluation techniques has continued unabated for several decades speaks to their perceived value for generating useable knowledge. However, the limitations of such techniques have not been lost on critics. In the case of cost-benefit analysis, features of the technique that make it so appealing—such as the reduction of all impacts to a common metric and the calculation of net social benefits—have also attracted criticism. In response, alternative methods for assessing the impacts of new policies, such as environmental and social impact assessments, have gained currency (Barrow 2000; Wood 1995). Similarly, widespread efforts have been made to promote the integration of gender and race analysis into policy development (Myers 2002; True and Mintrom 2001). In the case of evaluation studies, fundamental and drawn-out debates have occurred covering the validity of various research methods and the appropriate scope and purpose of evaluation efforts. Significantly, these debates have served to expand demand for policy analysis. Indeed, government agencies designed especially to audit the impacts of policies on the family, children, women, and racial minorities have now been established in many jurisdictions.

The rise of policy analysis has seen the development of several trends that have served both to embed policy analysts at the core of government operations and to expand demand for policy analysts both inside and outside of government. These trends have much to do with the growing complexity of economic and social relations and knowledge generation. Yet there is also a sense in which policy analysis itself generates demand for more policy analysis. For example, in Washington, DC, the growing population of policy analysts employed in the federal government bureaucracy during the second half of the twentieth century led to demand elsewhere for policy analysts who could verify or contest the analysis and advice emanating from government agencies. A classic example is given by the creation of the Congressional Budget Office (CBO). This office was established as an independent resource for Congress that would generate analysis and advice as a check on the veracity of the analyses prepared and disseminated by the executive-controlled Office of Management and Budget. The Government Accountability Office was also developed to provide independent advice for Congress (Wildavsky 1992). Among government agencies, the growing quality of the technical advice generated by some has typically promoted renewed effort on the part of others to build their analytical and advice-giving capabilities. When agencies must compete among themselves for funding of new programs—or for ongoing funding of core functions—a degree of learning occurs, so that incremental improvements are observed in the overall quality of analysis and advice being produced.

While these trends have been most observable in national capitals, where a large amount of policy development occurs, they have played out in related ways in other venues as well. For instance, in federal systems, expanding cadres of well-trained policy analysts have become engaged in sophisticated, evidence-based policy debates in state and provincial capitals. Cities, too, are increasingly making extensive use of policy analysts in their strategy and planning departments. At the global level, key coordinating organizations, such as the World Bank, the International Monetary Fund, the World Trade Organization, and the Organization for Economic Cooperation and Development have made extensive use of the skills of policy analysts to monitor various transnational developments and national-level activities of particular relevance and interest.

Today, the demand for policy analysis is considerable, and it comes both from inside and outside of governments. This demand is likely to keep growing as calls emerge for governments to tackle new problems. On the one hand, we should expect to see ongoing efforts to harness technical procedures drawn from the social sciences and natural sciences for the purposes of improving the quality of policy analysis. On the other hand, more people are likely to apply these techniques, reinvent them, or develop whole new approaches to counteract them, all with the purpose of gaining greater voice in policy making at all levels of government from the local to the global.

THE PURPOSE AND ORGANIZATION OF THIS BOOK

This book is intended as a core reading for students of policy analysis and a reference work for professionals who wish to build or refresh their skills as policy analysts. Government decisions—whether made at the local, regional, national or transnational level—profoundly affect the quality of people's lives. As awareness has grown of the powerful role that governments play in shaping our lives, people from a range of backgrounds have sought to understand and influence government policy making. Policy analysis as a discipline is supported by a central core of well-established analytical strategies (Stokey and Zeckhauser 1978; Weimer and Vining 2005). But new approaches to thinking about policy are continually being introduced. People training to be policy analysts need to be familiar with a variety of analytical strategies, to know the strengths and limitations of these strategies, and to be able to explore how combining strategies might effectively support improved decision making in specific contexts. Aspiring policy analysts must be able to confidently embrace this disciplinary complexity while striving to clarify problems and indicate appropriate strategies for addressing them.

This book is designed to help students build their analytical capacity. It is distinctive from other books on policy analysis because it introduces a broader set of analytical strategies than is typically the case. In particular, it offers a pathway to policy understanding that does not assume a background in microeconomics, and that is attuned with the approaches being used by analysts in and around government at all jurisdictional levels. The book also espouses a project-based learning model, and early chapters offer readers guidance on how to set up and execute their own original policy projects and how to present advice based on their analytical work.

Following this chapter, the book is divided into three sections. The first section offers an overview of policy analysis. It consists of six chapters. Having worked through these chapters, readers will have a sound understanding of the role of government in society and how policy analysts can help decision makers to improve the quality of government actions. Individual chapters cover what policy analysts do, what governments do, objectives of government action, how to manage policy projects, how to present policy advice, and how to do ethical policy analysis.

The second section of the book introduces a range of analytical strategies. The chapters in this section explore major approaches used by policy analysts to gain insights into policy problems. It is rare to find more than a few of these strategies being employed in any given policy project. However, the more familiarity we have with them and how to use them, the better equipped we are to use the right strategy at the right time. The chapter topics include coverage of markets and market failure, government failure, comparative institutional analysis, cost-benefit analysis, gender and race analysis, and implementation analysis.

The final section of the book contains a chapter intended to help readers improve their analysis as they move forward in their careers. It offers practical advice on how to develop as an analyst and advisor. The goal here is to help new policy professionals support their own learning and close the gap between knowing what policy analysis involves and actually becoming a very effective policy analyst.

The chapters of this book have been arranged so that the topics covered in each follow a logical sequence. Those who read the chapters in the usual serial fashion will discover many ideas that will improve their practice as policy analysts and advisors. But the book need not be read chapter by chapter. It can also be thought of and used as a compendium of concepts and techniques that are central to the work of policy analysts. Every chapter is deliberately self-contained and can be read individually with no loss of value in the treatment of its specific topic. So, as an addition to the policy analyst's bookshelf, this book represents a resource that can be regularly consulted when the need arises. For example, a person at the start of a policy project will find it useful to review the content of Chapter 5, "Managing Policy Projects." Likewise, a person looking ahead to the implementation challenges associated with a newly developed policy will find helpful insights in Chapter 16, "Implementation Analysis." All of the chapters contain suggestions for further reading. These suggestions are intended to be especially helpful to those who need to expand beyond the introductory coverage of material that is offered here.

The structure of this book is similar to the structure of courses that I have taught over many years, introducing policy analysis to final-year undergraduate students, first-year graduate students, and people already working in the field of public policy who have sought to enhance their analytical skills. The book is supported by a website containing regularly updated additional support materials.

CONCLUSION

We live in exciting times. The continuous streams of problems, discoveries, social and technical changes we see often present challenges and dilemmas for governments everywhere. But often, government decision makers do not have the time to fully explore the implications of changes in the world around them, and the problems and issues that emerge out of change. The rise of policy analysis has been propelled by changing social, economic, political, and environmental conditions. In the future, the increasing integration of economies and societies, referred to generally as globalization, can be expected to generate new sets of policy problems (Sandler 2004; Tabb 2004). In this regard, the changes associated with globalization echo the dynamics that were observed in federal systems from the late nineteenth century well into the twentieth century. During that period, increasing commerce across state and provincial borders and the emergence of intensive interjurisdictional competition prompted new considerations of the role of government in society (McCraw 1984). Extensive effort also went into determining what levels of government were best suited to performing different functions (Derthick 1979; Tyack 1974).

New times introduce new problems and questions. Drawing lessons from the past, it seems clear that many new policy problems will arise on government agendas in the coming decades. While globalizing forces will be responsible for generating many of these challenges, the challenges themselves will be manifest at all levels of government, from the local upward. As in the past, people both inside and outside of government can be expected to show intense interest in these policy challenges, and they will call for further supply of innovative and high-quality policy analysis.

This book is written for people motivated to make the world a better place, for those who recognize that governments play a major role in promoting positive outcomes. Policy analysis is challenging work. Appropriate and sound solutions developed to address a particular set of problems at a given time can turn out later to be undermined by changing conditions. In a context characterized by change and complexity, it is important for thoughtful, careful analysts to contribute new insights and advice that help decision makers to better interpret problems and choose effective responses. This book is intended to give aspiring policy analysts a set of skills that will serve them well both now and in the future. The material contained here is based on many important contributions that have been made over the past few decades to the emerging discipline of policy analysis. Taking what is available to us now, we work to build the future. The paths we will walk are yet to be defined. Where we are heading is never for certain. As we move forward, our destinations change, and we change too. To be consciously working to make our world a better place, working with others in the face of challenges and uncertainties, is difficult. But this is also a highly satisfying vocation, where our ongoing efforts—intertwined with those of others—can serve to improve the human condition.

Exercises

Problem definition occurs as people discuss the causes and consequences of situations that they find troubling. During these discussions, we often find different approaches being taken to explaining the problem. How we individually make sense of the world leads us to dwell closely on some aspects of problems, while paying little attention to other aspects. As a result, it is common for conflict to arise during problem definition.

1. In groups, list three or four issues that have been in the news recently. Discuss how they have been presented and who has offered their opinions on each matter. What perspectives have been dominant? Are there other sides to these issues that have not been focused upon?
2. Return to the lists made in item 1. Should government intervene to solve the problem? Could some other workable solutions be found to the problem?

Further Reading

Bardach, Eugene. (2008). "Introduction." In *A Practical Guide to Policy Analysis*. New York: Chatham House.

Mintrom, Michael, and Phillipa Norman. (2009). "Policy Entrepreneurship and Policy Change." *Policy Studies Journal* 37(4): 649–667.

Radin, Beryl A. (2000). "A Portrait of the Past" and "Policy Analysis Today: Dualing Swords." Chapters 1 and 2 in *Beyond Machiavelli: Policy Analysis Comes of Age*. Washington, DC: Georgetown University Press.

Stokey, Edith, and Richard Zeckhauser. (1978). "Thinking About Policy Choices." Chapter 1 in *A Primer for Policy Analysis*. New York: W. W. Norton.

PART I

Overview of Policy Analysis

2

What Policy Analysts Do

The Story So Far ... We have reviewed key steps in producing policy analysis, the emergence of policy analysis as a discipline, and how this book approaches the topic.

Here ... We consider what policy analysts do. Mostly, they assess policy problems and propose solutions with the goal of helping government decision making. The chapter focuses on the specific activities that policy analysts engage in as they develop effective advice. The career options available to policy analysts are also discussed.

THIS CHAPTER REVIEWS
- The social function of policy analysis
- Where policy analysts are employed
- How policy analysts contribute to public decision making
- Common competencies and attributes of successful policy analysts
- Why being a policy analyst is an appealing career choice

Construed most broadly, policy analysis is the study of how government actions affect our lives. Policy analysts consider how institutional arrangements in society affect our practices and, in turn, how these practices contribute to observed outcomes—for other individuals, groups, society as whole, and our environment.

Human beings are infinitely creative. When we are able to peacefully engage with each other within communities, across broader collective groupings, and across national borders, we have enormous capacity to achieve great things. Yet so much of what is creative, wonderful, and worthy of celebration about the human condition is contingent upon systems and structures that work to guide our thoughts and actions. Those systems and structures allow us to work together and avoid doing harm both to ourselves and to others. Scholars commonly refer to these systems and structures as institutions.

What are some common systems and structures that guide us in our daily lives? The languages we use to communicate and think, the days of the week, the time, codes of dress, payment systems, expectations from family members, rules of the workplace, the procedures of the schools or other learning institutions we or our children attend, the means of transport available to us, the availability of food, and the availability of clean water are some of the most obvious. Importantly, when we begin to trace back from all of the systems and structures that guide us in our daily lives, we soon see how laws and the actions of governments exert influence over how we behave in the world. Governments are rarely totalitarian, in the sense of using significant force or the threat of it to keep us all in check. But governments do a lot to guide and constrain us, as individuals and as groups.

This chapter offers an overview of what policy analysts do. The typical employment locations of policy analysts are also noted. This leads to a discussion of how policy analysts contribute to public decision making. To contribute effectively, policy analysts must display a range of competencies and attributes. These are reviewed at a fairly general level—more details concerning specific competencies are given throughout subsequent chapters of this book. In discussing what policy analysts do, it is also fitting to consider why a career as a policy analyst holds appeal. Several features of public policy work make it attractive as a career option, both for those yet to embark on their careers and for those considering a career change.

A key point to appreciate about policy analysis is that no matter where you start from, you will always find something about your background, your training, or your experience that is relevant and helpful to doing this kind of work. Another key point is that you can never know enough to be an exemplary policy practitioner. The problems, puzzles, and issues that arise for those with policy interests and advice-giving responsibilities present ongoing challenges. For policy analysts, there is always a new gauntlet being thrown down, challenging you to develop yourself further and, in turn, improve your practice.

THE SOCIAL FUNCTION OF POLICY ANALYSIS

Policy analysis is usefully thought of as both a discipline and as a practice. The discipline of policy analysis is comprised of all the efforts that have been made over the years to formally codify and pass on knowledge of public policy and how to most effectively interpret it, develop new policy proposals, and secure policy change. The discipline of policy analysis has grown primarily through the efforts of academics working in a range of disciplines, but who all share interests in the actions of governments and how they affect social practices and broader outcomes. In contrast, the practice of policy analysis is manifest through the day-to-day actions of people who—while working in a range of settings—are principally employed to offer insights and advice to decision makers on government actions and their consequences. In this discussion of policy analysis and its social function, I focus on the contributions made by practitioners of policy analysis. Of course, good practice is informed by advances in knowledge supported by university-based research and research-informed teaching.

Policy analysis, at its best, stops decision makers from making ill-considered choices. Human beings display a great desire to attain order in their immediate environment. They also like to be helpful. All of this is good, but it can often prove troublesome. The nub of the issue is this: In our desire to achieve order, we sometimes make limited and inappropriate use of information. We use a range of mental shortcuts—or heuristics—to guide our decision making. At their best, decision rules that rely on pattern matching across similar contexts and replicate in one place what worked well elsewhere can be incredibly efficient. Indeed, such mental shortcuts are what allow us to accomplish consistently good results in many day-to-day activities. But sometimes our confidence in our own decision-making abilities can let us down. We become overconfident and base our decisions on inappropriately limited information. We do not reflect on how routine thinking can blind us to different ways of considering particular situations (Nisbett and Ross 1980; Thaler and Sunstein 2008).

If we are able to break free of routine thinking, we can see situations in new ways. We can consider the range of possible responses to those situations, and the appropriateness of any specific response, given the relevant context. When we put the brakes on hasty decision making, it is likely that our chosen actions will end up being more beneficial to those we are trying to help than would otherwise have been the case. Policy analysis, as practice, embodies the belief that if we call a stop to our instinctual reactions, assess the situation, and think hard about it, then we will increase the odds that good outcomes will result. But what if there is a crisis? Even in the midst of crisis it is important to curb instinctual reactions. The good policy analyst enjoins us to take a deep breath, take time to think, talk to others, collect more information, reflect upon it, and then, after that, choose a course of action. Interestingly, when such a disciplined response becomes ingrained in the thinking of individuals and organizations, the time delay between making a hasty decision versus making a well-informed one can be relatively short. Yet the quality difference between those decisions can be vast. And the flow-on effects of a hasty versus a well-informed decision can be enormous (Collins 2001; Heifetz 1994).

The most significant social function of policy analysis is to support improved decision making by those who have been elected or appointed to act in the interests of the public within a given jurisdiction. Policy analysts contribute to this broader social function through their daily efforts across a range of settings in and around government. This social function can make important contributions to society by improving the quality of collective choices. Additionally, being supported by robust processes of information gathering, analysis, and deliberation, all good decisions leave trails of knowledge, evidence, and practical know-how that can help to inform future decision making. Further, good decisions have cumulative effects within specific policy areas, in that they can result in public policies that serve as platforms for subsequent good decision making.

At a practical level, individual policy analysts contribute to this broader social function through specific actions. All policy analysts approach particular problems or puzzles using particular analytical strategies. Typically, policy analysts are very conscious of the analytical strategies they are using, why they are using them, and how they differ from other alternative strategies that could have been used to approach the same problem or puzzle. Policy analysts seek to identify the likely consequences of particular government choices. Sometimes, when policies have already been adopted and implemented, policy analysts will work to identify actual policy consequences. Policy analysts usually take care to describe and interpret specific problems. Context is always critical to understand. The better able policy analysts are at understanding a problem, its context, and how the problem and context interact, the better able they will be to suggest effective strategies to address those problems (Kingdon 1984; Rochefort and Cobb 1994).

Policy analysts take seriously the notion that any given problem could be addressed in multiple ways. So they tend to think carefully about alternative responses to problems. Importantly, policy analysts need to have an appreciation for the relative social and political acceptability of alternative responses to particular problems. Sometimes, technically feasible solutions will not be socially or politically acceptable. In such cases, introduction of such a solution might fail. So, again, sensitivity to context matters. Sound efforts to accurately anticipate consequences are essential to the development of good policy advice. Even in instances where decision makers do not seem open to alternative solutions to particular policy problems, effective work that lays out the consequences of the desired solution can reduce the possibility of unintended consequences emerging.

WHERE POLICY ANALYSTS ARE EMPLOYED

Depending on how broadly we define policy analysis, we could end up suggesting that policy analysts can be found almost anywhere. For example, beyond policy analysts working for government agencies, many academics conducting research in universities could be said to be policy analysts, as could many journalists, public commentators, consultants, and advisors in private companies. The range of people who could be said to conduct policy analysis is wide because many people do have an interest in considering, analyzing, and writing about aspects of the role that governments play in society. Note that, as mentioned in Chapter 1, many of these people who conduct policy analysis do not necessarily have "policy analyst" in their title.

To better define who produces policy analysis and where those people are employed, I suggest that we draw distinctions based on what people spend their time doing, why they do it, and who they perceive as their audience. Among academics, people from a range of disciplines spend time thinking about and conducting original research on the relations between governments and other institutions and organizations in society. While their work will be targeted to an audience comprised mainly of their academic peers and students working within the same specific field, it is likely that some component of their work will have policy relevance. At that point, each individual academic needs to decide how much he or she wants to engage with the world of policy debate, discussion, and development. Very often, policy-relevant research does not reach a policy audience simply because that audience was never perceived as the primary audience for such work. In general, if academics working on policy relevant topics wish to have direct policy influence, they must find venues for such influence (Friedman 1995). So they will often seek to publish the results of their work in ways that appeal to and engage effectively with a practitioner audience. Sometimes, they will set aside their more pure research work and undertake policy work for a time, where they use their skills with the deliberate purpose of having a policy impact (Bernanke 2005).

For several decades now there has also been an ever-growing set of academics who have been deliberately creating a disciplinary field identifiable as policy analysis. These academics tend to be associated with schools of public policy or public administration. They see themselves as teaching future generations of policy practitioners. They also see their research as intended primarily to advance knowledge of how to address policy problems. Such policy scholars tend to be much more actively engaged with the policy practitioner community than the more varied set of scholars noted earlier.

Policy analysts as practitioners are mainly employed by government agencies. Within those agencies, their work can range widely, both with respect to the policy substance and the kind of analytical work being performed. Thinking of the policy process as involving problem definition, agenda setting, policy adoption, policy implementation, and program evaluation, we find that policy analysts are employed by agencies to contribute to aspects of policy work at each of these steps.

In general, the scope of the work performed by a given policy analyst in government depends on the nature of the agency where they are employed and the size of the governmental jurisdiction. For example, a policy analyst working in the economic development agency of a small local government is likely to have few colleagues. Consequently, such a policy analyst will get to work on many aspects of the policy issues that come to the agency. The work is all likely to focus on issues of economic development within a small territorial region. This might prove constraining in the longer term. But in the shorter term, working on policy problems from the problem definition stage right through to implementation and evaluation can create many opportunities for the development of important analytical skills. In contrast, a policy analyst working in a large central agency of a state or national government, such as a department of management and budget, is more likely to be engaged in analytical work to support government and legislative decision making concerning the adoption of new policies. It will usually also be the case that policy analysts employed in this kind of role will focus on specific substantive policy areas. However, there is likely to be more scope for rotation over time to working on different substantive issues within the same agency.

There is a tendency among government policy analysts to move among agencies. These moves can take place all within specific levels of government. For example, people might choose to make their careers within national or state or local government. In these cases, career aspirations can often be met without any relocation. Others might find that their areas of substantive interest span across levels of government. As a result, they might move during their careers among levels of government. Often, this will require relocation.

Finally, many policy analysts work as consultants. Operating through either self-employment or as part of a larger consultancy group, these policy analysts perform project work for client organizations. The client organizations can range from local governments through to agencies of state and federal governments, through to global entities, such as the United Nations or the World Bank. Often, consulting policy analysts will also develop advice for private sector companies and nonprofit organizations that seek advice on how changes in relevant government policies could positively or negatively affect their operating contexts.

HOW POLICY ANALYSTS CONTRIBUTE TO PUBLIC DECISION MAKING

Policy analysts do not usually hold power, in the sense that they have little ability to force others to do as they say. However, policy analysts can have major influence on people who do hold power, such as elected decision makers. Typically, top public decision makers are incredibly busy. They find themselves required to make decisions on many important issues without having time to gather all the necessary background information that would guide them in making good decisions. That is where policy analysts become crucial. Policy analysts are employed to give to issues the serious attention and deep thought that busy decision makers do not have time for. Policy analysts usually do six things to generate high-quality advice for decision makers.

First, policy analysts take problems that are presented to them and spend time thinking about why they have been presented in specific ways, what their sources might be, and why they have arisen at this time. It is very important that policy analysts engage in this kind of problem definition work. Often, decision makers and members of the public describe problems in peculiar ways that can have more to do with how they gained attention in a specific context than with their match to a broader class of problems familiar to policy specialists. So effectively defining and categorizing problems is important work for policy analysts (Schön and Rein 1994).

Second, policy analysts consider the contexts from which policy problems arise. A good understanding of the specific policy context enables policy analysts to determine how particular solutions to a problem would be received by the decision makers they are advising, by the people who would implement the policy, by those who would be affected by it, and by the general public.

Third, policy analysts think in terms of causal relationships. Viewing problems as outcomes caused by various behavioral and contextual factors, policy analysts consider how specific policy interventions could reduce the frequency and severity of the problems at hand. Causal thinking leads policy analysts to trace out the processes that result in specific outcomes and the role that policies play—or could play—in shaping those outcomes (Stone 2002).

Fourth, policy analysts make explicit the kinds of concerns that they think should be given most attention when thinking about the problem at hand and possible solutions to it. There are no hard-and-fast rules about what criteria should be used to judge the merits of potential policy solutions to a given problem (Majone 1989). However, effectiveness, efficiency, fairness, and administrative simplicity have often served as broad criteria for comparing alternative policy actions. Thinking in terms of effectiveness is important because it leads us to consider the likelihood that a given policy intervention will have a significant impact on the problem at hand. A focus on efficiency leads us to consider how we can conserve scarce resources while still attaining our goals. Taking fairness into account reminds us that people will have different perceptions of policies and we should take care to ensure that any new policies do not exacerbate social divisions. Putting a focus on administrative simplicity can be helpful for reducing the chances that a new policy will be overly burdensome in terms of creating compliance costs, monitoring costs, management costs, and so on.

Fifth, policy analysts gather background information and use a range of analytical techniques to build their knowledge about the likely impacts of possible policy responses to the problem at hand. What information is gathered and how it is analyzed will depend to a large extent on the nature of the problem and the aspects of it that are of most concern to decision makers. This is where prior knowledge and experience can prove of great value to policy analysts. Often, the development of advice to decision makers will be strongly informed by knowledge of what approaches have worked in other contexts. Thus, policy analysts seek to tap into accumulated bodies of knowledge and experience to support their advice-giving efforts. A lot of policy work involves deriving original insights from either new information or information that has been around for some time. But policy analysts also engage in a large amount of synthesizing work, where they bring together work developed by others and seek to derive insights from it that will help them to propose effective responses to the policy problem at hand (Bardach 2008).

Finally, policy analysts communicate the results of their background work to the decision makers who have requested their advice. The quality of their efforts to communicate effectively can have enormous implications for the value that decision makers place on the advice that they receive. To earn their pay, policy analysts must be able to present their findings in ways that are as useful as possible to decision makers. This is quite different from telling decision makers what they want to hear. Very good advice might involve telling a decision maker that his or her preferred option is not the most appropriate. Effectively conveying this kind of message so as not to cause embarrassment or outrage on the part of the decision maker is all part of the art of being a good policy analyst. A lot is at stake with this communication task. After all, if it is done poorly, it might mean that months of hard, difficult work performed by a team of people might not receive the kind of attention from decision makers that it deserved (Mintrom 2003; Verdier 1984).

COMMON COMPETENCIES AND ATTRIBUTES OF SUCCESSFUL POLICY ANALYSTS

Like many professionals, policy analysts need to have acquired a set of both technical skills and people skills in order to perform well in their role. This book introduces many of the analytical approaches that are commonly employed by contemporary policy analysts across a range of settings. Here, I mention broader competencies and attributes of successful policy analysts: a willingness to question received wisdom and to be persuaded by evidence, a reputation for good judgment, and the ability to convey trustworthiness. Policy analysts who regularly display these dispositions are likely to have significant policy influence through their work.

Policy analysts need to have well-developed critical abilities. Others in and around government might rush to judgment on the merits of specific solutions to problems. The weight of public opinion might suggest that a given solution would be the most politically acceptable. Policy analysts who simply parrot conventional wisdom, even when they do so using the language of policy discourse, bring nothing useful to the table. Policy analysts are at their best when they question the proposals being put forward by others, when they take the time to explore why problems are being presented in specific ways. Policy analysts should routinely consider the possibility that alternative approaches to problem framing might be valid and that alternative solutions—including those that have not featured in discussions to this point—might have merits. Of course, displaying skepticism toward conventional wisdom and giving critical scrutiny to other people's favorite ideas can get a lot of people annoyed. That does not mean policy analysts should hold back their critiques. Rather, policy analysts need to develop the ability to raise hard questions and offer alternative points of view in ways that promote constructive discussion and debate. This can be challenging, but it is necessary if you want to improve the quality of government decision making.

Policy analysts must display good judgment. While it is important not to be swayed by conventional wisdom or populist positions, policy analysts should never ignore them. The more aware we make ourselves of the context we are operating within, the more we appreciate the concerns and preoccupations of decision makers, the better attuned we are to the political landscape, the better able we will be to offer our advice in ways that make it truly helpful to those who have requested it. In practice, how might good judgment be displayed? Consider a political climate where public opinion polls routinely indicate citizen opposition to higher taxes and where decision makers have recently been taking steps to reduce the numbers of people employed in government. In such a climate, it would be unwise for policy analysts to propose new policies that would require recruitment of more government employees and that would add to the annual budget. However, if the analytical work undertaken on the issue at hand suggested that the expensive new policies were significantly superior to any alternatives that had been considered, then the advice could be worked up in a fashion that would make it more acceptable. For example, rather than simply proposing more spending on top of current expenditure totals, the policy analysts involved could investigate ways to make savings in related areas of government activity, so that those savings could offset the costs of the new policies. Approaches could also be explored that would keep the costs of the new policies as low as possible. In this instance, good judgment would be displayed by tailoring what you consider to be the best policy solution to meet the circumstances. That is quite another thing from backing off and suggesting a lesser solution that—while you do not like it—you think will be more politically palatable.

Finally, policy analysts must be trustworthy. Trustworthiness is a function of both character and competence (Covey 2006). It is not enough to be honest but incompetent. Nor is it appropriate to be analytically competent but to play fast and loose with evidence. All policy analysts must work at building their reputations as people able to offer decision makers the best policy advice they can get, given the problems or concerns they face. Typically, we build up such reputations over a period of time and through multiple interactions. Once you have established a reputation as a trustworthy advisor, it is vital that you continue to display the good character and the analytical competence for which you are trusted. Even the smallest, silliest mistakes can be highly damaging, and it can take a lot of effort to rebuild a reputation for trustworthiness (Goldsmith 2007). Working in close association with others who are trustworthy is probably the best way to stay honest and retain your analytical edge. At a minimum, you need to be able to have people around you to talk with about your work and your actions, and to give you guidance when you have your moments of self-doubt or weakness.

WHY BEING A POLICY ANALYST IS AN APPEALING CAREER CHOICE

Engaging in policy analysis can be challenging work. Whether we choose to work on a problem of our own volition or because someone else gives us a problem, we almost always have to go through a major learning process to produce sound analysis and to derive useful advice based upon it. Like a lot of work associated with complex decision making, it requires us to be comfortable with uncertainty and to get beyond black-and-white thinking and start "thinking gray" (Sample 2002). It requires that we develop confidence in our abilities to establish and pursue effective analytical strategies, especially when problems are new and limited work has been devoted to understanding and addressing them. Because the world is continuously changing, governments must continuously develop solutions to new kinds of problems. For creative people who like challenges, this is a great environment to work within. You also get a sense that you are contributing to the common good and making a positive improvement to our collective existence. That matters.

Over the years that I have worked as a policy analyst, consultant, and trainer, I have met many other policy analysts who have derived great satisfaction from their work. One thing I have found particularly interesting is that people who become involved in policy work come from highly diverse backgrounds. A variety of subjects taught at universities offer knowledge, skills, and experience that can be usefully applied to conducting policy analysis. Similarly, experiences, skills, and knowledge acquired through a broad range of occupations can create a sound platform on which more specific policy analytic skills can be acquired and developed. Although policy analysis has a strong disciplinary core to it, the range of problems that policy analysts confront in their work mean that few, if any, skills acquired elsewhere are ever wasted when people decide to pursue a career as a policy analyst.

Policy analysis is a social activity. Often, policy analysts work in teams, where different people bring different kinds of skill, knowledge, and expertise to the table (Mintrom 2003). In addition, as the work proceeds—developing background knowledge of a problem, exploring feasible solutions, and communicating recommendations—policy analysts find themselves interacting closely with other professionals. For my part, I know this is one of the great joys for me of policy work, but I know that is true for many other people I have met along the way.

Finally, through building your skills as a policy analyst, you also build a set of skills that are highly transferable to a range of other contexts. For this reason, working as a policy analyst can be highly attractive as an early or mid-career option. By developing yourself as a policy analyst, you can open many doors for your ongoing career.

CONCLUSION

Policy analysis is important work. The world is complex, and a huge amount of human effort goes into developing systems that allow us to effectively negotiate with our environment and thrive. Many of those things that people do to make the world a better place occur outside of government. However, governments do a lot to set the terms upon which people and organizations interact. Policy analysts ensure that governments make smart decisions. Increasing evidence is emerging to show that institutional structures are what make the most difference to the economic development of countries and the quality of the lives of those who live in them (Helpman 2004; North 1981). Again, government is not responsible for all of those institutional structures. But governments can have significant influence on how well those institutions function. Policy analysts contribute in a vast range of ways to improving government functioning. They are called upon to take the time to think deeply about problems and to generate appropriate ways to address them. The work itself is challenging and, in many ways, never finished. But it represents an important and influential way that people can apply their knowledge and skills toward making the world a better place.

Exercises

1. List specific tasks of policy analysts. Ask people to discuss what they think would be the hardest or most challenging part of each task, what would be most enjoyable about each task, and so on.
2. Based on what you know from current affairs portrayed in the media, make a list of policy problems. Then make a list of the majors in the class. Randomly assign major to problem, and consider how someone with this major might view a problem and how he or she could shed light on it.

Invite a Guest to Class

It can be inspiring for students to have practicing policy analysts come to talk with them. Those who have been working as policy analysts for a decade or more are often able to offer insights on the ways that the work changes them, as well as the ways that they feel they have made a difference through their work. If you decide to invite a guest, find ways to get members of the class involved. For example, one group could work as the "search agency," identifying an appropriate person and extending an invitation. Negotiating a mutually agreeable time and format for the visit can take some work. Another group could work in advance to solicit questions that members of the class would like to ask the guest. From here, the group could select five questions for the guest and ensure that the guest has them in advance of the class visit. A third group could work on logistics, ensuring that all the right equipment will be in the room for when the guest comes, that the guest has directions to the campus, has access to visitor parking, and knows who will escort them to the meeting room. A fourth group could be responsible for taking notes during the visit and writing a one-page summary of key points or insights for circulation to the whole class after the visit. This group could also be assigned responsibility for drafting a note of thanks to be sent to the speaker following the visit. Doing all of this will turn it into a special occasion. You want the guest to enjoy the visit and for students to make the most of it. Done well, this event could become a model for similar events with other visitors later in the course.

Further Reading

Bernanke, Benjamin S. (2005). Remarks at "Panel Discussion: The Transition from Academic to Policymaker." Annual Meeting of the American Economic Association, Philadelphia, Pennsylvania, January 7. Retrieved from http://www.federalreserve.gov/newsevents/speech/2005speech.htm.

Covey, Stephen M. R. (2006). "The One Thing That Changes Everything." In *The Speed of Trust,* 1–40. New York: Free Press.

Mintrom, Michael. (2003). "Policy Analysts and People Skills." In *People Skills for Policy Analysts,* chap 1. Washington, DC: Georgetown University Press.

Schön, Donald A., and Martin Rein. (1994). "Intractable Policy Controversies." In *Frame Reflection: Toward the Resolution of Intractable Policy Controversies*, chap. 1. New York: Basic Books.

Thaler, Richard H. and Cass R. Sunstein. (2008). "Biases and Blunders." In *Nudge: Improving Decisions about Health, Wealth, and Happiness*, chap. 1. New Haven, CT: Yale University Press.

3

What Governments Do

The Story So Far... We have considered the purpose of policy analysis, the steps involved in the development of policy advice, and the attributes of effective policy analysts.

Here... We review the range of policy actions that governments can take. Governments seek to improve social outcomes. Policy analysts play a vital role in advising how that might be done. Good policy analysts must have a sound working knowledge of what policy actions could be taken to address any given policy problem.

THIS CHAPTER REVIEWS
- The role of government in society
- The importance of cooperation and coordination without coercion
- The range of policy actions taken by governments
- The increasing complexity of issues facing societies and governments

Wherever they are located, policy analysts engage in efforts to understand specific contexts, problems in them, how aspects of current government policy relate to those problems, and the likely effects of changes to government policy. To do their work well, policy analysts need to have a sound understanding of what governments do and what they are capable of doing. Part of being a good policy analyst is the ability to imagine plausible alternative scenarios to those that confront us, and to explain to others the relative strengths and weaknesses of different proposals for addressing a particular problem. This chapter offers an introduction to the role of government in society. It begins with a broad consideration of the social context and institutional structures with which governments must interact. At this early stage, emphasis is placed on the importance of achieving cooperation and coordination in society. Government cannot be expected to take responsibility for ensuring good outcomes in all situations. However, by taking actions that offer clear guidance to others and, in many cases, serve to structure human interactions, governments can do an enormous amount to promote positive social outcomes.

Following these preliminary comments on the role of government in society, the largest part of this chapter is devoted to a review of policy actions that governments can take. This review will become an important reference point for much of the discussion in this book. From here, we are able to discuss rationales for using specific policy instruments and ways to identify and compare the merits and drawbacks of policy alternatives. Therefore, this chapter provides an important foundation for our subsequent explorations.

A clarification of terms is necessary. *Policy instruments* are specific interventions that governments can make to change a given set of social interactions. For example, prohibiting public drunkenness and empowering police officers to arrest offenders represents a policy instrument intended to promote social order. A *policy action* is taken whenever a change occurs that involves a policy instrument. This definition opens the possibility of policy actions that introduce, adjust, or remove specific policy instruments. Elimination of a prohibition on public drunkenness represents a policy action. So, too, is extending the prohibition, as is changing the severity of punishments for offenders.

THE ROLE OF GOVERNMENT IN SOCIETY

At the most general level, governments do for society those things that would be unlikely to be achieved simply through the efforts of citizens or small groups of citizens. This suggests that there are limits to how far a society can advance through sole reliance on decentralized, private, voluntary, individualized decision making and actions. Government represents a binding form of collective action. In contrast to decentralized, private, voluntary, individualized efforts, government policy making and government activities are characterized by centralized, public decision making. The decisions made by governments apply to all citizens. They are intended to mobilize and coordinate collective action.

Governments are often described as social institutions. In this portrayal, government systems serve to produce and police the rules that govern other aspects of social activity. Organizations in society develop and evolve in ways that are shaped and constrained by the presence and actions of the government. However, governments are not the only source of social institutions. Many other social institutions exist and, while aspects of those institutions are often subjected to government efforts to guide and constrain them, their autonomy from government remains well understood. Major examples include the family, organized religions (churches), and systems of commerce (markets). Historically, many of the big disagreements in society have centered on the influence that different institutions—such as the government, the church, the market, and the family—should have on individuals, their development, and the choices they make. Indeed, the boundaries between different institutions, and questions concerning the appropriate level of influence that each institution should have on individuals, continue to be hot spots for a great deal of social conflict and policy debate. Issues of power, control, freedom, fairness, identity, and justice often emerge in these hot spots.

Why do governments exist? The answer that emerges here is that governments are necessary to facilitate the advancement of human potential in the face of limitations presented by individual or group actions, even as those actions are shaped by other significant institutions in society. Government at its best sets the terms for peaceful coexistence. Structures of government are intended to provide venues for the resolution of conflicts within society and to protect society from external hostilities. Many of the significant contributions to political thought have involved extensive discussions of the need for governmental structures and the forms they should take. Major examples include Aristotle's *The Politics,* Niccolo Machiavelli's *Discourses* (1499), Thomas Hobbes's *Leviathan* (1651), John Locke's *Second Treatise of Government* (1689), Baron de Montesquieu's *The Spirit of the Laws* (1748) and *The Federalist Papers* (1788). For a useful overview of works in this tradition, see Cahn (2010). Hay, Lister, and Marsh (2006) deliberately draw linkages among these classic contributions and more contemporary approaches to theorizing the role of government in society. The body of public choice literature represents efforts by political scientists and economists to more precisely explain instances where voluntary attempts to achieve collective action fail and how they might be most effectively addressed through government interventions. For useful overviews of public choice, see Heckelman (2004) Mueller (1997, 2003), and Stevens (1993).

ACHIEVING COOPERATION

Cooperative action is crucial to human advancement. Governments can do a lot to set the terms for ensuring human interactions will be cooperative. However, there are limits to what can be achieved by government. As a society, it is preferable to have people know the right thing to do and to do it autonomously than to have a constant need to monitor and correct people's behavior. The reason is simple. If we can conserve the amount of resources that we put into checking on inappropriate behavior, then more resources can be devoted to social advancement. Indeed, when human cooperation works well, there is much that is marvelous about it (Axelrod 1984). As Adam Smith (1776) noted long ago, the daily coordination without overt coercion that occurs with respect to family life, organizational behavior, and commercial activity is staggering. When we add to that the acceleration of international trade, web-based interactions, and contemporary systems of transportation, we find much to marvel at. Yet often we take this coordinated action for granted. That is exactly as it should be. When systems are working well and we are able to use them effectively, we contribute to human advancement.

For government decision makers and their policy advisors, the continuous challenge is to ensure that our ways of organizing social and economic activity are as effective as possible. Of course, differences arise as to how we define effective-ness and so we need ways to promote productive discussions of our differences. Systems of representation and democratic governance are central to these efforts. Once we have the necessary knowledge and skills in place, policy analysts can contribute in many ways to productive discussions of this sort.

A REVIEW OF GOVERNMENT POLICY ACTIONS

Over centuries, governments have developed increasingly sophisticated means of structuring interactions in society and promoting continuous social and economic advancement. In what follows, a review is offered of major contemporary policy instruments. For introductory purposes, I here discuss these various instruments individually. However, in practice, it often happens that governments devise policy responses to specific problems that involve combinations of the instruments noted here. This makes sense because all policy instruments have strengths and weak-nesses and, given a particular context, looking for complementary ways to com-bine instruments might result in better overall outcomes than would be the case otherwise. In subsequent chapters we discuss further issues around instrument selection and creative combinations of approaches to addressing policy problems.

Market Making

There are at least three senses in which governments act as market makers. In discussions of the role of government in society, it is common for markets and governments to be characterized as completely separate institutional structures. Many times, that kind of characterization is reasonable in the sense that it allows us to focus on key distinctions between markets and governments and to discuss government measures that could improve the functioning of specific markets. However, when markets and governments are characterized as separate institu-tional structures, the implication then emerges that markets could operate on their own in the absence of government. In fact, markets cannot operate without sup-port from some minimal government structures. This is the first sense in which governments engage in market making.

To operate efficiently, markets depend upon clearly specified property rights and a system of rules and procedures that allow for effective enforcement of those property rights. That suggests a need for a legal system and a police force to uphold the rule of law. Markets also need a monetary system so that people can use cash as a medium of exchange. Stability of this monetary system is impor-tant. For example, it is crucial that inflationary pressures are limited so that people can make accurate predictions about the future value of goods and services. This calls for creation of government infrastructure, in the form of a central bank. It also requires systems of banking regulation that ensure people have peace of mind when engaging in transactions or planning for future transactions. Broadening out from this focus on the legal system and monetary system, we also see that governments must seek to create safe and peaceful conditions for their citizens.

Only under such conditions can markets develop and commercial enterprises flourish and expand. This suggests the need for government to keep defense forces that maintain their territorial integrity. In addition, governments need to develop systems of diplomacy both to avoid the potential for future conflicts and to support the kind of friendly international relations that allow national businesses to engage in productive trade with partners in other countries. Negotiation of free trade agreements represents important contemporary examples of ongoing governmental efforts to advance market development. So governments allow markets to operate. That is the first meaning of market making. It applies to the economy and markets in general.

The second way that governments engage in market making concerns efforts to facilitate or improve the functioning of specific markets. Often, this is achieved by removing impediments to market activity, what are often termed **market failures**. For example, if some parties to transactions routinely have more information than others and tend to use this information to their advantage, then it is possible that the market will implode. Here, **information asymmetries** are the source of trouble. The market for used cars offers a classic case. Often, incentives exist for associations of sellers or buyers or even nontrading third parties to provide information or establish other market conditions that allow the market to function (Akerlof 1970). But if those remedial actions by private parties do not transpire, then government action may be called for. This could take the form of requirements for traders to reveal information or the creation of rules concerning fair trade practices.

In other cases, when specification of property rights is difficult, the functions of particular markets might also be jeopardized. The problem emerges because of **negative externalities**, or harmful spillover effects on others of trading activities between a limited set of actors. For example, airports create a lot of noise due to the sound of jet engines during takeoff and landing. Governments can work to promote air travel while respecting the needs of residents. In the best cases, this can occur by requiring that airports be located where few people will be affected by the aircraft noise. In other cases, compromises might be worked out where flight paths alternate across different neighborhoods or curfews on flights are imposed during certain hours of the night. These efforts to manage the negative aspects of airport development allow for explanation of the market for air travel. In the absence of such government action, a range of problems and conflicts could arise, having negative effects for both economic development and the well-being of citizens.

A third sense in which governments act as market makers has become more common in the past few decades. As knowledge of market processes has deepened, government actors have sought ways to create market-like systems, or **quasi-markets,** to allocate goods, services, and rights that would have otherwise been allocated by some form of more centralized government action. For example, governments now offer many services on a fee-for-service or user-pays basis. Toll roads provide an obvious case. Indeed, governments have increasingly considered ways to balance traffic flow on toll roads by charging more for use of them when demand is highest. Governments also use vouchers as a method of subsidizing the uses that citizens make of services, while creating competitive dynamics in service supply. Instances of voucher use designed to generate new markets can be found in education, training, and health care. Finally, rights to the use of otherwise public resources, such as the airwaves, fisheries, and water, have increasingly been distributed through auction-like systems, where the rights go to the highest bidders. There is huge potential for creativity in this third kind of market making. Indeed, the development of emissions trading schemes and other ways of creating markets for waste products offer important recent examples.

Taxes

All governments impose taxes. In the first instance, they do so to raise revenues that fund all their other activities. Taxes make it possible for governments to develop policies and manage their organizational structures. Taxes can come in a wide variety of forms, including income taxes, business taxes, sales taxes, property taxes, and fees for services. The most important thing to note about *revenue-raising taxes* is that they need to be designed to have limited impact on citizens' behavior. If income taxes reduced work incentives or led people to hide the true amount of their income, then this would make it difficult for governments to achieve stable, predictable revenues. The general insight that emerges here is that governments should try to avoid imposing taxes at levels that are popularly perceived as unfair or onerous.

From the perspective of policy design, the more interesting kinds of taxes are those that are imposed with the deliberate aim of changing behaviors. These are often called *excise taxes*. Classic examples include taxes imposed on cigarettes and alcohol. Other examples include fines for traffic infringements or other illegal behavior. Employers can be served with stiff penalties, for example, if they fail to maintain a safe workplace, as specified in relevant rules. As many people have observed, taxes are pervasive in society. They usually require payment in the form of a percentage of the value of a transaction or as a lump-sum payment.

Much to the chagrin of the average citizen, the opportunities are almost endless for policy analysts to be creative with designing taxes. In general, good tax design involves thinking carefully about the effect that the tax will have on behavior. It is also important to think in terms of *compliance costs*. The easier it is for taxes to be paid, the better. Taxes imposed to raise revenue should be as painless as possible. But taxes that are imposed deliberately to reduce socially undesirable activity should be perceived as painful. Pain is the point. Their pain is intended as an incentive for behavioral change in directions perceived as socially desirable.

Subsidies

Governments provide subsidies to citizens, nonprofit organizations, and businesses. Subsidies are cash transfers. A subsidy occurs whenever an individual or entity receives cash from the government that is not a payment for service.

Subsides can also come in the form of *service provision*. For example, people may receive a service at no cost or at greatly reduced cost. In such cases, no cash payments go back from the government to the recipients, but the recipients do experience a benefit equivalent to an injection of cash into their bank account. As with a tax, the intentions behind any given subsidy will matter greatly for how it is designed and administered.

Some subsidies are designed as *social cushions*, to help people or organizations during difficult, transitional times. In the first instance, they are not intended to change behavior. For example, former full-time employees who lose their jobs and are required to search for new employment might reasonably be expected to live on any savings they have while looking for a new job. However, they might be entitled to a government benefit. In some countries this is referred to as unemployment insurance. In others, it might be called the unemployment benefit. In all cases, it is a subsidy in the form of a cash payment. Most importantly, the subsidy is designed to assist a person to cover the costs of living with dignity during temporary unemployment. The subsidy is not intended to change behavior. It would be a policy failure, for example, if those deemed eligible for the subsidy were to claim it and promptly abandon their job search in favor of taking a holiday at the expense of taxpayers. To guard against such eventualities, most subsidies of this kind come with strings attached. There is typically a stand-down period between job termination and eligibility for a benefit. There are also typically limits on how long a benefit will be paid. In addition, to reduce benefit abuse, eligibility requirements often include evidence of actively seeking work or being in some kind of training.

Many subsidies are designed to encourage behavioral changes on the part of individuals and organizations. These payment "carrots" operate as mirror images of excise tax "sticks." A vast array of examples exists of governments using *subsidies as incentives* to promote desired behaviors. For individuals, many subsidies can appear almost invisible. For example, they might come in the form of co-payments from the government to general practitioners so that patients rarely need to cover the full cost of seeing doctors when they are ill. The reasoning behind subsidies of this sort is that it is better to have patients establish contact with the health-care system shortly after the onset of illness than to put off seeking help until trauma strikes, which could require the more costly options of emergency treatment and hospitalization. As another example, governments often subsidize public transport in the expectation that if travel to work by bus or train becomes cheap enough, more people will switch from commuting in private vehicles. For firms, many governments provide incentives for investment in research and development. The subsidies can come in the form of lump-sum payments, or *tax rebates*. Tax rebates are also sometimes called tax expenditures, in the sense that the government subsidizes specific behaviors through a system that effectively reduces the government's tax collection. Tax rebates are an attractive means of conferring subsidies because they involve limited administration compare with systems where taxes are collected and then subsidies are paid out again.

Regulation

Governments care greatly about the behaviors of individuals, families, nonprofit organizations and firms. Often, governments impose sets of rules on what is considered appropriate behavior. These are referred to as regulations. Government regulation can come in many forms and be intended to address a variety of issues.

Procedural and *technical regulations* are frequently used to achieve greater safety and higher standards of professional practice in society. In all cases, such regulations are intended to reduce the possibility of negative social consequences or harm arising from specific activities. Licensing represents a classic form of regulation. We are prohibited from driving a car without a driver's license. The obvious reason for this is that if we were not held to specific standards of practice and knowledge concerning driving, we could easily end up being a danger to ourselves and others on the road. Individual professionals and organizations in many industries are also subject to regulation of their practices. For example, significant bodies of building regulations specify the construction methods and materials that must be used in development of particular structures. Individuals associated with the building industry, such as plumbers, electricians, and engineers, must all have up-to-date operating licenses and are usually required to hold specific forms of insurance to cover catastrophic events that might arise out of malpractice. Finally, organizations that engage in activities with the potential to put members of the public at serious risk are subject to extensive regulation. Airlines, bus companies, and taxi companies must all follow detailed rules about operating procedures. These can range from provisions concerning length of time a pilot or driver can operate without a break to maintenance requirements and record keeping.

Economic regulations are often used by governments to guide and constrain the activities of businesses in sectors where, for technical reasons, it is most feasible for just one or a small number of suppliers to be operating. This is a form of market failure called *natural monopoly*. Historically, large infrastructural industries such as electricity, railroads, and airlines have during parts of their development been subjected to significant regulation with regard to pricing arrangements and other aspects of their relations with consumers. Often, as industries mature and more knowledge emerges of how they operate, it becomes possible for government regulations to be reduced. Deregulation must be handled carefully, however. By significantly altering the general operating contexts for industries, deregulation typically ushers in periods of structural adjustment. These can have unintended consequences, such as the jeopardizing of continuous service, even when the longer-term results of a deregulatory move might be highly positive for consumers.

Social regulations cover yet another broad field of human endeavor. They can include rules concerning appropriate disposal and recycling of household waste, how much noise people can make in their neighborhoods, censorship of films and literature, the eligibility of two people for marriage, and appropriate ways to discipline children, among many other things.

A significant concern that arises whenever regulations are imposed is that they might reduce the potential for innovation to occur within the regulated area of activity. Sometimes this is referred to as *technical lock-in*. Critics of heavy-handed, or "command-and-control," regulation have proposed that alternative mechanisms be used to promote those behaviors expected to yield desired social and economic outcomes (Friedman 1962; Schultze 1977). For example, recent efforts to reduce greenhouse gas emissions have tended to make use of both regulation and tax-based incentives programs (Hahn 2009).

Direct Service Supply

Governments often take responsibility for providing services for public use. This direct service supply is most readily observed in cases where it would be difficult to imagine adequate service provision occurring if the matter were left to nongovernment entities to resolve. Another way to put this is that a lot of the responsibilities for service provision that fall to governments do so because they have ended up in the "too hard" basket of society. Of course, once governments have established the infrastructures and procedures necessary to support direct service supply, it often happens that ways can be found to place some of the responsibility for supply back into private hands. But the point remains that in the absence of government actions, service supply could well have been patchy, poorly coordinated, or nonexistent. Examples of direct service supply include most local government services, such as water supply, sewage systems, roads and parks. They also include national defense, the legal system, and police services. The development of the welfare state saw the increasing involvement of governments in the direct supply of public schooling and, in many countries, health services.

When considering government involvement in direct service supply, it is useful to think of it as consisting of two broad functions. The first is funding. Governments raise taxes to fund these services. In some instances, they might require some part of the costs associated with service supply to be paid for by service recipients. So, for example, the basic infrastructure of water supply is usually funded by government. However, individual households are required to make payments for water supply that are related to how much water they use. Sometimes this funding function of government is also referred to as service provision. That is, governments, through funding, make service provision possible.

The second broad function of government in direct service supply is service delivery. This is where government employs the service providers and coordinates the creation and maintenance of the facilities that allow for service delivery. With respect to the water supply example, this means that governments often manage the reservoirs, pumps, and pipelines that supply water to households. They also employ the workers who maintain these systems and who interact with consumers.

In all cases of direct government supply, governments take responsibility for both service funding and service delivery. However, consideration of service funding and service delivery as being separable functions has led to a range of cases where governments have moved toward using other parties to engage in service delivery (Horn 1995; Osbourne and Gaebler 1992). In the case of public schooling, it remains commonplace around the world for governments to both fund and supply schooling. Most teachers are paid as government employees, and school buildings and grounds are treated as government property. However, cases can also be found where funding and supply are separated. School voucher programs introduce the possibility of public funding of schools with private supply (Moe 2001). In this instance, companies or nonprofit organizations establish schools and employ the teachers. The ongoing viability of the schools depends on their ability to attract revenue, which is directly related to their ability to attract and maintain government-funded students.

Funding and Contracting

The conceptual distinction drawn between funding for service provision and actual service delivery introduces a significant question: When should governments do things for themselves and when should they purchase services from others? This can also be thought of as the "make-or-buy" decision (Donahue 1989). Interestingly, all of us face this kind of decision in our own households. Should we cook a meal at home tonight, or should we go to a restaurant? Should we clean the car, or have someone do it for us? Should we try to do all the planning and arranging for an important family celebration, or should we leave it to a professional event planner? Reflecting on the pros and cons of our answers to questions like this can yield some insights into the kinds of issues and trade-offs that governments must confront when they address the "make-or-buy" decision.

In many instances, governments act as the funders of services but leave service supply to contracted third parties (Savas 1987). Those third parties, that can be either corporations or nonprofit organization, serve as intermediaries between the government and the service recipients. The practice of funding and contracting has been attractive to many governments—from the national level to the local level—because it has been considered a useful way to reduce the costs of service supply. For example, a local government might fund garbage collection but contract private companies to do the actual work of regularly collecting and disposing of domestic waste. Those contract agreements might last for a period of several years before a new call is made for private companies to bid for the contract for the next time period. The likelihood that there will be competition for the service contract increases the likelihood that each company bidding for the contract will seek to offer the best package of proposed services and cost.

Funding and contracting reduce the number of people officially on government payrolls and hold the promise of promoting competition, organizational innovation, and the pursuit of efficiency gains in service delivery. However, contracting itself requires that careful effort and, hence, significant resources are devoted to contract specification, contract negotiation, and the monitoring of service provision. Often, with time, governments gain more experience with contracting and with knowing how to manage contracting problems. A lot of issues must be considered. For example, in contexts where it is likely that services from one provider will be substituted for those of another, it is important that part of the contract negotiation work involves a request for interested parties to carefully detail how they will manage the transition in service supply from one party to another. A vast array of examples of funding and contracting can be found. These range from management of parks, schools, and public transport to airport security services, transportation of prisoners, and the operation of prisons.

Partnering and Facilitating

Concerns about the growing size of government and the need to make efficiency gains have provided the major impetus for moves among governments to contract with third parties for the delivery of services. But recognition of the limits of government and the possible strengths of nongovernment entities has also grown over the past two decades. The confluence of these two streams of thought has resulted in an emerging tendency for governments to make use of two relatively new policy instruments. These are, first, partnering with other entities to deliver services and, second, playing a facilitation role with the aim of bringing together and helping to strike up mutually beneficial dialogues among actors in the nonprofit and voluntary sectors that do a great deal to support individuals, families, and groups that might otherwise rely upon government for support services.

Partnering can happen at various levels of government, although to date it has probably been more commonly found in local government settings (Rosenau 2000). Partnering occurs when a government agency enters an agreement with other entities to work together to produce a specific outcome. For example, a state government might offer seed funding for a new research facility and propose to match dollar-for-dollar contributions made by universities and industries, up to a set amount. Such a partnering effort recognizes that the state stands to gain from research that has commercial relevance, but that universities and particular industries stand to gain as well. Often these partnerships are established with the purpose of achieving a specific goal. Once that goal is achieved, the partnership is dissolved. Yet aside from proving beneficial in terms of allowing a goal to be reached that would not have been reached in the absence of the partnership, partnering can also produce spin-off gains at a procedural level. For example, when a government agency partners with another organization, it provides opportunities for personnel from both to work alongside each other, gain operational insights from each other, and share ideas and experiences. Such informal processes of learning can be helpful for both parties, opening the possibilities for each to make informed adjustments to aspects of their organizational goals and standard operating procedures.

Facilitating occurs when governments promote meetings and forge formal or informal alliances among organizations that share a common goal or common set of goals. For example, a government might wish to improve the quality of water in a particular river system. To do this effectively might require identifying a range of local organizations—many of whom might be voluntary—and finding ways to get those actors working together to pursue agreed goals. This form of government action is based on an understanding that governments typically have more resources to draw on—in terms of expertise, networks of contacts, records, and so on—than do other organizations. At the same time, such action is also informed by the realization that local nongovernmental actors often have much better knowledge and understanding of specific aspects of their context and local needs and concerns than governments could ever acquire without becoming highly intrusive. The actual work of facilitating typically involves identifying and contacting relevant actors, organizing meetings, helping groups to deliberate together around shared goals, and helping to set and monitor the series of activities that will allow those goals to be reached. Skills in working with others, delegating, resolving conflicts, and so on are extremely important for this kind of policy intervention (Forester 1999).

Information and Social Marketing

The quality of human decision making is influenced both by the quality of information that people have to base their decisions on and their abilities to effectively process that information. To a significant degree, efforts to carefully present information to people can serve to compensate for cognitive limitations (Thaler and Sunstein 2008). Therefore, the quality of information and the effectiveness of its presentation are vital keys to promoting good social outcomes. Governments engage in a variety of efforts to support improved decision making on the part of citizens.

It is commonplace for the producers of goods and services to have more information about their products than average consumers. This need not be a problem unless the producers are tempted to use informational differences to their strategic advantage. Often, producers will recognize for themselves the value in sharing product information with consumers. But to help consumers make well-informed purchases, governments frequently apply regulations requiring producers to reveal specific product details. For example, most food packaging now includes a table or list of the main ingredients of the product and notes any ingredients that could adversely affect people's health.

Governments can use other instruments to improve citizen decision making. For example, organizational report cards are increasingly being used to help citizens compare service provision on a variety of attributes (Gormley and Weimer 1999). It is now common to find government websites with detailed comparative information on the quality of schools, health-care services, and so on. Of course, other nongovernment entities also produce report cards. College guides are a classic example, as are guides to the differing qualities and attributes of automobiles. So it is possible for adequate information to be provided in many cases without government efforts. But sometimes it is easier for governments to collate and present relevant information than it would be for nongovernment actors to do so. This is because governments tend to amass high-quality information as part of their efforts to ensure accountability for the spending of government money and their routine monitoring efforts.

Organizational report cards, at a minimum, present comparative information and leave it to consumer-citizens to draw their own conclusions. However, it is also common to find report cards being supported with advice-giving narratives. A variation on this is government provision of advice for citizens and for other organizations. For example, many governments either fund or actually produce websites and supporting literature and activities designed to give advice on a range of topics. Government websites can be found offering advice on how to establish and run businesses and how to address common business problems or concerns. Websites offering advice on how to stay healthy are also common, as are websites that offer advice for parents on good practice for child-rearing or for raising happy, energetic, community-minded teenagers.

A further variation on the advice-giving efforts of government involves the use of public information campaigns (Weiss and Tschirhart 1994). A broader description is social marketing. Here, governments make use of various media formats with the explicit goal of shaping citizen attitudes in the hopes that these will promote positive behavioral changes. Examples include marketing campaigns to promote safer driving. At any given time, the package of activities involved in a campaign of this kind might include graphic television advertisements, pamphlet drops in schools and workplaces, and use of billboards along highways. Actors dressed as the grim reaper have been known to appear near danger spots on main highways during holiday periods. Other examples of social marketing include efforts to change people's drinking habits and to put people off smoking. Often, all of these marketing efforts serve to reinforce the goals of other policy instruments, such as fines for driving infringements, taxes on alcohol and tobacco, restrictions on who may buy certain goods, and regulations prohibiting consumption of particular products in specific places.

Frameworks and Strategies

Governments seek to promote improved social and economic outcomes for citizens living within their jurisdictions. To do this, they must find productive ways to engage with citizens and other social entities. Often, this involves governments making regulations or introducing new services, subsidies, or taxes. The tendency for governments to promulgate frameworks and strategies simultaneously displays awareness, on the one hand, that there are limits to what governments can do to create change and, on the other, that governments are well placed to offer social and economic leadership. Branding a region as "the next Silicon Valley" or "the Smart State" sends a signal to citizens and businesses that the government is serious about shaping a particular regional identity. The implication is that activities having a clear or even tangential connection to this brand will be viewed favorably by government.

Frameworks and strategies can take a variety of forms, from simple locational branding efforts to detailed initiatives that might join aspects of social marketing with the introduction of a variety of new subsidies, efforts to forge new partnerships, facilitate network development, and so on (Mintrom and Wanna 2006). For example, government efforts to promote economic transformation and knowledge-based economic development might be initiated by publication of a strategy document. This might be followed by the announcement of a set of new subsidies for businesses engaging in research and development in specific areas. It might also be accompanied by new, targeted funding to universities designed to encourage them to build partnerships with local firms to speed up the development of promising scientific discoveries into new, profit-making technologies. The presentation of the framework and continuous reference back to it is intended to set the broad terms upon which relevant organizations will interact and engage in mutually beneficial activities. Within government, these types of efforts can do quite a lot to break down parochial, blinkered thinking and promote more inter-agency coordination and collaboration around shared goals.

The effectiveness of these policy instruments depends greatly upon the energy and focus that lead agencies bring to their application (Bardach 1998). At their best, they can do a great deal to promote coordinated cross-agency and cross-sector collaborations. However, their weakness is that they are based solely on powers of persuasion with no supporting mechanisms to compel coordinated action. At their worst, then, frameworks and strategies can start to look like variants on social marketing. Viewed cynically, they can appear as window dressing, in the sense that they indicate governments are taking an issue or problem seriously, while in reality few new policy initiatives or government resources may be devoted to the cause.

Summary

This review has sought to give a basic introduction to the most important contemporary policy instruments used by governments. Table 3.1 offers a checklist of what governments do. It is expected that this table will prove helpful as a reminder

Table 3.1 A Checklist of Government Policy Actions

Market Making	Regulation	Information and Social Marketing
• Setting the general context	• Technical	• Advisory services
• Addressing specific market problems	• Economic	• Service report cards
• Using vouchers and auctions	• Social	• Advertising
Taxes	**Direct Service Supply**	**Frameworks and Strategies**
• Raising revenues	• Funding provision	• Branding
• Excise taxes, fees, and fines	• Service delivery	• Coordinating actions
Subsidies	**Funding and Contracting**	• Promoting cooperation
• Income maintenance	• Contract specification	
• Targeted assistance	• Contract negotiation	
• Tax rebate	• Contract monitoring	
• In-kind transfer	**Partnering and Facilitating**	
	• Seed and matching funds	
	• Achieving shared goals by working with others	

of the broad array of possible ways that governments might seek to address specific problems. As noted here, some instruments are obviously best suited to addressing particular sets of problems and are not so good at addressing others. However, there are many times when brainstorming around the possibilities for taking unusual approaches to matching policy instruments to problems can lead to breakthrough thinking about ways forward with developing proposals for policy change.

INCREASING COMPLEXITY

Our inherent desire to achieve order and to seek improvement in the human condition has led to many incredible inventions during the course of human history. Democratic government and the capitalist system represent exemplary cases of what has been achieved through inventiveness and sustained efforts to make things better. Humanity is fallible; we are not angels. Despite that, we have made progress in terms of advancing human development. Interestingly, advances in human endeavor—across a spectrum of activities—often reveal new problems that must be managed if those advances are to have their biggest positive impacts. For example, advances in transportation technology and in diplomatic relations have opened many new possibilities for global trade. However, with increasing trade come risks of increased exploitation of people, violations of human rights, fraud of many kinds, and other criminal activity. The great positive prospects of expanded global trade must therefore be balanced against some of the negative elements. This situation forces governments—and policy analysts employed by them—to think seriously about ways to use policy instruments to guide and constrain developments in ways that lead to better outcomes all around.

Much the same can be said for advances in computing and information technology. The wonders of the Internet bring with them new opportunities for exploitative and criminal behavior. Likewise, astonishing advances in biotechnology, genomics, and nanotechnology all must be supported by advances in policy thinking. In all cases, these advances bring with them both opportunities and threats. Recognizing this inevitability about human advancement, we see that the work of policy analysis and development can never be expected to remain predictable or to be perfectable. Increasing complexity brings with it increased need for careful thinking about policy issues. This is an important reason that we need to augment our knowledge of policy instruments and what policy interventions have worked well in the past with a constant curiosity about future directions and their implications for policy design. Human development brings increasing complexity. As such, it brings continuous challenges for policy analysts.

LOOKING AHEAD

Gaining familiarity with the things governments do is important to your development as a policy analyst. To develop your analytical capacity, it is important that you are able to readily determine how policies applied in a given context to address a specific problem approximate to one or more of the generic policy instruments discussed in this chapter. Having identified the instrument or instruments currently in use, you can then begin to develop your knowledge around both their general strengths and weaknesses, as discussed in the relevant literature, and their strengths and weaknesses as they have been applied in the context of interest to you. The more you learn about policy instruments and effective ways to make use of them, the better able you will be to propose creative solutions to specific policy problems.

Exercises

1. In small groups, write down a local example of each of the things governments do, as summarized in Table 3.1.
2. In your groups, identify a policy problem that could be addressed in several different ways, using different policy instruments. Try to think of at least three different ways that the problem could be addressed.

Further Reading

Bardach, Eugene. (2008). "Appendix B: Things Governments Do." In *A Practical Guide for Policy Analysis*. 3rd ed. Washington, DC: CQ Press.

Friedman, Milton. (1962). "The Role of Government in a Free Society." In *Capitalism and Freedom*, chap. 2. Chicago: University of Chicago Press.

North, Douglass C. (1990). "An Introduction to Institutions and Institutional Change." In *Institutions, Institutional Change and Economic Performance*, chap. 1. New York: Cambridge University Press.

Osborne, David, and Ted Gaebler. (1992). "Catalytic Government: Steering Rather than Rowing." In *Reinventing Government: How the Entrepreneurial Spirit Is Transforming the Public Sector*, chap. 1. Reading, MA: Addison-Wesley.

Salamon, Lester M. (2002). "The New Governance and the Tools of Government Action: An Introduction." In *The Tools of Government: A Guide to the New Governance*, ed. Lester M. Salamon, chap. 1. New York: Oxford University Press.

Weimer, David L., and Aidan R. Vining. (2005). "Correcting Market and Government Failures: Generic Policies." In *Policy Analysis: Concepts and Practice*, chap. 10. Upper Saddle River, NJ: Pearson Prentice Hall.

4

>✐◯

Objectives of Government Policy Actions

The Story So Far... We have reviewed the nature of policy analysis, what policy analysts do, and the policy instruments that are available for governments to use in addressing policy problems.

Here... We review common objectives of government policy action. These provide rationales for the use of specific policy instruments. Many different arguments can be made for policy action. It is useful for policy analysts to be aware of these arguments. Different policy instruments tend to be used, depending on the rationales given for policy action. But we rarely find one-to-one relationships between government objectives and policy instruments.

THIS CHAPTER REVIEWS

- Approaches to discussing government policy action
- Human flourishing as an objective of government
- Improved institutional performance as an objective of government
- Efficient resource allocation as an objective of government
- Equity among citizens as an objective of government
- Problem definition and agenda setting

W hy do governments do what they do? That question has preoccupied scholars of politics and government for centuries. My purpose in this chapter is not to summarize what the great books have said on this topic. However, as policy analysts, we do need to lift our vision above the technical level; we need to be able to say more about why particular policy approaches might be adopted than simply that a given instrument seems good, given the problem at hand. Many people, from a range of backgrounds, seek to engage in discussions and debates concerning public policies. As policy analysts, we can enhance our practice by improving our ability to understand how others think about public policy issues and why they use specific language to discuss particular issues or problems.

Sometimes, policy analysts are portrayed as narrowly technical participants in policy discussions. Undoubtedly, some policy analysts approach their work narrowly. However, if we seek to add significant value to policy discussions, then we need to broaden our perspective. Take the example of an excise tax, as introduced in Chapter 3. Speaking in a narrow, technical way, we could say that the purpose of a tax on alcohol is that the government wants to provide a disincentive for excessive drinking. We could then perform estimates of the relationship between the margin of the tax and observed outcomes in consumer behavior. But by looking more broadly at the matter, we begin to think about ways that government actions can protect individuals and those around them from harm. We begin to ask questions about bigger social goals and the things that government can do—through the use of policy instruments—to advance those goals. In so doing, we start to think in comparative terms about alternative policy instruments and the strengths and weaknesses of each, given our broader social goals. Eventually, we might still conduct a test allowing us to estimate the relationship between the margin of the tax and observed outcomes in consumer behavior. But along the way, we are likely to have discovered new ideas about the issue at hand.

This chapter offers an approach to considering objectives of government policy action. I do not discuss the original state of nature and how we might get beyond it. Thankfully, we have moved on. Today, the predominant form of government in the world is one that is based on democratic representation, with representatives receiving expert advice from professional staff. Governments recognize the power of markets. It is also generally agreed that choice in the marketplace and choice among candidates in elections are both consistent with the pursuit of a harmonious society, in the face of significant individual differences in preferences (Dahl 1998). As globalization has brought with it increasing flows of people across national borders, we also find multiculturalism becoming a fact of life in many places. The pursuit of effective ways to manage multiculturalism and, hence, promote positive social outcomes, is an important role for governments, and one in which policy choices can do a lot to help or harm those efforts (Kymlicka 2007). Increasingly, we also find governments around the world wrestling with environmental concerns and issues associated with the pursuit of sustainable development (Roosa 2008).

At the broadest level, public policies represent efforts by governments to structure human behavior through the application and enforcement of rules, and by other actions, such as the supply of specific kinds of goods and services (Bok 1996; Ostrom, Gardner, and Walker 1994). When public policies are put in place, they typically result in substitution of public decision making for private decision making. To be more comprehensive, we might say that public policy choices revolve around this question: *When should centralized, public decision making augment or even supplant decentralized, private decision making?* The question is a normative one. That is to say, it cannot be answered entirely with reference to evidence. Any answers we put forward will be informed—either implicitly or explicitly—by value judgments. Being human, policy analysts make value judgments all the time as private citizens. In their professional role, policy analysts also make value judgments. However, acting as professionals, they should strive to make their value judgments explicit or to put their value judgments aside and assess the matter at hand in a fashion that is as objective as possible. It is important to be explicit about values and how they might guide decision making. In highly partisan contexts, it is possible for policy analysts to add considerable value to policy discussions and debates by taking care to expose relevant values and reveal, to the extent that it is possible, the likely outcomes that would result from pursuing policies that adhere to those values.

But how do we tackle questions of power in society? People in power positions in society are likely to exercise that power when it is expected to help them to achieve goals that they desire (Mayhew 1974). This matters for policy making. It raises the possibility that policy analysis and advice based upon it will be ignored. When policy analysts are employed by powerful people who direct them to discuss policy alternatives in specific ways and ignore relevant evidence, there is not a lot that can be done. You could politely suggest that the decision at hand would gain more support if the accompanying analysis were sound and as free as possible from political influence. And, in general, we might note that expanding knowledge of public policy development and how to perform careful policy analysis can be a democratizing, empowering act. Good quality information and objective analysis—appropriately coupled with smart advocacy efforts—can change power relations. It can also take a long time (Weiss 1980, 1992).

The chapter proceeds as follows. First, it presents an approach to thinking systematically about government action. Next, it is proposed that government action is generally intended to promote human flourishing. This leads into a discussion of social institutions and their relationships with government. Here, it is argued that public policies are designed to address instances of institutional failure, which can be found across institutional forms, including families, markets, businesses, nonprofit organizations, and governments themselves. This broad understanding of the objectives of government action helps us to explain why public policies often operate on moral dimensions, as well as efficiency and equity dimensions. Out of this discussion, an inventory is drawn of key objectives of government and some related goals. These are what typically motivate the development and implementation of public policies. While not intended to be exhaustive, the inventory offered here is more inclusive than the set of objectives often associated with government action in earlier books on policy analysis.

DISCUSSING GOVERNMENT POLICY ACTION

In popular discussions of governments and of public policies, a range of words are used almost interchangeably to describe government actions. This section

Table 4.1 Defining Key Terms

TERMS	DEFINITIONS	EXAMPLES
Objective	A significant desired achievement that is a focus of activities and that requires major investment of resources and effort.	*Individual:* To earn a university degree. *Public:* To reduce traffic congestion in a particular city.
Strategy	A coherent plan that breaks specific objectives into sets of goals and indicates the actions that will support goal attainment.	*Individual:* My semester-by-semester course plan. *Public:* Our five-year plan for improved traffic flow.
Goal	A specified, measurable achievement that, when met, contributes to the achievement of a broader objective.	*Individual:* To pass this university course. *Public:* To improve public transport on the currently busiest route.
Action	Any activity that requires time and other resources.	*Individual:* Studying for an exam *Public:* Putting more frequent bus service on the currently busiest route.
Purpose	How an action contributes to a goal or objective.	*Individual:* Studying improves exam performance. *Public:* A more frequent bus service helps people switch from using cars to using buses.
Rationale	A reason given for taking a particular action, linking it to a goal or objective.	*Individual:* Passing this exam will help me to pass this course and gain a degree. *Public:* More buses will reduce traffic congestion.
Policy	A rule intended to promote consistency of action, given specific conditions.	*Individual:* Whenever I have an exam, I study for it. *Public:* We have allocated additional funds to allow more frequent bus services on the currently busiest routes.

offers a systematic way of drawing distinctions between some key terms. It also shows how those terms relate to one another. The central focus of this chapter is objectives of government policy action. *Objectives* are here portrayed as desired achievements or social outcomes. Once specified, these objectives provide a focus for government activities. Those activities tend to require major investment of resources and efforts. Improving institutional performance, promoting efficient resource allocation, and pursuing social equity all represent broad objectives of government action in almost all settings. Often, governments specify their objectives using *strategy* documents. These represent efforts to portray sets of *goals* associated with the pursuit of particular objectives. These goals are usually more specific and more easily measured than broader objectives. Often, strategy documents also state *actions* that governments intend to take in pursuit of specific sets of goals and particular objectives. When actions are discussed, attention can be devoted to the *purposes* of those actions.

The purpose of an action is simply the way that it is seen as contributing to a goal or objective. Discussions of actions can also lead to the stating of *rationales*. A rationale is a reason or justification given for taking a particular action. Importantly, rationales serve to link actions back to goals and objectives. A statement of purpose tends to be quite factual, operating at the technical level mentioned earlier. In contrast, a statement of the rationale for an action can be more subjective in nature. One action might be accorded multiple rationales.

A *policy* can be thought of as a rule intended to promote consistency of action, given specific conditions. As individuals, all of us can have our own policies. These are the commitments we make to ourselves about how we intend to behave in the world. *Public policies* operate in the same way. They are the commitments that governments make on the behalf of their citizens concerning public action. Public policies, then, are rules that generate consistent government actions in response to specific conditions.

Table 4.1 summarizes this definition of terms and offers a set of individual and public examples to show the relevance of the terms to our individual practices and the practices of governments. Although it might seem pedantic to lay out these terms in this fashion, it is helpful to try to be precise and systematic in our use of language. Indeed, this is the starting point for development of an approach to exploring policy issues and problems that we will frequently return to throughout subsequent chapters of this book.

PROMOTING HUMAN FLOURISHING

As individuals, we appear to have an inherent desire to advance ourselves. Human history, for the most part, is the story of advance in the quality of human life and the stretching of human potential. In families, that desire for advance is manifest in the ways that adults nurture children and young people. Often, we observe people deferring present gratification so that they can invest in their own development or in the development of others around them. In the realm of business, we observe this same desire for advance. It is common to hear people say that businesses care only about the bottom line, about making profits for shareholders. Of course, businesses do have to care about profitability. Yet that drive to achieve monetary success serves as a powerful motivator for business leaders to deliver products and services that customers like. As such, whatever the private motives of business leaders, those motives contribute to broader social outcomes. Here, I equate the striving for advancement of ourselves and others with the desire to promote human flourishing.

At the outset of this chapter, I posed the question, "Why do governments do what they do?" Now we can state our first answer to that question. Governments do what they do because they seek to promote human flourishing. This objective of government is manifest in the pursuit of a variety of related goals. For example, governments at all levels have created structures and systems to promote social and economic advancement. Governments do an enormous amount to encourage human freedom. Consistent with this, they also support individual initiative and make investments that serve to support and celebrate human creativity and curiosity. The efforts to promote human flourishing are not solely geared toward individuals. Governments also take many actions intended to promote a sense of community. These can range from the support of education to advancement of democracy, the adoption of local planning rules, and the creation of social welfare systems. At the broadest level, then, much government activity—and hence, the making of public policies—is conducted with the objective of promoting human flourishing.

PROMOTING EFFECTIVE INSTITUTIONS

Governments do much to shape and support social institutions. At the broadest level, institutions can be thought of as the rules of the game that dictate how we should conduct ourselves in a broad range of situations (North 1990). Often, individuals operate as parts of organizations that can be seen as coordinated efforts to flourish or advance within the rules of the game as established by institutions. In contemporary society, the three most influential sets of institutional arrangements are those relating to the family, the marketplace, and government itself. These institutions, in their various manifestations, serve to shape and guide our individual and collective behaviors. While they impose significant constraints on us, institutions also serve to facilitate productive and creative activity. Often, we become blind to those institutions and their influence upon us. Think, for example, of the ways that our commitment to the use of a common language influences our behavior. As we write and as we talk, we constantly confront rules of grammar that shape and constrain how we communicate. At the same time, that set of basic rules opens space for an infinite amount of creative activity. The same can be said of the legal system, the monetary system, and codes of moral practice.

By embodying a set of fixed rules, institutions reduce uncertainty. They allow individuals and organizations to develop standard operating procedures for performing effectively within their chosen contexts. When people take action, institutions provide feedback that either affirms or negates those actions. Actions that are affirmed tend to be repeated. Those actions that are negated quickly cease. Institutions, and the feedback they give, therefore promote social learning and stability (Hodgson 1998).

Institutions change slowly because the whole point of their existence is to promote stability. Several important insights flow from here. First, institutional stability promotes the phenomenon of path dependency (David 1994; Pierson 2000). In practice, this means that where we start out from significantly affects subsequent developments. For example, the rules that state the side of the road on which one drives an automobiles must have, among other things, influenced the design of automobiles, the planning of roads, the development of car parks, and the siting of malls. To try to introduce a switch now would be a costly and unpopular exercise.[1] But a second insight arises here. That is, many of the design aspects of institutions are arbitrary. While path dependencies have developed around the side of the road that automobiles must be driven on, we must also note that in some countries people drive on the left-hand side of the road; in others they drive on the right. What practice is correct? There is no right or wrong answer. But once the institutions are in place, you flaunt the rules at your peril.

While institutions are slow to change, pressures do sometimes emerge that indicate a need for change. Evolution in social norms or innovations in other parts of the broad institutional structure of society can generate such pressures. For example, employment conditions in advanced industrial countries have progressively improved over time. Discrimination in hiring practices has declined, the length of the typical workweek has been reduced, workplace safety has been enhanced, health insurance and retirement benefits have been introduced, and employers have become more flexible in granting employees holiday leave or leave associated with specific sets of circumstances, such as new parenthood, sickness, or family bereavement. Some of these changes have come about through competitive pressures in the labor market. Employers have had to make improvements in the conditions of work to remain attractive to potential employees. However, other changes have come about because employee groups lobbied governments to enforce improvements in working conditions.

Through the rules and structures that they develop and maintain, governments do a lot to support nongovernmental institutions in society, such as the family and the marketplace. Given the powerful role that governments can play in supporting institutions, it is often government that people turn to when they seek to promote institutional change. Many public policies can be viewed as efforts by

---

[1] In 2009, Samoa switched from right-hand traffic to left-hand traffic. The idea was to allow the import of cheaper used cars from Japan and New Zealand, rather than the more expensive used cars from the United States. The switch met with major protests. The government called a national holiday for people to get used to the switch. A New Zealand car crash investigator predicted a dramatic increase in smash ups in the immediate aftermath of the change.

governments to reform and improve the workings of the broader set of institutions in society.

Beyond promoting human flourishing, the pursuit of effective institutions represents a key objective of government. Toward that end, we find governments doing a great deal to protect citizens and their possessions. This is done through development and maintenance of defense systems, of efforts to advance and maintain the rule of law, and of efforts that promote democratic principles in society. Through their public policy efforts, governments also encourage effective institutions in the form of well-functioning markets and the expansion of markets into new areas. Through public policies, governments also do much to protect families and to support families in their efforts to raise and nurture healthy, happy children.

Even as governments shape and support other social institutions, governments themselves operate as institutions. That is, government reduces down to a set of rules and a range of organizational structures designed to develop and maintain those rules. Significantly, the efforts that governments have made over the centuries to support social and economic development have resulted in the growth of government systems. Observers have long noted that, for all the good that governments clearly do in society, elements of government systems can grow outdated, redundant, or problematic over time. The literature on government failure offers many examples of how the institutional structures of government can come to generate negative social outcomes. That is a matter we return to in Chapter 11.

To conclude this preliminary discussion of institutions and institutional failure, three points deserve emphasis. First, although institutional change can come about without government engagement (Ostrom 1990), governments are the most powerful and efficacious force in society for promoting institutional change. The centralization of authority and amassing of power associated with modern government have produced this situation. Because governments have acquired a significant level of power and legitimacy in society, it is common to find groups of people turning to government for action, even when other organizations in society could potentially take remedial actions to improve specific situations. Second, in the pursuit of the objective of securing effective institutions, it is important for governments to continuously look for ways to improve their own effectiveness. Therefore, it is common to find governments pursuing the goal of improving public management and governance arrangements (Ingraham 2007; Kettl and DiIulio 1995). Consistent with this goal, administrative simplicity and efficiency often become goals for governments. When governments introduce new public policies, as well as seek to promote a range of other objectives and goals, administrative efficiency and simplicity are often accorded high priority.

PROMOTING EFFICIENCY

Efficient use of resources is generally taken to mean usage that produces the least amount of wastage. The Italian economist Vilfredo Pareto (1848–1923) made a significant conceptual contribution to our understanding of efficiency. According to

Pareto, an economic system is inefficient if a change in the allocation of resource would result in some individuals becoming better off without anyone becoming worse off. A *Pareto improvement* is said to occur when a change in the resource allocation has this kind of positive effect. Many actions designed to increase efficiency are consistent with seeking to make Pareto improvements. For example, when we engage in comparison shopping, with the aim of purchasing everything on the shopping list without paying above the minimum price for a given item, then we are acting as intuitive efficiency experts. Likewise, when we seek to work more efficiently, or do housework more efficiently, we are motivated by the goal of saving time. We try to improve our situation without making things worse for others. A specific allocation of resources is *Pareto efficient* when no improvement for one person could be made without another person being made worse off. In practice, that is quite a restrictive definition of efficiency, because the prospects for harmless gains occurring are often limited. Subsequent contributions to welfare economics refined notions of efficiency and resource allocation. For our purposes, it is useful to know about the *Kaldor-Hicks compensation test*. This test proposes that a move intended to improve efficiency is reasonable even if it means that some people benefit and others lose. So long as the winners could compensate the losers and still become better off, then the move would be considered appropriate. Significantly, this compensation test does not require that any compensation actually occur.[2]

We care about efficiency in our actions and our allocation choices because it is generally accepted that we live in a world of scarce resources. At any given moment, this is true. As individuals, we each face limits on our use of money and the amount of time at our disposal. As collectivities, we again face constraints. However, due to human discovery, creativity, and innovation, over time we have been able to expand ways that we make use of the resources that we have. For example, efforts to transform public property—such as grazing space for cattle or land for planting crops—into private property have resulted in more efficient use of resources. Discoveries that have allowed the development of metals, plastics, and semiconductors have contributed massively to the quality of human life. Governments can do a lot to promote economic advance and, hence, the overall advance of human society. On this score, efforts by governments to support the development and expansion of markets have been critical. As noted in Chapter 3, governments take a range of actions designed to allow markets to operate. These include the development of property rights, legal systems, national defense forces, police forces, diplomatic services, and monetary systems.

As market-based systems of commercial activity develop and evolve, governments are often called upon to develop policies that promote more efficient outcomes. For example, when the benefits of a good or service are not fully captured by those who pay for them, there is a tendency for people to underestimate the full value of their purchases. Likewise, when the costs of a transaction are not fully

---

[2] Most textbooks on intermediate microeconomics will discuss this compensation text. See Hicks (1939) and Kaldor (1939).

covered by those who pay for a product, there is a tendency for people to consume more of it than would be the case if they did face all the costs. Situations like this are often remedied by policy actions. Those actions serve to promote economic efficiency.

Historically, governments have taken a range of actions that have supported work on the part of individuals and firms that would not have occurred in the absence of that support. While arguments can be made that individuals and firms should assume all the risk associated with their actions, society as a whole has frequently benefited from the development of products that had their origins in work supported by governments (Wade 1990; Weiss 1998). For example, research work undertaken in universities, national laboratories, and agencies of governments have generated major benefits to society (Geiger 1993; Stokes 1997). Short-term costs have produced long-term benefits. Many of these benefits have resulted from work of discovery and innovation. Other benefits have flowed as by-products of those activities. In the short term, some of the government investments made might have appeared to have had little or no payoff. However, longer term, their benefits to society have been vast. Viewed broadly, then, pursuit of efficiency is not simply about conserving the resources at our collective disposal. Penny-pinching is not always the most efficient practice. The pursuit of efficiency also involves thinking carefully about how to make wise investments in the hopes that they will generate more resources. The introduction and maintenance of systems of public education and public health can be viewed as examples of efforts that have done this. Further discussion of the ways that governments can address problems in markets is presented in Chapter 10.

As part of government efforts to promote efficiency, it is important that government resources are used well. By definition, revenues raised through taxes take some opportunities for expenditure decisions away from individuals so that collective decisions can be made. The better able governments are to operate well using limited resources, the less need they will have to draw on taxes to cover their operations. Efforts to "reinvent" government and many ongoing reform efforts are motivated by the desire to reduce the costs of government and achieve more efficiency in the use of current resources (Lynn 2006; Osborne and Gaebler 1992). Such actions need not imply that the way things were done in the past were inappropriate. Rather, if we view human society as being in a state of continuous evolution, then we can quickly grasp that systems established to address a particular set of problems at a given time might well need to be reformed or even abandoned at a later date. Much of the literature on government failure, which is reviewed in Chapter 11, explores cases in which problems have arisen because old ways of doing things have become entrenched in the practices of governments.

PROMOTING SUSTAINABILITY

The environmental movement, manifest in the actions of various interest groups across many countries, has had a huge effect during the past few decades in changing how people think about human activity and its broader impacts. Increased knowledge of the effects of pollution, of how atmospheric emissions contribute to global warming, and how consumer and industrial waste pose ongoing hazards have prompted government action to encourage sustainable development. Sustainability has become a significant consideration across a range of areas of commercial, government, and household activities. Governments have tended to spur others to action through the introduction of new regulations, taxes, fees, subsidies, and other incentives schemes (Klyza and Sousa 2008; Rabe 2004).

Among other things, in pursuit of the objective of promoting sustainability, governments have made commitments to a variety of related goals. These include encouraging environmental protection and encouraging the use of renewable sources of energy. Recycling and other incentive programs have been established to discourage the wasteful use of resources. Once a sustainability mindset is adopted, many areas of human activity become subjected to scrutiny. For example, while efforts to have people switch from commuting in private automobiles to commuting on public transport were once pursued mainly to reduce traffic congestion, now such efforts are being additionally justified based on the need to reduce reliance on nonrenewable sources of energy and to reduce carbon emissions.

Questions arise concerning the compatibility between the pursuit of sustainability and efforts to promote social and economic advancement. Viewed simplistically, sustainability concerns could be interpreted as calling for people to significantly change their current lifestyles and join a "back-to-nature" movement. More sophisticated interpretations are needed, of course. After all, the pursuit of human flourishing is predicated on people's commitment to advance our current conditions, not return us to more simple ways of living. Fortunately, many people are now seeing the sustainability challenge as a great motivator to innovation (Esty and Winston 2006). In this, there is much that governments can do to lend support. For example, they can offer more assistance to promote forms of scientific inquiry and technological development intended to contribute to the broader goal of creating more sustainable ways of living in the world. The basic logic here is that, while human civilization has made many incredible advances over time, we now must pay attention not just to keeping up the momentum but to ensuring that, as we do so, we act in ways that ensure the positives of future development will always outweigh the negatives. The challenges are great, but they also create exciting puzzles for policy analysts to address. Many of those puzzles will require the creation of multidisciplinary teams to think seriously about aspects of sustainable development.

ADVANCING HUMAN RIGHTS

As we have noted so far, governments can do many things to promote human flourishing. Among these, a very significant component involves efforts to protect and advance human rights. The Bill of Rights that comprises the first ten amendments to the Constitution of the United States has been a vitally important document for advancing and protecting human rights in the United States during the intervening centuries since it was adopted in 1791. Successive governments of the United States have sought to act in ways that are consistent with the spirit and letter of the Bill of Rights. The Bill of Rights has been instrumental in protecting the freedom of citizens to worship as they see fit, to exercise freedom of speech, to be treated respectfully by government agents, to be fairly tried in courts of law, and to be protected from cruel and unusual punishments.

The Universal Declaration of Human Rights, adopted by the General Assembly of the United Nations in 1948, has served to promote the advancement of human rights around the world. Indeed, along with seeking to act in accordance with the Universal Declaration, many governments have also adopted their own human rights acts. Throughout its thirty articles, the Universal Declaration enumerates a range of rights that individuals should enjoy throughout their lives. The document recognizes the inherent dignity of all people and their equal and inalienable rights. It argues that no distinctions should be made among people on the basis of race, color, sex, language, religion, political or other opinion, national or social origin, property, birth, or other status. In the Universal Declaration, education is to be made available freely to all, and should be compulsory, at least at the elementary level. In addition, all people are to have the right to work, to free choice of employment, to just and favorable conditions of work and to protection against unemployment.

With accelerated processes of globalization, the flows of people across borders have significantly increased. Now, more than ever, it is common to find many people living and working in countries that are different from their countries of birth. People bring with them into new contexts their prior cultural assumptions, customs, and beliefs. While many people adapt to their new cultures, others go to great lengths to protect and pass on their cultural heritage. The multiculturalism that emerges from these processes introduces many opportunities for the advancement of human flourishing, for individuals to be exposed to different and exciting approaches to living a good life. Yet multiculturalism can also bring with it clashes of views about appropriate social practices and how we should engage with one another (Gutmann 1994; Kymlicka 2001). As part of their efforts to advance human rights, government everywhere must find effective ways to mediate among the competing claims that different groups make for the recognition of their cultures and practices that are integral to them. The policy challenges opened up are significant, and they deserve deep thought. Often, they are leading policy analysts to draw upon frameworks and approaches to thinking about problems that are innovative and that differ significantly from the traditional tools of policy analysis. These matters are discussed in more detail in Chapter 14, "Gender Analysis," and Chapter 15, "Race Analysis."

PROMOTING SOCIAL EQUITY

People care about fairness. Everyone wants to feel that they are being treated fairly. Most people also like to see other people treated fairly. Indeed, efforts to advance human rights have been motivated, to a large extent, by people's innate sense that fairness matters. We might also say that, just as we judge people by how they treat others who are weaker than them and who can do nothing to help them, so we judge whole societies by how well they treat their weakest citizens (Rawls 1971). People who care about social equity look at the distribution of resources in society and ask, "What's fair?" The question cannot be answered in a single, objective way (Hochschild 1981). However, a number of common approaches have been developed to help us to think about issues of social equity and how they might be addressed.

A starting point for thinking about social equity is the realization that people come into the world with different endowments of talent. These affect our life chances. Further, the environments we are born into also greatly influence how well we will be able to grow, develop, and ultimately take care of ourselves (Shonkoff and Phillips 2000). Why does this matter?

Stark differences in our starting positions in life can have major implications for the distribution of resources in society. Although well-functioning markets can appear miraculous in the ways that they serve to promote the efficient allocation of resource in society without centralized coordination, markets operate on the assumption that people have the resources to engage in trades. If you are unable to engage in a trade, because you do not have enough resources to bring to the table, then you will not be able to purchase desired goods. Often, we just have to live with this. Most of us will never be wealthy enough to purchase highly valued art works, for example. This need not be a source of concern. But we must surely become concerned when lack of resources leads people to be unable to keep themselves, their children, or other dependents fed, decently clothed, and living in healthy housing. Indeed, as society becomes more sophisticated and our expectations of what constitute basic necessities are raised, our definition of what constitutes poverty will continually change. While absolute measures of poverty are always relevant, relative well-being is what we really need to focus upon in society. For many people today, lacking an automobile or a computer with a high-speed internet connection renders them distinctly disadvantaged in society.

A commitment to respecting the human dignity of all people and the sanctity of life would lead us to conclude that efforts should be made to help those who cannot help themselves (Sen 2001). When we show respect for the human dignity of others, we affirm our own humanity and our own sense of self-respect. How can we feel truly good about our lives when we know that elsewhere in our society, or elsewhere in the world, other people are suffering and dying because they lacked opportunities and resources that were available to us?

Beyond these appeals to our humanity, two somewhat more instrumental reasons can be offered for respecting the human dignity of all people and the sanctity of life. First, many stories can be found of incredibly gifted and talented individuals who started life in difficult circumstances but who were fortunate to benefit from a lucky break or from the benevolence of others. As a society, we gain immeasurably from the fully developed gifts and talents of other human beings. Note also that the quality of our lives today owes much to the actions, the creativity, the discovery, and the tenacity of great people in history. Given this, we should look for ways to encourage all individuals to develop themselves in ways that allow them to reach their full potential.

A second instrumental reason for respecting the human dignity of all people is a concern for maintaining the legitimacy of the social order. If a broadly shared view develops in society that the governing structures are unfair, then this can lead to high levels of social unrest. In turn, this can have implications for social harmony and for economic and social advance. It can be expedient therefore, in the interests of preserving current institutional structures, to ensure a reasonable degree of social redistribution that reduces significant wealth disparities.[3] Interestingly, this legitimacy argument can also serve to support government provision of benefits that extend to many groups in society, even when an income test would suggest that no such benefits are needed for many people. For example, government support for students attending university, no matter how well off their families might be, has sometimes been viewed as a way that governments ensure the ongoing support of the welfare state by those who would not normally stand to benefit from it.

Equality of opportunity is viewed as a basic right for all people in many countries. For this reason, governments do a lot to provide income support to poor families, based on the number of children they have. Governments also make heavy financial commitments to maintain systems of free public education and health care services. All of these efforts clearly do much to reduce inequality in society.

Arguments based solely on the need to ensure equality of opportunity do not take account of the possibility that people will suffer serious hardships throughout their lives, some of which can impede their subsequent life chances. As a result, many governments make provisions for benefits and forms of support for citizens that go well beyond promoting equality of opportunity. Rather, they seek to offer a reasonable level of comfort to all people, no matter how well or poorly they have worked at achieving self sufficiency in life.

When thinking about social equity and how to address disparities in the well-being of people, we also need to take into account incentives issues and our concern with achieving efficient social outcomes (Blinder 1987; Okun 1975). While very good reasons can be found to give various forms of public assistance to people who are poor, or who are in temporary situations of difficulty, we must also look for ways to help people to achieve self-reliance. From the perspective of those engaging in social redistribution, a worry arises that some number of people might seek public support when, if no such support were available, they would make the effort to seek gainful employment and support themselves. This concern that people might cheat the system typically leads to the development of elaborate approaches to screening people to ensure that only the truly needy receive assistance. Approaches are also developed to try to reduce the reliance that people might place on forms of public assistance. For example, limits are often placed on the number of weeks, months, or years that people can draw upon government

---

[3] See Weimer and Vining (2005: 146) on preserving institutional values.

benefits. Many systems of income support also come with requirements, such as the expectation that all people who receive support will be actively seeking work or will participate in work programs. The need for systems like this, and the cost of employing people to manage them, adds to the administrative costs associated with achieving fairer social outcomes.

Table 4.2 provides a summary of the six key objectives of government reviewed here. For each objective of government, the table includes the related goals discussed in the text.

Table 4.2 Key Objectives of Government and Some Related Goals

OBJECTIVES	RELATED GOALS
Human Flourishing	• Promote social and economic advancement • Encourage human freedom • Support individual initiative • Promote a sense of community • Support and celebrate human creativity and curiosity
Effective Institutions	• Protect citizens and their possessions • Maintain the rule of law • Maintain and advance democratic principles • Encourage effective market processes and the expansion of markets • Protect families and the work of social reproduction • Improve public management and governance arrangement
Efficiency	• Protect and encourage the market system • Maintain effective rules and regulations concerning commercial practice • Achieve efficiency in the management of government-owned enterprises • Promote administrative efficiency in government
Sustainability	• Encourage environmental protection • Encourage use of renewable sources of energy • Discourage wasteful use of resources • Assist scientific discovery and technological innovation • Support international initiatives to protect the planet
Advancing Human Rights	• Respect the sanctity of human life • Maintain safe and civil societies • Promote rights of minority and marginalized groups • Protect individual freedoms • Encourage democratic participation • Respect and celebrate social diversity
Social Equity	• Promote equality of opportunity • Respect the human dignity of all people • Meet the needs of those who are least well off • Provide social safety nets and transitional assistance • Encourage self-reliance

PROBLEM DEFINITION AND AGENDA SETTING

Policy debates often revolve around specific problems and how they should be addressed. Just as path dependency in institutional arrangements means that any direction we take in the development of institutions will be heavily influenced by our starting points, so too we find that the trajectories of policy debates are heavily influenced by initial problem definition. A significant literature has developed over the past few decades exploring the strategies that political actors use to influence policy agendas (Mintrom and Norman 2009). Problem definition is recognized as central to agenda setting. Interestingly, among scholars, there is debate about the dynamics of problem definition itself. A key question arises: *In the absence of knowledge concerning potential solutions to problems, how good are we at identifying policy problems?*

A common view among policy scholars is that we need to have a sense of the range of alternative approaches beyond the status quo if we are to see particular problems as able to be addressed through government actions (Cobb and Elder 1983; Kingdon 1984; Wildavsky 1979). Take the case of workplace safety. In the absence of knowledge about ways to protect workers from harm in specific places, such as construction sites, we might simply assume that accidents and fatalities on the job are just part of our social condition. However, once we know that accidents and injuries can be reduced when specific safety procedures are followed, then accidents and injuries change from being part of our social condition to being policy problems. The policy question becomes this: What should be done to protect workers on construction sites? Thinking in terms of objectives of government action, we find that efforts to protect works can contribute to a number of such objectives and related, more specific, goals of government.

Among participants in policy debates, it is common to find people using a range of rationales to support their proposals for specific government actions. Policy analysts need to take care to understand the arguments that people construct, the rationales they put forward to justify specific policy prescriptions, and where the lines of policy disagreement are being drawn. All of us approach issues and problems with particular predispositions. Our backgrounds, our training, and our present occupations all significantly influence our thinking on any given matter. Donald A. Schön and Martin Rein (1994) refer to these as predispositions as *frameworks*. In their view, differences in the frameworks that people bring to specific problems can become the source of "intractable policy controversies." To get beyond those controversies and to start addressing the problems at hand, it is necessary for those involved to reflect on why they take the views they take and why others differ. Schön and Rein contend that by working through a process of "frame reflection," we can ultimately find ways to get beyond difficult policy disputes.

Earlier in this chapter, we discussed the importance of policy analysts broadening their perspective beyond a focus on narrow, technical aspects of policy issues. This discussion of problem definition and agenda setting suggests that policy analysts can enhance their contribution by first recognizing the potential for many discussions of policy problems and issues to escalate into policy controversies. Potentially, policy analysts can contribute to the effective management of conflicts through the ways that they work with other participants in policy debates. As a start to this process, in any given situation when a policy problem has been identified, policy analysts should take care to understand and interpret the ways that other people are talking about that problem and the ways it might be addressed. Having thought about key objectives of government is useful preparation for this kind of work.

Tension and debate are both positive when they lead to better outcomes than would have occurred otherwise. But tension and debate must be wisely handled if they are to lead us to those better outcomes and not to intractable policy controversies. We need to become adept at representing preferred alternatives for policy action, revealing pathways to effective compromise, and helping others to engage in productive discussions that identify good, positives steps forward that can lead to broad agreement. As more voices are added to policy conversations, and the backgrounds and concerns of those weighing into those conversations grow more diverse, a major challenge emerges. But it is an important challenge for policy analysts to embrace.

WORKING WITH OBJECTIVES, GOALS, AND PUBLIC POLICIES

As policy analysts, we seek to help policy makers to make well-informed, sound policy decisions. Work on policy problems starts with problem definition. Typically, during discussions of the problem, the knowledge people have about it, and how to interpret that knowledge, people make statements that reveal the objectives and related goals of government that are considered relevant. Suppose that the policy problem concerns how best to meet the educational needs of high school students who are performing poorly and who are at risk of leaving without any qualifications. At the broad level of government objectives, reasonable arguments could be made that addressing this problem would contribute to the promotion of human flourishing, effective institutions, human rights, and social equity. More specific goals, relating to these objectives and clearly of high relevance to the policy problem, could then be stated. From this process of identifying relevant objectives and related goals, it is useful to distill a short list of the most important goals associated with addressing the problem. Once we have identified the short list of relevant goals, they serve as the criteria against which we judge the merits of proposed policy responses.

The discussions and debates that circle around policy problems are often messy and unstructured. Policy analysts need to appreciate that disciplined thinking is not always a top priority for other people. More important, we need to respect that differences in perspectives on a problem are helpful because when views differ and we have to discuss them, we often attain new insights that might not otherwise have emerged (Page 2007). We should also note that as we engage in thinking about a policy problem and talking about it with other people, it is likely that our ideas will evolve. In our efforts to add value to policy discussions, we need to do our best to effectively state the nature of the problem at hand, state plausible policy alternatives for addressing it, and indicate the criteria that we will use to judge the proposed alternatives. But it is important to remember that achieving a degree of clarity concerning a policy problem and ways to address it usually takes time. Things get messy, and then they get clearer.

Once we have the problem clarified, the proposed alternatives lined up, and the criteria for judging alternatives finalized, we can then move to gathering, generating, and systematically presenting evidence about just how well each possible policy alternative will perform against the criteria of interest. The section of this book devoted to analytical strategies (Part II) offers advice on how to go about this process of building knowledge on policy alternatives. With appropriate information in hand concerning the likely effectiveness of alternative policy approaches, given the problem to be addressed and the criteria we care about, we can do a lot to further support effective policy making. In particular, we can discuss the different merits of different policy alternatives and the *trade-offs* associated with choosing one alternative over the others. We can also consider immediate versus longer-term effects of introducing different policy alternatives. Here, we should ask question like this: If we adopted this alternative, what would be the most immediate consequence? Looking ahead, what secondary effects could we expect the policy to have? Broadly, what long-term effects will this policy have? Posing questions like this opens up the possibility that we could improve our analytical work and our advice giving by developing and presenting *policy scenarios*. These are short narratives that carefully indicate the key anticipated effects of introducing a specific policy alternative. We will discuss the development and presentation of scenarios in more detail in the chapters on analytical strategies.

Throughout this chapter, emphasis has been placed on the value of bringing objectives and goals to the surface of policy discussions. Listening to people and trying to understand why they see policy problems in specific ways and how they justify their preferred policies can be enormously helpful to you. Such efforts will significantly inform your approach to portraying the problem, developing a set of alternative policy approaches to addressing the problem, and proposing criteria on which to judge the merits of each alternative. But sometimes during the policy analysis and design work, it can actually be helpful to find ways to downplay the importance of discussing policy goals and rationales. This seemingly odd situation will arise when different parties participating in policy development show signs of agreement on a specific policy alternative, even though their reasons for that agreement are distinctive—and, possibly, even contradictory.

One thing you rapidly learn as a policy analyst is that there is no such thing as a perfect policy. Given this, it is often better to run with an alternative that definitely offers a step in the right direction, even if it does not represent an ideal solution. If policy makers can agree to such an alternative and implement it, then the possibility always remains for subsequent refinements. Almost always, a partial solution is better than no solution at all. By implication, this means that at some point during the discussion of policy alternatives, you might find value in easing off the focus on goals and rationales. Of course, this should not be taken as advice to skip that broader discussion altogether. The only people who try to stifle discussion from the outset are those who know that they are too intellectually weak to win arguments. You do not want to play that game, but you must be aware of how people will seek to control agendas and stifle debate (Bachrach and Baratz 1962; Dixit and Nalebuff 2008; Riker 1986).

CONCLUSION

Fierce debates frequently emerge concerning directions of government action. This review of government objectives helps us understand why that is so. Through their actions, governments can make significant contributions to the quality of human life. At the same time, the actions government take often mean that those goals and values held dear by some members of society become open to strong challenge from others in society who hold different goals and values. Sometimes, our goals and values might be similar, but we express them very differently. This can lead to misunderstandings. The tensions and debates that circle around policy making open important spaces into which policy analysts can enter and, potentially, do a lot of good. Worthy objectives of government, pursued effectively, can generate many positive outcomes. Those outcomes can be realized not just in present times but often long into the future as well. As policy analysts seeking to add value to policy making, we need a clear sense of the key objectives of government. We also need to be sensitive to the ways that other people make their arguments and the need for compromise in public debates. When we adopt a broad perspective on government policy action and combine it with an ability to engage in careful, focused analysis of policy details, we can become valued, influential contributors to many public policy discussions. At such times, we face the real prospect of contributing to ongoing human flourishing. That is a good thing to do.

Exercises

1. In Chapter 3, "What Governments Do," the following checklist was used to summarize government policy instruments. We have now considered the rationales for government actions, and they are summarized in the Table 4.2.

   In small groups, choose two objectives of government from Table 4.2. What policy instruments could governments use to pursue the two objectives you have chosen? Consult the checklist of what governments do (Table 4.3) to help you formulate your answers. Be prepared to summarize your discussion for the broader group.

Table 4.3 A Checklist of What Governments Do

Market Making	Regulation	Information and Social Marketing
• Setting the general context	• Technical	• Advisory services
	• Economic	• Service report cards
• Addressing specific market problems	• Social	• Advertising
	Direct Service Supply	**Frameworks and Strategies**
• Using vouchers and auctions	• Funding provision	• Branding
	• Service delivery	• Coordinating actions
Taxes	**Funding and Contracting**	• Promoting cooperation
• Raising revenues	• Contract specification	
• Excise taxes, fees, and fines	• Contract negotiation	
	• Contract monitoring	
Subsidies	**Partnering and Facilitating**	
• Income maintenance	• Seed and matching funds	
• Targeted assistance	• Achieving shared goals by working with others	
• Tax rebate		
• In-kind transfer		

2. Problem definition and agenda setting tasks tend to generate a lot of political activity. Often, policy analysts seeking to contribute to problem definition are called upon to engage in aspects of conflict resolution. Together, try to answer these questions:

- Why do efforts to define problems often create conflicts?
- Can you think of local examples of conflicts that have arisen over the definition of a policy problem?
- What constructive things could policy analysts do to help people resolve their disagreements about the definition of problems?
- What major challenges for policy analysts arise from the political nature of problem definition?

Further Reading

Dovers, Stephen R. (1996). "Sustainability: Demands on Policy." *Journal of Public Policy* 16: 303–318.

Frederickson, H. George. (1990). "Public Administration and Social Equity." *Public Administration Review* 50: 228–237.

Morse, Jennifer Roback. (1999). "No Families, No Freedom: Human Flourishing in a Free Society." *Social Philosophy and Policy* 16: 290–314.

Rochefort, David A., and Roger W. Cobb. (1994). "Problem Definition: An Emerging Perspective." In *The Politics of Problem Definition: Shaping the Agenda.* ed. David A Rochefort and Roger W. Cobb, chap. 1. Lawrence: University Press of Kansas.

Thaler, Richard H., and Cass R. Sunstein. (2008). "When Do We Need a Nudge?" and "Choice Architecture." In *Nudge: Improving Decisions about Health, Wealth, and Happiness,* chaps. 4 and 5. New Haven, CT: Yale University Press.

5

+⌒

Managing Policy Projects

The Story So Far... We have considered the nature of policy analysis, what policy analysts do, the range of policy instruments that can be used to address policy problems, and common objectives of government policy action.

Here... We explore how the discipline of project management can helpfully inform the work of policy analysts. Often, policy analysts do their work through projects. When we know how to effectively structure and manage a policy project, we are more likely to produce high-quality work on time and be valuable assets to those with whom we work.

THIS CHAPTER REVIEWS

- Key elements of project management
- How to develop a policy project proposal
- How to work with other policy literature
- How to effectively manage your time

A lot of the work of policy analysts involves investigating problems or issues from a unique perspective. While similar work might have been done at another time or in another place, the particular conditions will not have been identical to those that now apply. Further, most policy work must be performed within a set time frame. In addition, policy work often requires a team of people to contribute to its development. These characteristics of policy work mean that it can usefully be approached in project terms. We might use other words to describe what we are doing. For example, we might talk about our current assignment or engagement or report. But whatever we call it, it remains project work.

As such, we can improve our ability to produce high-quality policy analysis if we bring to it a project management mindset.

This chapter presents an approach to managing policy projects. The approach can be used by students undertaking a policy project as part of their work for a university course. Or it can be used to guide project work being done by people employed as policy analysts. Project work represents a great way to apply our present knowledge and skills and to acquire more knowledge and skills along the way. That is why I require students in my university courses on policy analysis to plan and complete a policy project in parallel to the lecture sequence. In those courses, before I introduce many of the analytical strategies presented in this book, I ask students to prepare a project proposal relating to a topic of their own choice. As the course evolves and the students learn about different analytical strategies, they often start to apply one or more of those strategies in their project work. Almost always, when their projects are completed and they submit their policy reports, students will tell me that they wish they had known more about a particular analytical strategy before they began their work. Sure, that would have been good. However, I am convinced that without being challenged and excited by their project topics, the students would not have been so eager to engage with the analytical strategies presented to them. When we are wrestling with problems, our minds open up. Our desire to meet the challenge generates greater perceptual acuity. We grow more curious about what lies before us and get better at recognizing potential pathways to needed solutions.

Seeing the good results of introducing project work early in a policy course has informed my decision to place this chapter on managing policy projects in the overview section of this book. That is also the reason for placing the chapter on presenting policy advice directly after this one.

THE DISCIPLINE OF PROJECT MANAGEMENT

Project management represents a disciplined effort to achieve a desired goal or set of goals. The planning and control techniques encompassed under the project management rubric can be applied to a broad range of activities. The defining characteristics of projects, as opposed to routine activities, are that projects have clear beginnings and endings, and the products of projects are expected to be unique. Project work, then, is very often highly creative work that involves the solving of new and complex problems. Such work can quickly become unwieldy, especially when it involves large numbers of people. This is why project management is critical.

Fundamentally, project management is all about achieving desired goals in the most efficient manner possible. When time and resources are plentiful, individuals and organizations can afford to be somewhat relaxed and unsystematic about the ways they go about accomplishing their goals. But the reality is very different for most individuals and organizations, when deadlines and budget constraints are ever present. The techniques that make up the discipline of project management were developed to maintain timeline and budgetary control of complex and strategically important engineering projects. They were subsequently refined through application in a range of endeavors, such as the development of computer systems and software and their installation in large organizations. Today, the discipline of project management is applied across many industries (Heerkens 2002). As you become familiar with the discipline of project management and consciously apply it in your work, you will gain insights and experience that will serve you well throughout your career.

The project management process is typically portrayed as having four key steps: (1) project initiation, (2) project planning, (3) project execution and control, and (4) project closure. Each of these steps requires the project manager to follow a variety of procedures, all with the aim of making the project run smoothly, so that the desired goal will be attained on time, within budget, and at the expected level of quality (Cook 2005).

Project Initiation

Projects often start with a conversation, an e-mail exchange, or a formal requirement in a university course or a degree program. The project initiation step involves figuring out who will take responsibility for the project work (the project manager) and who will oversee the project, support it, and receive the final products (the project sponsor). Generally, through discussions between the project manager and the project sponsor, issues are worked out around matters such as the broad focus of the project, its scope, how long it will take, and what resources will be available for it. The project initiation step ends when the project sponsor and manager agree that they have a viable project topic and the resources to support the project work. For policy projects, it is commonplace for the project initiation phase to end with a short document (about a page in length) setting out the broad terms for the project. This is sometimes called the *project charter*. It is useful, even at this stage, to give the project a name, so that it can be readily identified and so that any people who will be brought on as team members to work on it will know from the outset what it is about. It is important that this document conveys a sense of why the project is being undertaken, the need it is intended to fill, and what related work has been done previously. Formal roles and resource and skill requirements should be noted also. With this document completed, a formal decision can be made concerning whether or not the project will proceed.

Project Planning

With the big questions of project topic and responsibilities settled, project planning can begin. Typically, you should expect to devote about one-tenth of the total project time to the planning step. This step involves the project manager producing a detailed project proposal. This document sets out as systematically and thoroughly as possible the goals of the project, how those goals will be achieved, who will be involved in the project, how much it will cost, the project time frame, what will be delivered as the end products of the project, and a discussion of how any risks to the project will be managed. The following guidance is offered on how to develop a policy project proposal.

Project Execution and Control

This is the part of the project that will take the most time. How smoothly project execution and control runs will depend significantly on the quality of effort that has already gone into project planning. Throughout project execution and control, documents produced during the planning step can guide day-to-day activities. Ideally, the project manager should have a kind of "project dashboard." This will clearly indicate how the project is proceeding in terms of the extent to which it is meeting expectations around time use, expenses, and quality. For example, it is very useful with any project to be able to continuously check actual project progress against planned progress. Such a dashboard can also help the project manager to monitor risks and to remain mindful of the needs and concerns of the project sponsor and others who might have a stake in the project and its possible stakeholders.

Project Closure

The close-out step of the project is where all the end products or deliverables of the project are finalized for handover to the designated recipient. Toward the end of a project, there can be a tendency for people associated with it to begin thinking about the next big thing and to lose their focus. It becomes crucial for the project manager to keep the project on track to the end and to pay close attention to the details that will make the difference between attaining good project outcomes and attaining excellent ones. As well as getting everything ready for delivery, during the project closure step it is important that several other matters are given attention. Effort should be made to ensure the project documentation is well organized. With good documentation in place, should subsequent questions arise about any aspect of the project work (such as the sources of data or how analytical results were obtained), it will be easy to find the answers. Effort should be made to manage relationships associated with the project. Some form of low-key celebration is always a good way to mark the end of a project and to increase the likelihood that goodwill created during the process will be sustained into the future. Finally, it is always good to be reflective about how the project process ran and how it could have been improved. The more that you can build a conscious learning process into your projects, the more able you will be to gain control of your self-development (Austin 2004).

DEVELOPING A POLICY PROJECT PROPOSAL

A policy project proposal, once established, serves as the guidebook to the project. It should be clear enough about how the project is to be conducted that you could give it to somebody else who was not involved in development of the proposal and—assuming they had the required skills—they would be able to do it, based on the content you have provided. Creating a task list is the core element of project planning. Once this has been done, the other planning activities flow logically from it. The task list sets out all the key tasks that must be completed in order for the project to achieve its objectives. The next step in the process involves estimating task durations. This can be quite tricky work, because the duration of tasks will often depend on the abilities of the people who will perform them. Once tasks have been assigned, work can start on the project budget. Some other elements of project planning are also important for many projects. For example, project managers must often conduct project risk assessments.

Once the project proposal has been completed, it should be presented to the project sponsor for approval. With that approval, the document becomes equivalent to a contract between the project manager and the project sponsor. In effect, the agreement is as follows: *If, as the sponsor, you agree with this project proposal and contribute resources for its completion, then, as the project manager, I agree to ensure the project is completed on time and on budget, with a set of deliverables that meet your expectations for quality.* Clearly, for the project manager, the proposal represents a high-stakes kind of document. The more thorough the planning, the greater the chances that the project will meet with success. From a career management perspective, project failures can be costly. That is why thoroughness during this planning phase is essential. The project manager should worry about everything.

The project proposal states what is to be done and how it will be done. The work undertaken to prepare this document must be thorough. However, the actual document should be kept as brief and as simple as possible. For many policy projects, the proposal should probably be no longer than around three to ten pages.

The proposal should set the tone for the project. It should be written in a way that encapsulates all the thinking and planning to this point. But it should also communicate the excitement, relevance, and potential of the project. This is especially important for helping to promote a sense of collective purpose if the project work is to be completed by a project team. But it is also important for stakeholders that this document clarifies what the project is designed to accomplish and how that will happen. In drafting this document, you should strive to make it engaging reading. All policy project proposals should contain the following items listed. Additional items will often be added depending on the actual policy substance of the project. So the items here should be considered the minimum necessary for effective project management.

A Project Summary

A good proposal begins with a clear statement of what the project is going to do, why it is worth doing, and what is likely to be achieved through completion of the work. The summary should demonstrate that the project addresses a clearly defined topic, issue, or problem. When possible, it is good to portray the scope of the phenomenon of interest (for example, through the use of statistics). In general, this is the place where you need to make a convincing argument for why this is a relevant and important public policy topic. Careful background reading and investigation will be required to develop a summary that indicates your familiarity with the subject of the project. Usually, the summary should be no more than about a page in length.

A List of Project Objectives

The project objectives should be clearly stated. This can be done with a short introductory paragraph followed by a set of bullet points, each of which marks a specific objective. Here are some examples of policy project objectives:

- Document the different ideological positions that interested parties bring to this issue.
- Establish a policy history, listing key events and policy initiatives during the past five years.
- Identify and summarize results of previous studies relating to this issue, as it has arisen elsewhere.
- Create a framework to assess the impact of a user fee on track use in the park.
- Estimate the impact of a user fee, and generate alternative policy approaches.

In some cases, it can be useful to support each statement of an objective with a short explanation. Developing a set of clear, specific project objectives typically requires a reasonable amount of careful thought and focused background work. Achievement of the project objectives should make it possible to produce the project deliverables or products.

A List of Project Deliverables

This list states exactly what the project sponsor will get from this project. With policy work, this usually means some kind of report or presentation of evidence and analysis. A list of project deliverables might look like this:

- A final report on the project and its findings
- A briefing, supported by a PowerPoint presentation and/or video
- A two-page summary document for circulation to stakeholders and the media

As with the listing of project objectives, it can be useful to support each statement of an objective with a short explanation.

A Project Task List

This is a central feature of the policy project proposal. In its final form, it sets out in a logical order all of the key tasks that must be completed to achieve the project objectives and produce the deliverables. Before beginning to create the project task list, you must make sure that the project's objectives and the deliverables of the project are well understood. It is also good to have a clear sense of the budgetary and time constraints facing the project, because these will help to condition just how involved any aspect of the project will become.

Task lists are sometimes referred to as the *work breakdown structure* of a project (Black 2004; Cook 2005). Brainstorming about what work needs to be performed to complete the project is the most useful way to get started on the task list. To help with this, it is useful to draw some basic diagrams. Figure 5.1 offers a good start to the thought process of breaking down the work. It forces you to answer the following question: What are the three key tasks associated with undertaking this project? Figure 5.2 shows how this way of thinking could be applied to breaking

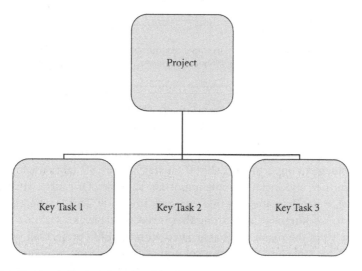

Figure 5.1 The Logic Underlying a Work Breakdown Structure

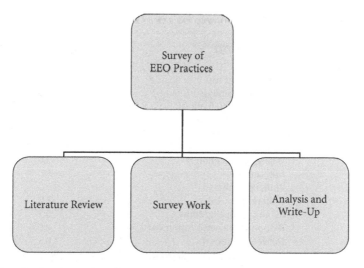

Figure 5.2 Getting Started on the EEO Survey Project

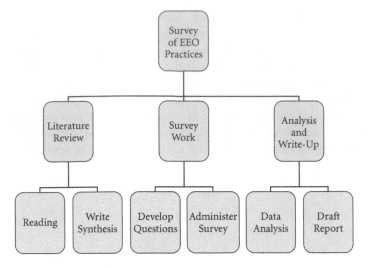

Figure 5.3 Refining the Work Breakdown Structure for the EEO Project

down the work for a project intended to discover what firms are doing to create equal employment opportunities (EEO) for staff. Figure 5.3 takes the logic of this diagram further, and includes some important subtasks. Of course, after a while, continuing to use diagrams like this can grow unwieldy. This is when it is useful to switch to working with something that is recognizable as a task list. Table 5.1 presents a list of the major tasks associated with the EEO project, all in a logical sequence. This table also contains a column of task duration estimates. The task duration column can serve as the basis for development of the project timeline.

Table 5.1 The Task List for the EEO Survey Project

TASK SEQUENCE	DESCRIPTION	DURATION ESTIMATE (DAYS)
1	Literature review	5.0
2	Synthesize findings	2.0
3	Develop research questions	0.5
4	Identify sample frame	1.0
5	Develop questionnaire	2.0
6	Conduct survey	10.0
7	Dataset preparation	3.0
8	Data analysis	2.0
9	Write up analysis	1.0
10	Draft report	3.0
11	Submit for quality control	0.5
12	Respond to reviewer comments	2.0
13	Deliver final report	0.5
	Total Project Time	**32.5**

Creating a task list is a learning process. It is good to develop a draft, take some time away from it, and then come back to refine it. Further, asking others to review and add to a task list is very helpful. It is critical that nothing important gets left out. If it does, then that will have implications for determining the length of the project and the project budget. It might also jeopardize the overall success of the project. Early in the development of the task list, there is no need to logically order the list of tasks. Eventually, however, this will become important. In particular, as you begin to develop a schedule for the project work, you need to be sure you understand which tasks must be completed before others can begin. Thinking along these lines represents the start to exploring ways to minimize the overall length of the project.

Once you have established a task list that appears thorough and logical, a new set of issues need to be addressed. These include the following:

- How much time should be estimated for completion of each task?
- What skills will be called for to complete each task?
- In the case of teamwork, to whom should each task be assigned?

A Preliminary Time Budget

This can consist of one basic sentence supported, when appropriate, with a sentence or two explaining which tasks will take the most time. As in Table 5.1, the projected duration should emerge from the task list. However, there will be times when the project deadline is externally imposed, in which case the duration is constrained. This can have implications for the scope of the work. For example, if the project associated with the task list depicted in Table 5.1 had to be completed within 20 working days, then you would have to revise how much time could be devoted to each task. Because the limit of 20 days is considerably less time than the original estimate of 32.5 days, it is likely that you would have to also revise the overall scope of the work and how you would accomplish it. The survey work, currently expected to take 10 days, might have to be scaled back.

A Project Timeline

This maps the list of tasks to actual weeks and months ahead. The project timeline should take into account competing activities. Most projects are completed against a backdrop of other work activities. Project timelines should also take into account the time that others will take to read your work and comment on it, holiday time, and some additional time to manage unanticipated problems for the project.

Biographical Statements

From the perspective of the sponsor, stakeholders, and team members, it is useful to provide a short biography for each member of the team, explaining what they bring to the project and what each is expected to do. These statements should be no more than about 100 words in length. They should present each team member and his or her skills and previous experience in a highly positive way. That is important for helping to build a "can-do" culture for the project and project team.

Table 5.2 A Project Proposal Checklist

☑   Has clearly defined the central topic, issue, or problem.
☑   Has given evidence that relevant background reading and preliminary
       information gathering has occurred.
☑   Has listed the project objectives.
☑   Has stated what final product or products will be delivered.
☑   Has developed a project task list that systematically defines and
       logically sequences the major research tasks ahead (e.g., reading, information
       gathering, analysis, and writing).
☑   Has produced a preliminary time budget and timeline.
☑   Has introduced the project team and specified task responsibilities.
☑   Has estimated project-related costs.
☑   Has noted any project risks and how they will be managed.

A Project Budget

This should contain only as much detail as the sponsor and any funder would require. Often, one column for tasks and another for costs would be sufficient. When a preset amount has been granted for the project, the budget should indicate how that amount will be allocated.

A Risk Assessment

It is useful at the start of a project to consider what possible risks could arise during the project. Having made a list, it is possible to determine which are most serious and which have the most likelihood of happening. It is also a good discipline to think about how risks could be reduced and, if they did eventuate, how they would be managed. For many project proposals, risk assessments and a statement of how risks will be managed can be contained in a paragraph.

Table 5.2 presents a Project Proposal Checklist. A list like this can be very helpful for ensuring that the proposal contains all relevant information about the project and its scope.

TRANSITIONING TO PROJECT EXECUTION AND CONTROL

By the end of the project planning step you need to have established a project repository or folder. This will be comprised of a dedicated computer folder with subfolders within it. I suggest that the files in the project folder be minimally organized into subfolders capturing the four steps of project management: (1) initiation, (2) planning, (3) execution and control, and (4) close-out. Other files will be kept relating to the substance of the project. For example, you will usually find it helpful to develop files for storing copies of papers, reports, and articles relevant to your project. Often, you will also want to develop a set of data files and logs. Table 5.3 lists items for inclusion in your project management files.

Table 5.3 Items for Inclusion in Project Management Files

1 Initiation	3 Execution and Control
• Drafting documents	• Progress reports
• The project charter	• Meeting notes
2 Planning	• Log of advice received and actions taken
• The task list	• Actual project schedule
• Project timeline	• Actual project budget
• Project budget	**4 Close-Out**
• Risk plan	• Deliverables
	• Lessons learned
	• Close-out checklist

CONSTRUCTING PROGRESS REPORTS

Progress reports are short documents, running to just a couple of pages. They are used to formally report how the project is going and how progress compares with the original project timeline and budget. Most importantly, progress reports provide opportunities for you to reflect on what you have accomplished so far and what steps you must take to successfully complete the policy project. From the perspective of the project sponsor, these documents provide opportunities to monitor your progress and ensure that you have put an appropriate amount of thought and effort into your project. The progress report also provides another formal opportunity for you and the sponsor to discuss the work and what things you can do to ensure that the end result is as good as possible. A progress report might include the following items:

- A preliminary abstract of around 150 words that states the policy topic, establishes its relevance, explains the goal of the study, reviews the research approach, and anticipates the study findings.
- A 200-word narrative on what you have accomplished to date. If necessary, include in this narrative some description and justification of any departures that have been made from the proposed topic.
- Credible evidence that the major project tasks are being accomplished (e.g., reading, information gathering, analysis, and writing).
- A brief review of questions and potential critiques that others could raise concerning the validity of your project work. Explain how you are seeking to address those possible doubts and objections. Think especially of those people that you expect will disagree with your conclusions. How can you present your work in such a way that opponents would still welcome your basic contribution?
- A preliminary table of contents for the final report. It would be helpful to annotate this with a brief (i.e., one sentence or so) comment on the content of each section.
- An updated timeline, noting potential bottlenecks and how to avert them.

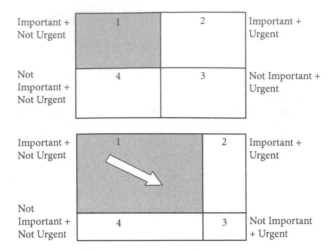

Figure 5.4 Filtering and Prioritizing Demands on Our Time

MANAGING YOUR TIME

So far in this chapter, the focus has been on broader issues of project management and planning. Developing a project proposal and incorporating a timeline into it is a very good step toward the effective management of our time. However, we need to ensure that our day-to-day practices are effectively linked to the achievement of our bigger goals. Without paying attention to how we manage our time in the short term, it is easy to let other demands crowd out our ability to act in ways that support achievement of goals like the completion of a major project. This section offers some guidance on how to effectively manage your time so that plenty of clear space can be created and protected for the pursuit of bigger goals.

The basic problem we face is how to make sense of all the demands on our time. As a first step toward managing our time, it is useful to develop some filters. A common approach is to label incoming tasks according to their importance and their urgency (Covey 1989). When we do this, we can build a simple two-by-two table, containing four cells. See the top half of Figure 5.4. Policy project work is important work that, up until the deadline for delivery of the key outputs, is typically not urgent work. It falls into Cell 1. The problem we face is that work falling into Cells 2–4 continually poses pressures that, if unchecked, would reduce the size of Cell 1. Ideally, we should seek to increase the proportion of our time we devote to important and nonurgent work, as depicted in the bottom half of Figure 5.4. Among other things, we can work toward this by taking the following actions (Mintrom 2003).

Make "To Do" Lists

Get into the habit of making lists of things to do. With all demands on your time set out, you can more easily manage how you will address them. I have also found that it is useful to estimate how long any given task will take. Breaking the tasks into short chunks (e.g., thirty minutes or less per task) can help with planning.

Prioritize Among Activities

If at all possible, you should order the items on your "to do" list based on their overall importance. Try to make a habit of keeping your best time for your most important activities. So think about when you are most alert and energetic, and devote a big chunk of that time to your project work. Attend to the less important thing when your energy is starting to flag. You might even find that switching your attention for a short time can help you to build up your energy levels again.

Batch Routine Tasks

We often complain about interruptions without recognizing our own ability to manage our time. If you find that you get easily distracted by e-mail, then it makes sense to turn off your e-mail or its notification systems. Most messages do not require instant responses. Checking messages every couple of hours during the workday allows you to avoid a major source of distraction. The same logic can be applied to other activities. In general, it is good to try to batch together small tasks and do them all in one go, rather than letting them cut into your quality project time.

Think About Opportunity Costs

The opportunity cost of any activity is the additional value you would gain from switching from working on that activity to working on something more valuable to you. Whenever possible, you should organize your time so that every activity represents the best use of your time at that moment. Of course, there are always going to be some obligatory things that we will consider a waste of time. It is important to find ways to be as economical as possible in the time allocated to those things.

Think in Marginalist Terms

When you reach a logical break in a task, it is useful to consider how much time you have before your next commitment and how you could best use it. With an ever-present "to do" list, it is easy to make the most of small amounts of "spare time." A fifteen-minute stretch before an appointment might not be time enough to devote to an aspect of a project, but it might be a very good amount of time for running an errand, returning a phone call, or answering a few e-mails.

Take Care of Relations with Others

Any miscommunications, misunderstandings, or disagreements with other people around us can end up wasting a lot of time. Given this, it is important that you reduce the possibility of problems arising. The better your relations with others, the easier you will find it to focus on your work.

Manage Your Downtime

Few of us are always zippy and excited about our work, even the parts of it that we love most. And all of us have days when, due to tiredness or ill health, we might not be able to devote our usual levels of energy to our work. Given this, it is good to have a few routine tasks—the nonurgent and nonimportant stuff—that we can attend to when we do not have what it takes to do the more important work. Having a "to do" list and a good sense of the overall task list for a project can increase the odds that you will be able to clock up some achievements, even when the day does not get off to a good start.

The key insight about time management to emerge here is that we can improve control of our time through the use of simple models and tools. By filtering tasks according to their importance and urgency, and applying some discipline around how we choose what to attend to at any given time, we can make quality time for our project work. We can increase our overall productivity. That can give us an important competitive edge over others.

WORKING WITH POLICY LITERATURE

Policy analysts, like researchers, never work in isolation of ideas and evidence produced by others. When we begin a policy project, it is as if we are entering a room where a conversation is already taking place. People will want to know how what we have to say is relevant to that conversation. Given this, we need to make sure that we are making contributions that are fresh and that will get members of our intended audience to sit up and take notice. Reviewing what other people have written on the topic of interest to us is an important starting point. We cannot hope to contribute anything deemed original and important if we do not first have a sense of what others have said before us. For any given policy project, the nature of the relationship it has to previous work will be unique. However, some general approaches to working with relevant literature can be deduced. They can help you to position your work effectively and clearly demonstrate how it is adding value to the current state of relevant knowledge.

As you begin to review policy literature, you will often find that only a limited amount has been written directly on the topic of interest to you. That is fine. But, given this, you also need to look for ways to connect what you have to say to broader policy issues and topics. One of the best things that you can do is to answer this question: *Of what broader class of issues or problems does my particular topic represent a specific instance?* In working to answer this question, you are really working to link the particular with the general. The more that you become familiar with public policy scholarship and examples of social scientific writing, the more you will see that this is a very common strategy for researchers. We cannot hope to know a great deal about large topics. Therefore, we strategically choose topics to work on that represent specific instances of more general issues and problems.

In seeking relevant literature for a given policy project, it is helpful to start out broadly and then narrow your focus. It is good to think about linkages to policy literature on specific types of problems and particular types of policy instruments. Books and academic journals can prove a good starting point. But you should also reflect on how the problem came to your attention and the particulars of the present case. That will lead you to explore current sources of information that can include newspaper articles, websites, and documents produced by policy analysts working in the same or related areas. You will likely find yourself making good use of information on the websites of government agencies and think tanks, as well as information acquired using traditional library search tools.

The challenge when building your knowledge and documenting it in a literature review is to link information and ideas from individual sources to broader themes and concerns. Inevitably, you need to read and make notes on individual pieces of work. But you should choose carefully those pieces you will focus upon. And when working with each document, you must also be judicious about what aspects of it you will extract for your own records. This process will involve continually reassessing the linkages between specific details and the big picture.

As you read a given document, it is helpful to take notes. However, the notes should not be extensive, and it is important to make your notes with the end purpose in mind. Most policy reports do not contain long discussions of relevant literature. It is more likely that you will find it helpful to refer to the existing literature in a few paragraphs. For example, when writing up the background section, you will most likely want to mention past approaches to the issue at hand or similar issues. A literature review will help you to acquire information both on how issues have been approached in a theoretical or conceptual fashion and on how actual policies in specific settings have been motivated by aspects of the problem at hand. Literature reviews can also prove valuable for helping you to justify your choice of analytical techniques and your use of evidence in later sections of your report. So a lot of documents presenting original policy analysis do not have a specific section called "literature review." Rather, references to other literature and review of specific ideas, evidence, or methods are spread throughout the work and are introduced when it is strategically appropriate to do so.

Given the way that we make use of literature in policy documents, I suggest the following approach to recording the contributions of specific books, book chapters, articles, and policy reports. Create a summary template to guide your reading. Make notes in this template as you read, and make sure to write up your final set of comments as soon as you can after you have completed the reading of the document. Most summaries should be short (one to two pages). Within your summary, try to answer these questions:

- What is the key point made in this work?
- What are the author's driving assumptions?
- What theory or theories guide the study?
- What evidence is presented?
- How is it analyzed?

As you read and summarize documents for your project, look for themes that cut across them. For example, you will begin to be able to answer questions like this:

- What questions have been addressed in the existing literature?
- What gaps in knowledge remain?
- What are the points of convergence in the existing literature?
- Where is there divergence?

Looking at how to further shape your own project, it is important to think carefully about knowledge gaps and how to most effectively address them. A sound effort to review relevant literature will help you to identify the most important contribution that you could make and the most fruitful approach to making it. The approach of writing up a set of brief summaries can be supported with development of an overview summary, which again does not need to be long. This is a way of drawing connections between works. You will probably find tables or diagrams helpful as you seek to perform this kind of synthesis work.

CONCLUSION

Designing, doing, and completing a policy project can give you a great sense of accomplishment. Projects also provide excellent opportunities for learning, both in a self-directed fashion and from others with whom your projects lead you to interact. But project work can also be difficult and challenging. This chapter has been developed as an introduction to policy project management. By following the suggestions contained here, you should be in a strong position to effectively plan and execute a range of projects in which you are the person who will do most of the work. Of course, the substance of any project will always present uncertainties and issues that you will need to address. Knowledge of project management techniques does not eliminate the difficulties. But it can make it easier for you to place those difficulties in perspective and effectively figure out how to address them in ways that will keep the whole project viable. As you develop more competencies around project management, you will become ready to manage bigger projects involving coordination across a range of people and groups. Among other things, that kind of work requires skills in team building, conflict management, and the ability to manage effective meetings.

Exercises

1. In small groups, reflect upon your past practices when working on projects. In what ways could you incorporate insights from project management into your practice as a policy analyst?
2. Together, discuss ways that you go about managing your time. Make a list. Check your list against the items listed in the section of this chapter called "Managing Your Time." On reflection, what is one thing you would most like to change to improve your management of your time?

The Class Project

Three of the forthcoming analytical strategy chapters in this book (Chapter 12, "Comparative Institutional Analysis"; Chapter 13, "Cost-Benefit Analysis"; and Chapter 16, "Implementation Analysis") contain suggestions at the end for running class projects. Of course, class projects could be developed around applying any of the analytical strategies introduced in this book. The three I have made suggestions for just seem to be obvious cases in which a lot of people could effectively participate in one collective effort. Further, gaining "hands-on" exposure to working with these analytical strategies can increase people's attractiveness as candidates for policy analyst positions. I suggest when undertaking a class project that you consciously adopt a project management mindset. Among other things, this will lead you to systematically identify tasks to be completed in the project, establish a project timeline, assign tasks to individuals or groups, and establish reporting standards. Upon completion of a class project, all class participants will be able to legitimately claim that they have experience in undertaking a policy project and working with others to generate a project deliverable. Employers show keen interest in job candidates who have experience in doing team work and who understand the basics of project management. Since project management involves joining planning techniques with effective use of people skills, several chapters of Michael Mintrom's (2003) *People Skills for Policy Analysts* (Washington, DC: Georgetown University Press) represent relevant reading. These include the chapters on working in teams, interviewing informants, and giving presentations.

Further Reading

Austin, Robert D. (2004). "Project Management as Process." In *Managing Projects Large and Small*, chap. 1. Boston, MA: Harvard Business School Press.

Cook, Curtis R. (2005). "Project Planning Basics." In *Just Enough Project Management*, chap. 3. New York: McGraw-Hill.

Knopf, Jeffrey W. (2006). "Doing a Literature Review." *PS: Political Science & Politics* 39(1): 127–132.

Mintrom, Michael. (2003). "Managing Your Resources." In *People Skills for Policy Analysts*, chap. 2. Washington, DC: Georgetown University Press.

6

✦

Presenting Policy Advice

The Story So Far... We have considered the nature of policy analysis and how policy analysts can use the discipline of project management to increase their ability to produce high-quality analytical work within agreed time frames.

Here... We focus on how policy analysts can most effectively present the evidence that they have collected and their analytical work. The degree of effort that policy analysts take to understand their audiences and meet their needs strongly affects their ability to influence policy making.

THIS CHAPTER REVIEWS

- The importance of clarifying audience needs
- How to structure a policy report
- How to develop and present policy recommendations
- How to effectively present evidence
- Using goals/alternatives matrices
- How to develop presentations and oral briefings

olicy analysts inform and add value to policy making through their written work, their presentations, and their briefings. For junior policy analysts especially, all forms of communication with those they are advising tend to be highly formal. It is only as policy analysts gain experience and respect as trusted advisors that the level of formality of engagement with decision makers may fall. At all times, policy analysts need to be seriously concerned to present themselves and their work in a highly professional manner. This is part of what it takes to gain the trust of those for whom you work.

This chapter offers an overview of key elements in presenting policy advice. Among other things, the chapter explores the importance of knowing your audience and the questions of central interest to audience members concerning a policy problem and options for addressing it. The chapter also discusses the need to work within reporting conventions, but to look for angles that can be used to increase the impact of a policy document. Although new channels for advising are continually emerging, carefully developed, readable policy reports remain the core means by which policy analysts present their arguments to their target audiences.

A reasonable expectation might be that a chapter like this on presenting policy advice would appear near the end of the book. The implication would be that having first gained a sense of the various analytical strategies you can use as a policy analyst, you can now focus on how to bring your work together into a policy report. But because high-quality written work is the coin of the realm for policy analysis, I believe it is appropriate to discuss it early on in the process of imparting policy training. As we will see working through this chapter, the expectations and needs of our primary audience must always serve as the central reference points during the development of our work. The understanding of audience and audience expectations is the point from which all further questions and decisions flow concerning the design of a policy project and the development of advice based upon it.

CLARIFYING AUDIENCE NEEDS

The more clarity we can gain concerning who we are writing for, what that audience needs to know, and when our advice is needed, the better able we will be to deliver useful work. The following comments from a politician concerning advice giving make the point well. "Advisers can exercise better judgment if they have a better understanding of the context in which they are making those judgments." This politician expressed the desire to have top advisors attend meetings of decision makers. "We want to make sure that the Cabinet committees are operating with the best information available and that the work that's being undertaken by the government agencies on our behalf is absolutely in tune with the thinking."[1]

The policy report is a means of conveying what you know and what you think about the topic, problem, or issue that has been the subject of your policy project. When you write it, you must do so with the needs of your target audience firmly in mind. Your audience will have certain interests and expectations about your work. Even when you have spent enormous amounts of time gathering particular pieces of information, it is not always appropriate for you to share all that information with your audience. You cannot hope to present everything that you have done and everything that you have learned.

---

[1] See Oliver (2008).

In preparing policy advice, it is useful to start with the end goal in mind. Key questions arise:

1. Who will comprise the primary audience for this work?
2. What questions will be uppermost in the minds of audience members?
3. What would be the most powerful way to address these questions?
4. By when do they need my advice?
5. Given time constraints, what analytical strategies are possible and appropriate?

By gaining answers to questions like this, we can decide the scope and originality of the analytical work we should perform. As such, early into the process of doing our analysis, we can also achieve a degree of clarity around what kind of end products we will be delivering. If we have been given three months to produce a policy report, then we should be expecting to deliver a very careful piece of work that is based on the highest quality analysis. In contrast, if advice is needed urgently by the end of the week, then we must significantly scale back our ideas about what kind of report we can produce. In policy work, timeliness is as important as substance, so it is important that we continuously weigh what is possible, given the time constraints, and act accordingly.

STRUCTURING A POLICY REPORT

We think by writing. Author E. M. Forster is credited with having asked, "How can I know what I think till I see what I say?" Given that we think and learn through writing, it is important to avoid procrastinating before you begin work on your policy reports. With my own writing, I like to begin with a clear sense of the basic structure that my work will follow. Therefore, once I have gathered most of my evidence together, I usually take some time to think about the structure of the paper or report or book chapter that I plan to write. Of course, as I work through the drafting process, I often find that I want to alter the initial structure and that I need more evidence than I have already gathered. But the structure or outline serves as an excellent prompt to writing. I have also found that with a clear structure developed, I need not start writing at the beginning. In fact, I tend to begin my writing where I figure it is easiest to write. So, often I will write up my analytical framework section or my research methods section before writing the introduction to my work. Actually, on bad writing days, I try to keep the momentum going by working on things like formatting and the bibliography. After all, these things have to be taken care of at some point.

In what follows, I provide some suggestions for how to develop a policy report. But the basic requirements can be readily outlined.

1. Provide a clear summary of the matter that you have worked on.
2. State the issues that you believe need to be better understood.

3. State the research questions that motivated your project.
4. Describe how you went about seeking to answer those questions (i.e., review your analytical strategy).
5. Provide your answers and draw out the implications that your answers hold for public policy settings.
6. Ask yourself, what kind of document would I have most liked to have come across when I began this work? In many cases, your policy report should be *that* document.

Because you are closer than anyone else to the background, evidence, and analysis associated with your project, you are likely to be the best judge of how to most appropriately structure your final policy report. However, there are some basic items that should appear in all such documents. A list of those items follow. Deviation from this list may make sense on some occasions, but you should be very clear as to why you would do that.

Abstract or Executive Summary
This summary should state the problem you have analyzed, why your intended audience should care about it, the approach you have taken to analyzing it, and your principal findings. It should be around 200 words in length.

Table of Contents
Unless your report is just a couple of pages long, it is useful to include a table of contents. This is especially useful for quickly conveying to your audience the structure of your report and the argument contained within in. You should usually expect that some readers will get no further than scanning the abstract and table of contents. So it is important to use these elements of your report to help to draw your audience into your work.

Introduction
The introduction will lead off the main body of your policy report. This is where you explain why this topic is important and why your target audience should care about it. You should also use this introduction to provide a brief overview of the structure of your report. Since you are not writing a mystery, you should give your reader a clear sense of what is to come, and the basic conclusions that you have reached through your analysis.

Background
In this section, you review the problem that you have chosen to analyze. If possible, try to summarize both the evolution of the problem and the current situation. It is often useful here to report some basic data that will help readers to get a sense of the nature of the problem. You should also review what other analysts have previously said about this particular problem, or similar problems. It is good practice to draw connections between this particular manifestation of the problem and other problems of this kind. Thus, your background section can be thought of

as both a review of the problem and a review of the relevant literature concerning this particular problem or problems of this sort.

It is important to think carefully about ways to structure this section so that you effectively draw your intended audience into the issue and explain how others have thought about the issue up to this point. It is also useful to think of this background section as the place where you strive to cut through all that has gone before and create "blue sky" for yourself. That is, you should make sure that you show where previous policy efforts and previous scholarly work have been lacking, and clearly define the knowledge gap that your efforts have been designed to fill.

Analytical Strategy

Policy analysts should always be explicit about how they have chosen to think about and analyze a specific policy problem or issue. The analytical strategy section of your policy report gives you the space to do that. This is where you show and justify to your audience the analytical approach that you believe is most suitable for generating fresh insights into the problem at hand. Try to keep the analytical strategy section fairly narrowly focused. It is important to remember that you simply cannot tackle every aspect of a policy issue. The analytical strategy section need not be extensive, but you should highlight within it the assumptions driving your analysis, the key criteria used to judge policy alternatives, the scope of your analysis, and the limitations of your work.

Analysis and Findings

In this section, you take your chosen analytical strategy and apply it to the topic you have presented in your introduction and background sections. This is the section of the policy report where you must describe the steps you followed to investigate the policy problem. Thus, it is quite possible that your discussion here will be somewhat technical in nature. This will be the case no matter whether you are presenting case study or quantitative work. How did you come to choose the cases you are working with? Why is your analytical strategy valid? You should provide sufficient documentation of your work so that someone else, by following the steps you report, would readily be able to replicate the analysis (and hopefully, come up with much the same set of findings). Despite the need for accuracy and specificity here, it is always important to try to keep a narrative flow and to keep things as clear as possible for your readers. Without going overboard, think carefully of ways that you might include tables or diagrams that effectively summarize aspects of your analysis and your findings.

Discussion

This is where you stand back from the details of your analysis and findings and return to the "so what?" question. What implications do you draw from your findings? How sure are you that these implications are valid? These are the sorts of things you should write about here. Where relevant, you might want to make connections back to the previous work of others (say, comparing and contrasting your main finding with the previous findings that other policy analysts or research-ers have reached). However, by now your policy report should be dwelling pri-marily on what you have to say, based on your original work, not on what others have said.

After you have developed an initial draft of your discussion section, it is good practice to approach what you have written from a highly critical perspective. Think about the policy issue in question and the array of people and interests who have sought to contribute to discussions of that issue in the past. What kinds of concerns or critiques are different groups of people likely to raise when they see how you have approached the issue and the conclusions you have reached? Of course, some possible critiques will be more serious than others. If you attempted to anticipate and address all possible critiques, you could end up writing a different report and finding that your unique perspective has been all but buried. Balance is important. Try as much as you can to anticipate and address major criticisms. This should lead you to be even more careful about how you make use of evidence, the conclusions you draw from it, and how far you can go in making any predictions or generalizations. Within limits, the more accurate you are in anticipating cri-tiques and the more thorough you are in addressing them in advance, the stronger your policy report is likely to be.

If you have written your policy report with the goal of prompting policy changes, then ideally each part of this discussion should logically lead up to a clear recommendation. Place these recommendations in the discussion, and try to use language that also allows the recommendations to stand alone. If you pay careful attention to your use of language here, then you will find that you can also pull each recommendation out of the text and it will still make sense.

Policy Recommendations

In some instances, you will wish to include recommendations that emerge sys-tematically from your research and analysis. Each recommendation should be no more than a sentence in length. Try to avoid making too many recommendations. Concision is helpful. Your recommendations should be specific to your target audience, and they should be action-oriented, prescribing observable behavioral changes. As a set, your recommendations should flow from one to the other, and they should appear highly coherent. It is important to list the recommendations in a separate section in the report. But, as noted previously, including each rec-ommendation as the logical end point of parts of your discussion section is also important for showing your readers the logic and evidence upon which each rec-ommendation has been based. From conversations over the years, I know that quite a few policy analysts often start drafting their reports by setting out some of the recommendations they plan to make. I have done this myself at times and found it useful for gaining clarity in a report and in helping me to structure the dis-cussion section. The focus on recommendations can also lead you back to explor-ing ways to improve the presentation of your analysis and findings. Occasionally, you will find that a recommendation that you would like to make is not adequately supported by evidence. In such cases, you might consider going back to your analysis and refining it. If there simply is not sufficiently strong evidence to support your recommendation, then you will have to abandon it. However, this practice can be very useful for forcing you to make your analysis as robust as possible.

Conclusion

To bring your policy report to a satisfactory close, it is important that you briefly reiterate the point of the analysis, what you did, your main findings, and the broad thrust of your findings. Often, through our policy analysis, we come to conclude that more analysis is needed. This is a good place to indicate what you believe would be fruitful next steps in the study of the problem you have investigated. By the time you have done all the other writing, it is often tempting to power out a brief and somewhat perfunctory conclusion section. Try to resist that urge. The conclusion is a good place for you to really play up your contribution and set the agenda for further policy work.

Table 6.1 A Policy Report Checklist

☑ I have given my policy report a clear title consisting of ten words or less. I have avoided being clever or cute.

☑ I have included an abstract or executive summary. This is around 200 words long and it conveys the essence of the whole project. It states the policy topic, establishes its relevance, explains the goal of the analysis, reviews my analytical approach, and notes my key findings.

☑ I have included a brief table of contents directly after the abstract. This visually conveys the logical structure of the whole policy report.

☑ I have identified the intended audience, and I have written in an appropriate style, given the needs and expectations of that audience.

☑ I have made a strong, evidence-based argument concerning the relevance and importance of the topic being addressed.

☑ I have shown how my specific topic relates to broader policy themes or issues.

☑ I have made appropriate use of policy analysis concepts and analytical strategies. I have argued for why my approach is appropriate, given the problem, question, or issue at hand and the current state of knowledge.

☑ I have anticipated questions and potential critiques concerning the validity of my analytical strategy, and I have sought to address them. I believe that if other policy analysts and researchers (even those with different points of view) were to examine this topic, problem, or issue using similar procedures, they would come to much the same conclusions that I have reached.

☑ I have developed several clear, actionable recommendations for the intended audience of the study. These recommendations flow logically from the discussion section of the policy report.

☑ I have made appropriate use of citations and footnotes, and I have included a separate section at the end of the report called "Bibliography."

☑ I have asked a friend or colleague to read my report and check the presentation, grammar, and spelling. The presentation, grammar, and spelling are flawless.

Other Items

Aside from the previous sections, most policy reports should contain a carefully developed *bibliography*, and all your analytical work should be meticulously documented. (*Technical appendices* are good places to document your analytical work, as necessary.) Although the work should be technically proficient, you should also strive to produce a clear, visually appealing, and well-structured document.

EFFECTIVE PRESENTATION OF EVIDENCE

At its core, policy analysis involves collecting together information, making sense of it, extracting new insights from it, and then conveying those insights to others. Often, when policy analysts have done their work well, the final results can appear clear and simple. Here, a dilemma arises. On the one hand, we are driven by a desire to let other people know that we are clever and that we have done a lot of work. On the other, it is always a mistake to present you work in a dense and detailed fashion. You want to be informative and helpful to your audience, not intimidating. So seeking clarity is exactly the right direction in which to head, even if it means that occasionally someone might misjudge the degree of thought and effort that you have put into your work. On this point, the economist John Kenneth Galbraith is credited with having said that his papers achieved a sense of effortless writing on about the fifth draft.[2]

Part of good writing involves making well-judged decisions on how to most effectively present evidence. As you proceed with a policy project, you will often find it helpful to develop tables, lists, or diagrams that allow you to summarize the material and information. When you are able to lay out information in a systematic fashion, it becomes easy to take stock of what you know and what gaps remain.

Among other things, when working on policy projects, I have found it useful at times to create policy histories. As part of the process of making sense of an issue, it is a good discipline to establish the sequence of events and past policy decisions that have contributed to the current situation. Using a list, timeline, or table can be a good way to clarify what has happened before and to identify linkages between previous events. There may be times when some refined version of this history could be included in your final report, although you probably will not want to cover the historical material in extensive detail. Where you judge it appropriate, you could draw upon this material to write a background paragraph or two. Sometimes, you might want to support this with a simple figure setting out key policy events or an appendix containing a more detailed history.

Figures, tables, and diagrams are especially helpful in policy reports when they clearly establish key relationships of interest to your audience. For example, an organizational chart might be useful at times to indicate the set of relationships

---

[2] See Krugman (1993).

among agencies and other stakeholders that support delivery of current services in a specific policy area. At other times, a diagram can be useful to depict the way that you see linkages between a specific problem and the policies that could address it.

Figures, tables, and diagrams can also be important for allowing you to present your analysis in clear, easily digestible ways. Very often, good visual tools of this type can become the focus of conversations among decision makers. That is exactly what you want. So it is worth thinking very hard about how you can use a particular visual device as a central organizing feature of your analysis and your policy report. As we move into our review of analytical strategies, more advice will be given on how to present evidence and analysis in your policy reports. Here, however, it is important to mention a very helpful tool: the goals/alternatives matrix.

Goals/alternatives matrices, while somewhat clumsily titled, offer an invaluable presentational tool for policy analysts. When thinking about problems and policy alternatives that could address them, we need to find ways to weigh the merits of the different approaches. In some instances, an obvious one-to-one relationship might be found between a policy problem and the right policy instrument to address it. In most instances, however, several policy solutions could be effective. Goals/alternatives matrices allow us to compare policy instruments with regard to selected criteria. As noted in Chapter 4 on objectives of government policy action, a variety of criteria could be used to judge the merits of policy alternatives. The most commonly used are efficiency, equity, and administrative simplicity. But other criteria can be used, such as implications for personal freedom, human dignity, social harmony, and environmental sustainability. Working on a case-by-case basis, we are likely to find some policy goals to be relevant in some instances and not in others. Note that trade-offs among these goals are likely to have to be made. For a given problem, we can enter our judgments of the various policy alternatives into the cells on the matrix. By doing this, we accomplish two things.

First, we can establish some goals that can help us in developing our discussions of a policy problem and how it might best be addressed. Our discussion of policy instruments in Chapter 3 offers a starting point for thinking about a set of alternative approaches to address a given policy problem. Our discussion of objectives for government policy action in Chapter 4 offers a starting point for thinking about criteria against which to judge the merits of each policy alternative. The review of analytical strategies presented in Chapters 8 through 15 offers advice on how to assemble the evidence about likely policy outcomes that can complete the cells in goals/alternatives matrices. A great benefit of working with a matrix as you proceed with your project work is that it allows you to very rapidly assess where your needs for evidence on outcomes have been met and where gaps remain to be filled. It is very important to strive to find appropriate ways to ensure that summary evidence of anticipated performance of each policy alternative on each goal is easily comparable with the performance of the other alternatives on each

Goals: (*i.e., the criteria used to judge the relative merits of policy alternatives*)	Policy Alternatives:		
	A Tax or Fee	*A Regulation*	*Provision of Information*
Efficiency	Summary of evidence on efficiency of a tax or fee.	Summary of evidence on efficiency of a regulation.	Summary of evidence on efficiency of provision of information.
Equity	Summary of evidence on equity effects of a tax or fee.	Summary of evidence on equity effects of a regulation.	Summary of evidence on equity effects of provision of information.
Simplicity	Summary of evidence on administrative simplicity of a tax or fee.	Summary of evidence on administrative simplicity of a regulation.	Summary of evidence on administrative simplicity of provision of information.

Figure 6.1 The Basic Structure of a Goals/Alternatives Matrix

goal. This summary evidence might be provided in verbal form, in the form of a ranking (e.g., high, moderate, low), or in numbers (e.g., expected costs, expected number of communities affected).

A second virtue of goals/alternatives matrices is that some version of them can usually be incorporated into the final policy report. At this stage, when you are presenting information for your audience, you might want to reduce the number of options presented and criteria used from the broader set that were explored during your analysis. A well-developed, clean, and straightforward goals/alternatives matrix can serve as a simple visual summary in your policy report of more complex points made in your discussion section. Figure 6.1 presents the basic structure of a goals/alternatives matrix. There is a lot of room in such a structure for adaptation to the specifics of the problem or issue that you are working on.

REFLECTING ON THE CONTRIBUTION

Although it is important to follow a logical structure in your policy reports, you should not let the structure come to dominate your argument. Sometimes, policy analysts get so caught up in the form of their expression that readers can almost miss the most significant aspects of the contribution that is being made.

As you work on your policy report, think carefully about the nature of the contribution that you are making. What are you saying here that is unique? How does what you say differ from what has previously been said on this matter? How can you highlight the uniqueness and importance of your contribution? Once you have answered these questions for yourself, look for ways to organize your report so that members of your target audience will readily grasp the uniqueness and importance of your message.

Of course, a solid contribution is one in which the validity of the analysis can be readily verified. Tell people what you know. Sometimes, to maintain your reputation for integrity, it is important to be up front as well about what you do not know. Be careful to explain the methods that you have used to come to your conclusions. You must convince yourself and your audience that if others were to do the same work, they would come to similar conclusions.

THE SIGN-OFF

Eventually, you will arrive at the point where you have successfully completed your policy report. It is ready to go. It is important at this time to break your instinctual desire to just be done with it. The sign-off is the point at which you are prepared to place work in the public domain and let others judge you by it. You should never sign off in haste. If at all possible, give yourself an additional day or so to check over your work in a leisurely fashion to ensure that it really is as good as you want it to be. At this stage it is a good discipline to ask yourself, "How could I make this even better?" In asking the question, you open yourself to the possibility of being struck with an exciting, bold possibility for improvement. Obviously, at this late stage in the process, you should not be thinking of major structural adjustments or changes in your use of evidence. But you might become aware of changes that would be worth a little more time.

Before doing the sign-off, it is important to think about reputation management. Many people submit their work—policy reports, research papers, theses, and dissertations—without putting sufficient effort into inspecting it for quality. Whether you like it or not, people make judgments—about you, your intelligence, your commitment, your energy levels, and so on—based on your work. Given this, it is essential that you treat every piece of work you do as a way to maintain and advance your reputation as an excellent, careful analyst and researcher. Rather than adopt a self-centered approach to your work, you need to try to gain some distance from it and think about how others might respond to what you have done. This is one way to begin effectively managing your reputation. In a competitive world, you cannot afford to have people forming anything other than highly positive judgments about your abilities.

Fortunately, in many organizations that produce policy analysis, good processes of quality assurance are in place. This means that it becomes routine practice for all analytical work and draft policy reports to be subjected to careful review by peers or by senior colleagues. If you are working independently—which is often the case for students—there are still things that you can do to ensure the final policy report is in good shape. Whenever possible, I propose that students work with one or two others and swap their near-completed drafts, inviting advice on how to make improvements. Almost always, peer review will allow us to gain fresh insights into problems in our work and effective ways to address them.

DEVELOPING PRESENTATIONS AND
ORAL BRIEFINGS

To expand the influence of their policy analyses and advice, policy analysts frequently need to present their work in multiple venues using multiple delivery techniques. In this regard, it is common for policy analysts to be asked to accompany the delivery of final policy reports with a formal presentation or a more informal oral briefing. Working on such presentations and briefings represents another way that you can gain feedback and insights concerning effective ways to structure your overall argument and the delivery of evidence. Sometimes, through preparing a presentation or discussing the content of our policy reports in a forum or meeting, we might realize that we need to make further refinements to the report itself. For example, by working on a PowerPoint presentation and seeking to create a clear diagram that sets out key aspects of the policy problem, we might strike upon a visual representation that could—upon further refinement—become a valuable addition to the policy report itself.

As with the development of the policy report, development of presentations and oral briefings should always begin with a careful assessment of audience needs, time constraints, and the most important outcome that you can realistically hope to achieve through this form of engagement. In general, with presentations and briefings, it is better to keep things clear and concise than to bombard your audience with a large amount of information. As much as possible, treat the initial part of the presentation and briefing as a way to clarify key points and set the stage for a lively, engaging discussion with your audience.

As the presenter, you need to know everything about your topic in great detail. Actually, the definition of a *policy wonk* is someone who knows everything backward (w-o-n-k = k-n-o-w backward.) But the presentational trick is to figure out ways to impart just the right amount of information in just the right sequence that it will be well received by your audience. Ideally, you wish to draw audience members into an intelligent, well-informed discussion of the policy issue at hand.

Before you develop your presentation or briefing, it is important that you know about the room where it will take place, about how many people might be present, the audiovisual facilities available, and how long you will have to present. Even if PowerPoint facilities are available, there can be times when it is more productive to have a conversation in which people refer to a handout as you talk. This is especially the case when you are giving a briefing to just a few people. In other words, it is important for you to understand the presentational conventions that will be guiding how your audience will respond to your work. It is most important that you do your best within established guidelines for presenting. Once you have mastered those conventions, it is perfectly fine to deviate from them somewhat (say, by introducing an original video clip), but only if you are sure that a degree of innovative presentational practice will definitely enhance the impact of your work.

When structuring presentations and briefings, I have found the following questions helpful to prompt my thoughts about how best to organize my materials.

- What will be the main concern for my audience?
- How much time will I have to talk?
- What are the major messages I want to convey?
- What findings emerge from my analysis?
- How does my analysis support those findings?
- What actions do I recommend based on my analysis?
- How do I respond to objections that might be raised to my findings and recommendations?
- What is the best possible outcome that could occur from this presentation? How can I maximize the odds that this outcome will happen?

When developing your presentation or briefing, it is useful to draft a text that contains a brief narrative response to each of the topics or questions you seek to address. You can then work from this text to develop a PowerPoint presentation, a handout, or a set of notes for yourself. Keep things simple, but make sure that you have the ability to elaborate on your statements if necessary. In preparing for oral briefings, I now tend to develop flashcards for myself that contain material that is readily committed to memory. This allows me to be articulate on my feet, without having to focus on notes. But it is always good to have notes or a brief handout available to guide discussion. Likewise, when giving presentations to bigger groups and using PowerPoint, it can be helpful to develop a one-page handout that summarizes the main points you plan to make. Often, it is easier to convey details in printed form than on a PowerPoint slide.

THE IMPORTANCE OF CREATIVITY

Policy analysis requires us to blend technical competency with high levels of creativity. Often, in working with evidence, we have to make do with what we have, find ways to use existing information or data in new ways that allow it to serve as relevant evidence for our analyses, and so on. Likewise, when presenting our policy advice, the possibilities are vast for putting our creativity to good use. I strongly encourage people to be creative in how they approach working with policy problems and how they go about presenting their work. This is not an invitation to cut corners on the technical quality of your work. Rather, the general orientation is driven by a belief that high-quality technical work, combined with high levels of creativity in all aspects of the policy project, can result in policy reports and advice giving that is well received by the audience and that will inform sound decision making.

Presently, a lot of approaches to the development of policy reports—especially within government agencies—appear to be heavily informed by practices that were developed long before recent advances in information technology occurred. There is a lag in the degree to which policy advising has made use of the possibilities opened up by, for example, web technology, video technology, and so on. I predict that the next decade will see major advances in how policy advice is developed and presented. All of us can play a part in moving things forward in exciting ways that significantly add to the value of the policy advice being given.

The difficulty we struggle with is that always we must work within predefined norms and expectations concerning the acceptable presentation of evidence and reporting formats. Part of becoming a trusted and highly valued policy advisor involves never giving surprises to the people for whom you are working. An implication is that you should always strive to do work that will be judged highly acceptable against the standard organizational norms. Beyond that, if you can see ways to push the boundaries of current practice and—in so doing—set new standards for high-quality work, then go for it. Sometimes, we can make effective breakthroughs on projects that are somewhat low visibility and low priority, hence also low risk. Pushing the boundaries there might allow you to set new standards by example that can then begin to filter into standard operating procedures concerning more significant policy work.

CONCLUSION

Excellent policy advisors tend to have finely honed presentation skills. Such skills, of course, are never a substitute for excellent analytical skills. But when a policy analyst is very good at producing high-quality analysis and has strengths in communication, the combination can be powerful. The material in this chapter is intended to help you master some of the basics of presenting policy advice. As you become more acquainted with policy work and the policy reports produced by others, you will develop a sense about what works well, given the area and policy circles you are working within. It can be particularly useful to your self-development to keep a folder of excellent work produced by others. This might include several examples of great policy reports. You might add to it examples of great tables or figures that you have encountered. After observing a very effective presentation, it is also good practice to write notes for yourself documenting what you think made it good, and recording strategies or approaches that you might emulate in your own work in the future. Alternately, taking ten minutes with others to diagnose the elements of a particularly good presentation that you all witnessed can be both instructive and fun.

Exercises

1. In small groups, have everyone reflect on some of the best policy reports that they have seen. What presentational features of the reports made them really good? Have everyone in your group share their thoughts. Together, make a list of up to five things that you think are important features of good policy reports. Please be ready to share your list with the full group. Reflecting on the discussion about good policy reports, what do you think you'll do differently when you next work on a policy document?

2. Sometimes, preparing an oral presentation or developing a one-page memo about your policy project can lead you to make some useful changes to the full policy report that formed the basis for these smaller activities. Why do you think that is? Given this, what could be a good practice for you to build into the development of policy reports?

Invite a Guest to Class

As noted in Chapter 1, students can become inspired when practicing policy analysts come to talk with them. When you are covering the topic of presenting advice, having a policy analyst talk about this aspect of his or her work with the class could be quite valuable. Getting the perspective of a decision maker or former decision maker regarding "what works" with policy advising could also be valuable. Given that technology changes have been opening up opportunities for whole new ways to be used for delivering advice, it could be fun to have students brainstorm together about innovative ways to deliver policy advice. Ideas coming out of this session could then be introduced during the meeting with the visitor, as a way of taking the discussion to a more creative, exploratory level. See my suggestions at the end of Chapter 1 for ways to involve the class members in arranging a visit by an invited guest.

Further Reading

MacRae, Duncan, Jr., and Dale Whittingham. (1997). "Aiding Choices with the Criteria/ Alternatives Matrix." In *Expert Advice for Policy Choice*, chap. 5. Washington, DC: Georgetown University Press.

Miller, Jane E. (2004). "Seven Basic Principles." In *The Chicago Guide to Writing about Numbers*, chap. 2. Chicago: University of Chicago Press.

Mintrom, Michael. (2003). "Giving Presentations" and "Writing for Multiple Audiences." In *People Skills for Policy Analysts*, chaps. 5 and 8. Washington, DC: Georgetown University Press.

Weimer, David L., and Aidan R. Vining. (2005). "Goals/Alternatives Matrices: Some Examples from CBO Studies." In *Policy Analysis: Concepts and Practice*, 4th ed., chap. 15. Upper Saddle River, NJ: Pearson Prentice Hall.

7

Doing Ethical Policy Analysis

The Story So Far... We have explored the work of policy analysts and how they can effectively advise governments on their choices of policy responses to pressing policy problems.

Here... We observe that decision makers trust policy analysts to carefully assess policy options and to give them honest, objective advice. We consider the ways that policy analysts might exhibit strong ethical behavior in their work. By doing this, policy analysts can raise the quality of policy discussion and debate in their specific areas of interest.

THIS CHAPTER REVIEWS
- The need for ethics in policy analysis
- Previous approaches to considering ethics and policy analysis
- Five ethical principles to guide your work as a professional policy analyst
- How those principles can be applied at each step of doing policy analysis

In contemporary society, economic and social processes are shaped by vast numbers of complex and subtle interactions between private, decentralized activities and the activities of governments. Like the demand for many professional services, the demand for policy analysis arises from knowledge gaps. Government decision makers, such as a cabinet ministers or councilors, continuously confront public problems for which solutions must be found. Typically, those decision makers adopt new public policies or adjust current policy settings to address the problems at hand. Outside of government, decision makers in many nongovernmental organizations also seek policy analysis. Such decision makers rely on policy analysis to help them interpret how changes in government policies could affect their operating contexts, revenue streams, and the cost of doing business.

The knowledge gaps that drive demand for policy analysis also create problems of trust. Over the centuries, government decision makers have developed various ways of structuring bureaucracies and using systems of checks and balances to reduce concerns about the trustworthiness of advisors (Kelman 1988; Le Grand 2003). Yet even when such systems are in place to promote honest and high-quality work, verifying the merits of advice given by policy analysts can be costly. The good motives and actions of individual advisors therefore remain a key to good governmental decision-making processes. Decision makers must be assured that the policy analysts who advise them are acting with integrity. We can never be entirely sure that individual policy analysts will prove trustworthy. But steps can be taken to reduce the chances that they will behave badly. Those steps include carefully screening applicants for advice-giving roles, creating organizational cultures that promote truthfulness, and instructing policy analysts on good practice. This chapter offers suggestions for how to do ethical policy analysis.

For the purpose of the current discussion, we will focus on the work of policy analysts serving as advisors to elected and appointed decision makers in government. This simplification allows us to discuss the practice of policy analysis in the context in which most of it is performed, without the need to continually discuss exceptions. Even so, much of what is said here will be relevant to policy analysts serving any clients, be they public or private decision makers. It is also useful to remember that ethical questions are almost always context-specific. So the broad treatment of ethical issues offered here is intended as an invitation to consideration of dilemmas in many instances.

The next section offers background to our explorations of policy analysis and ethical practice. Consideration is then given to how aspects of ethical practice can inform each of the essential elements of policy analysis. The overall argument is that policy analysts should avoid shaping their work in ways that simply reinforce prevailing views in local policy conversations. Although such an approach is pragmatic in some ways, it can reduce the usefulness of policy analysis. At their best, policy analysts maintain critical distance from political debates—not to the extent that they become disengaged, but so they can view problems in fresh ways and offer evidence and insights capable of creating bold changes in policy thinking. Performing like this, policy analysts can exhibit trustworthiness while also infusing policy conversations with ideas and analyses that can promote significant, positive change in policy-making communities.

POLICY ANALYSIS AND ETHICAL PRACTICE

Citizens expect government decision makers to address problems caused by private, decentralized aspects of social and economic interactions, others caused by governmental processes, and yet others caused by unintended, negative interactions between public and private activities. Those decision makers face knowledge gaps concerning the nature of the problems and how they might be tackled. Decision makers also must be careful that any responses to given problems represent workable solutions. As Charles Wolf cautioned, "the cure may be as bad as the illness" (1979a: 133). Policy analysts are employed to close knowledge gaps that inhibit effective policy making. As the discipline of policy analysis has evolved, a consensus has emerged on how policy analysts conduct their work. Here, I follow the six steps of policy analysis first presented in Chapter 1. Policy analysts add value to decision-making processes when they do the following:

1. Engage in problem definition
2. Propose alternative responses to the problem
3. Choose criteria for evaluating each alternative policy response
4. Project the outcomes of pursuing each policy alternative
5. Identify and analyze trade-offs among alternatives
6. Report findings and make an argument for the most appropriate response

In my portrayal of policy analysts, emphasis is placed on their role in closing knowledge gaps for government decision makers. But this is rarely straightforward. Policy analysts have some discretion when considering how to define a problem and the nature of the analytical work that flows from there. They also face many choices when they develop their policy reports and present their advice. Further, policy analysts face choices over the extent to which they consult with stakeholders during the policy development process. Even when consultation is required, everyone knows that stakeholder engagements can be perfunctory. Sometimes, consultation can be used primarily for pushing specific solutions rather than for genuinely listening to stakeholders and understanding their concerns.

Among other things, policy analysts acting ethically must strive to promote outcomes that are good for society. They must also be transparent about the choices embodied in their work. Contemporary notions of ethical practice are informed by a range of philosophical and religious ideas that have been discussed and developed through the ages. In this chapter, we draw from that tradition to develop five ethical principles that can guide the practices of individual policy analysis. However, before turning to those principles, it is useful to review three highly influential ethical perspectives.

Universalism tells us that there are certain appropriate behaviors and that those behaviors should be followed without any reference to the mediating effects of context. The Ten Commandments fit the universalism model.[1] The Golden Rule offers another example of universalism and has been proposed by many religions and cultures. It is summed up in the words of Jesus: Do unto others as you would have them do unto you.[2] Immanuel Kant presented a variation of the Golden Rule: "Act only in accordance with that maxim through which you can at the same time

---

[1] See the Old Testament books of the Bible: Exodus 20:1–17, and Deuteronomy 5:5–21.
[2] See the New Testament books of the Bible: Matthew 7:12, and Luke 6:31.

will that it should become a universal law."[3] Universalism promotes persistence and consistency, but it is difficult to apply because exceptional circumstances abound. The focus is on strict adherence to a code of practice; the assumption is that this will generate desirable outcomes.

Utilitarianism focuses on outcomes: the maximization of pleasure and the minimization of pain. Here, consequences of actions are considered to be more important than whether those actions fit a universal code of practice. The perspective is most closely associated with the thinking of Jeremy Bentham and John Stuart Mill.[4] Within the utilitarian perspective, individuals are expected to promote attainment of the greatest good for the greatest number of people. There are many instances where deviations from a universal law would be justified within this perspective. For example, there may be times when failing to attend to the neediest people in a group allows effort to be devoted to securing the best outcome for the group as a whole. Utilitarianism is easily understood and is frequently used. However, outcomes are often difficult to predict, and people might have different views about the likely consequences of an action.

Altruism requires that love of others serve as our ethical standard. People are not treated as the means to an end; they are what matter most. Altruism guides us to always take account of the position of the least advantaged person and make that position as dignified and comfortable as possible. This perspective has been espoused by many people who have dedicated their lives to working among the poor or who have used their political careers to promote the social circumstances of the least fortunate. While informed by imperatives that characterize universalism, altruism takes account of context. Difficulties surround the application of this perspective, because people can disagree on what is best for others.

The three ethical perspectives mentioned here offer distinctive views on what individuals should care most about. Should we follow a strict code of practice, focusing on good process? Should we care most about maximizing the outcomes of society? Or should we attend most to the fair treatment of the least fortunate person? A crucial part of the ethic of being a good policy analyst involves helping others to better understand the choices they face and the likely consequence of any given course of action. At the level of the individual professional, we also need to be aware of the choices we face in our daily practices. When would it be appropriate for us to follow universal principles? When would it be more appropriate for us to focus on outcomes? When should we pay special attention to the situation of those who could be most harmed by the advice we give? Identifying the ethical dilemmas we face in our work and discussing them with others around us can serve to improve the overall quality of the analysis we do and the advice we give. We can be better people as a consequence of this kind of reflexivity, and offer better support to government decision makers. Inevitably, though, there will be times when our efforts will fall short of what could be expected of us. At such times, my

---

[3] See Immanuel Kant ([1785]1997, chapter 11).
[4] See John Stuart Mill (2003).

suggestion is that we follow the advice of the great Stoic philosopher Epictetus. "Human betterment is a gradual, two-steps-forward, one-step-back effort. Forgive others for their misdeeds over and over again.... Forgive yourself over and over and over again. Then try to do better next time."[5]

Other policy scholars have considered how policy analysts might use ethical perspectives to guide their work. The literature falls into two camps. In one, consideration is given to the practices of policy analysts themselves. In the second camp, consideration is given to how policy analysts can integrate ethical frameworks and analysis into the development of policy advice. A common concern is that policy analysts do not make sufficient use of ethical analysis to guide their comparisons of policy options. The concerns of each camp were neatly represented in articles published back-to-back in an issue of *Policy Analysis and Management* that appeared several decades ago.

Representing the camp concerned with doing ethical policy analysis, Guy Benveniste (1984) argued that a code of ethics should be developed for policy experts and advisors. Benveniste recognized the power and status that policy analysts can accrue because of the knowledge that they hold. He worried that individual policy analysts could become enamored with playing the game of political influence. In doing so, they could undermine their legitimacy as sources of independent expert knowledge. Benveniste argued that an effective code of ethics would cover the scope of responsibilities, what should be done about identifying and managing conflicts of interest, how issues of secrecy and the exposure of information should be managed, how policy analysts should manage consultation with stakeholder groups, and how decision-making processes should be conducted during crises (Benveniste 1984: 569). Benveniste recognized that establishing a code of ethics would be difficult and that many decision makers and policy analysts would see little point in its adoption. He noted, for example, that recipients of policy advice are usually powerful political actors, which distinguishes them from the clients of other professionals, such as lawyers and doctors. In the latter cases, the asymmetries of power and knowledge between clients and professionals are more pronounced than in the case of policy advising and tend to run in the favor of the person rendering the services.

Representing the camp calling for greater application of ethical principles as guides to the analysis of public policies, Douglas J. Amy (1984) suggested that the strong emphasis on policy analysis as a technical exercise, combined with issues of administrative structure, reduced the opportunities for such work to be developed. In the decades since Amy considered this matter, there has been considerable growth in the contributions made by ethicists to policy debates across a range of policy domains. For example, in the introduction to their book *Public Policy*, Michael E. Kraft and Scott R. Furlong (2007) note the ways that ethical considerations inform aspects of health-care policy, environmental policy, and foreign policy, along with public policies relating to other fields of human activity.

---

[5] Epictetus (1994: 99).

The present chapter falls in the camp concerned with doing ethical policy analysis, the camp Benveniste (1984) defined. The goal here is to consider ways that policy analysts exhibit ethical behavior in the conduct of their work. Models for this kind of exercise can be found in cognate areas of professional practice. For example, a literature exists exploring how social scientists can be ethical in their practices. As well as covering topics such as informed consent, confidentiality, and the researching of sensitive topics, this literature covers motivations for conducting social science research, the need for competency among researchers, and appropriate reporting of research findings (Reynolds 1979; Frankfort-Nachmias and Nachmias 1996). Within the field of program evaluation, efforts have been made to develop standards (Sanders et al. 1994). Among other things, these include standards for designing evaluations, collecting information, engaging in analysis, and reporting results.

Policy scholars David L. Weimer and Aidan R. Vining (2005) have offered a useful guide for how policy analysts might exhibit professional ethics through their work. To do so, Weimer and Vining proposed that policy analysts be viewed as performing one of three roles: the objective technician, the client's advocate, or an issue advocate. Each policy analyst can be seen as holding fundamental values, such as commitment to analytical integrity, responsiveness to the client, or adherence to one's conception of what is socially good. At any given time, policy analysts might view themselves as performing more than one of these roles and show joint commitment to analytical integrity, their client, and their own values. But ethical dilemmas often arise. Weimer and Vining explore how policy analysts might respond to values conflicts, noting available options. These range from discussion of those conflicts with the client to resigning from a given role, and even showing disloyalty to the client.

This chapter builds on prior contributions and explores how ethical challenges arise at each step in the process of doing policy analysis. As such, it offers the prospect of reducing the tendency for policy analysts to profess an ethical orientation and good intentions, while routinely engaging in practices that undercut the contributions they could make to improving policy discussions and promoting high-quality public decision making.

ETHICAL PRINCIPLES FOR POLICY ANALYSTS

Most general ethical principles hold relevance for people in both their private lives and vocational settings. Contributions to the contemporary literature on leadership and management emphasize the importance of ethical behavior for supporting effective team processes, organizational transformation, and the emergence of cultures of excellence.[6] Here, five ethical principles are introduced: integrity,

---

[6]See, for example, Warren Bennis (2003), Stephen M. R. Covey (2006), Stephen R. Covey (1991), Jeffrey J. Fox (2002), Laurie Beth Jones (1995), John P. Kotter (1996), John C. Maxwell (1999), Robert E. Quinn (2000), Steven B. Sample (2002).

competence, responsibility, respect, and concern. In selecting this set, I have followed Thomas G. Plante (2004). While other principles are relevant, these five offer a sound basis from which to explore the ways that a focus on ethics can promote good practice among policy analysts. Having set out these principles for policy analysts, I employ them to assess how policy analysts might act ethically at each step in the process of doing analytical work.

Integrity

When people act with integrity, they are directed by an internal moral compass. They strive to do the right thing in any given situation and to achieve consistency in their intentions and actions across contexts. Thomas G. Plante (2004) has suggested that "integrity is the foundation for living an ethical life" (61). In his view, people display integrity when they follow high standards of honesty, and when they show commitment to the values of justice and fairness. People of integrity do not seek selfish, short-term gains through opportunistic actions that harm others. Rather, they take the view that their commitment to honesty and fairness will produce the best outcomes all around. Evidence from cognitive psychology suggests that people have fine-tuned skills for detecting when others are not being honest with them (Kramer 1999; Meyerson, Weick, and Kramer 1996). As a result, acting with integrity can lay the foundations for building long-term relationships of trust and mutual support (Covey 2006).

Policy analysts are called to advise decision makers about the nature of the public problems they must confront and the relative merits of alternative responses. In all cases, decision makers must have faith that the policy analysts have performed their work with integrity. Advice based on limited engagement with appropriate evidence, lack of consideration for how various policy approaches will affect different groups of people, and limited attention to good design and implementation could result in poor outcomes both for those affected by the policies and the decision makers who adopted them. This is why policy analysts must act with integrity. Adherence to the values of honesty, justice, and fairness is important. Being around others who exhibit integrity can also help to reduce the risk of behavioral lapses.

Competence

A strong relationship exists between competence and ethical behavior. When you talk or act as if you can do something, then the qualities of honesty and integrity dictate that you can actually do it. It is dishonest for anyone to say they can do something when they cannot. Most professionals have specialized knowledge and skills, making them highly competent in a narrow set of areas. To undertake work outside your specialization carries the risk that you could fail at it. In some professions, such as medicine and engineering, incompetence could result in serious injuries and the loss of lives.

In the field of policy analysis, the level of knowledge and skill required to perform competently will depend on the substantive area of focus. However, all policy analysts should aspire to delivering high-quality work, to do so without unnecessary cost, and to continuously improve their analytical skills. Seeking feedback from clients, working with mentors, and identifying high-quality work to emulate are some useful strategies that policy analysts can use to strengthen their competencies. Often, the nature of the analytical task will require that teams of policy analysts work together, so that all team members can contribute in their areas of expertise without straying into territory where their skills would be inadequate. Policy analysts also have reason to form teams with specialists from other fields who possess substantive knowledge and skills relevant to the analytical task. The teamwork required by many policy tasks illustrates the importance of policy analysts building people skills that complement their technical expertise. The skills of working effectively in teams, communicating with a range of stakeholders, and managing conflict are highly relevant to the work of policy analysts (Mintrom 2003).

Responsibility

Taking responsibility means acknowledging the part you play in contributing to anticipated or observed outcomes. It is commonplace for people to willingly accept the credit when good outcomes occur but to deflect blame for poor outcomes. People who take responsibility do more than accept that they are accountable to others. They tend to be proactive, striving from the start to achieve good outcomes. They also quickly acknowledge instances in which their actions or lack of action created problems. They then do what they can to make good on past mistakes. Making good can range from sincerely apologizing for what happened to doing all that is necessary to address and fix the problem. Acknowledging problems you have caused and undertaking service recoveries takes courage. It can also mean spending valuable resources to make things right. However, when such actions are taken with good grace, they not only serve to mend endangered relationships but they can even strengthen them (Covey 2006; Quinn and Quinn 2009).

Policy analysts face many situations in which responsible action is called for. They face choices about how thoroughly they will investigate policy problems and explore creative ways to address them. When policy analysts recognize and respect the trust that decision makers place in them, they can scope their work and conduct it in ways that break with conventional wisdom and offer new insights for policy design and implementation. Of course, there will be times when policy problems are neither significant enough nor novel enough to justify extensive new work being performed. Part of being responsible involves taking the time to listen to decision makers and evaluate their willingness to pursue significant policy innovation. Responsible policy analysts work to develop good relations with those they are employed to advise. They look for appropriate ways to close knowledge gaps. They also work quickly to defuse problems or misunderstandings that arise because of their actions.

Respect

When we show respect for others, we acknowledge their humanity, their dignity, and their right to be the people they are. Respect means being considerate and appreciative of others. It means treating others as you would like to be treated (Plante 2004). It is relatively easy for us to respect others when we like them, when we have known them for a long time, and when we share with them common views and interests. The tough part of respect is looking for the humanity, the good, and the reasonableness in people who our gut instincts led us to despise. Hard as it is, part of being an ethical person involves seeking to understand others, to appreciate how they see things. The quality of forgiveness can be especially valuable as an aid in such efforts. So, too, can patience, particularly when it means slowing down the pace of our actions and listening hard.

Respecting others is an important attribute in policy analysts. First, policy analysts need to respect others whom they engage with when they are conducting their analysis and developing ideas for ways to address policy problems. Often, policy debates grow heated because of the different interests at stake (Schön and Rein 1994). While it can be challenging, policy analysts can gain valuable insights into effective policy design by listening closely to others, even when they profoundly disagree with what they are hearing. Respecting others and turning conflicts into opportunities for learning can be a way to promote creative problem solving (Quinn and Quinn 2009). Second, policy analysts need to respect the lives, the needs, and the aspirations of the people who will be directly affected by policy change. Often, policy analysts work to develop policies that will significantly affect the lives of people with whom they share little in common. At such times, showing deep respect for the views, feelings, and hopes of others can be vital for resolving differences. Making conscious use of gender analysis or analytical strategies that take account of differences across racial groups and people of different ethnicities can serve as useful starting points for recognizing social differences and their policy implications. Marianne Williamson, who proposes love as a key to addressing the world's problems, has observed, "It's amazing how positively people respond when they feel respected for their thoughts and feelings. Learning to feel such respect—and to actually show it—is key to a miracle worker's power" (2004: 175). We might add that, in the cut-and-thrust of policy disputes, showing respect for others can be both courageous and transformative.

Concern

Living an ethical life requires that we show concern for others, and not just those who are close family members or friends. Concern means caring about, showing an interest in, and being involved in the lives of others. When people devote their lives to working with and advancing the interests of the poor, they demonstrate exceptional levels of concern for others. Without making that level of sacrifice, many people—through their work, their philanthropy, and their acts of altruism—do an enormous amount to help others to live better lives.

Policy analysts often choose their vocation because they are concerned for the lives of others and they want to make a positive difference in the world. As such, many policy analysts share a people-focused orientation that has roots in the same goodwill toward others that can be found among people in the caring professions, such as doctors, nurses, teachers, counselors, and social workers. However, the day-to-day work of policy analysis can easily become rarefied and removed from the lives of those who will be affected by policy change. This suggests that value lies in policy analysts gaining exposure to the communities that their policies affect. By keeping the lives of others salient to themselves, policy analysts can remain alert to the impacts of their work.

DOING ETHICAL POLICY ANALYSIS

Policy analysts are called to close knowledge gaps faced by decision makers. Given inherent information asymmetries in these relationships, decision makers must place trust in policy analysts to act ethically. Having discussed five ethical principles for policy analysts, we now explore the implications those principles hold for the actions of policy analysts at each step in their work.

Ethical Problem Definition

Problem definition is inherently political work. Rarely do the objective facts of a problem situation receive uniform interpretations from all relevant stakeholders (Majone 1989; Rochefort and Cobb 1994). At this most preliminary stage of conducting policy inquiry, policy analysts face choices about the conduct of their work. Those choices are significant, because how problems are defined strongly influences which policy responses are likely to gain serious attention and which will be brushed aside. How should ethical policy analysts act at the problem definition step? First, they should identify relevant stakeholder groups and learn how members of those groups see the problem and how they would like it to be addressed. Second, they should assess their findings and identify the key lines of disagreement. Based on this information, they should engage in more collection of basic information about the nature of the problem, its causes, and feasible solutions that might be available to address it. All of this information should be assessed and synthesized into a problem statement. It should be shared and discussed with the decision maker, with the goals of conveying potential risks associated with the development of policy solutions, achieving clarity around how the decision maker views the problem, and getting support for moving ahead to other steps in the analytical process. High levels of integrity and competence are required of policy analysts at this stage, to avoid conflicts based on stakeholder perceptions of exclusion or beliefs that a favored solution has already been selected and that everything else will be spin.[7]

---

[7]James Verdier (1984) noted that "analysis that comes early in the process can usually have much more impact than that which comes later.... Economic analysis at this stage can help frame the terms of the debate and structure the options that are presented. At later stages, politics tends to dominate analysis. Economic analysis is then used the way a drunk uses a lamp post, for support rather than illumination" (426–427).

Ethical Construction of Alternatives

Introducing a range of alternative policy responses to a problem can be done in ways that significantly advance policy discussion and good decision making. The subject of how we identify relevant solutions to problems has been considered at length, both by scholars of decision making and political scientists (see, e.g., Cyert and March 1963; Jones 2001; Kingdon 1995). Typically, solutions and problems come intertwined. That is, when feasible solutions become apparent, perceptions of problems change and arguments are made that government action is necessary. For example, as treatments have been discovered for life-threatening diseases, arguments for government funding of those treatments has grown compelling. Likewise, evidence of the life-preserving effects of airbags in cars has produced compelling grounds for airbags to become a required feature of all new cars. We see in these examples that the suitability of the fit between solutions and problems tends to change over time, predicated on the flow of evidence and of technical innovations. A challenge for policy makers involves avoiding the adoption of policy responses that lock in present technologies and potentially inhibit the discovery of improved solutions. Another challenge is the way that interest groups tend to promote their favorite solutions to problems, even when evidence suggests that those solutions might not produce the best outcome for the greatest number of people.

What is an ethical approach to constructing the set of alternative policy solutions? First, we should acknowledge that there are limits to how many alternatives can be considered in any decision-making process. Three or four would seem a reasonable number. To promote useful discussion, alternative approaches included within the set should each be quite distinctive, so that decision makers can get a good sense of the range of possibilities open to them. Second, we should include alternatives that appear most relevant, given the problem and discussions surrounding it. If an alternative is well known to be favored by key stakeholders, then it is appropriate to include it—or a close approximation to it—in the set. Decision makers will need to know how it stacks up against other alternatives. Third, the set of alternatives should be constructed taking account of the broader financial context. For example, when government spending is highly constrained, there is little point in proposing costly policies without accompanying the proposal with suggestions for cost savings in other areas. Fourth, the construction of alternatives offers an opportunity for policy analysts to broaden policy discussions. Learning about approaches tried in other jurisdictions or in other related areas of policy can help analysts to devise innovative policy solutions (Mintrom 1997; Mintrom and Norman 2009). This shows evidence of both competence and concern. Finally, we should treat our analysis as a vehicle for facilitating discussion of additional alternatives. If, on reviewing our advice, decision makers request more alternatives to be considered that build on those already presented, that should be treated as good feedback.

Ethical Selection of Criteria

Policy analysts are required to weigh the relative merits of alternative policy responses to any given problem. To do this in a systematic fashion, they must establish a set of

criteria for judging each alternative, and then make sure that they assess the anticipated performance of each alternative on each criterion of interest. It is common for
policy analysts to analyze policy alternatives using three criteria: efficiency, equity,
and administrative simplicity. Taken together, these criteria lead us to consider the
relative costs of each alternative, the fairness by which different groups of people are
affected by each alternative, and the relative degree of burden that each alternative
would place both on those required to implement it and those required to comply
with it. There is good reason to believe that the use of these three criteria is both
sound and ethical. However, focusing only upon them can limit policy analysis in
unhelpful ways. It is often important to assess policy alternatives in terms of their
implications for personal freedom, human dignity, social harmony, and environmental sustainability. When should other criteria be introduced? The development
of policy analysis as a discipline has seen increasing calls by various groups to have
their interests and their concerns reflected in the criteria used to judge policy alternatives. While there is no conceptual limit to what criteria might be applied, in practice we need to keep our analysis manageable. Reflecting on the concerns expressed
by stakeholder groups who have weighed in at the problem definition stage is helpful
here. It can lead to development of a set of evaluative criteria that is appropriately
suited to the context. Discussing with others what they care about and how their
concerns could be captured in the evaluative criteria is a good way to show both
respect and concern during the process of policy development.

Ethical Prediction of Outcomes

Decision makers need high-quality information on the likely effects of adopting
specific policy solutions. The challenge for policy analysts is to generate that information, paying careful attention to the criteria judged most appropriate. Policy
analysts can employ various methods to gather existing information, generate new
information, and analyze the information to predict likely policy effects. Several
ethical concerns arise. First, all analytical work requires that we make simplifying
assumptions, that we make estimates when good data is not present, and that we
work with models that, at their best, only approximate real-world processes. None
of this is a problem, so long as we carefully document our work and have others
peer review it. Other people should be able to follow our analytical procedures and
come to much the same conclusions. They should also be able to clearly understand the limits of our analysis. Strong technical work should be accorded value by
decision makers. However, analysts should never try to hide behind technical matters or try to win support for a favored solution using opaque but smart-sounding
analysis. Second, because we know that there is room for fudging of evidence, we
should work to promote high standards of technical ability and clarity of explanation in our work. This raises the bar for those who would be happier to win policy
disputes by playing fast and loose with the evidence.

Ethical Analysis of Trade-Offs

Through the work of predicting outcomes, policy analysts will usually form judgments about the relative merits of each alternative and the trade-offs associated

with pursuing one over the others. It is important that these trade-offs be made explicit. Policy analysts should also be prepared to state their views on which policy alternative would be most appropriate in the given context. Doing so can be clarifying to decision makers. Just as important, it forces the analyst to work hard at making his or her arguments for the choice they favor. The most effective way to do this is to make the strongest possible argument for each alternative, rather than paying more attention to a favored position and doing limited or sloppy analysis of the other alternatives. Exposing your work to peer review is a further check on the validity of your evidence and arguments.

Ethical Reporting Practices

Knowledge gaps can be closed only when relevant information is presented in ways that work for the decision makers. If a busy decision maker requests that all material be initially presented in an oral briefing and a one-page memo, then the onus is on the policy analyst to meet that requirement. Meeting such a requirement can take a lot of careful thought and effort. Policy analysts need to become adept at writing and presenting their work for multiple audiences (Mintrom 2003). It is both ethical and smart to tell the same story in multiple ways, so long as the story remains consistent across the audiences being reached. Having said this, it is clear that any organizational conventions around reporting must be met. Working at different ways to present your work to different audiences is an important means of showing respect to others. But throughout, policy analysts must be sure that they also have a version of their report that they feel most comfortable with, that pulls together in one place all the documentation associated with the analytical process. Increasingly, we can make use of technology to produce reports in which different audience members can choose the features of the analysis that they wish to focus on. To do this well is likely to mean working with experts in website design, communications, and marketing. That is what is required when we take responsibility for improving policy discussions and when we desire to help others understand the problems they face and how policy changes can address them.

CONCLUSION

Knowledge gaps provide the primary rationale for the work of policy analysts. At its best, their work can enlighten decision makers concerning policy problems and effective ways to address them. Given the nature of these knowledge gaps, decision makers must trust that the information provided to them is based on sound, honest work. Asymmetries in expertise create the potential for problems to arise. For example, policy analysts might deliberately narrow the definition of a problem, limit the selection of alternatives to address it, or place undue weight on cost issues, when other criteria should be made salient.

This chapter has discussed how policy analysts might develop and deliver their work in accordance with sound ethical principles. By adhering to the proposed approaches, policy analysts can find ways to advance and even transform policy conversations. It is important that policy analysts understand the political contexts within which they operate. But it is disappointing when apparent contextual constraints are used to justify analytical work that does little more than support the political consensus of the day. Policy analysts should be bold. In particular, when exploring alternative policy responses, they should aspire to being creative, looking for innovative solutions from elsewhere that could usefully inform local policy discussions. This way of doing policy analysis does not depart greatly from standard approaches. But it sets us in a direction that can promote significant, positive change. More than most people in society, policy analysts can catalyze new thinking on policy issues. To do so is ethical. In a world filled with challenges, where routine responses yield limited gains, such work is urgently needed.

Exercises

1. Suppose that you were working as a policy advisor in a government agency and other people around you acted unethically in how they developed their policy advice or how they made decisions. What actions could you take?
2. Think about an area of public policy that is of interest to you. What ethical dilemmas could or do arise for policy analysts working in this area? How could such dilemmas be overcome?
3. Divide into two groups and debate the following proposition: "Policy analysts should not be expected to hold higher ethical standards than other professionals in society."

Invite a Guest to Class

How do policy practitioners wrestle with ethical issues in their work? What advice would they like to share with people aspiring to be professional policy analysts? The challenges of doing ethical policy analysis suggest rich subject matter for consideration by an invited class guest. See my suggestions at the end of Chapter 1 for ways to involve the class members in arranging a visit by an invited guest.

Further Reading

Benveniste, Guy. (1984). "On a Code of Ethics for Policy Experts." *Journal of Policy Analysis and Management* 3(4): 561–572.

De Leon, Peter. (1995). "Democratic Values and the Policy Sciences." *American Journal of Political Science* 39: 886–905.

Epictetus. ([circa 55–135 AD] 1994). *The Art of Living: The Classic Manual on Virtue, Happiness, and Effectiveness, A New Interpretation by Sharon Lebell.* New York: HarperCollins.

Kramer, Roderick M. (1999). "Trust and Distrust in Organizations: Emerging Perspectives, Enduring Questions." *Annual Review of Psychology* 50: 569–598.

Plante, Thomas G. (2004). "What Is Doing the Right Thing?" In *Doing the Right Thing: Living Ethically in an Unethical World*, chap. 2. Oakland, CA: New Harbinger.

PART II

Analytical Strategies

8

Introduction to the Analytical Strategies

The Story So Far... We have explored how policy analysts can effectively advise governments on policy choices. But often information gaps will exist that can be closed only by policy analysts doing original analysis.

Here... We begin exploring the analytical strategies that policy analysts can use in their work. Effective application of analytical strategies is crucial when you wish to contribute in fresh, creative ways to policy discussions. This chapter previews the organization of the chapters to come. It also offers a quick guide on when to use various analytical strategies.

THIS CHAPTER REVIEWS

- The structure and contents of the analytical strategies chapters
- The connection between the use of analytical strategies and the general steps in policy analysis
- When to use each analytical strategy

Policy analysts have the potential to add value to policy making in a variety of ways. It is important to be able to define problems, to consider how those problems might be addressed, and to develop and present useful advice to decision makers. But it is the careful and appropriate use of various analytical strategies that distinguishes policy analysts from other actors in and around the policy-making process. Analytical strategies give us the building blocks for developing unique pieces of policy analysis. The better we understand the strategies and how and when to apply them, the more useful we will be to those around us. Aside from the final chapter, each chapter in the rest of this book introduces a specific analytical strategy and explains how to use it.

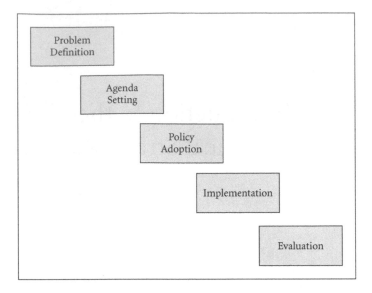

Figure 8.1 Stages in the Policy-Making Process

   This introductory chapter offers an overview of the analytical strategies. It situates the strategies in the context of the steps generally followed when doing policy analysis. It also offers a preview of the structure of the analytical chapters. The set of actual policy studies that are highlighted as applied examples in these chapters are also introduced. By the end of this chapter, you should understand why policy analysts need to be familiar with a range of analytical strategies. You should also be better able to judge what analytical strategies to use, given the policy problems and challenges that interest you, or that you have been asked to address.

POLICY ANALYSTS IN THE POLICY-MAKING PROCESS

Policy analysts can make their contributions to policy making at many points in the process. Here, we discuss the kinds of contributions that can be made. We do so by dividing the policy-making process into stages.

   Policy-making processes are always contextually specific. For example, those found at the local government level exhibit many differences from those found at the national level. Many differences can be found across policy-making processes used in different countries. That said, scholars of public policy have often found it

----

[1] Anderson (1975), Jones (1970), and Peters (1986) popularized use of the stages model as a way of conceptualizing the policy-making process. Paul Sabatier (1991) has criticized the model's representativeness of the policy-making process, primarily because of its assumption of strict linearity and lack of consideration of feedback loops (see also Jenkins-Smith and Sabatier 1993). For pedagogical purposes, however, it is a useful model to work with. It also has face validity.

helpful to use a simple model to characterize the policy-making process.[1] In this model, the process is divided into five stages—problem definition, agenda setting, policy adoption, implementation, and evaluation—as illustrated in Figure 8.1. A linear progression is assumed in this model, and this seems a reasonable assumption. Before policy adoption occurs in decision-making arena, such as council chambers, legislatures, and parliaments, some form of agenda-setting activities must have occurred to draw attention to the policy proposals. Before agenda setting can occur, an issue or problem must become salient. So we can see here that a logical progression runs through the first three stages. It is also reasonable to claim that a policy must be adopted before it is implemented, and the evaluation makes sense only when a policy has been put in place at the implementation stage. Critiques of this linear conception of the policy-making process have dwelled on the observation that policy-making processes are also characterized by feedback loops and multiple iterations. This is where the clean boundaries of the stages in Figure 8.1 become blurred. However, the linear model of the policy-making process works well for our purposes here.

THE ANALYTICAL STRATEGY CHAPTERS

The analytical strategies are covered in a set of chapters that follow a common structure. The structure is presented in Table 8.1. Here, a brief overview is provided of the content of each chapter.

Chapter 9: Analysis of Markets

Because markets are vital mechanisms for the allocation of goods and services in society, policy analysts must have a good understanding of how markets work.

Table 8.1 Common Structure of the Analytical Strategies Chapters

Introduction
When this analytical strategy can be used.

An Overview of the Analytical Strategy
Background on the analytical strategy and a review of key conceptual issues relating to it.

Using the Strategy as an Analytical Framework
How to effectively position this strategy as the central component of a policy project and report.

Steps in Applying the Analytical Strategy
A logical list of steps to follow when doing this kind of analysis.

An Applied Example
The logical list of steps to follow are applied and discussed, with reference to a published study in which the strategy represents the central component of the original analytical work.

Advice for Analytical Practice
A set of suggestions that can improve the application of this strategy.

This Strategy and Other Analytical Strategies
Consideration of how this strategy can be combined with other strategies introduced in this book.

This chapter reviews individual, firm, and market behaviors. It explains how policy analysts can use the analysis of markets to understand the effects of contextual changes. It lays the foundation for thinking about relations between market processes and government policy settings.

Chapter 10: Analysis of Market Failure

This chapter reviews ways that markets can sometimes fail. Market failures often stem from information problems, poor specification of property rights, or technological challenges. Market failures can provide justifications for policy responses.

Chapter 11: Analysis of Government Failure

This chapter considers insights that have emerged from the literature on government failure. This literature reminds us that when governments seek to address problems of decentralized decision making, sometimes the cure can be worse than the illness. We consider how policy analysts can reduce the prospect that their policy proposals will result in government failure.

Chapter 12: Comparative Institutional Analysis

Use of comparative institutional analysis, which compares actual working institutional arrangements, can provide powerful evidence for supporting the development of effective public policies. This chapter explains how to conduct comparative institutional analysis.

Chapter 13: Cost-Benefit Analysis

Cost-benefit analysis is a vital tool for supporting informed choices concerning adoption of public policies. It can be combined with other analytical strategies, like comparative institutional analysis, to offer rich insights into the likely consequences of alternative policy proposals. This chapter provides an overview of how to conduct cost-benefit analyses.

Chapter 14: Gender Analysis

This chapter considers how policy analysts can improve their awareness of policy effects by paying attention to gender differences. Policy analysts must be vigilant to avoid the perpetuation of social disadvantage based on discrimination and seek ways to eliminate it. We discuss the importance of recognizing gender differences and efforts to reduce undesirable differential impacts of policies on women and men.

Chapter 15: Race Analysis

Aggregate statistics often reveal stark differences across racial and ethnic groups with respect to the attainment of desired social and economic outcomes. Several concerns are raised when some groups in society appear systematically disadvantaged. From the perspective of social equity and the promotion of human rights, all people should be able to enjoy equality of opportunity and be free from discriminatory practices. From the perspective of effective institutions and economic efficiency, it is preferable for society that arbitrary forms of disadvantage and discrimination are eliminated. This chapter considers how race analysis can be used to promote improved social and economic outcomes.

Chapter 16: Implementation Analysis

Application of implementation analysis can increase the chances that new policies will perform as intended, that they will not be undermined by opponents, and that they will not create unintended negative consequences. The chapter reviews key elements of implementation analysis.

USE OF APPLIED EXAMPLES

Each of the analytical strategy chapters contains an applied example illustrating how the strategy has been used to generate insights concerning a real-world situation. In each case, the steps proposed for applying the analytical strategy are used as a template for interpreting and discussing the real-world application. Table 8.2

Table 8.2 The Analytical Strategies and the Applied Examples

Analysis of Markets
How the introduction of mobile telephones improved efficiency in the South Indian fisheries
(Robert Jensen, *Quarterly Journal of Economics,* 2007)

Analysis of Market Failure
Problems of information asymmetry in the market for child care
(Naci Mocan, *Journal of Population Economics,* 2007)

Analysis of Government Failure
Regulatory failure and the railroads in Britain
(Martin Lodge, *Journal of Public Policy,* 2002)

Comparative Institutional Analysis
How competition in schooling promotes innovative school practices
(Michael Mintrom, *State Politics and Policy Quarterly,* 2001)

Cost Benefit Analysis
The cost of HIV/AIDS to businesses in southern Africa and how it can be reduced
(Sydney Rosen et al., *Harvard Business Review,* 2004)

Gender Analysis
A British study of how women are disadvantaged in the workplace
(Savita Kumla and Susan Vinnicombe, *British Journal of Management,* 2008)

Race Analysis
A test for racial discrimination in the setting of automobile insurance rates in California
(Paul Ong and Michael Stoll, *Journal of Policy Analysis and Management,* 2007)

Implementation Analysis
Implementation of the U.S. Pollution Prevention Act
(Suna Bayrakal, *Social Science Journal,* 2006)

offers an overview of the applied examples that have been matched to the analytical strategies. All of the applied examples are drawn from contemporary publications in policy-relevant scholarly journals.

THE ANALYTICAL STRATEGIES AND GENERAL STEPS IN POLICY ANALYSIS

In the earlier chapters that provided an overview of policy analysis, it was noted that a consensus has evolved in the discipline of policy analysis concerning how policy analysts conduct their work. The consensus can be encapsulated in the following steps, which closely follow steps suggested by Edith Stokey and Richard Zeckhauser (1978) and Eugene Bardach (2008). Policy analysts add value to decision-making processes when they do the following:

1. Engage in problem definition
2. Propose alternative responses to the problem
3. Choose criteria for evaluating each alternative policy response
4. Project the outcomes of pursuing each policy alternative
5. Identify and analyze trade-offs among alternatives
6. Report findings and make an argument for the most appropriate response

The general steps in policy analysis can all be brought together in the development of goals/alternatives matrices. Chapter 6, on presenting policy advice, introduced these matrices. As well as being helpful for allowing us to rapidly summarize extensive analysis in simple tabular form, goals/alternatives matrices can provide useful focus during the development of analytical work. Figure 8.2 indicates how analytical strategies can be used to generate information for inclusion in a goals/alternatives matrix. Notice that policy analysts will typically face a lot of options when deciding what analytical strategy or strategies to employ to generate needed information. However, most policy analysis must be performed in a limited amount of time. Given this, care must be taken to select one analytical strategy or one combination of strategies that is most likely to produce the most relevant information, given the problem at hand. Goals/alternatives matrices offer a useful way to summarize evidence generated through use of the analytical strategies. The cells in the middle of the matrices must contain our assessments of expected outcomes. These matrices allow you to keep track of what evidence you have gathered on outcomes and where gaps remain to be filled. Policy analysts need to offer advice concerning the trade-offs associated with pursuing one policy option over others. Goals/alternatives matrices, when used in combination with appropriately chosen analytical strategies, allow us to assess the trade-offs among valued goals, given the pursuit of each alternative. The matrices reduce the complexities of deciding what alternative seems most appropriate, given the selected criteria, projected outcomes, and anticipated trade-offs.

Goals:	Policy Alternatives:		
The policy analyst selects and lists here the criteria to be used to judge the relative merits of the selected policy alternatives.	The policy analyst selects the set of policy alternatives that will be given careful consideration in a specific piece of analytical work. Here, three alternatives are suggested: (1) A tax or fee; (2) A regulation; and (3) Provision of information.		
	Projected Outcomes:		
	A Tax or Fee	*A Regulation*	*Provision of Information*
Efficiency	The policy analyst should seek to complete the three cell entries in this row by summarizing evidence on projected outcomes developed using, for example, market analysis, analysis of market failures, analysis of government failure, cost benefit analysis, and/or comparative institutional analysis. We should be able to compare across the cells in this row to determine which policy alternative will likely produce the most efficient outcome.		
Equity	The policy analyst should seek to complete the three cell entries in this row by summarizing evidence on projected outcomes developed using, for example, market analysis, cost benefit analysis, comparative institutional analysis, and/or gender and race analysis. We should be able to compare across the cells in this row to determine which policy alternative will likely produce the most equitable outcome.		
Simplicity	The policy analyst should seek to complete the three cell entries in this row by summarizing evidence on projected outcomes developed using, for example, analysis of market failure, government failure, comparative institutional analysis, and/or implementation analysis. We should be able to compare across the cells in this row to determine which policy alternative will likely produce the most administratively simple outcome.		

Figure 8.2 Using Analytical Strategies to Complete Goals/Alternatives Matrix

Trade-offs: Having generated the information on projected outcomes, it is possible to then discuss the relative merit of each policy alternative and the trade-offs between attainment of desired goal associated with pursuing any one alternative over the others.

Table 8.3 Mapping Analytical Strategies to Stages of the Policy-Making Process

STRATEGY	PROBLEM DEFINITION	AGENDA SETTING	ADOPTION	IMPLEMENTATION	EVALUATION
Market analysis	*				
Analysis of market failure	*	*			
Analysis of government failure	*	*		*	*
Comparative institutional analysis	*	*	*	*	*
Cost-benefit analysis		*	*		*
Gender analysis	*	*	*		*
Race analysis	*	*	*		*
Implementation analysis			*	*	

WHEN TO APPLY EACH ANALYTICAL STRATEGY

No absolute rules exist that dictate the circumstances under which the use of one analytical strategy should trump the use of others. However, it is clear that different kinds of analytical contributions are called for at different stages of the policy-making process. Table 8.3 maps the analytical strategies covered in this book to stages of the policy-making process introduced earlier in this chapter. It is intended as a guide for choosing among strategies to apply. Reasonable people could disagree about the mapping I have done here. Mostly, we should use a table like this to help convince ourselves and others that our use of a given analytical strategy is appropriate, given the nature of the analytical task we are confronting.

CONCLUSION

Effective policy analysis requires both good technical skills and good judgment. Those who are familiar with a range of analytical strategies have great capacity to illuminate problems and add value to policy discussions. However, good judgment ensures that analytical capabilities are appropriately directed and that the right analytical strategies are used given the problem at hand. The chapters to follow are intended primarily to support development of technical skills. Good judgment comes through experience and by critical reflection on the contexts other analysts confronted and the choices that they made concerning the use of analytical strategies.

9

Analysis of Markets

The Story So Far... Policy analysts strive to make fresh, creative contributions to policy discussions.

Here... Because markets are vital mechanisms for the allocation of goods and services in society, policy analysts must have a good understanding of how markets work. This chapter reviews individual, firm, and market behavior. It explains how policy analysts can use the analysis of markets to understand the effects of contextual changes. This lays the foundation for thinking about relations between market processes and government policy settings.

THIS CHAPTER REVIEWS

- Consumer choice and the demand side of the market
- Firm behavior and the supply side of the market
- Equilibrium in markets
- Comparative static equilibrium analysis
- Price signaling and interconnected markets
- When and how to use market analysis in policy work

Policy analysts need to understand market processes. If we think of all items that are available for use by people in society as resources, then we can note that a range of mechanisms exist in society for resource allocation. In families, it is common to find those who have the greatest ability to amass resources beyond the family to engage in allocation of resources within the family. For example, parents make use of their time and their financial resources to ensure—as best they can—that their children are sheltered, well fed, secure, and able to develop into well-adjusted, productive adults. In firms and other organizations in society, executives make decisions about the allocation of resources based on the desire to see the organization continue to function effectively in contexts subject to continual change or competitive pressures. Governments also serve as extremely important institutions for allocating resources in society. Government leaders make many decisions that have major implications for resource allocation in society. The defining characteristic of governments is that they embody powers that allow them to make allocation decisions, to direct that those decisions be implemented, and to see that intended outcomes occur. Government decision making about resource allocation is centralized, it is done on behalf of all citizens living within the specified jurisdiction, and the decisions are publicly recorded. Within all of these venues where decisions about resource allocation are made (families, firms, other organizations, and governments), power differences and the possibility of coercion are ever present.

In markets, resource allocation decisions are decentralized. They are made by individuals or by firms. The decisions are private—there is no expectation that others will be consulted before choices are made. Markets are characterized by the demands of consumers and by supply from producers. Coordination in markets is achieved through the price mechanism. Price adjustments in markets send signals to potential buyers and sellers concerning the best decision to make—how much of a given commodity they will buy or sell at the prevailing market price. At their best, markets facilitate coordination of resource allocation without coercion (Friedman 1962).

This chapter provides an overview of market processes. It begins with a discussion of individual choice and how market demand for any given commodity is derived from the aggregation of individual demand curves. Consideration is given to decision making in firms, which helps us understand the derivation of market supply curves. The chapter then presents a discussion of market equilibrium and the analytical value of comparing markets before and after a change. That kind of comparative work is called *comparative static equilibrium analyses*. What some people have called "the miracle of the market"—the ability of markets to support widespread coordination of decentralized, individual plans—is then discussed with reference to the ways that conditions in one market can have a domino effect on the conditions in related markets. The chapter also includes suggested steps for conducting basic market analysis. The application of these steps is demonstrated in an applied example. This is followed by further advice for analytical practice. The material presented in this chapter serves as crucial background to the discussion of market failure contained in the chapter to follow.

Policy analysts need to know the conditions that allow markets to work well and when markets are the most appropriate mechanism for resource allocation in society. At the outset, we should note that markets cannot operate effectively without the underlying rules of the game being set by governments. At a minimum, governments are expected to establish and enforce property rights, have a stable money supply, and promote fair trade. Sometimes markets require additional government policy action to improve their performance. There are also cases in which government allocation of resources is preferable to reliance upon markets as allocation devices.

AN INTRODUCTION TO MARKET ANALYSIS

By taking the time to work through the idealized behaviors of consumers and producers and the implications of their behaviors for market outcomes, we can gain insights into the broad relevance of terms and processes that both economists and policy analysts use to describe and explain human behavior. There has been much discussion in the past about the ability of people to make sound, or rational, decisions (Friedman 1953; Moe 1979; Simon 1955, 1991). In economic modeling, it is commonplace to find simplifying assumptions being made about people and the contexts they exist in that can seem quite unrealistic or even unreasonable. In the models presented in this chapter, six assumptions are made.

1. All parties to a trade are assumed to have full knowledge of relevant information. If they do not, then there is a possibility that one party will deliberately manipulate relevant information with the goal of gaining at the expense of other parties.
2. All costs and benefits associated with a trade are assumed to be reflected in the market price. If they are not, then it is possible that the trade is indirectly benefiting or harming others.
3. Property rights are assumed to be appropriately specified. When property rights are not well specified, disputes could arise over what actually was exchanged in any market transaction.
4. Expressions of preferences are assumed to be sincere. When people say that they are willing or unwilling to buy or to sell at specific prices, they mean it. Another way to put this is that our models do not allow for strategic behavior, in which people deliberately lie or withhold relevant information with the intention of gaining from the gullibility of others.
5. No buyer or seller can manipulate the prices at which items are traded. If a buyer or seller could manipulate prices, then that would suggest they have a lot of power relative to other market participants.
6. There is no coercion. The models introduced here assume that all parties participate freely in their transactions. If people would prefer not to participate, they need not. This assumption implies that markets are democratic, that they distribute power evenly across buyers and sellers.

As we work through the model of consumer choice and the market model, we will find that we can gain a variety of insights that are useful for real-world analysis, even if those models are built around strong assumptions. The development of economic analysis has often been driven by economists' efforts to explore the effects of making changes in one or a few of the assumptions built into such models.

Consumer Choice and the Demand Side of the Market

We begin with the simple *model of choice*, in which the focus is placed on the choices open to an individual consumer. Standard economic models assume that individuals are driven by self-interest and that they seek to maximize their gains, subject to contextual constraints. The model of choice helps to reinforce several common economic concepts used frequently by policy analysts. These include *incentives, marginalism, opportunity cost*, and *trade-offs*. This model also reveals systematic aspects of individual-level consumer choices that affect aggregate market demand. Following standard approaches to modeling consumer choice, this model assumes a world containing just two goods. We want to keep the model simple, but we need to give our consumer choice, so a two-good world is an effective way to proceed. Assume further that the individual in this two-good world receives income and that he or she must spend it on some combination of the two goods. (It is useful to keep two specific goods in mind, such as coffee and chocolate. In other words, imagine a world in which your budget is devoted entirely to purchasing some combination of coffee and chocolate. *Disclaimer:* This is a thought experiment, not a recommended lifestyle.) In this model, each good is defined by just two attributes: quantity and price. Note, for example, that quality is assumed to be fixed. The individual consumer is assumed to have a fixed income and to spend it all. Some notation is useful.

- Good A (e.g., chocolate) has price P_A and quantity purchased is Q_A
- Good B (e.g., coffee) has price P_B and quantity purchased is Q_B
- Income = Y

With this information, we can start to define the choices available to the individual. To move in that direction, we define a **budget constraint**. This represents the combinations of Good A (chocolate) and Good B (coffee) that the individual can purchase, subject to the individual's fixed income, the fixed price of A, and the fixed price of B. The budget constraint is as follows:

$$Y = P_A Q_A + P_B Q_B.$$

Suppose that the individual were to purchase none of Good A (chocolate). If

$$Q_A = 0,$$

then

$$Y = P_B Q_B.$$

This implies that

$$Q_B = Y/P_B.$$

Likewise, suppose that the individual were to purchase none of Good B (coffee). When

$$Q_B = 0,$$

then

$$Y = P_A Q_A.$$

This implies that

$$Q_A = Y/P_A.$$

We can now graph the budget constraint. It appears in Figure 9.1. The budget constraint establishes the combination of goods A and B that the individual can purchase, given the fixed income, Y. Note that the consumer can purchase any combination of A or B on or below the budget constraint line. Therefore, the triangular area defined by the budget constraint and the space below it is called the feasible purchase set.

Discussion of the budget constraint becomes interesting when we consider the effects of a change in the price of one of the goods or a change in the individual's income. Suppose that the price of Good A (chocolate) rises from P_A to P_{A+}. The effect on the budget constraint is portrayed in Figure 9.2. Here, the original budget constraint line is labeled 1 and the new budget constraint line is labeled 2. The increase in the price of Good A (chocolate) has served to reduce the size of the feasible set. Now suppose that the individual's income falls from Y to Y-. This generates a new budget constraint labeled 3 in Figure 9.2. The fall in income could be due to a drop in pay or to the imposition of an income tax. For our purposes, the source of the fall in income is not important. What matters is that the fall in income reduces the size of the feasible set. From the point of view of ability to

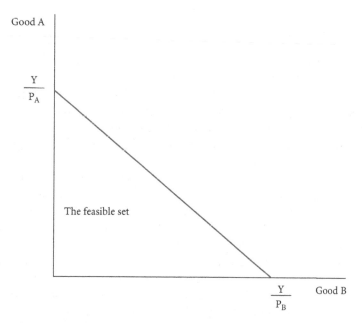

Figure 9.1 The Budget Constraint

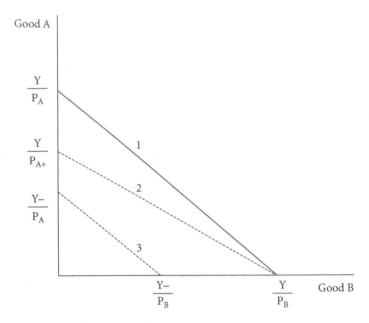

Figure 9.2 Changes in the Budget Constraint

make purchases, we see that an increase in the price of a good is equivalent to a fall in income. In both cases, these changes reduce options available to the consumer. In contrast, when prices fall, they have an effect equivalent to an increase in income. That is, both a fall in the price of a good and an increase in income result in the individual facing more consumption choices.

This simple result offers an explanation for why people engage in comparison shopping. When we manage to find a lower price for a good, say Good A (chocolate), this has the equivalent effect as receiving an increase in income. Indeed, people seem to devote more time to comparison shopping to find the lowest price of a good when the good is considered to be a big-ticket purchase.

The model of choice also explores consumer preferences. Before we turn to that, it is helpful to reflect on the general effects of consumption of any given good. Economists say that individuals gain utility from the consumption of goods. Utility can be thought of as the pleasure or satisfaction that we derive from consuming. Importantly, economists make the assumption that all of us experience diminishing marginal utility during the consumption of any good. Think about anything you like to consume and the pleasure or satisfaction you get from it. Perhaps you thought of chocolate or coffee. When we desire to consume something and we purchase it, we typically find that we gain the most pleasure or satisfaction near the beginning of the act of consumption. No matter what it is we are consuming, and no matter how much of it we are potentially able to purchase, after a while we will find ourselves gaining fewer and fewer increments of pleasure and satisfaction from each unit we consume. Total utility continues to increase, but the rate

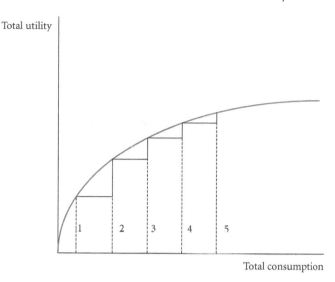

Figure 9.3 Portraying Diminishing Marginal Utility

of increase slows with additional consumption. See Figure 9.3. At some point, we might wish to stop consuming this particular thing (chocolate) and switch to consuming something else (coffee).

You can probably think of cases in which people—perhaps you—seem to derive plenty of pleasure or satisfaction from consumption of a good, even if they have already consumed a lot. Such cases can be accommodated in this model. The assumption is that marginal utility derived from consumption of a given good will decline as additional units are consumed. So the assumption refers to the general curve of the line linking consumption with overall utility. The line will be concave, even though at the initial stages of consumption (which might be longer for some people than for others) the line will appear straight. (Watch how much chocolate people eat, how much coffee they drink. Our preferences are all a bit different, but generally we will get most pleasure or satisfaction from the initial taste.)

The insight that we all experience diminishing marginal utility as we consume any given thing informs the second part of the development of the model of choice. This is where the individual's consumption preferences concerning the two goods, Good A (e.g., chocolate) and Good B (e.g., coffee), are mapped. We do this using an indifference map, characterized by a set of convex lines called *indifference curves*. As with the line that maps total consumption with total utility when consuming one good (see Figure 9.3), the slopes of the indifference curves will differ depending on the preferences of the individual consumer. However, indifference curves always take a convex shape, as portrayed in Figure 9.4. It is important to note that utility is assumed to increase with a move outward on the diagram. This means that individual consumers are always assumed to want to locate themselves on the highest possible indifference curve. (A world with lots

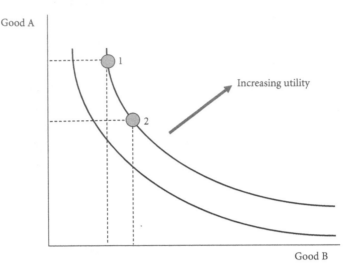

Figure 9.4 The Indifference Map and Indifference Curves

of chocolate and lots of coffee is better than a world with less of each.) Note also how the notion of diminishing marginal utility is captured in Figure 9.4. Consider the outermost indifference curve. At Point 1, the individual would be consuming a large amount of Good A (chocolate) and a relatively small amount of Good B (coffee). The indifference curve shows that this individual would be indifferent between the combination of Good A and Good B at Point 1 and the combination of Good A and Good B at Point 2. The dotted lines make clear that, in making such a switch, the individual would be prepared to trade-off a relatively large amount of Good A (chocolate) for a relatively smaller amount of Good B (coffee).

The model of consumer choice is complete when we bring together the budget constraint (representing consumption options) and the indifference curve map (which represents consumption preferences). The complete model is presented in Figure 9.5. We can now use this model to explore the drivers of individual consumption decisions. Figure 9.6 reproduces the model of choice, but this figure shows an additional indifference curve. This figure can be used to help us explore the concept of opportunity cost and how this relates to the making of trade-offs. Suppose that the consumer chooses to purchase the combination of Good A (chocolate) and Good B (coffee) represented by point G in Figure 9.6. Point G is on the budget line, so all income is being used to obtain this combination of goods. However, this is not the best purchase decision. The consumer could attain a higher level of utility while still remaining within his or her budget constraint, spending the same amount of money. Point H shows the combination of Good A (chocolate) and Good B (coffee) that yields the highest obtainable utility, given the fixed levels of income and the fixed prices of Good A and Good B. The consumer faces an opportunity cost by spending at Point G. In this case, the opportunity cost is the difference in the utility that could be derived from the purchase combination

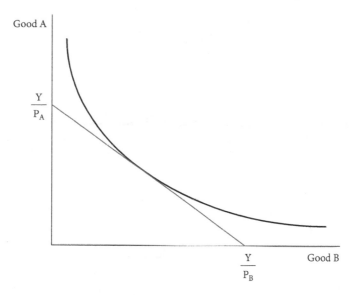

Figure 9.5 The Model of Consumer Choice

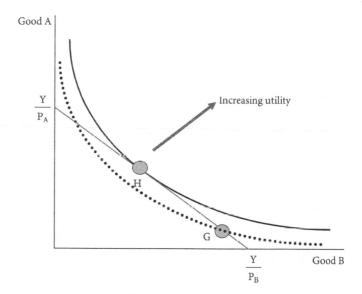

Figure 9.6 Portraying Opportunity Cost and Trade-Offs

at Point H minus the utility actually experienced at Point G. Because the consumer faces an incentive to attain the highest available level of utility, it is appropriate to trade off some amount of consumption of Good B (coffee) for a greater level of consumption of Good A (chocolate). When the consumer purchases the combination of goods represented by Point H, no opportunity cost exists. The

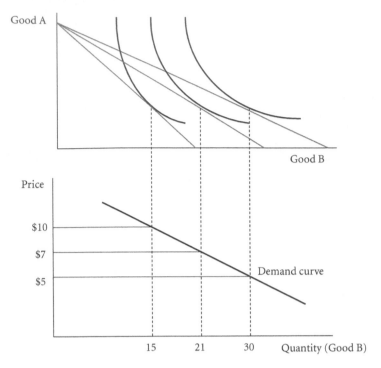

Figure 9.7 Deriving the Consumer's Demand Curve

consumer would have no regrets about the consumption choice, because it is the best that could have been made given existing preferences and constraints. We also see from this example that gains in utility can often be made without spending more money and without changing the set of goods we consume. Those gains come from the reallocation of spending through better consumption choices. An important insight emerges here for policy analysts. That is, finding ways to eliminate opportunity costs can be an effective way to attain better outcomes without spending more money.

Before moving on from the model of choice, we can use it to show the logic behind the downward slope of demand curves for individual consumers. Consider Figure 9.7. The top of the figure presents a model of choice in which three different levels are set for the price of Good B. For each new price of Good B, a new budget constraint must be drawn. The intersection of each budget constraint with a new indifference curve indicates the point of optimal consumption for the consumer given fixed preferences, fixed income, and fixed prices. Figure 9.7 next shows dotted lines from the model of choice to a graph in which the quantity of Good B is marked on the horizontal axis and the price of Good B is marked on the vertical axis. Consistent with the model of choice, we see that as the price of Good B falls, the quantity demanded increases. (Alternatively, we could say that when the price of Good B increases, the quantity demanded falls). That logic stands behind all portrayals of the demand-side of the market. We will next explore this further.

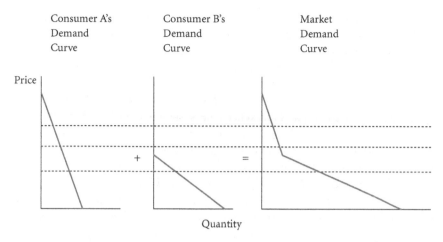

Figure 9.8 Deriving a Market Demand Curve

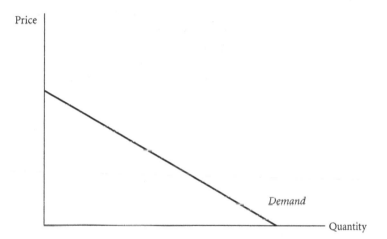

Figure 9.9 The Typical Market Demand Curve

Market demand for a good is sometimes referred to as *aggregate demand*. It represents the sum of all the demand curves for individual consumers. Figure 9.8 shows how we derive the market demand curve for any good. For ease of exposition, in this simple case, the demand-side of the market is composed of just two buyers. When the demand curve for Consumer A is added to the demand curve for consumer B, the result is the market demand curve. Here, we see a kink in that market demand curve. Generally, however, we simply portray market demand for any good using a straight, downward-sloping line.[1] The market demand curve

[1] The aggregate demand line tends to straighten out as more individual demand lines are added. The simple market model assumes lots of consumers, since it also assumes that no single market participant, acting alone, can affect the market price.

reflects an economic law. That is, market demand for a good will decline as the market price increases. A typical market demand curve is presented in Figure 9.9.

The market demand curve maps the total demand expected in a given market, at a specified price. Shifts in price result in shifts in quantity demanded. Shortly, we will explore how market demand and market supply work together to produce market-clearing prices. But before we do that, it is useful to consider other factors that might affect demand in a market. We have already seen that changes in individual income levels will change consumption patterns. All else assumed fixed, we expect that an individual whose income increases will respond by demanding more of a given good. Likewise, a drop in income is expected to translate into a drop in the demand for any given good. Aggregating this insight, we expect that the market demand curve will shift outward to the right when a large proportion of consumers experience increases in their incomes. This effect is portrayed in Figure 9.10. Importantly, we see here that, at any given price, say, p_1, the aggregate demand for the good is now increased from q_1 to q_2. Another way to put this is that, in aggregate, consumers would now be prepared to pay price p_2 for quantity q_1, where previously, they were prepared to pay only p_1. By the same logic, a fall in income across a large group of consumers is expected to results in a shift inward to the left of the market demand curve. At any given price, aggregate demand for the good falls. Shifts like the kind presented in Figure 9.10 can also be explained by changes in consumer preferences. For example, changing fashions in clothing, food, and entertainment can see shifts in consumer demand that are not the result of changes in relative prices.

It is also useful to note here that consumption patterns relating to some goods are more price-sensitive than others. A market demand curve that is steeply sloped indicates that consumers are, in aggregate, less sensitive to price changes than in cases in which the demand curve has a gentle slope. Demand for luxury goods

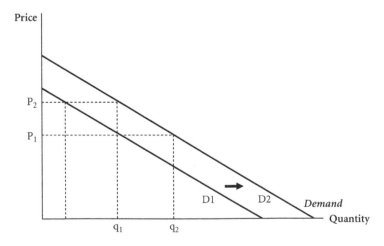

Figure 9.10 Portraying a Shift in the Market Demand Curve

is said to be very price-sensitive; in contrast, demand for "essential" goods is less price-sensitive. Economists talk about elastic and inelastic demand curves. An insight for policy making that falls out of this is that sales taxes imposed on basic consumption items are likely to have less effect on consumer behavior than sales taxes on luxury goods.

Firm Behavior and the Supply Side of the Market

In standard economic models, firms, like individual consumers, are assumed to be motivated to maximize gains subject to contextual constraints. Firm owners also need to recognize the opportunity costs they face—in this case, it is the best returns they could have received on their investment had they not allocated it to the firm. Finally, many elements of operations of firms are subject to the law of diminishing marginal returns. The decision making of firms, then, can be complicated, and this is the subject of a whole subbranch of economics called *industrial organization* (Cabral 2000; Pepall, Richards, and Norman 2008). Here, we consider the rudimentary issues confronting a firm entering a market.

Before any firm can supply goods or services for sale, the owners must incur set-up costs. These are the costs associated with, for example, renting premises, purchasing equipment, and developing business systems. These set-up costs, or fixed costs, remain the same whether the firm sells a small quantity or a large quantity of its products. As the firm begins to produce more and more units of product, the set-up costs are spread. Because of the set-up costs, the average cost of producing each individual unit tends initially to drop with each additional item produced. Firms also face variable costs of production. Initially, these costs might decline per unit produced, because the teamwork in the firm produces efficiency gains with each item produced. However, after a while, those variable costs can

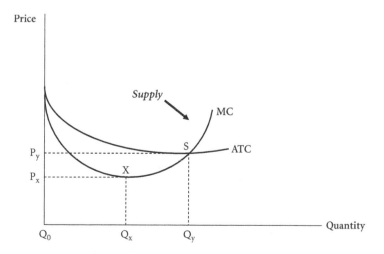

Figure 9.11 Determining When a Firm Will Profitably Produce

start to rise. This logic is captured in the marginal costs of a firm, which are the additional costs associated with producing each additional unit.

The production choices facing a typical firm are depicted in Figure 9.11. The figure indicates that, following outlay for set-up costs, the average total cost of the production of each unit of output falls with each unit produced (see the downward sloping region of the average total cost curve, ATC, between Q_0 and Q_y). Meanwhile, marginal costs of production fall with initial levels of output, because teamwork produces efficiency gains. However, after a while, the marginal cost of each unit of output starts to rise again (see the upward sloping region of the marginal cost line, MC, beyond Q_x). Firm production becomes profitable only when the marginal cost of production is greater than the average total cost of production, ATC, and marginal revenues equal marginal costs. Here, marginal revenue can be equated with the price received for a unit of output. Note in the figure that if the price received were P_x, then the firm would not be able to operate profitably. While marginal revenue would equal marginal cost at point X in the figure, the total costs of production would not be covered (the average total cost curve, ATC, is above the marginal cost curve, MC). Only when price exceeds P_y will the firm enter the market. The supply curve for this firm therefore begins at point S in Figure 9.11. The supply curve for the firm is the marginal cost curve (MC) when it is above the average total cost curve, ATC.

Market supply, or aggregate supply, of a given good or service represents the sum of all the supply curves for individual producers participating in that market. Figure 9.12 shows how we derive the market supply curve. Here, to keep things simple, the supply side of the market is composed of just two sellers. The market supply curve is the sum achieved when we add the supply curve for Producer A and the supply curve for Producer B. The differences in the slope and intercept of the supply curves for each of the individual producers reflect differences in the efficiency of the operations of each producer. As we will see, these differences can have significant effects on the profits that each producer derives from its market

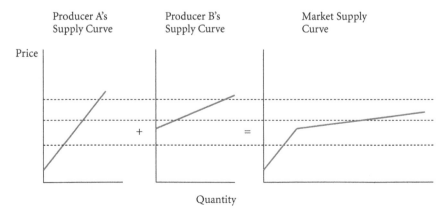

Figure 9.12 Deriving a Market Supply Curve

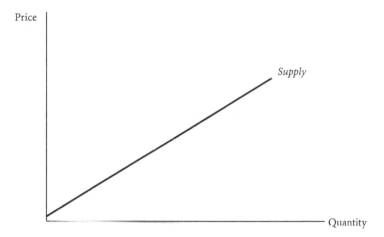

Figure 9.13 The Typical Market Supply Curve

engagement. The supply curve portrayed in the last panel of Figure 9.12 is kinked. However, market supply curves are generally portrayed as straight, upward-sloping lines.[2] The market supply curve reflects the economic law that market supply will increase as the market price increases. A typical market supply curve is presented in Figure 9.13.

The market supply curve maps the quantity of a good or service that will be supplied to a market, given the prevailing market price. Movements up and down the line are a function of the market price. When the market price is low, less of the good or service will be supplied. As the price rises, quantity brought to market also rises. In reality, the supply of goods and services in any market can be affected by more than the prevailing market price. Figure 9.14 portrays a situation in which the original market supply curve (S1) moves inward. By comparing the original market supply curve (S1) with the new one (S2), we see that, for any given price—say P_1—the quantity supplied has fallen—from Q_1 to Q_2. Alternately, we might say that this shift in the supply curve means that for the same quantity to be supplied now as before—say Q_1, then the market price would have to rise from P_1 to P_2. What could explain a shift in the market supply curve? The usual explanation is that some or all of the firms in the market have experienced increases in the costs of supplying their products. For example, the shift in the supply curve from S1 to S2 could be the result of an increase in the cost of electricity or the imposition of a tax on a key factor of production, such as a property tax. We have not depicted it here, but market supply

---

[2] The market or aggregate supply curve tends to straighten out as more individual supply lines are added. The simple market model assumes lots of producers, since it also assumes that no single market participant, acting alone, can affect the market price. These features of the market or aggregate supply curve mirror those of the market or aggregate demand curve discussed earlier.

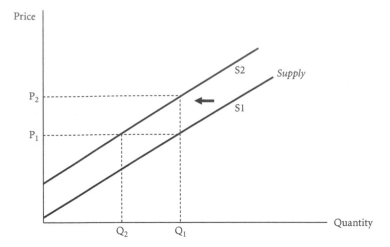

Figure 9.14 Portraying a Shift in the Market Supply Curve

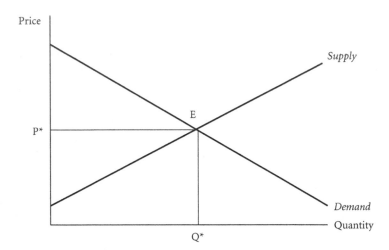

Figure 9.15 Portraying a Market in Equilibrium

curves can also move outward, so that, for each quantity of the product to be supplied, the required market price is lowered. (This would be equivalent to a shift from curve S2 to curve S1 in Figure 9.14.) Efforts on the part of firms to innovate in their production processes and drive down the costs of supply can drive this kind of shift. Because changes of this kind can yield increased profits for producers, all producers face strong incentives to find ways to economize on costs and to pursue innovations in their production processes. Observed reductions in the price of computers and all forms of consumer electronics during recent decades can be explained by innovations on the part of producers in those markets.

Equilibrium in Markets

The market model is completed when the market demand and market supply curves are superimposed on each other. The point where the two curves intersect defines the point of market equilibrium. This is the stable point in the market, where the plans of all participating producers and consumers are perfectly aligned. Figure 9.15 portrays a market in equilibrium. The equilibrium price, or market-clearing price, is defined as P*. At this price, the quantity sold, Q, and the quantity purchased, q, are equal, and are represented by the equilibrium, or market-clearing quantity, Q*.

With the basic market model developed, it is useful to introduce the concepts of consumer and producer surplus. These are identified in the market model portrayed in Figure 9.16. First, consider *consumer surplus*. In the figure, this is represented by the triangle defined by the three corners: a, P* and E. In this market, all consumers buy the quantity of goods that they desire at the stable, equilibrium price, P*. However, the demand curve indicates that some consumers would have been prepared to pay considerably more than they were required to pay. Consumer surplus, then, is comprised of the difference between the prices people were willing to pay and the price they actually paid for the specific good or service. *Producer surplus* is represented in the figure by the triangle: b, P* and E. The supply curve indicates that some producers would have been willing to sell their goods or services in this market at prices below the equilibrium, or market-clearing price, P*. The difference between the price producers required to bring forth supply and the equilibrium price comprises their producer surplus. It is pure profit. The bigger the difference between the price required to bring forth supply and the actual price received, the greater the profit to the individual producer. Taken together, consumer surplus and producer surplus are said to represent the *social surplus* generated through market exchange. When a market is in equilibrium, the social surplus is maximized.

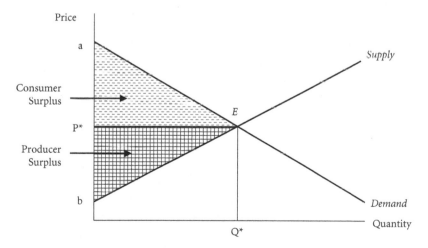

Figure 9.16 Consumer Surplus and Producer Surplus

Comparative Static Equilibrium Analysis

Having developed and discussed the basic market model, we will now explore how it can be used to conduct comparative static equilibrium analysis. This kind of simple analysis can offer useful insights into the nature of market dynamics. Consider a case in which the current market price is sufficiently low that there is excess demand. The case is represented in Figure 9.15. Assume that the current price is P_1. At this price, market demand is high, at q_1. Many consumers see the low price and exhibit a willingness to buy at that price. However, because P_1 is relatively low, few producers are prepared to bring forth the supply at that price. In fact, the quantity supplied is shown to be Q_1. The size of the excess demand in the market is given by the difference between q_1 and Q_1. The condition of excess demand is unsustainable. What happens next illustrates the power of what Adam Smith called "the hidden hand" of the market. At the prevailing price of P_1, some buyers who would have been willing to pay a higher price for the good start to bid up the price. As the price begins to move upward from P_1, two things happen. First, some consumers drop out of the market, because the price goes higher than the level at which they are willing to buy. Second, the upward movement in the price sends a signal to producers. Now, drawn by the incentive of making a profit, producers show more willingness to supply to the market. As the price moves upward, as some consumers fall away, and as more producers enter the market, the condition of excess demand is eliminated, as seen in Figure 9.17. The market reaches its equilibrium—its point of stability—when the price is just sufficient that all consumers who want to buy at that price and all producers who wish to sell at that price can do so. The plans of all buyers and sellers are perfectly aligned.

To further explore the use of comparative static equilibrium analysis, we will consider a market subject to a demand-side shift. The situation is depicted in

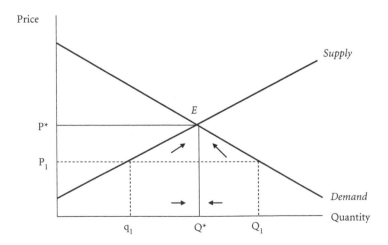

Figure 9.17 From Excess Demand to Market Equilibrium

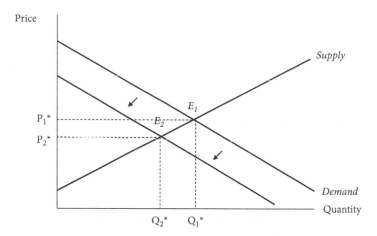

Figure 9.18 A Shift in Demand and the New Market Equilibrium

Figure 9.18. Many markets are subject to shifts of this kind, as consumers change their behavior. For example, a general decline in economic activity might lead households to spend less on items considered to be luxuries, such as dinners at high-quality restaurants or holidays at resorts. Or a general decline in economic activity could result in the deferral of some routine purchases, like the replacement of a car with a new one, or the updating of large household appliances. Originally, the market cleared at equilibrium point F_1, where the equilibrium price was P_1^* and the equilibrium quantity traded was Q_1^*. After the shift in consumer behavior, the market reaches a new equilibrium, E_2. At this point, the new, stable price is P_2^* and the new, stable quantity traded is Q_2^*. What happened in the shift from E_1 to E_2? First, for whatever reason, a large number of consumers came to the decision that the price P_1^* was too high for them to keep paying for this good. So those consumers dropped out of the market. As demand at the prevailing price, P_1^*, dropped, a situation of excess supply emerged. As a result, some producers would not have been able to sell at the prevailing price, P_1^*. Some of them would have dropped out of the market; others would have dropped their price. On the demand side of the market, this drop in price would have been sufficient to bring some buyers back to the market. The result is the new equilibrium price P_2^*. At this lower price, less trading occurs than before (i.e., the total traded now is Q_2^* rather than Q_1^*). But the price mechanism has again worked to achieve perfect alignment among the plans of all buyers and sellers. Everyone who wants to buy in the market at price P_2^* does so; likewise, everyone who wants to sell in the market at price P_2^* does so.

Price Signaling and Interconnected Markets

In a famous article on market processes, Friedrich von Hayek (1945) observed that "in a system where the knowledge of the relevant facts is dispersed among many people, prices can act to coordinate the separate actions of different people" (p. 526). In Hayek's view the signaling work of prices in markets was astounding. Price signals solved allocation problems that would stretch the capacity of any alternative method. Prices provide incentives for individuals to make choices that bring whole systems into equilibrium. The coordination work of prices can be appreciated by reflecting on markets for goods that are substitutes and markets for goods that are complements. First, consider **substitute goods**. We use substitutes when we do not have any of the things we immediately wanted. Examples include consuming soy milk rather than dairy milk, using plastic bottles as substitutes for glass bottles, or aluminum cans as substitutes for tin cans. Consider the case of two substitute foods: say, fish and chicken. If the local price of fish increases (the whole supply curve shifts upward to the left) then, all other things being held constant, local demand for fish will fall. Some people will stop eating fish. Because chicken is treated as a substitute for fish, we can expect that some of the people who previously consumed fish will now switch to consuming the substitute, chicken. (The whole demand curve for chicken moves upward to the right.) The result is that the price of chicken rises. The resulting market shifts in consumption practices occurred purely through consumers responding to price signals, not because someone played some complicated coordination role.

Consider now the case of **complementary goods**. These include things like surfboards and wetsuits, shoes and socks, cereal and milk. Air travel and hotel accommodation also tend to be complements. Suppose that the price of air travel rises rapidly, perhaps due to a rise in the cost of jet fuel. This can be characterized by a shift upward and to the left by the supply curve. As a result, the demand for air travel will fall. But because a lot of people who travel by air use hotels at their destinations, we can expect that the demand for hotel accommodation will drop (the whole demand curve for hotel accommodation will shift down and to the left.) As a result, hotels will face incentives to lower their prices. While no fundamental change has occurred in the market for hotel accommodation, the complementary nature of hotel accommodation and air travel makes the hotel market sensitive to changes in the price of air travel. Again, we see broad system effects driven by price signaling. These observations about price signaling and interconnected markets suggest that analysis of markets should always take into account the possibility that observed changes in one market are driven by more fundamental changes in another.

Assumptions of the Market Model Revisited

The models of consumer choice, firm behavior, and market processes presented here are premised on many simplifying assumptions. Indeed, all model-building exercises share a common feature with fiction writing. That is, they discard a lot of real-world details so that close focus can be placed on fundamental relationships and processes, with a view to gaining new insights into them. For people interested in the design and development of public policies, all this effort to simplify things can seem frustrating. We live in a messy, difficult world. Surely our analytical methods should take account of that. The good news is that they often do. Economists have given large amounts of attention to adjusting and augmenting simple economic models so that they can generate new insights into the complexities of real-world processes. But the important point is that clear understanding of complex situations starts with simplification and focus (Krugman 1993).

Among other things, our discussion of market processes led to the following conclusions. First, at the equilibrium price, the plans of all buyers and all sellers in the market are perfectly aligned. Every producer who was prepared to sell at the equilibrium price gets to do so. This means that there is no excess supply. Also, every consumer who was prepared to buy at the prevailing price gets to do so. This means that there is no excess demand. The result is economic efficiency. This coordination of individual, decentralized decision making is facilitated by the signals given by the market price and the incentive-driven actions of the market participants.

But suppose we are talking about the market for food. Everyone needs to eat, but some consumers might not be able to participate in the market because they have no money, and no means of making it. That points to a big problem with the market model. Markets are very good at the allocation of resources in society when everyone can freely choose whether or not they wish to participate in those markets. But markets do not work as mechanisms for redistribution among our initial endowments. Societies cannot expect markets to solve the problems of the poor. When considering social equity problems and how they might be addressed, we immediately see a limitation of market processes. But we might also say that to criticize markets on those grounds is unreasonable, because that is not their primary purpose. This does not suggest that we should ignore problems of social equity; only that it is inappropriate to expect markets to effectively address them.

As noted at the start of this chapter, six key assumptions are contained in the models presented earlier. Let us reconsider them.

1. All parties to a trade are assumed to have full knowledge of relevant information. If they do not, then there is a possibility that one party will deliberately manipulate relevant information with the goal of gaining at the expense of other parties to the trade.
2. All costs and benefits associated with a trade are assumed to be reflected in the market price. If they are not, then it is possible that the trade is indirectly benefiting or harming others.
3. Property rights are assumed to be appropriately specified. When property rights are not well specified, disputes could arise over what actually was exchanged in any market transaction.
4. Expressions of preferences are assumed to be sincere. When people say that they are willing or unwilling to buy or to sell at specific prices, they

mean it. In other words, the models do not allow for strategic behavior, where people deliberately lie or withhold relevant information with the intention of gaining from the gullibility of others.

5. No buyer or seller can manipulate the prices at which items are traded. If a buyer or seller could manipulate prices, then that would suggest they have a lot of power relative to other market participants.

6. There is no coercion. The model assumes that all parties participate freely in their transactions. If they would prefer not to participate, they need not. This assumption implies that markets are democratic, that they distribute power evenly across buyers and sellers.

From a policy-making perspective, things get interesting when features of any given market do not conform with this set of basic assumptions about market processes. When market processes are undermined, rationales emerge for some form of government intervention to rectify the problem and support improved market functioning. This is a topic that we will discuss in detail in the following chapter on the analysis of market failures. For now, it is important to remember, however, that markets always depend upon government to set the underlying rules of the game. At a minimum, governments are expected to establish and enforce property rights, to have a stable money supply, and to promote fair trade.

USING MARKET ANALYSIS AS AN ANALYTICAL FRAMEWORK

The foregoing introduction to market analysis, while rudimentary, offers a starting point for using market analysis as an analytical framework. Policy analysts frequently must consider the comparative merits of market versus governmental allocation processes. In a given situation, the operative question will be this: Should allocation decisions be left here to decentralized actors driven by private motives, or should they be augmented—or even supplanted—by government decision making, motivated to promote good collective, public outcomes?

As a start to that kind of analytical thinking, it is useful for policy analysts to consider the effectiveness of market processes in the absence of any significant government intervention. Often, governments are called upon by citizens to influence market processes, because some people do not approve of the currently observed outcomes. Given this, policy analysts need the capability to diagnose the current market situation. For example, New Zealand is a country that, like many others, is heavily dependent on other countries for much of its gasoline supply. When local gasoline prices experience a rapid increase—which can often happen—it is almost inevitable that advocates for consumer groups or for the poor will call for government action. In short, people do not like high gasoline prices and they would like the government to lower them. Using market analysis, we could begin to isolate possible causes of the observed increase in gasoline prices.

- World demand for gasoline has increased and there has been no change in world supply, so the world price for gasoline has risen. Companies supplying gasoline to the local market have faced higher prices on the world market.
- World supply of gasoline has declined, but world demand has remained the same, so the world price for gasoline has risen. Again, companies supplying gasoline to the local market have faced higher prices on the world market.
- There has been no change in the world market for gasoline, but the local currency has depreciated in value against other world currencies. Companies supplying gasoline to the local market must now pay more local dollars than before for the same quantity of gasoline purchased at the unchanged world price. The effect is a local price rise.
- There has been no change in the world market for gasoline and no change in the currency, but local demand has temporarily increased, leading to temporarily increased prices. As soon as the companies supplying gasoline to the local market can increase their inventory capacity and bring forth more supply at the world price, the local price will fall back to previous levels.
- One of the companies supplying gasoline to the local market has ceased its operations, temporarily reducing the supply of gasoline to the local market. This has caused local prices to rise.

By considering possible causes of the observed increase in the local price for gasoline, policy analysts can begin to determine whether government action is necessary and what kind of action could be appropriate. Some long-term problems with supply could suggest a need for government action. For example, if it was found that the companies supplying gasoline to the local market were acting strategically to limit local supply and drive up local prices, then that would suggest grounds for government action on the supply side of the market. In contrast, if the problem appeared to be a short-term spike in prices due to exchange rate fluctuation, then the government would probably consider taking actions on the demand side of the market. For example, it could temporarily reduce the sales tax on gasoline, thereby reducing the local cost to all consumers. Or it could seek to help the neediest in society by distributing vouchers for a gasoline subsidy to people who are already entitled to some form of government assistance via income maintenance programs.

In sum, the tools of market analysis can prove highly effective for guiding policy analysts to think hard about the effects, scope, and underlying causes of observed problems in markets.

STEPS IN MARKET ANALYSIS

Market analysis can be undertaken for many reasons. Many academic economists analyze markets because they are simply curious to identify regularities in the behaviors of consumers and producers under specific conditions having to do with information, the state of technology, or market structure. Policy analysts have more practical reasons for engaging in the analysis of markets. Typically, they do so to understand whether grounds exist for government interventions and, if such grounds do exist, what kinds of interventions would be appropriate. Here, several general steps are proposed for conducting market analysis. The following section offers an example of their application.

Step 1. Identify the phenomenon of interest. The analysis must be motivated by a specific question or concern. Among other things, market analysis might be motivated in the following ways. An unexpected price change needs to be explained. An industry is in decline, and people wonder why. Consumers have complained about unfair prices and suspect discrimination. People wonder how adoption of a new technology will affect an industry. Because market analysis can easily grow complicated, the scope of a study must be defined before the investigation starts.

Step 2. Consider the behavior of consumers and producers. How markets perform, in terms of the efficient allocation of resources, depends on the behavior of both consumers and producers. So while the phenomenon of interest to us might be associated most closely with either the demand side or the supply side of the market, it is always useful to consider how both sides contribute to observed outcomes.

Step 3. Think in terms of comparative statics equilibrium analysis. When we conduct comparative statics equilibrium analysis, we compare stable market positions at different points in time and discuss the dynamic processes that take us from one of those positions to another. This snapshot, before-and-after approach can offer helpful insights without requiring the modeling of the actual change processes, which can quickly become complex.

Step 4. Collect and analyze the relevant information. Working through the steps to this point is a useful way to specify hypotheses to be tested and to develop a general research design. That preliminary work can then guide efforts to collect relevant information about the market of interest and the behavior of actors within it. The information can then be analyzed to detect patterns and draw conclusions about the phenomenon of interest.

Step 5. Draw implications for government action. Once the basic analysis has been done, it is then possible to stand back and consider what, if any, implications the findings hold for government action. Knowledge of the performance of markets can be valuable to the design of public policies. Policy prescriptions concerning interventions into markets—or the supplanting of market processes—should always be based on thorough analysis of appropriate evidence. While market analysis will often grow complicated, it is vital that the implications of the analysis are presented in ways that can be easily understood.

AN APPLIED EXAMPLE

This section highlights analysis contained in the following:

Robert Jensen. (2007). "The Digital Provide: Information (Technology), Market Performance, and Welfare in the South Indian Fisheries Sector." *Quarterly Journal of Economics* 122: 879–924.

Most of us could not imagine life without our mobile telephones. Quick conversations or the exchange of text messages routinely help us coordinate with others. More generally, we might say that both consumers and producers value new technologies for their ability to save time, labor, and money. Surprisingly, however, evidence on the economic gains flowing from technological change has often been only anecdotal. Robert Jensen, a development economist, explored the effects of mobile telephone adoption on local beach fishing markets in the state of Kerala, in southwest India. The study, based on weekly surveys over a period of several years, allowed Jensen to determine the economic impact of the adoption of mobile phones by fishermen. Jensen observed that, through improved information, on any given day fishermen were able to determine the best place to sell their fish, based on local demand and supply conditions. Because mobile phones were introduced into different parts of Kerala at different times, Jensen was able to observe the different outcomes associated with mobile phone adoption, comparing changes both within single markets and across markets. Jensen found that mobile phone use by fishermen improved their operating efficiency, increased their profits, and led to less variation in daily prices across the set of markets. It also reduced wastage of catches. In addition, Jensen found that these changes on the supply side of the Kerala fishing market resulted in improved outcomes for consumers. His findings strongly indicated that there was an overall economic improvement from the use of mobile telephones. In what follows, we trace the steps of Jensen's market analysis.

Figure 9.19 offers a simple stylization of Jensen's findings. The adoption of mobile phones reduced the fishermen's costs of doing business. This led to a shift in the aggregate supply curve from S_1 to S_2. Assuming no change in aggregate demand, the supply-side change led to more fish being traded at a lower price. In Figure 9.19, the move from market equilibrium E_1 to equilibrium E_2 is associated with more fish being bought and sold (Q_2 is greater than Q_1) and a lower trading price (P_2 is smaller than P_1). Notice that this change on the supply side generates an increase in social surplus; that is, the sum of producer and consumer surplus. Producer surplus—the total profits of all the fishermen—increased from the area of the triangle P_1E_1B to the area of the triangle P_2E_2C. But consumers gained too, because of the reduction in the market price for fish. In Figure 9.19, the shift of the aggregate supply curve from S_1 to S_2 increases consumer surplus from the area of triangle P_1E_1A to the area of triangle P_2E_2A.

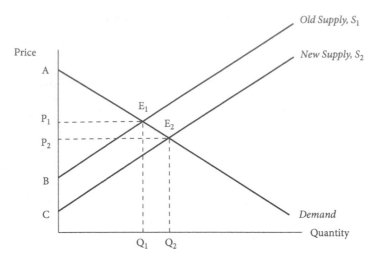

Figure 9.19 How Information Technology Improved Outcomes in the South Indian Fisheries

Step 1. Identify the phenomenon of interest. Jensen's goal was to understand the market effects of the adoption of mobile phones. Jensen knew that when market information is limited, it is possible for a product to sell at different price levels. This is what he originally observed across the beach fishing markets dispersed along the coast of Kerala. Fishermen would return to their home market, often missing out on the higher prices that they could have received at a different market nearby, and sometimes having to dump their catch due to lack of local demand. Jensen anticipated that use of mobile phones would result in better market information and, hence, more efficiency. With adoption of mobile phones, the fishermen would learn while still offshore which local market they should return to with their catch, to ensure a good selling price and to avoid waste. By exploring this instance of technology adoption and its economic consequences, Jensen aimed to provide new evidence that would be relevant to thinking about the effects of technological adoption for efficiency in a broad range of markets, not just the local fishing markets of Kerala, India.

Step 2. Consider the behavior of consumers and producers. Jensen's primary focus was on the changing practices of fishermen. His focus on the supply side of the market led him to conclude that adoption of mobile telephones produced better coordination among the fishermen at sea and people at the local markets. From here, he could explore the ways that this use of technology improved the overall function of the fishing market and eliminated wastage. Because he was also interested in the overall economic gains associated with use of the new technology, as a secondary element of his study, he also considered consumer behavior.

Step 3. Think in terms of comparative statics equilibrium analysis. Jensen's approach to studying the beach fishing markets in Kerala was consistent with the use of comparative statics equilibrium analysis. He was able to observe trading prices and quantities of fish brought and sold across different beach markets on the same days. He was also able to observe prices and quantities in each of the local sites across time. With this kind of information, he could then analyze the effect of the adoption of mobile phones among fishermen. Because mobile phone networks were established at different time points for different regions along the coast, Jensen had many opportunities to compare market outcomes with and without mobile phones. He could observe differences in outcomes across time at specific beach market sites. He could also study contemporaneous differences across those sites where mobile phones were in use by fishermen and those sites where the technology had not yet become available.

Step 4. Collect and analyze the relevant information. The study design involved administering surveys to a random sample of fishing boats at a set number of sites along the coast. The surveys were conducted each week over a period of several years. For each fishing boat, questions were asked concerning the number of fish caught, the market of sale, the quantity sold, the sale price, the time of the sale, costs, where they fished that day, and whether they used a mobile phone. This information was sufficient for Jensen to develop a clear sense of the functioning of the local fishing markets and the effects of the adoption of mobile phones. To estimate outcomes for consumers, Jensen combined his survey-based information on changes in market prices with information from annual household surveys, which allowed for estimation of the market demand curve. From here, estimates could be made about changes in consumer surplus.

Step 5. Draw implications for government action. In this specific study, Jensen noted that the observed improvements in market performance and overall social welfare were driven by changes in the practices of private individuals and firms. The introduction of mobile phones was an initiative of private companies that were not receiving government subsidies. However, the study presents a useful way of estimating the effects of adoption of new technology in a market. Such evidence could be used to make the case for government actions, such as the temporary use of subsidies (say, interest-free loans) to help producers adopt new technologies that are expected to generate economic gains for producers and consumers alike.

ADVICE FOR ANALYTICAL PRACTICE

When analyzing markets, it is useful to bear in mind the following points.

- Build your analysis around a central question concerning the behavior of market participants.
- Sketch simple diagrams to structure your initial thoughts about the processes of interest.
- Study trend information on the market price over time.

- Design the analysis to allow before-and-after comparisons.
- Identify how consumers and producers interpret price changes.
- Consider the sensitivity of the market to changes in related markets.
- Identify factors that drive decision making by consumers and producers.
- Consider how government actions could or do influence market outcomes.

ANALYSIS OF MARKETS AND OTHER ANALYTICAL STRATEGIES

Contemporary societies rely greatly on markets for the efficient allocation of resources. Because they function through decentralized decision making and they promote freedom of individual choice, markets provide venues for people to develop a sense of efficacy, to create, and to flourish. They reduce the need for centralized coordination in many areas of human engagement. As such, they free up the capacity for governments to manage the harder societal challenges that cannot be resolved through the aggregation of private actions. Policy analysts need to have a good appreciation of market processes.

This chapter has highlighted the strengths of markets. We will next consider market failures, which often provide grounds for greater government involvement in the allocation of resources. Throughout our discussions of other analytical strategies, we will continually return to questions about the relative virtues of centralized versus decentralized decision making. We will also make regular use of concepts that have their origins in the analysis of market processes. That is why policy analysts will benefit from knowing the basics of market analysis. The material in this chapter has been designed to offer a rudimentary knowledge upon which more sophisticated understandings can be developed.

CHAPTER CONTENT REVIEW: A SELF-TEST

1. Holding other things unchanged, if the price of a good increases, what will happen to consumer demand for that good?
2. Suppose that an aggregate consumer demand curve for a specific good is observed to shift upward and to the right, indicating that, for any given price, more consumers are now prepared to buy the good. What plausible explanations could be given for this observed change?
3. How is excess supply in a market characterized? Explain the adjustment process that is expected to eliminate the condition of excess supply.
4. Using the concept of producer surplus, explain what incentives firms face to lower their production costs through innovative management techniques.
5. Using the concept of complementary goods, explain how a decline in fish stocks in the Great Lakes could affect the local hotel industry.

Exercises

1. Consider a policy project that you are working on. What market processes are relevant to the problem or issue at the center of the problem? How could a discussion of consumer and producer behavior help guide your thinking about the problem or issue? What effects do price signals or the lack of such signals have here?

2. The *Economist,* the *New York Times,* and the *Journal of Economic Perspectives* all regularly publish short articles that cover economic issues without using extensive technical language and details. Working in small teams, locate up to five recent articles from these sources. Together, decide on one that you would like to discuss in class. Focus on the nature of the analysis reported in the article and how that analytical approach could be applied more generally.

3. The annually awarded Nobel Prize in Economic Sciences is the most prestigious award in the economics profession. The Nobel Foundation website lists all the recipients of this award and contains clear explanations of the economic work for which the awards were made. Consider ways that you could use information from this website as the basis for a series of group discussions about key contributions to economics. The discussion could be preceded by a brief overview ("What's the Big Idea?") and a consideration of its implications for policy analysis ("What's in It for Us?").

4. Markets are a central focus of economic analysis. Think about a particular topic area that interests you (e.g., education, health, the environment, urban development, gender differences, multiculturalism). Now do a search for recent economics articles that relate to your area of interest. You will most likely need to make use of a variety of keywords to do this. Collect the abstracts of five articles. What do they tell you about fruitful ways that market analysis has been applied in this area? Does this exercise make you think of some ways to integrate market analysis into your policy research?

The Policy Research Seminar

Organize a research-oriented seminar that will run for about ninety minutes, preferably with some light refreshments. Invite up to twelve people, and make sure you have a mixture of experienced researchers, junior researchers, and graduate students. The purpose of the discussion should be to develop ideas for the design of policy research projects that give a central place to market analysis. The project ideas should be sufficiently interesting and original that each could form the basis of a significant research paper, dissertation, or thesis. Have participants come to the seminar having read both this chapter and Robert Jensen's (2007) article. You might structure the discussion around the "Steps in Market Analysis" section presented in this chapter and applied in the overview of the Jensen study. Many other recent journal articles could have been highlighted in this chapter. Prior to the group meeting, you might have several participants locate other interesting articles that present original analyses of markets. Discussions of this sort tend to work best when the group has a clear goal. I suggest this outcome statement: "By the end of this meeting, we will have identified five possible topics for new research projects that involve market analysis. We will have sketched out basic research designs for at least two of those projects." Brainstorm to get some ideas flowing. Hold the more skeptical, analytical comments until later in the seminar. Ideally, some members of the discussion group will follow up on the meeting and continue to develop, perhaps collaboratively, research designs that build from the readings and the discussion. This is a good way to promote original policy research inspired by the best contemporary applications of quantitative and qualitative research methods. For additional advice on how to run effective meetings of this kind, see Mintrom (2003) and Kelley (2001).

Further Reading

Bernanke, Ben S. (2005). Remarks at "Panel Discussion: The Transition from Academic to Policymaker." Annual Meeting of the American Economic Association, Philadelphia, Pennsylvania, January 7. Retrieved from Speeches of Federal Reserve Officials, located on the website of the Board of Governors of the Federal Reserve Board System.

Friedman, Benjamin M. (2008). "Chairman Greenspan's Legacy." *New York Review of Books* 55 (4, March 20). This is a review of Alan Greenspan's memoir, *The Age of Turbulence: Adventures in a New World.*

Friedman, Milton. (1962). "The Relation between Economic Freedom and Political Freedom." In *Capitalism and Freedom,* chap. 1. Chicago: University of Chicago Press.

Greenspan, Alan. (2008). "The Making of an Economist." In *The Age of Turbulence: Adventures in a New World,* chap. 2. New York: Penguin Books.

Hayek, F. A. (1945). "The Use of Knowledge in Society. *American Economic Review* 35: 519–530.

Krugman, Paul. (2007). "Who Was Milton Friedman?" *New York Review of Books* 54 (2, February 15).

Mankiw, N. Gregory. (2008). "How Markets Work." In *Principles of Microeconomics,* 5th ed., part 2. Mason, OH: South-Western Cengage Learning.

10

✦◯

Analysis of Market Failure

The Story So Far... Many of the key objectives of government can be pursued through efforts to support the effective functioning of markets. Often markets work well with only a limited amount of government support. But sometimes the limitations of markets create problems that call for significant government action.

Here... We review ways that markets can sometimes fail. Market failures can stem from information problems, poor specification of property rights, or technological challenges. Market failures often provide justifications for policy responses. We discuss generic responses.

THIS CHAPTER REVIEWS
- Information asymmetries
- Externalities
- Public goods
- Natural monopolies
- Social equity concerns

When they work well, markets are highly effective and efficient institutions for the allocation of resources in society. Yet, aside from the most basic barter systems, all markets rely on government actions to help them function. At a minimum, markets require governments to establish and maintain property rights and to supply a common currency. The upshot is that government involvement in market processes should be viewed on a continuum, running from setting basic rules of the game to significant levels of intervention and control. Further, instances arise where market processes simply cannot achieve socially desired goals. In such instances, societies call on governments to perform allocation roles.

Here, we consider generic instances where markets do not perform efficiently. We then discuss what actions can be taken to address observed problems. Governments can, and often do, undertake supportive actions in specific markets to allow them to generate more socially desirable outcomes. But efforts to enhance the performance of markets are by no means the sole domain of governments. Often, private actors try to improve things. When we consider the potential for markets to fail, it is always important to assess ways that private actors could address those failures themselves.

The existence of firms tells us something important about markets and their performance. Ronald Coase (1937) wondered, if markets are so effective at resource allocation, why firms exist at all. Coase concluded that market participants often face high costs of organizing activities in a fully decentralized system, even when the relevant markets are performing efficiently. Take, for example, the large-scale production of any goods or services requiring multiple inputs. Examples can range from making meals to making cars to educating people. Entrepreneurs seeking to create those products in purely market settings would need to engage in a lot of search effort, figuring out who to buy from and where the lowest prices are. They would also have to preside over complex, many-to-many contracting agreements. Such costs of coordination within the marketplace are called *transaction costs*. When entrepreneurs establish firms, they typically write a set of labor contracts between themselves and their employees. This action reduces the organizing costs for all employees. The efficiency gains achieved by the entrepreneur can be converted into profits. Note, however, that the entrepreneur now must incur a range of management costs. So we can say that the fundamental trade-off that entrepreneurs face when they decide to move coordination from the marketplace into the firm is a trade-off between transaction costs and management costs. Because it is always possible for the entrepreneur to revert to using the market as the site for coordination efforts, organization in the firm must remain more efficient than use of the market.

In the previous chapter, we noted that producers face incentives to innovate and generate efficiencies in their production processes. From this present discussion, we see that innovation around the actual organization of production—that is, managerial innovation—can be an important way to maintain competitiveness. This discussion of the rationale for establishing firms also hints at the vast range of ways that people and organizations continually seek to promote efficient social outcomes. They look for ways to make markets work better or to adjust their actions so they can use existing market arrangements more effectively. That said, there are times when even the most resourceful efforts on the part of decentralized individuals do not allow them to adequately address market failures. This is when significant government actions are necessary.

Our discussion here begins with instances in which markets work, but the outcomes are not socially desirable. We then consider instances in which, due to difficulties establishing property rights or other technical challenges, markets do not function. From there, we discuss instances in which, despite the generally efficient functioning of markets, socially desired goals are not met. For example, market processes often serve to exacerbate social inequality. Because most members of society care about the promotion of values like equality of opportunity, government actions are used to attain goals that would not be attainable through reliance on markets or on any other form of decentralized interactions. In sum, the purpose of this chapter is to provide an overview of the limitations of markets, how those limitations can be analyzed, and the kinds of things governments typically do to address them.

AN OVERVIEW OF MARKET FAILURE

It is useful to start by reviewing the key assumptions of the market model, introduced in Chapter 9. The model is built on strong assumptions; that is, assumptions that are often contradicted by evidence. We can summarize them as follows.

1. All parties to a trade have full knowledge of relevant information.
2. All costs and benefits associated with a trade are reflected in the market price.
3. Property rights are appropriately specified.
4. Expressions of preferences are assumed to be sincere.
5. No buyer or seller can manipulate the prices at which items are traded.
6. There is no coercion.

When market operations are consistent with these assumptions, the result is economic efficiency. At the equilibrium price, the plans of all buyers and all sellers are perfectly aligned. There is no excess demand and no excess supply. All those who want to buy and all those who want to sell at the prevailing price do so. But what happens when the market model's assumptions are contradicted by evidence? Economists have carefully explored how the conduct of market participants and market outcomes change when specific assumptions are relaxed. Collectively, that analytical work provides the intellectual spine for discussions of the kind presented here.

Market failures present rationales for government action. That is why it is vital for policy analysts to understand when markets are susceptible to failure and what might be done to promote more socially desirable outcomes. Knowledge of how markets work and how they can fail is useful for guiding investigations into many social and economic problems. Policy analysts would be wise to routinely consider ways that market failures might be contributing to problems of interest to them. Table 10.1 provides a summary of market failures and potential government actions. The discussion that follows explores each of the forms of market failure included in the table.

Information Asymmetries

Problems can arise when the parties to a transaction have different levels of relevant knowledge about the qualities—or attributes—of the good or service to be

Table 10.1 Market Failures and Potential Government Actions

MARKET FAILURE[a]	POTENTIAL GOVERNMENT ACTIONS[b]	RELEVANT GOVERNMENT OBJECTIVES[c]
Information Asymmetry	• Market making • Regulation • Information and social marketing	• Human flourishing • Efficiency
Positive Externality	• Market making • Subsidies • Regulation • Partnering and facilitating • Information and social marketing • Frameworks and strategies	• Human flourishing • Efficiency
Negative Externality	• Market making • Taxes • Subsidies • Regulation • Partnering and facilitating • Information and social marketing • Frameworks and strategies	• Human flourishing • Efficiency • Sustainability
Common Pool Resources	• Market making • Taxes • Regulation • Partnering and facilitating	• Effective institutions • Efficiency • Sustainability
The Need for Collective Provision	• Market making • Taxes • Subsidies • Direct service supply • Funding and contracting	• Human flourishing • Effective institutions • Efficiency • Sustainability • Advancing human rights • Social equity
Natural Monopoly	• Market making • Regulation • Subsidies • Direct service supply • Funding and contracting • Partnering and facilitating	• Effective institutions • Efficiency • Sustainability
Social Equity Concerns	• Market-making • Taxes • Subsidies • Direct service supply • Funding and contracting • Partnering and facilitating • Information and social marketing • Frameworks and strategies	• Human flourishing • Advancing human rights • Social equity

[a] Details in this chapter.
[b] See Chapter 3 for details.
[c] See Chapter 4 for details.

supplied.[1] When one party is in a position of relative ignorance, they are vulnerable to the other party exploiting the knowledge gap and cheating them. Many real-world transactions involve information asymmetries. In the absence of corrective efforts, the existence of information asymmetries can threaten to collapse market processes. Given this, incentives exist for people to supply relevant information, or give assurances, to encourage confident trading.

For many transactions, information asymmetries are not an issue. This is the case when the significant attributes of the good being traded can be fully observed before any money changes hands. Consider a baseball cap. Before you buy, you can check the fit and the quality of the stitching, and quickly decide how cool you will look wearing it. Any goods where you can rapidly form accurate judgments about the quality and suitability of what is on offer are called *search goods.* Markets for search goods tend to function efficiently.

For many goods, and for most services, it is difficult for consumers to form accurate judgments of all relevant attributes until after their first purchase. These are called *experience goods.* We have to experience the good or service before we can accurately judge its worth. However, by the time we get to form an accurate judgment, we will have already paid for the good. After the experience, we can accurately answer these questions: Had I known what I know now, would I have purchased this product? Would I have been willing to pay the price that I paid for it? A takeout meal offers a classic, everyday example of an experience good. You select items from the menu, order them, pay for them, and collect your purchase all before you get to know just how good it will taste. Of course, once you have gained experience with relatively inexpensive goods with few attributes to make judgments about, this experience means that, next time you shop for them, the goods in question will be more like search goods to you. But things like takeout meals are never going to set you back too much, so if you take a risk and do not like what you get, it is not a big deal. Compare this with purchasing a secondhand car. You are looking at the car. You like the model and color. The person selling it to you says that the sole previous owner was the local librarian who used it only to drive to church on Sundays. Are you about to buy a great car or a clunker? Here you have a major problem of information asymmetry.

As David Weimer and Aidan Vining (2005) have pointed out, some goods and services are most accurately categorized as *post-experience goods.* These are items in which accurate judgments about their value can be made only sometime after they were purchased and consumed. Many forms of education fall into this category. Sometimes, it is not until people have graduated from high school or from university and started their careers that they attain full awareness of the quality and worth of their courses. This concept is captured in the opening line of a song by Paul Simon, "Kodachrome" (1973): "When I think back on all the crap I

---

[1] My discussion of information asymmetries owes debts to Akerlof (1970), Barzel (1989), contributions to Pratt and Zeckhauser (1985), and Weimer and Vining (2005). My initial thinking on this matter was also advanced through development of my contributions to Teske et al. (1993).

learned in high school, it's a wonder I can think at all." On a more positive note, it is common for people to reflect back on their education and realize how much a specific teacher or professor served to influence and affirm specific life choices or career choices. Life choices that are understood to have very harmful long-term health effects, such as smoking, can be thought of as an activity that can generate post-experience bad outcomes.

For analytical purposes, we will focus here on information asymmetries associated with experience goods. We will also consider the nature of the private actions and the actions that governments can take to rectify this form of market failure. Consider the characterization of a market with uninformed consumers, portrayed in Figure 10.1. Suppose it is the market for hotel rooms in a city where tourists experience high levels of petty crime and robbery but are unaware about this ahead of their visits. Assume that the market is currently in equilibrium at point E_1, where the market price is P_1 and the quantity traded is Q_1. If tourists were fully knowledgeable of relevant information ahead of making their travel plans, then, at any given price level, demand for hotel rooms in this city would be lower than is currently the case. Informed consumption choice would lead to less tourism in this city and a lower market-clearing price for hotel rooms. The equilibrium point in the market with informed consumers would be E_2. Here, the market price would be P_2 and the quantity traded would be Q_2.

Figure 10.1 offers important insights into the effects of uninformed consumption. At equilibrium E_1, consumer surplus is represented by the triangle BE_1P_1. Producer surplus is represented by the triangle P_1E_1F. However, notice the shaded triangle, defined by E_1AE_2. This triangle represents the ***deadweight loss*** to society of uninformed consumption. Had they been appropriately informed when making their purchase, a group of consumers would not have traveled to the city and stayed in hotels there. The shaded triangle portrays the loss to society as a whole caused

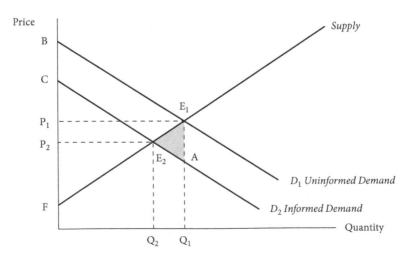

Figure 10.1 A Market with Uninformed Consumers

by this uninformed choice. When consumers become informed, and the market equilibrium moves to E_2, several things happen. First, consumer surplus becomes defined by the triangle CE_2P_2. Producer surplus becomes defined by P_2E_2F. Now, there is no deadweight loss. In addition, this shift removes a large section of producer surplus, defined by the trapezoid $P_1E_1E_2P_2$. The section of producer surplus that existed with uninformed demand represents the gain that the producers—in this case, the city's hoteliers—gained at the expense of the uninformed tourists.

The situation portrayed in Figure 10.1 reveals that consumers face incentives to become informed. As they do so, they increase their ability to make choices that are consistent with their preferences. Further, they reduce the ability for producers to gain at their expense. We also see that society as a whole gains from informed consumption. That is because informed consumption reduces the likelihood of misallocation of scarce resources, represented by the deadweight loss associated with uninformed consumption. This offers a justification for government actions to reduce information asymmetries in circumstances in which private actions are not effective.

Often, providers of goods and services face incentives to reduce information asymmetries. For example, in a city where tourists experience high levels of petty crime and robbery, hoteliers could strive to reassure travelers that a stay with them will be safe and relaxing. The big concern for sellers of goods and services is that lack of consumer trust will lead to the collapse of demand. But if there is no demand, then the notion of the market collapses. George Akerlof (1970) wrote a classic article on this topic, in which he highlighted potential problems in the used car market.

Akerlof noted that there is always a large price difference between new cars and those that have just left the showroom. He invited us to consider a world with just four kinds of cars: new cars and used cars; good cars and bad cars. (Bad cars are sometimes called "lemons"; hence Akerlof's title: "The Market for 'Lemons.'") When a person buys a new car, he or she faces a fixed probability, q, that it is a good car and a probability of $(1-q)$ that it is a lemon. However, after gaining experience as car owner, the driver can assign a new probability to the event that the car is a lemon. This estimate is likely to be more accurate than the original estimate, which was based on limited information. Now, if this owner were to sell the car, then the owner would have better information about its probability of being a lemon than any potential buyer. But good used cars and bad used cars sell at the same price because potential buyers cannot tell a good one from a bad one based on a cursory search. These circumstances result in all used cars selling for less than new cars. The owner of the used car, who believes it is good, cannot sell it and receive a price reflecting the true value of the car. The price received will be the average price for all used cars, which is less than the average price of a new car. The owner is better off keeping the good used car for two reasons. First, the price received for it would not be sufficient to purchase a new car. Second, any used car purchased would be expected to have a higher probability of being a lemon than the probability of being a lemon that the owner assigns to their current car, based on experience with it. The owner of the used car is locked into ownership of it. By this logic, the only people who would sell used cars in this market are those who believe that they could do better through trade. Those people will be the ones who own lemons and know they are lemons; and no one will want to buy their cars from them. In the absence of corrective action, the market will not function.

Arkelof suggested that the dynamics at play in the market for used cars are characteristic of those in many situations in which people desire to buy and sell experience goods. The scope of application here is vast. The general argument fits the dynamics of markets for many commodities and services. It is also applicable to many labor market transactions and to markets for financial instruments, such as the purchase of bonds and shares. Information asymmetries can lead to market failure. People will be unwilling to engage in trades; the whole notion of a market is jeopardized.

The focus in this discussion has been on instances in which sellers have more information than buyers. But it is also applicable in some instances in which buyers have more relevant knowledge than sellers and they use it to their advantage. Examples include reckless and thrill-seeking drivers presenting themselves as good customers to rental car firms, people with serious medical conditions failing to report their condition to health insurers, parents of children with special needs not advising school administrators, and aspiring hijackers boarding planes dressed like corporate lawyers. Reflecting on these examples, it is clear that sellers of services who are vulnerable to exploitation by customers typically take significant efforts to reduce the information asymmetries. Rental car firms require detailed information on renters, and they tend to charge more to renters who share the demographics of the drivers who most often have collisions. Health insurers require people to obtain medical tests from designated professionals prior to applying for an insurance policy. Many other examples exist of how market actors seek to close information gaps.

Scholars sometimes use *principal-agent models* to assess instances of information asymmetry that arise in many situations in everyday life, business, and politics (Campbell 2006; Laffont and Martimort 2002; Pratt and Zeckhauser 1985). Here, it is assumed that the agent, who is employed by the principal, has more information than the principal and might use it to advantage. For example, decision makers must worry about the competency and honesty of their advisors. That problem strikes close to home. It plagues relations between decision makers and members of their policy analyst staff. The issue was discussed in Chapter 7.

Early consideration of information problems in insurance markets led to the use of two terms. *Adverse selection* arises when somebody deliberately withholds information or lies to win a contract. For example, a person seeking a high-powered role as a government science advisory might state that he or she holds a PhD, when, in fact, the dissertation is incomplete and unlikely to ever get finished. *Moral hazard* arises when, having signed a contract, a person acts in ways that are not in the interests of the other party. For example, new employees might take advantage of a generous sick leave policy by frequently phoning in sick, especially on Mondays or Fridays. In this way, they obtain long weekends without cutting into their annual leave entitlements. But they do so at the expense of the employer. Basically, they are stealing because they can. See Pratt and Zeckhauser (1985) for more discussion of adverse selection and moral hazard.

Rectifying Information Asymmetries

Information asymmetries can lead people to make choices that are not in their best interests. They can allow some people to benefit at the expense of others. They can result in the misallocation of scarce societal resources. They can also threaten the whole existence of markets. People who lack confidence that their transactions will be in their interests may decide to avoid trading with anyone other than trusted family members or friends. But if all goods and services could be transformed into search goods, then information asymmetries would dissolve. All parties to trades would have full knowledge of relevant information. So long as other assumptions of the market model were met, markets would perform to allocate goods and services efficiently. The challenge, then, is how relevant information about experience goods could be conveyed in ways that would render them search goods.

If we assume that information can be provided to transform experience goods into search goods, then we also need to consider who should provide that information. There are several possibilities. Depending on the conditions in specific markets, there will be times when buyers face incentives to acquire more information. Often, consumers rely on word-of-mouth information, the advice of friends, or observations of the actions of others to guide their own actions (Bikhchandani, Hirshleifer, and Welch 1992). At other times, intermediaries might use their knowledge of specific goods and services to develop low-cost ways to promote informed consumer choice. Vast numbers of examples now exist of market intermediaries providing product information to consumers. Those examples include the many guidebooks that are available to help tourists to effectively plan and manage visits to places that are new to them. Rankings of colleges, universities, and graduate programs help people make choices about where to obtain their degrees. A great deal of information is also available to help people make informed choices about places to live, cars to buy, movies to see, books to read, airlines to fly, and so on.

Because they want to encourage consumers to buy from them, sellers face incentives to share information relevant to the trade. Use of accreditation services, membership in exclusive professional groups, and affiliation with chains of service providers all represent ways that sellers seek to reassure customers that trading with them will produce a good experience. For example, a restaurant owner positioned near an interstate junction may seek to acquire a lot of business from visitors passing through. Becoming the local franchise for a recognized national chain of restaurants is a common way to convey relevant information about a particular restaurant to people who have no previous experience dining there. This observation helps us to understand the predominance of brands and chains in mass societies. They serve to rapidly convey vital information to consumers.

Individuals use the acquisition of educational qualifications to reduce information asymmetries in the labor market. Holding well-regarded qualifications from reputable institutions allows people to signal to potential employers key information about their knowledge and work ethic. It is interesting to observe how rapidly university hiring committees can work through a stack of applications for faculty openings. As buyers, the committee members use various decision-making shortcuts—or heuristics—to short-list candidates. Of course, they desire to carefully read selections of the work of potential colleagues, to meet with them, to observe them present their research, and so on. The candidates' campus visits are designed to help extract significant information about how each candidate would likely perform as a colleague. However, these intense efforts to understand the "products" on offer are preceded by actions that turn potential colleagues into search goods. This is not a situation to bemoan or take personally. It is the reality of how people come to work efficiently in situations characterized by information asymmetries.

Despite these many ways that market actors seek to transform experience goods into search goods, there are times when the nature of the information asymmetries makes government actions helpful. Four general forms of government action will be considered here. All of them represent forms of market making, because they are intended to address specific market problems and set the general context for mutually beneficial trade. First, regulations can be enforced to require sellers to disclose relevant product information to consumers. Second, governments can seek to educate consumers to be discerning shoppers for specific goods and services. Third, governments can collect relevant information about product quality and disseminate it to consumers. Finally, governments can regulate the entry of providers into specific industries, thereby seeking to reduce the risk of buyers being harmed by low-quality products or services.

Regulation forcing disclosure of relevant product information is common. For example, most items of children's clothing contain labels that indicate whether the material they are made from is fireproof. Such labeling is especially important on clothing for babies and young children. Likewise, most food packaging contains information about ingredients and nutritional value. Such information reduces the likelihood that people who have specific food allergies will be harmed through unwitting consumption of items they would normally avoid. In some countries, government regulations require providers of professional services—such as legal work, accounting, dental surgery, and car maintenance—to provide clients with cost estimates before they perform proposed work. The work can proceed only after the providers have obtained signed agreements from the client. Many governments around the world, in efforts to reduce consumption of cigarettes, have now required cigarette manufactures to place very bold messages and graphic images on cigarette cartons, stating and illustrating the harmful long-term effects of smoking.

Governments sometimes try to help consumers become more discerning in their purchasing choices. These actions are less coercive than regulatory actions.

For example, governments routinely run public information campaigns designed to portray smoking as bad for your health. Public information campaigns can be used in a range of ways to help consumers make more informed choices. Consider the case of financial advising. At some point in their lives, most people could do with help in figuring out how to better manage their debts and how to effectively implement a savings plan in anticipation of retirement. Yet it is well known that information asymmetry problems plague the market for financial advising (Oehler and Kohlert 2009). In response, some government agencies have sought to educate consumers on how to manage their relations with financial advisors. In one such case, the Consumer Financial Education Body in the United Kingdom offers a free "Moneymadeclear" guide for consumers. The cover reads, "No selling. No jargon. Just the facts about getting financial advice."

We noted earlier the prevalence of actions by market intermediaries to generate travel advice, rating systems, report cards, and league tables. Because governments routinely collect large amounts of information on the services that they fund and provide, it is now common for them to make that information publicly available in ways that promote informed choices on the part of citizen-consumers. It is particularly important for governments seeking to promote markets in the delivery of public services that they generate information to help people make good choices. Parents in many places can now use information supplied by governments to learn about the comparative performance of local schools (Schneider, Teske, and Marschall 2000). Generation of report cards and league tables can also serve as a way to promote improved service delivery (Gormley and Weimer 1999). When accurate information is publicly available and citizens can choose among service providers, powerful incentives can be created for managers to instigate service quality enhancement efforts.

Finally, for many decades, governments have addressed problems of information asymmetry by regulating the entry of people into professions and firms into industries. Professional licensing and certification has been used as a tool to establish minimum standards of service provision in a range of areas, including health care, schooling, and construction. Regulation of firm entry into specific industries has been justified on a range of grounds, including the prevention of harm to citizens. Safety regulations pertaining to service providers in the transportation sector offer an example of how regulation can compensate for consumer ignorance. Stringent requirements on who can operate an airline and on the frequency of aircraft maintenance may seem pedantic to libertarians. But they offer the public reassurance that all airlines will meet appropriate safety standards. Such reassurance has played its part in expanding the budget airline market and opening more travel options for consumers.

Scholars of human decision making have noted the difficulties people often face when processing available information. Sometimes, the strategies we use to interpret what we see, hear, or read can lead us to make poor choices, even when the cues that would help us make good choices are right there for us to work with (Nisbett and Ross 1980; Thaler and Sunstein 2008). Policy analysts can gain a lot from considering the prescriptions for information provision, or "choice architecture," that have emerged from these studies. At the most general level, this means thinking hard about not just what information people need to make good decisions but how to structure its provision so that people rapidly grasp the key points. For example, because most people are familiar with the meanings of green, yellow, and red traffic signals, following such color coding in organizational report cards could help people quickly figure out the service providers they should avoid and those they should consider using. More generally, consider the car dashboard as a metaphor. Car dashboards convey essential information to drivers. In many other situations in which we are interacting with complex systems that we barely understand, simple dashboards would make life easier. The design question then becomes this: Given the challenge people are facing in a given situation, if we could give them a dashboard, what information would it convey, and how would it do it? Testing out alternative ways of providing information in trials with actual citizens and consumers, observing how people work with that information, and listening closely to feedback, can help in the development of powerful approaches for reducing information asymmetries.

The term *caveat emptor* literally means "let the buyer beware." This discussion of information asymmetries has shown that there are many instances in life in which people find it difficult to make adequately informed consumption decisions. In such cases, buyers need to become better informed. However, efforts to become better informed are often costly to the individual. Here, we have considered a range of ways that buyers, sellers, and market intermediaries attempt to transform experience goods into search goods. While often such nongovernmental practices will do a lot to promote efficient market outcomes, a variety of instances remain in which government actions can be desirable. We have considered several generic approaches that governments can use to rectify information asymmetries.

Positive Externalities

The market model assumes that all costs and benefits associated with a trade are reflected in the market price. However, it is common to observe cases in which transactions generate spillover effects on others who are not directly involved. These effects are usually referred to as *externalities*. They arise when property rights are not appropriately specified. The existence of externalities can reduce the ability of markets to perform efficient allocation of goods and services. Externalities can be either positive or negative. They can be generated either by the actions of producers or the actions of consumers.

Let us consider two cases of positive externalities. A positive externality from production occurs when, as a result of their market transactions, producers generate benefits to others who do not pay for them. For example, universities and undergraduate colleges often produce positive externalities for the towns, suburbs, or cities where they are located. While students pay tuition and housing fees to the place of higher learning, they also tend to spend money in the local restaurants, bars, and shops. Further, the need for faculty members to live close to their workplace often has positive effects on local house prices. Beyond these things, Richard Florida (2005) has noted the significant knowledge economy gains that can come to such locations, with talent, technology, and tolerance creating fertile ground for innovative business development. An indicator of the magnitude of this positive externality is offered by the case of Merced, California. In 1995, the Regents of the University of California announced their selection of Merced in California's Central Valley as the site for development of a tenth campus, with a projected student body of 25,000. The new campus opened a decade later, in 2005. In the interim, people started to view the new campus development as a savior to a historically poor region of California. Local property prices boomed for several years. While that initial boom proved temporary, many people continued to see the new campus development as promising a brighter future for the region.

Now consider a positive externality from private consumption or investment. When families ensure that their children are well educated, this generates immediate and long-term private benefits for those children. They develop knowledge and skills that allow them to more fully participate in all manner of social and economic activities. But there is a public or social benefit that everyone in a society gains when children are well educated. That positive social benefit creates an incentive to try to ensure that all children in society receive at least some minimum level of education. Of course, ensuring education of all children can also be justified on equity grounds, but for now we wish to focus solely on the justification accorded by the existence of a positive externality.

Figure 10.2 portrays a market with a positive externality from consumption. Let us assume that this is the market for schooling. The market is at equilibrium, E_1, where quantity Q_1 of schooling is traded at price P_1. However, schooling generates a positive externality. The demand curve, which portrays marginal private benefits (MPB) to schooling, sits below a parallel line, which portrays the marginal social benefit (MSB) of schooling. The difference between the marginal private benefit and the marginal social benefit represents the amount of the positive externality. Note, however, that with consumption at the level of Q_1, there is a deadweight loss to society. This is portrayed in the figure by triangle AE_2E_1. The deadweight loss is the unrealized benefit to society that accompanies consumption of schooling at Q_1. The loss could be eliminated by a move to a higher level of consumption, Q_2. Given the supply of schooling portrayed by the supply curve in Figure 10.2, the move to consumption at Q_2 would be accompanied by an overall increase in the price of schooling, to P_2. The new market equilibrium point would occur at E_2. Because there is a social gain from this increased consumption, a justification exists for public funding to support it. That public funding could come in the form of a subsidy to parents. The appropriate subsidy would be equivalent in magnitude to the area covered in the figure by trapezoid $P_2E_2E_1P_1$. With parents receiving a subsidy to support sending their children to school, the market for schooling would generate an efficient result, with no unrealized benefits.

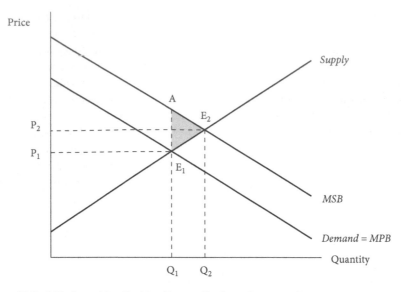

Figure 10.2   A Market with a Positive Externality from Consumption

Rectifying Positive Externalities

Private decision makers often face incentives to internalize externalities, thus eliminating spillover effects. For example, the owners of orchards benefit from bees pollinating their trees. In turn, beekeepers benefit from their bees having plentiful sources of nectar. It is therefore common to find beekeepers and orchardists deliberately cooperating and colocating their activities. However, when the magnitude of an externality is sufficiently high, when it affects a large group of people, and when feasible private solutions are not forthcoming, good grounds can exist for government action. In the two cases of positive externalities presented here, broader groups of people can benefit from the actions of smaller groups.

Because, by definition, positive externalities yield social benefits, better social outcomes can be achieved through encouraging the activities that generate the externalities. The challenge is to determine appropriate forms of government action. It would be wasteful to make incentive payments to people to do things that they would do anyway of their own accord. It would also be wasteful to make incentive payments when the desired amount of positive externality has been realized. Therefore, an efficient policy instrument would identify the set of consumers or producers needing incentives to do the things that will generate positive externalities. In practice, this can be difficult. Once people know that an incentive is available to them, they might act strategically so that they will receive it. Policy designers need to be aware of this. At the same time, it is usually better to design simple policies that are easy to administer, knowing that there will be some efforts to game the system, rather than developing elaborate policies that require a lot of resources just to manage them.

Positive externalities are commonly addressed by making a government subsidy available to those who generate them. By funding the subsidies from general taxes, the government creates conditions in which the costs of funding the activity are shared around, just as the benefits are. Note also that subsidies can be provided in ways that ensure the people who derive the most benefits from the activities still cover a greater proportion of the costs of funding them than do others. For example, governments often provide subsidies to help people attend university. However, individuals are still expected to pay most of the cost of attending university, because they are the ones who will receive the university qualifications. Those qualifications benefit them the most, because they pave the way for them to attain jobs that are higher paying than those they could have attained in the absence of the qualification.

Sometimes, subsidies to individuals are accompanied by regulations requiring them to engage in the activities that generate the positive externalities. For example, in most countries, the schooling of children is heavily subsidized. But families are not given a choice about whether or not their children can attend school. Regulations typically require that all children within a certain age range receive formal education. Sometimes, government subsidies to promote activities with positive externalities are provided in ways that create markets. For example, it is common to find individuals or households receiving vouchers that allow them to spend the government subsidy at any qualified supplier of their choice. Sometimes, governments target information and social marketing toward people whose choices they seek to influence. This can be done to nudge people toward making socially desirable private choices. Information provision and social marketing can be done as an alternative to providing subsidies or in conjunction with doing so (Thaler and Sunstein 2008).

Governments can use subsidies and regulations when seeking to influence producers that generate positive externalities. But they can also develop creative ways to partner with others. For example, public-private partnership arrangements are now common in a range of areas (Rosenau 2000). Governments offer some funding support to assist private providers supply goods or services that generate positive social outcomes. At a softer level, governments sometimes seek to reduce social coordination problems that would otherwise hinder the provision of specific goods or services with positive externalities. For example, it is now common to find governments working with representatives of the local tourism industry to "brand" a region to make it more attractive to visitors. Done well, efforts of this kind by governments can generate good leverage from limited amounts of government funding.

Negative Externalities

Like positive externalities, negative externalities can be generated either as untraded by-products of the production process or by other people's consumption. Consider a market with a negative externality from production. The case is illustrated in Figure 10.3. Suppose that this is a market for electricity production

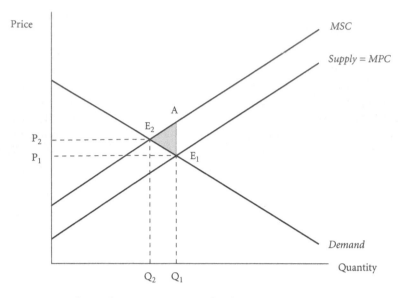

Figure 10.3 A Market with a Negative Externality from Production

in a jurisdiction bordered by several other jurisdictions. All electricity there is produced through the use of coal-fired power stations. The coal-burning plants produce emissions of ammonium, carbon, nitrogen, and sulfur that contribute to local atmospheric pollution, acid rain in nearby jurisdictions, and global warming. These are negative externalities that are not accounted for in the local price of electricity. In Figure 10.3, quantity Q_1 of electricity is traded at a prince of P_1. The supply curve represents the marginal private cost (MPC) of producing the electricity. However, the marginal social cost (MSC) is higher, represented by the line in the figure that parallels the supply curve. The difference between the two lines portrays the unaccounted cost to society of the power plant emissions. The deadweight loss to society is captured in triangle E_2AE_1. The negative externality can be internalized by requiring the polluters to pay the cost of addressing the pollution. In effect, this move serves to equate the marginal private cost with the marginal social cost of producing the electricity. That could be done in a variety of ways. But whatever solution is used, it is expected to result in an increase in the price of electricity and less electricity being traded. Effective internalization of the externality would lead to quantity Q_2 electricity being traded at price P_2. The new market equilibrium would be E_2. With this change, the deadweight would vanish.

Now consider an example of the actions of some consumers having a negative impact on the well-being of others. A fraternity house is located on a quiet suburban street, populated mainly by professional families. For the most part, there are few problems, because the residents of the fraternity house are hardworking. They seek to be high-paid professionals with families themselves one day. However, every few weeks, the fraternity house has a party, usually on a Wednesday or Thursday night. These parties run until around 3 AM, and they generate a lot of noise from loud music playing and voices shouting above it. Often, the professionals living on the street find the noise keeping them awake for much of the night. Inevitably, they end up being less productive at work the following day. To overcome situations like this, most towns and cities impose noise restrictions. As a result, a complaint can lead to a visit from a noise inspector. The people making the noise might be warned to quiet things down. If they do not comply, the source of the noise might be physically removed.

An interesting aspect of this case is that the number of people involved is relatively small. Potentially, the parties could get together and discuss ways to manage the situation without the need for government action. Ronald Coase (1960) discussed a number of scenarios in which negative externalities exist. Applying his analysis here, we might ask this: Who is creating the problem for whom? The story has been told from the point of view of noisy people keeping hardworking people awake at night. An alternative story could be told. That is one of people with a preference for quiet intruding on the interests of those who just now and then want to have some fun with friends. In the absence of public noise restrictions, the situation could be approached in a somewhat different manner. That is, we could calculate the cost of the harm that the party noise causes the neighboring families, in terms of broken sleep and lowered on-the-job productivity the following day. We could also seek to calculate the cost to the fraternity house residents and their friends of being denied the right to make noise that disturbs others. Based on this information, the groups concerned could seek to determine a solution. A variety of workable options could potentially yield net benefits greater than those achieved through recourse to a noise restriction. Elinor Ostrom's (1990) analysis of efforts by small groups of people to manage common pool resources indicates that nongovernmental, yet binding, solutions can often be found to negative externality problems. However, when the number of people involved grows larger, action by government is often required. Especially with established government systems in place, it is usually more efficient to turn to government to remedy a problem—like dealing with noisy parties—than to have local communities generate their own solutions. Coase (1960) proposed, "In devising and choosing between social arrangements we should have regard for the total effect" (p. 44). This is good advice that reminds us to be alert to the hidden costs—especially the hidden coordination costs—that could be associated with different private and public responses.

Rectifying Negative Externalities

A significant amount of thought has been given to ways of addressing negative externalities (see, e.g., Hahn 1989, 2009; Stavins 1997). In the case of pollution associated with generation of electricity by coal-fired power plants, regulations that force producers to use specific approaches to reducing emissions have long been a common practice. However, starting in the 1960s and 1970s, policy scholars started to question the merit of using "heavy-handed" regulation to achieve social goals (see, e.g., Dales 1968; Schultze 1977). As a result, over the past few decades, there has been a remarkable embrace of incentives-based approaches to addressing negative externalities. For example, taxes are often used as instruments to discourage industrial pollution. More recently, tradable permits with auction rights have been introduced to reduce emissions of greenhouse gases. Even though it has been viewed by some as a failed effort to promote policy change, the Kyoto Protocol established in 1997 served to significantly advance innovation in the use of policy instruments to manage negative externalities.

Regulations hold a lot of appeal for addressing negative externalities. When agents of government establish appropriate procedures to address a problem, monitor compliance with those procedures, and impose penalties on noncompliance, those being regulated face strong incentives to do the right thing. That is why regulations are widely used to force producers to inform relevant parties of their accounting and production processes, to address public safety concerns, and to reduce the public nuisances caused by various forms of pollution. Yet a common concern with regulatory approaches to addressing negative externalities is that they do not provide sufficient incentives for producers to develop technologies that, through time, could eliminate the sources of the problems. Eugene Bardach and Robert Kagan (2002) have documented the highly adversarial relationships that can arise between government regulators and the producers they regulate. Sometimes, this can result in producers being penalized for taking actions that appear to improve their management of problems but, in so doing, take them out of compliance with aspects of the regulatory regime.

Informed by insights from economics, new policy instruments intended to reduce negative externalities move the focus away from compliance with prescribed procedures and onto attainment of the socially desired outcomes. For example, by imposing taxes, fees, or fines on producers that generate negative externalities, governments can create powerful incentives for those producers to limit the offending actions. Take the case of a carbon tax. Producers that generate atmospheric pollution can be taxed for doing so. (The easiest way to do so is to impose the tax at the place in the production process where accurate measurement can be done at low cost. This is usually not the tailpipe.) The tax creates an incentive for the producers to use less of the fuels that cause pollution. As a result, they might search either for ways to economize on fuel use in the production process or for alternative fuels that cause less pollution. The same desire to introduce incentives for producers to remove negative externalities lies behind the development of "cap and trade" systems of permitting pollution. Under these systems, producers are allocated free permits to pollute. Those who do not need to use all their permits can sell them at auction. Those who need more than their allocated amount can buy more, using the auction. This kind of system serves to reward those who do not pollute and punish those who do. Indeed, those who did not change their production processes would most likely be forced out of the industry. They would eventually find themselves unable to compete with other suppliers able to deliver products to consumers at lower costs, because those competing firms do not have to purchase permits to pollute. Creation of emissions trading schemes represents a form of market-making.

Negative externalities can also be addressed through policies that serve to persuade people, rather than control them or subject them to strong incentives. For example, sometimes governments use training programs and systems of incentives to help people and businesses switch away from activities that generate negative externalities. In such cases, governments provide subsidies with the aim of changing behavior. Cases include the provision of training programs that highlight ways to improve safety on construction sites. Efforts to address negative externalities in the social realm are also common. Programs to help people manage their anger, reduce their heavy consumption of alcohol, or to become more effective parents, are often fully or partially funded by governments. Also, it is common to find governments providing information to targeted groups or engaging in social marketing efforts that illustrate the social harm caused by specific behaviors. Government-funded advertising campaigns to remind people not to drive after consuming alcohol are motivated primarily by the desire to stop drunk drivers from harming others, and the major social costs that come with that. Increasingly, governments try to work with other organizations—both for-profit and nonprofit—to reduce the sources of negative externalities.

Public Goods: Common Pool Resources

So far in this discussion of market failure, we have focused on private goods. The most significant attribute of private goods is that those who own them can exclude others from their use. The presence of externalities—both when they are positive and when they are negative—is created by property rights problems. More specifically, the effective management of externalities always involves efforts to better specify, monitor, and enforce property rights. All efforts to internalize externalities are equivalent to defining boundaries and building fences. Sometimes, those fences have very sophisticated designs.

When property rights are impossible to enforce, by definition, they become public goods. People might like to claim that they are the owners of a good, but if they cannot monitor use of the good and enforce their property rights, then it is a public good. Here, we consider public goods that are common pool resources. For such goods, it is difficult to exclude people from using them or to limit how much they use them. However, consumption from the common pool resource is competitive, in the sense that whatever one person consumes from the common pool cannot be consumed by another. Common pool resources include naturally occurring things we all value, such as clean air, clean water, land, mineral deposits, forests, grazing animals, birdlife, the sea and the seabed, and fish in the sea. Throughout history, as human knowledge has developed and people have come to associate high value with common pool resources, two things have happened. First, people have come to realize that indiscriminate use of these resources can lead to their depletion. In the absence of appropriately specified property rights, individual actions motivated by self-interest can produce collectively undesirable outcomes. This is the reverse of the situation in market settings, where property rights are well specified and self-interested actions by all can produce good collective outcomes.

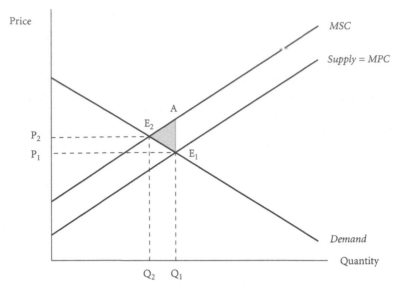

Figure 10.4 Characterizing the Effect of *Overconsumption* of a Common Pool Resource

The second key thing about common pool resources is that many disputes and wars have been fought to gain control over them. As human knowledge continues to advance, property rights problems will continue to emerge. The discovery of airwaves and what can be done with them represents a relatively recent example of the creation of a common pool resource. Increasingly, aspects of intellectual work are generating common pool resource problems. Appropriate responses involve the better definition of intellectual property rights and how rewards can be given to those who create or expand common pools.

We can explore the market failure problem here with reference to Figure 10.4. The figure is deliberately identical to Figure 10.3, which portrays a market with a negative externality from production. Economists adopt more sophisticated methods of modeling and portraying the dynamics associated with demand and supply of common pool resources.[2]

Suppose that Figure 10.4 portrays a market for fish in the sea, where no restrictions are placed on the quality of the catches that can be extracted. Note that this fishing example is representative of many cases in which a common pool resource exists and is vulnerable to overconsumption. The demand curve in the diagram is identical to that found in a standard market model. That is, as the price rises, the quantity demanded falls. The supply curve in the diagram is also the same as in a standard market model. This makes sense because we would expect that the cost of bringing fish to market would increase with increasing supply. To begin with, supplying fish to the market would be easy. However, to catch more

---

[2] See, e.g., Rosen (2007); Weimer and Vining (2005).

fish, fishermen would find it necessary to invest in more equipment, to go farther out from shore, and so on. In the figure, the market clears at E_1, where the market price for fish is P_1, and the quantity traded is Q_1. Notice, however, that there is another line that parallels the supply curve, but that sits above it. This line, labeled MSC, portrays the *marginal social cost* of fishing. The position of this line shows that the marginal social cost of fishing is greater than the marginal private cost, MPC, which is captured by the supply curve. The marginal social cost of fishing is higher than the marginal private cost because overconsumption serves to deplete the overall stock of fish.

The greater the overconsumption of fish, the greater the risk that the fishing stock will be run down to a level that is not sustainable. With no intervention to change this situation, we would expect several things to happen. First, with fewer fish available to catch, the marginal private cost of fishing would go up. Second, because each fish removed from the fishery further depletes the stock and the potential for the fish to reproduce and the stock to grow, the distance between the marginal private cost of fishing and the marginal social cost of fishing would grow larger. The private actions of many people, all responding to the incentives established in the situation, take them to an outcome that none of them want, but none of them can avoid. That is, complete depletion of the resource.

In Figure 10.4, the deadweight loss associated with the trade of Q_1 fish is represented by the triangle E_2AE_1. By finding a way to force fishermen to realize the marginal social cost of fishing, the supply curve in the diagram would move up. The new market equilibrium would be at E_2, where the market-clearing price is P_2, higher than P_1, and the market-clearing quantity is Q_2, lower than Q_1. At equilibrium E_2, the deadweight loss is eliminated.

Rectifying Problems with Common Pool Resources

Common pool resources create allocation problems because no mechanism exists to force individuals to act responsibly. People extract what they can while they can and ignore the future. The dynamics of the situation have been termed "the tragedy of the commons" (Hardin 1968; Ostrom 1999). In contrast, if private property rights could be assigned and enforced at little cost, then access to the resources could be restricted. Further, those holding private access rights would face strong incentives to manage their private property in a sustainable fashion. Fortunately, opportunities now exist to create effective systems for managing common pool resources. These opportunities have been created by improvements in knowledge concerning the characteristics of specific common pool resources and how to maintain them. They have been supported by the creation of government administrative systems and advances in information management systems. Today, a range of government actions can be taken to rectify problems with common pool resources. All of them transform access to common pool resources into a private good. These government actions include regulation, the use of taxes, introduction of market-like arrangements, and efforts to build management partnerships. When these government actions have their intended effects, they can establish stable economic and social relations. They can contribute to more efficient use of common pool resources. They can promote sustainability.

At a rudimentary level, simply restricting access to common pool resources can reduce the risk that they will be rapidly and indiscriminately depleted. Such action—equivalent to the fencing of the commons, or what historically was termed the *enclosure movement*—transforms the public good into a private good. Perhaps the most valuable aspect of this initial move is that it forces people to recognize the value of the resource. At that point, incentives arise for people to learn more about the resource, its size, the degree to which it is renewable, how renewal happens, and so on. For example, stakeholders associated with specific fishing areas, known as fisheries, have increasingly used scientific knowledge to help them understand how fish stocks reproduce. This has led them to develop more effective approaches to regulating access and educating people concerning ways that they can contribute to sustaining the fishery.

Because management of common pool resources can require a lot of information gathering, monitoring of activities, and enforcement work, policy approaches have been developed that require those seeking access to a given resource to pay significant access fees. Policies of this kind serve to combine regulation with targeted taxation. In variations on these fencing practices, governments will provide users with historical linkages to resources with tradable access permits. When such actions are taken, they serve to create markets for use of the common pool resource. Because the number of access permits and the rights granted within the permits are closely informed by knowledge of the resource, the market can operate effectively while promoting sustainability. Two variations on this approach also deserve mention. First, sometimes governments give contracts to private entities to manage a resource for a specified number of years. For example, a specific company might pay for exclusive rights to commercially manage a forest for fifteen years. During the contract period, the activities of the company would be carefully monitored. At the end of the contract period, new bids would be taken from forestry companies seeking to have exclusive rights to the forest. Whatever kind of market-like arrangement is established will depend greatly on the nature of the resource and knowledge of how best to manage it. A second variation on government efforts to efficiently manage common pool resources involves establishing partnerships with stakeholders. Sometimes, indigenous groups will claim the rights to manage some common pool resources. While such claims can create conflicts and tensions, they also present opportunities for creative problem solving. The comanagement of the Pacific Northwest Salmon Fisheries offers an example of what can be done (Singleton 1998). The state of Washington and over twenty Indian tribes have found a way to work together to manage the salmon stocks in the area. Because the state is closely involved in management, local groups can engage in strong conservation practices, safe in the knowledge that others are doing the same.

Elinor Ostrom (1999) has suggested that all policy initiatives designed to rectify problems with common pool resources should be treated as experiments. That is because complexities and idiosyncrasies associated with any given common pool resource will always open possibilities for problems and the need to develop appropriate responses. Given this, Ostrom also proposes that policy efforts be undertaken in ways that specifically allow for utilization of local knowledge and for knowledge transfer across the unique local settings. When governments are able to coordinate efforts and serve as conduits of good practice across domains of action, the chances are increased that evolution of sound resource management will occur.

Pure Public Goods: The Need for Collective Provision

So far, this discussion of market failure has highlighted three points. First, markets efficiently allocate private goods for which all relevant attributes can be assessed by simple observation. Second, informational advantages can encourage dishonest practice. Widespread fear of being ripped off can cause markets to collapse. Third, inadequate specification of property rights can inhibit market processes and encourage inefficient, socially undesirable choices. We see, then, that information problems represent a fundamental challenge to efficient market activity.

Pure public goods are nonexcludable and they are nonrivalrous in consumption. When a pure public good is provided to you, by definition, it is also provided to your neighbor. Further, your neighbor's consumption of the good has no bearing upon your enjoyment of it. When you are next lying on a beach, the warm sun on your face, the waves beckoning, and just a handful of people are present, think of this. The key difference between a pure public good and a common pool resource is that common pool resources are assumed to be rivalrous in consumption. The unit you consume leaves one less for me to consume. Notice that if there is plenty for everyone, then a common pool resource becomes equivalent to a public good. Notice also that a public good subject to congestion takes on the attributes of a common pool resource. That is, it becomes nonexcludable, but rivalrous in consumption.

To live well in society, we need a range of pure public goods to be established. For example, it is hard to imagine civilized existence without institutions supporting collective decision making, a common language, defense systems, legal systems, a police force, systems to ensure public safety, and a monetary system. We use governments to provide these public goods. To do so, governments raise general taxes.

It is true that public goods can often be supplied in small groups. In such cases, it is possible that a group can be privileged by the presence of one member who is prepared to pay the cost of supply of a public good that all then benefit from (Olson 1965). For example, a resident of a street that does not have streetlamps may decide to pay for the installation and maintenance of a couple of lamps. All residents of the street benefit, but only one pays. Small groups can also find voluntary ways to collectively supply public goods. However, such groups must be small enough that individual actions can be readily monitored to ensure that everyone is playing their part (Ostrom 1990). Once we move to the realm of large groups, it becomes difficult to sustain voluntary collective action. Some approaches that work involve having people form associations that supply private goods directly to members and that generate public goods as by-products of their private service provision. For example, unions and clubs provide private goods to members. That is what keeps them in business. However, they also supply public goods to members, in the form of advocacy efforts (Olson 1965; Sandler 1992). Such approaches all rely on private incentives to promote public, or semipublic, ends.

Governments supply pure public goods because, in their absence, significant collective action problems can arise. Those problems inhibit the development of functional markets for allocating public goods. The problems are caused by what we can now call the usual suspects. First, transaction costs arise. It is difficult to coordinate action in the absence of binding contracts, but to establish such many-to-many contracts would involve so much energy that little would remain to produce the public goods at issue. Second, the absence of private property rights ensures that people will benefit from supply of the good, regardless of whether they paid for it. Third, people can be sneaky with information. The market model assumes that expressions of preference are sincere. When they are, it is possible to derive a market demand curve. When people withhold relevant information, the market can collapse.

We know in many situations requiring two parties to contribute to a collective outcome that the best collective result arises when both parties contribute. Yet, in such cases, it often happens that one party would gain even more if it did not contribute but the other party did. Of course, because both parties face the same incentives to cheat, no contributions are forthcoming. The dynamics of the two-party situation are captured in the chicken game, which is a variation on the prisoners' dilemma game (Mueller 2003). Consider an example. Two people are neighbors. They share a boundary but do not have a fence. The fence would be a public good. One neighbor owns a dog and has a flower garden. The other owns a goat that produces milk. Without the fence, the dog tends to stray and to worry the goat, so that the goat stops producing milk. Meanwhile, with no fence, the goat likes to feed on the flower garden. The best outcome would be for both neighbors to contribute to building a fence. However, each neighbor faces a strong incentive to strategically declare no interest in a fence, and then wait for the other to stop all the bluffing and just pay for the whole fence, not bothering to seek a contribution from the neighbor. The problem is that, for a long time, these neighbors could be in a situation that neither of them wants.

Figure 10.5 characterizes the collapse of the market for a collectively provided good. It is designed to convey the logical market outcome of people strategically manipulating their expressions of preferences. In this case, it is assumed that everyone wants to be a "free rider" on the good deeds of others. Nobody will admit that they would like the good to be provided. As a result, no market demand can be established. Whatever market demand curve might have existed under sincere expressions of preference simply collapses, indicating that there is no demand. But because there is no revealed demand, no supply can be expected. In markets,

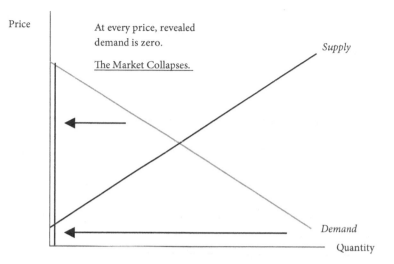

Figure 10.5 Characterizing the Collapse of the Market for a Collectively Provided Good

producers respond to incentives provided by the price mechanism. When no demand is revealed, no price signaling can occur. No basis exists for a market and so no good is supplied. Collective action—that is, action taken by government on behalf of all citizens—is the only way that the pure public good will be supplied. Markets cannot work here.

Arranging Collective Provision

Collective provision of pubic goods can contribute to many positive social and economic outcomes. Among other things, collective provision of public goods can promote human flourishing. It can help to support the development of effective institutions and encourage efficient use of resources. The resulting structures of government can promote sustainability, as they allow people to better manage their relationships with the world around them. We noted earlier that systems of defense, legal systems, and police forces are prime examples of pure public goods. We also know that institutions of this kind serve to protect and promote human rights. There are good grounds for contending that collective provision of pure public goods can promote social equity. Some of this depends on judgments about what government services comprise pure public goods. But to the extent that they involve actions that contribute to people's education and health, collective provision of public goods advances people's life chances.

Government provision of pure public goods requires the collection of taxes. Those taxes then fund the provision of the pure public goods. Often, pure public goods are both funded and directly supplied by governments. However, once the revenue has been collected, it is possible to have the services supplied by private actors working for the government under contract. Historically, many pure public goods have first been supplied by governments. However, as more knowledge about delivery systems and their management has grown, opportunities have arisen for governments to contract with other entities for service provision. In some instances, such as schooling and the provision of some health services, governments have engaged in market making. That is, they have chosen to give subsidies to citizens in the form of vouchers. Citizens have then used those vouchers to "shop" among public or private service suppliers to obtain the services that most suit their preferences.

A significant debate in twentieth-century economics concerned the question of efficiency in the supply of pure public goods by governments. Paul Samuelson (1954) contended that government delivery of public goods meant a large portion of national income must be allocated in "nonoptimal" ways compared with allocation in the private sector. Charles Tiebout (1956) responded with a theory of local expenditures. According to Tiebout, the possibility of efficient delivery of public goods increased when governments were forced to compete with one another for citizens and, hence, tax revenues. This would happen, Tiebout contended, when citizens were mobile and could choose among several jurisdictions in which to live. Tiebout's work laid the foundation for an extensive body of research refining our understandings of the dynamics of intergovernmental competition and the possibility of pure public goods being delivered in ways that reduce the potential for misuse of taxes and poor service quality. Contributions by Vincent Ostrom and Elinor Ostrom have been important to the development of that literature (see, e.g., Bish and Ostrom 1973; Ostrom 1990). Here we also find the intellectual grounding for studies of government efforts to apply contracting and privatization strategies to improve allocative efficiency in the provision of public goods (Cooper 2003; Donahue 1989; Savas 1987). A vast amount of room exists for policy analysts and policy scholars to design ways for improving collective provision of pure public goods.

Natural Monopolies and How They Can Be Managed

As well as containing strong assumptions about information, property rights, and expressions of preference, the competitive market model contains two other assumptions. First, no buyer or seller can manipulate the prices at which items are traded. Second, there is no coercion. We now consider instances in which violations of these final two assumptions produce market failures.

To begin, it is useful to define terms. A monopoly exists when there is only one producer of a good or service. The existence of the monopoly opens the possibility for the producer to manipulate prices. Given the profit motive, a monopolist will face incentives to exploit customers by charging artificially high prices. Often, monopolists seek to segment customers by their willingness to pay for goods or services. As a result, some customers are charged higher prices than others. Further, if a firm has a monopoly in some areas but not in others, then incentives exist for the firm to engage in cross-subsidization across markets. This means that the monopolist will charge high prices where they have the monopoly, but low prices where they have competition. Indeed, whenever monopolists are threatened by competition in a given market, they face incentives to price their products in that market below actual costs. This is called predatory pricing. If they can sustain this for long enough—using profits from other markets to cover their losses—they can successfully drive out competition. Airlines have often been accused of this kind of practice. They will charge high prices for tickets on routes where they have no competition while virtually giving away tickets on routes where competition is fierce.

The existence of monopoly need not be a problem, so long as the monopolist refrains from price manipulation. A key question is whether they will do so voluntarily or whether government regulation will be required to control pricing and other business decisions. The case for limited government action toward monopolies can be made on two grounds. First, William Baumol, John C. Panzar, and Robert D. Willig (1982) argued that monopolists will behave like competitive firms whenever other firms have the potential to start competing with them. Baumol et al.'s contestability theory can be used to justify apparent monopoly service provision in a range of settings. Second, the existence of monopolies is often a function of technology. This is a point we will return to in our discussion later. But for now, we can note that producers in competitive situations face incentives to innovate with technology. Technological advance can serve to break down monopolies. Often, through being sheltered from competition and by making big profits, monopolies grow complacent and do not keep up with technological developments. As a result, when competitors enter their markets with better products and better prices, the monopolists can have great difficulty responding to the pressure.

Natural monopolies arise when the costs of establishing service provision are high but the marginal costs of service provision are negligible. Historically, big infrastructural industries like the railroads, electricity, and telecommunications have been natural monopolies. Often, natural monopolies cannot be established without government support. Consider the case of a railroad company wishing to run a new set of tracks into a state where no trains currently operate. The costs of building those new tracks and the systems supporting them would be very high. Those costs would be incurred only if the railroad company believed that it could make future gains from the investment. Suppose that market analysis suggested that there would be strong demand for rail transport. But now a strategic dilemma could arise. If building new tracks into the state appeared attractive to one railroad company, it would be likely to appear attractive to other railroad companies as well. However, if more than one company built tracks into the state, there will be an overinvestment in track infrastructure. Further, expected competition would drive down the expected future gains from the investment, making the investment seem unattractive. But because all railroad companies that could potentially enter the state would recognize this strategic problem, a good chance would arise that no new tracks would be built at all. With the choice being either overinvestment with no profitable returns or the status quo, the status quo would dominate.

It is not immediately obvious from this example that the solution is government action. After all, there would seem to be possibilities for the companies involved to find a mutually beneficial way to work out how to make tracking into the state work. However, the concern will still arise that whatever is mutually beneficial to the railroad companies is not so good for potential customers. Next, we consider the kind of government actions that can be taken to manage natural monopolies. In responding to problems associated with natural monopolies, governments attempt to promote outcomes that would be similar to those that could be expected to result from allocation of goods and services through an efficient market. The major goals of government action, then, are the pursuit of efficiency, the creation of effective institutions, and promotion of sustainability.

Because society and the economy can greatly benefit from the development of industries requiring high levels of initial infrastructural investment, governments will often lend support to the development of those industries. They can do so through provision of subsidies to private companies. Usually, when these subsidies are given, regulations are also established to govern the actions of the companies and potential competitors. This ensures that the natural monopolies do not engage in price manipulation but that they are also protected from aggressive competition from other companies. When natural monopolies perform an important role in an economy, governments do not wish to see their operations jeopardized by the presence of "fly-by-night" companies that could try to erode their profitability in small, potentially lucrative parts of the business.

Historically, there have been many cases in which governments have served as the investors and owners of natural monopolies. In so doing, they have established state-owned enterprises. Governments in many countries have had experience owning their national railroad systems, their electricity industry, and other natural monopolies whose existence has been deemed critical to promoting economic development.

As technological changes have occurred and knowledge has developed about the performance of natural monopolies, governments have often sought ways to reform how they manage them. As a result, a range of efforts have been made to move the ownership of natural monopolies out of the hands of governments and into private hands. A range of efforts have also been made to establish public-private partnerships and other alliances between governments and private companies. All of these efforts have been taken with the goal of squeezing more efficiency and better performance out of large, strategic industries that started out as natural monopolies.

Social Equity Concerns and How They Can Be Addressed
In this discussion of market failure, we have considered situations in which the actions of private individuals, groups, or firms can jeopardize market performance. Potential responses have ranged from minor government actions to governments taking full responsibility for funding and providing goods or services. Social equity concerns led us to think differently about markets. One claim made about markets is that when they are in equilibrium, the plans of all buyers and all sellers are perfectly aligned. Everyone who wants to buy and everyone who wants

to sell at the prevailing price does so. But there is a problem. The market model is silent on what characteristics allow people to participate in the first place. All market participants must be able to offer things that others want—money, services, or goods. When people have nothing to bring to the market, they can expect nothing from it. This is not a case of market failure. But taking account of social values beyond the pursuit of efficient resource allocation, we see here a huge limitation in the performance of markets. Because social equity matters, people need to find nonmarket ways to help everyone live with dignity. Much of the time, this can be done through the institution of the family, or through the actions of individuals and groups who gladly give gifts of time, money, goods, or services to help others less fortunate. Governments can also help, and they do so in many ways. Our discussion in Chapter 4 of social equity as an objective of government considered a variety of relevant issues. Here, brief consideration is given to how governments can use specific policy approaches to promote social equity.

Governments use tax systems to raise revenue and distribute it in the form of benefits or entitlements to those who cannot generate their own incomes and who have no other viable means of support. Often, governments also fund and provide services that promote social equity. Systems of public education represent classic cases of governments promoting equality of opportunity by funding and actually operating public schools. Systems of public health, common to most developed countries, also see governments providing free health services to all members of society who require them. Together with income maintenance programs—unemployment benefits, welfare benefits, and pensions—these government actions are the backbone of the welfare state. Along with promoting the fair distribution of resources in society, they also promote human flourishing and advance human rights.

As governments have gained more experience in the management of welfare states and as more knowledge has been amassed on policy instruments and their effects, a variety of efforts have been made to reform and experiment with the funding and delivery of valued services. Along with providing financial support, governments put considerable effort into informing citizens of services to assist them attain greater independence (Epstein 2006; Weiss and Tschirhart 1994). Voucher programs are used to promote consumer choice and encourage quality- and efficiency-enhancing competition among service providers (Osborne and Gaebler 1992; Popovich 1998). Other contracting approaches are transforming governments from service providers into funders that rely on the local knowledge and expertise of nongovernment entities to work with people in need. Many different agencies of government and nongovernment organizations work simultaneously with targeted individuals and families. Sometimes they lack effective coordination. In response, it is now common to find governments developing frameworks and strategies to improve communications among service providers (Agranoff 2007; Goldsmith and Eggers 2004). Much fertile ground exists for policy scholars, policy analysts, and program designers eager to improve government activities that promote social equity. Many principles can inform such initiatives. At a minimum, all people should be treated with dignity, feel safe, know that they are loved, and be encouraged to achieve independence and make meaning of their lives. Others can help them in many ways. Governments have crucial roles to play. Such collective effort epitomizes the good society. The product is human flourishing—a wonderful thing.

USING MARKET FAILURE AS AN ANALYTICAL FRAMEWORK

Market failures present rationales for government action. Policy analysts should always consider ways that market failures might be contributing to problems of interest to them. The section to follow introduces a set of general steps for performing analyses of market failure. Those steps are then utilized in an applied example.

Markets are not the only institutions in society that can fail. For example, consider families. Societies depend greatly on families to do the work of social reproduction—that is, to give people opportunities to develop and prepare themselves for their social and economic activities. A lot of trust is vested in families. However, when families become dysfunctional—perhaps because of sickness, financial stress, or domestic violence—then it would seem appropriate for some kind of government action to be taken. Here, we have not considered cases of institutional failure other than market failures. Yet the review of market failures is helpful for giving us concepts that can be more broadly applied. Why should government care about dysfunctional families? The concept of negative externalities helps answer the question. When families do not operate effectively, they can create poor outcomes that affect many people, not just the relatives involved. Why is it so difficult for agencies to detect and work with dysfunctional families? The concept of information asymmetries helps here. For many reasons, people in dysfunctional families often do not want to tell others about the problems they are facing. Those reasons might include coercion, pride, or conditioning that leads people to think of their situation as normal. As people explore problems in different institutions in society, treating market processes and market failures as metaphors can be a useful way to gain fresh insights on those problems. Those insights can also suggest starting points for effective solutions.

STEPS IN THE ANALYSIS OF MARKET FAILURE

The eight steps presented here offer a logical procedure for analyzing market failures. Through their use, policy analysts can build knowledge of how consumers and producers are behaving and how their actions can be causing problems. This analytical approach also indicates how analysis of market failure can be combined with the investigation of effective government responses.

Step 1. Specify the good or service of interest. Careful analysis of market failure requires understanding the processes of interest and relevant behaviors of people involved in those processes. Specifying the good or service of interest represents an important prelude to that work. The primary question to answer is this: What are people buying and selling? If no trading appears to be happening, then a better question might be this: What is the demand here and how could it be addressed? Sometimes, our attention is first drawn to a set of interactions that are actually secondary or incidental to a trade. So this step can be difficult.

Step 2. Identify the consumers and producers and the location of their transactions. Once we have a sense of where money is changing hands, we can identify the consumers and producers of the good or service of interest. Knowledge of the consumers and producers can provide important insights into power relationships and market dynamics.

Step 3. Using the tools of market analysis, construct a simple model of how an efficient market would allocate this good or service. Markets work best when property rights are well specified, when spillover effects are negligible, when the most relevant attributes of the good or service can be rapidly assessed in advance of the trade, and when there are many buyers and sellers. Thinking through the match between the processes associated with allocation of the good or service of interest and a simple market model is an effective way to reveal the possibilities for market failure.

Step 4. State the market failure that you believe is present in this context. It is useful to begin with the broad categories of market failure introduced here: information asymmetry, externalities, public goods, natural monopoly, and social equity concerns. Often allocation problems are complex and several kinds of market failure could be present. In such cases, it is good practice to start your analysis with a focus on the market failure that you predict as the most significant source of problems in the given context.

Step 5. Analyze the actions of consumers and producers and how those actions contribute to market failure. Your selection of a market failure to focus upon gives you a theory to guide your observations of consumer and producer actions. It is important to break the situation down so that you can explore separately what is happening on each side—the demand side and the supply side—of the market. Starting with the demand side, ask the following: (1) What are the consumers doing that appears inconsistent with expectations from a simple market model? (2) Is this observed discrepancy consistent with the kind of market failure we believe is present? Having worked through the demand side, the supply side can be subjected to the same questions, with the word "producers" replacing the word "consumers" in the first question.

Step 6. Estimate the financial implications of the market failure, and note any other salient impacts. Market failures usually produce inefficient economic outcomes. Either too many or too few resources are devoted to an activity. Also, in most cases, one group of actors benefits at the expense of another. Estimating the financial implications of market failures can be difficult, but it is important work. When the nature of the situation and the effects of actions by producers and consumers are well understood, it is easier to assign monetary values to component parts of the problem. Having a sense of the financial magnitude of a problem is a starting point for considering feasible solutions. The costs of rectifying a market failure should never exceed the anticipated benefits. It is better to leave the problem alone until lower-cost responses can be developed.

Step 7. Identify efforts made by consumers, producers, and any other nongovernmental actors to address the market failure. Market participants often face significant incentives to address market failures. However, as decentralized actors with no ability to coerce behavioral changes in others, it is often difficult for those involved to achieve coordination at a scale sufficient to address the problem at hand. Information concerning the financial implications of a market failure can indicate what it is worth to people to improve the situation, and whether solutions will be developed by consumers, producers, or third parties.

Step 8. Suggest how government use of policy instruments could potentially address the market failure. Once the financial implications of the market failure have been estimated and the nongovernment efforts to address it have been assessed, consideration can turn to potential government actions to rectify the problem. It is essential to remember here that government action comes at a cost. Any resources that governments devote to addressing this problem are resources that could be used elsewhere. In general, efforts should focus on identification of minimal interventions and opportunities to "nudge" producers and consumers toward creating better outcomes. Because governments now have had a lot of experience addressing market failures, a huge amount of evidence exists concerning the effectiveness of different kinds of policy responses. It is much better to carefully design low-cost, relatively unobtrusive responses than to hastily impose government solutions that end up introducing new problems of their own.

AN APPLIED EXAMPLE

This section highlights analysis contained in the following:

Naci Mocan. (2007). "Can Consumers Detect Lemons? An Empirical Analysis of Information Asymmetry in the Market for Child Care." *Journal of Population Economics* 20: 743–780.

Over the past few decades, many countries have experienced significant expansion in formal provision of early childhood care and education. There are two main explanations. First, the participation of women in the paid workforce at rates approaching those of men has led to major changes in families and their caregiving arrangements. To maintain a reasonable standard of living, most households with young children now require all the adults present to be earning an income. Second, there has been a growing recognition of the benefits that infants and toddlers can gain from spending regular periods of time socializing with peers. Increasing numbers of parents also understand that a good education is vital to future economic and social success. They desire their children to perform well in school and value preschool services that prepare them for this.

The quality of preschool child care centers matters to parents. All parents want their children to be safe, well nourished, and happy. Many also care greatly that the centers their children attend offer environments that nurture cognitive and social development. Parents seek quality child care for their children because they are driven by love. Yet society as a whole has reason to worry about the quality of formal child care provision (Gormley 1995). High-quality child care can produce positive externalities, by giving children the foundational skills for later success in life. Low-quality child care can produce negative externalities. When infants and toddlers are subjected to neglect or abuse, the long-term personal and social consequences can be devastating. Concerns about social equity can also prompt broad interest in the provision of subsidized, quality child care for children from low-income families. Therefore, several justifications exist for widespread social concern about the quality of preschool child care centers. In practice, most child care centers are subject to government regulation. The operators must be licensed. Usually, the requirements for licensing contain provisions regarding the quality of the physical facilities, the ratio of staff to children, and the qualifications of staff members. It is also common for child care centers to receive government subsidies, and for those subsidies to be tied to measures of quality. Sometimes governments both fund and operate child care centers.

Naci Mocan (2007) observed that child care centers offer complex services and that, as a result, many parents might have difficulty distinguishing among centers on the basis of quality. Child care is a classic post-experience good, and room exists for information asymmetries that could be exploited by service providers. Mocan studied quality levels and parental choice strategies using evidence from 400 child care centers in California, Colorado, Connecticut, and North Carolina in the United States. From his research, Mocan concluded that parental inability to make fine-grained quality distinctions prompted overconsumption of low-quality services and underconsumption of high-quality services. Because it is relatively costly to provide high-quality services, centers are not motivated to do so in the absence of demand for it. According to Mocan, information asymmetries drive high-quality child care provision out of the market and leave a market filled with low-quality providers.

Step 1. Specify the good or service of interest. This is a study of the market for center-based child care provision, with a focus on how to distinguish among service quality levels.

Step 2. Identify the consumers and producers and the location of their transactions. Parents are the consumers. They act on behalf of their children, and they are assumed to make decisions based on obtaining the best services for their children, subject to the financial constraints they operate under. The producers are the actual operators of the child care centers. The transactions occur on the center sites.

Step 3. Using the tools of market analysis, construct a simple model of how an efficient market would allocate this good or service. Figure 10.6 depicts an efficient market for child care. The model assumes that child care is a private good with no externalities. Further, it assumes that service quality is uniform across providers. This removes the potential for problems generated by information asymmetries between producers and consumers. These simplifications transform child care into a private search good, in which all relevant attributes can be assessed prior to purchase.

Step 4. State the market failure that you believe is present in this context. The market failure of interest here is the existence of information asymmetry between the producers and the consumers. Child care centers (the producers) are expected to have more information on center quality than parents (the consumers), because parents are unable to spend significant amounts of time at centers to observe various dimensions of their operations.

Step 5. Analyze the actions of consumers and producers and how those actions contribute to market failure. Previous studies have indicated that parents are

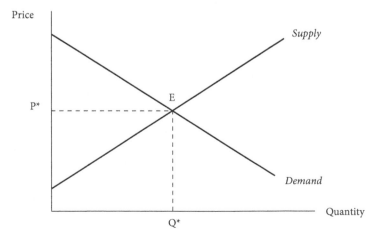

Figure 10.6 An Efficient Market for Child Care, with Uniform Quality

very sensitive to price in child care markets and that they display a low willingness to pay higher prices for higher quality services. At the same time, parents appear to have problems making quality distinctions among centers. Naci Mocan explored parental ability to assess center quality. Data collectors for the study obtained in-depth information on 400 child care centers through on-site visits. At each center, interviews were conducted with center administrators and owners, and reviews were made of center payroll and other records. Two trained observers also visited each center for a day to gather data on classroom and center quality. Structural quality was measured by variables such as staff-child ratios, group sizes, and the educational qualifications of the staff. Process quality was measured by studying, among other things, the nature of the interactions between the care provider and the child and the activities to which the child is exposed. The measures of quality were designed by psychologists. Parents associated with each of the child care centers were also surveyed. The surveys found that parents care a lot about center quality, as characterized by the variables noted previously. Parents were then asked to offer their judgments of the quality of the centers their children were attending, doing so through their responses to questions on the broad range of quality variables that experts also used to rate the centers.

Mocan found that parents consistently overestimated the quality of their children's child care centers compared to the rating given by the trained observers. Parents used a variety of strategies to develop quality judgments about centers. Often, these strategies led to false conclusions. For example, parents tend to judge more positively the quality of publicly supported centers compared with the quality of church-based or publicly regulated centers. The proportion of white children at centers was associated with parental perceptions of higher quality. Mocan found

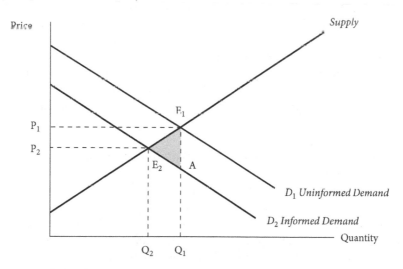

Figure 10.7 The Market for Low-Quality Child Care, Showing Uninformed Demand and Informed Demand

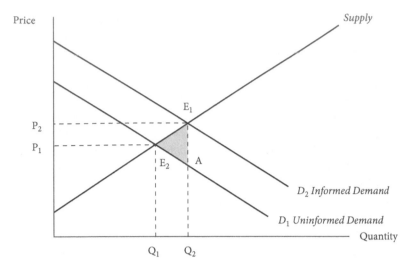

Figure 10.8 The Market for High-Quality Child Care, Showing Uninformed Demand and Informed Demand

that more educated parents appeared to make more accurate judgments of quality and were less prone to judging on attributes that had little relevance.

Figure 10.7 characterizes the market for low-quality child care. It shows that when parents are uninformed, more low-quality child care is purchased, and at a higher price, than would be the case if parents were accurately informed of service quality. The triangle E_1AE_2 represents the deadweight loss to society that occurs because too many resources are being allocated to an activity that is not socially desirable. In contrast, Figure 10.8 characterizes the market for high-quality child care. It shows that uninformed demand is lower than informed demand. If parents knew for sure how to distinguish between low-quality and high-quality centers, then the demand for high-quality centers would rise. More people would be prepared to pay more for the high-quality service. This would bring forth greater supply of high-quality services. The deadweight loss in Figure 10.8, triangle E_1AE_2, represents the unrealized social surplus that could come from greater use of high-quality centers. With informed demand, the deadweight loss vanishes.

Step 6. Estimate the financial implications of the market failure, and note any other salient impacts. Naci Mocan's goal was to document the existence of an information asymmetry between child care providers and parents. For this reason, he did not estimate the financial implications of the market failure. However, he did draw upon evidence produced by others to indicate the significance of research on this topic. For example, he noted evidence suggesting that high-quality child care programs reduce the likelihood of children enrolling in special education programs when they enter school, that they tend to improve the academic outcomes of children, and that they are generally associated with children's well-being. He also argued that if high-quality care increases the cognitive skills of children and their labor market opportunities as young adults, then high-quality child care today would benefit society tomorrow (Mocan 2007: 744).

Step 7. Identify efforts made by consumers, producers, and any other non-governmental actors to address the market failure. Naci Mocan concluded his article with the suggestion that "making information on quality obtained by expert observers available to parents has the potential of creating a remedy for this market failure" (p. 774). He did not comment on who might take responsibility for generating and disseminating that information. This would seem to be an instance in which expert intermediaries could provide the necessary information. Mocan noted that in 2004, the U.S. Bureau of the Census estimated that almost nine million children were enrolled in nursery school, preschool, and kindergarten. This would suggest demand for relevant consumer information on provider quality, especially in large metropolitan areas where quality-driven parental choice among centers would seem feasible.

Step 8. Suggest how government use of policy instruments could potentially address the market failure. This study suggested only that more information could be made available to parents. Potentially, other policy instruments could be used. For example, if high-quality child care was of high priority to governments, then targeted subsidies could be used to promote quality improvements. Strengthened systems of regulation and monitoring could also be used to this end. Inevitably, trade-offs would need to be assessed, taking into account policy effectiveness on the one hand, and costs on the other.

ADVICE FOR ANALYTICAL PRACTICE

Whenever a policy problem arises, it is useful to consider how it might represent a form of market failure. The following points can help guide effective analysis of market failures.

- Learning the background to a problem is a good way to identify what kinds of responses people have already used to address it. Try to avoid repeating what has not worked in the past.
- It is impossible to take full and accurate account of the costs of market failures. But any effort to identify costs and estimate their dollar values will be helpful. At a minimum, this can prompt others to try making better estimates.
- Often, market failures can be addressed with limited or no government actions. It is important to always consider what outcome would occur if government did nothing.

MARKET FAILURE AND OTHER
ANALYTICAL STRATEGIES

Sometimes, markets do not function as anticipated. Economic inefficiencies result. These market failures are caused by violations of one or more of the key assumptions of the market model. The existence of market failure is considered a necessary, but not sufficient, condition for corrective public policy actions. This is where government (*centralized, public*) decision making augments or supplants individual (*decentralized, private*) decision making. Here, we considered common forms of market failure that can serve as rationales for government actions. Because markets are fundamental institutions in society, their operations and the outcomes they produce hold implications for most other social and economic activities. Therefore, the analysis of market failure is a primary analytical strategy for use by policy analysts. Used in isolation, the analysis of market failure can generate many insights into policy problems. However, its usefulness can be greatly expanded when it is applied in tandem with market analysis and the analysis of government failure. In addition, the analysis of market failure can be combined to good effect with comparative institutional analysis and cost-benefit analysis.

Exercises

1. Consider one or two areas of public policy that interest you (e.g., transportation policy, education policy). Discuss what extent you think policy in these areas has been developed in response to the following:

   • Particular market failures
   • Social equity concerns
   • Other concerns (*specify*)

2. Ronald Coase (1937) suggested that even well-functioning markets have their limitations when it comes to organizing efficient production of goods and services. When coordination through markets becomes costly, there is justification for the formation of firms. Formation of private firms, then, can be viewed as a rational effort to improve on market outcomes. Following this same logic, we might contend that even when a type of market failure is observed, actions taken by producers, consumers, or nongovernmental third parties might address it. Government intervention should not be assumed to be the only viable response, although sometimes it will be. Can you think of some examples in which nongovernmental efforts have been made to address problems associated with the functioning of markets?

3. Together, make a list of local, state, or national government policy actions that appear to promote participation in markets by people who—in the absence of government action—could lack the ability to do so. Are such policy actions

restricted to promoting consumption of necessities? What do your answers tell us about the role of government in contemporary society?

The Policy Research Seminar

Organize a research-oriented seminar that will run for about ninety minutes, preferably with some light refreshments. Invite up to twelve people, and make sure you have a mixture of experienced researchers, junior researchers, and graduate students. The purpose of the discussion should be to develop ideas for the design of policy research projects that give a central place to the analysis of market failure. The project ideas should be sufficiently interesting and original that each could form the basis of a significant research paper, dissertation, or thesis. Participants should come to the seminar having read both this chapter and Naci Mocan's (2007) article "Can Consumers Detect Lemons? An Empirical Analysis of Information Asymmetry in the Market for Child Care" (*Journal of Population Economics* 20: 743–780). You might structure the discussion around the section "Steps in the Analysis of Market Failure" presented in this chapter and applied in the overview of the Mocan study. Many other recent journal articles could have been highlighted in this chapter. Prior to the group meeting, you might have several participants locate other interesting articles that present original analyses of market failures. Discussions of this sort tend to work best when the group has a clear goal. I suggest this outcome statement: "By the end of this meeting we will have identified five possible topics for new research projects that involve analysis of market failure. We will have sketched out basic research designs for at least two of those projects." Brainstorm to get some ideas flowing. Hold the more skeptical, analytical comments until later in the seminar. Ideally, some members of the discussion group will follow up on the meeting and continue to develop, perhaps collaboratively, research designs that build from the readings and the discussion. This is a good way to promote original policy research inspired by the best contemporary applications of quantitative and qualitative research methods. For additional advice on how to run effective meetings of this kind, see (1) Michael Mintrom's (2003) "Facilitating Meetings" in *People Skills for Policy Analysts* (Washington, DC: Georgetown University Press) and (2) Tom Kelley's (2001) "The Perfect Brainstorm" in *The Art of Innovation* (New York: Currency/Doubleday).

Further Reading

Akerlof, George A. (1970). "The Market for 'Lemons': Quality Uncertainty and the Market Mechanism." *Quarterly Journal of Economics* 84: 488–500.

Blinder, Alan S. (1987). "Needed: Hard Heads and Soft Hearts." In *Hard Heads, Soft Hearts: Tough-Minded Economics for a Just Society*, chap. 1. Reading, MA: Addison-Wesley.

Coase, R. H. (1974). "The Lighthouse in Economics." *Journal of Law and Economics* 17: 357–376.

Demsetz, Harold. (1993). "The Theory of the Firm Revisited." In *The Nature of the Firm: Origins, Evolution, and Development,* ed. Oliver E. Williamson and Sidney G. Winter, chap. 10. New York: Oxford University Press.

Hahn, Robert W. (2009). "Greenhouse Gas Auctions and Taxes: Some Political Economy Considerations." *Review of Environmental Economics and Policy* 3: 167–188.

Ostrom, Elinor. (1999). "Coping with Tragedies of the Commons." *Annual Review of Political Science* 2: 493–535.

11

Analysis of Government Failure

The Story So Far... Many key objectives of government can be pursued by efforts to promote efficient market outcomes. Sometimes, public policies are introduced that result in governments both funding and providing public services.

Here... This chapter considers insights that have emerged from the literature on government failure. This literature reminds us that when governments seek to address problems of decentralized decision making, sometimes the cure can be worse than the illness. We consider how policy analysts can reduce the prospect that their policy proposals will result in government failure.

THIS CHAPTER REVIEWS

- The coordination role of government
- The tendency for government to manage processes that fall into the "too hard" basket of other social institutions
- Nonmarket counterparts to market failure
- Concerns about undue influence, abuse of power, poor mechanism design, and technological lock-in
- Path dependency and its relevance

Across society, a range of institutional structures promote social stability. They allow people to pursue their own interests, through their decentralized, individual, and private actions. At the same time, these institutions resolve coordination problems, ensuring that everyone's individual pursuit of self-interest contributes to good collective outcomes. For example, the institution of the family does a lot to structure individual activities and align individual interests with collective interests. Markets, as institutions, also structure the behaviors of individuals or of collections of individuals. The organization of firms represents a very significant way that people engage in collective action to effectively participate in markets. Those actions also often serve to promote good collective outcomes. It is useful for us to think of governments as entities that structure institutional arrangements with the goal of further aligning decentralized, individual decision making with the promotion of desired social and economic outcomes. Understood in this way, we see that governments do a lot to establish the fundamental rules of the game for other institutions in society. Markets could not operate effectively without, among other things, safe and peaceful social relations, a common language allowing transactions to occur, a system of property rights and policing mechanisms to enforce those rights, and a stable money supply. These are things that effective governments supply. Thinking along these lines, we also realize that a lot of infrastructure supports our day-to-day activities, and that government actions contribute significantly to ensuring adequate procurement and maintenance of such infrastructure. Examples of that infrastructure include roads and highways, transportation systems, water and sewage systems, electricity and telecommunication systems, schools, health services, and so on. All around us, obvious signs exist of the vital roles that governments play in supporting social and economic cooperation and coordination.

We noted in Chapter 9 that well-functioning markets maximize the sum of consumer and producer surplus, also known as the social surplus. However, our discussion of market failure in Chapter 10 highlighted conditions whereby market transactions manifest problems. Those problems create wastage in the form of uncaptured social surplus. In any given market that is not operating perfectly, the uncaptured social surplus is also called deadweight loss. When markets are generating outcomes that are deemed to be unsatisfactory, or when markets simply cannot help us to realize desired social outcomes, then arguments can be made for government actions to be taken to improve the situation. For example, when a market is operating but is subject to market failure, then governments need to do more than maintain the underlying conditions that allow that market to function. Government interventions designed to improve the performance of specific markets can take the form of law changes, regulations, the imposition of taxes, the provision of subsidies, the provision of information, or other actions.

Economists have devoted a lot of attention to understanding market processes and government interventions intended to rectify market failures. In so doing, they have come to appreciate that government interventions can themselves create problems. This has led to a literature on the subject of nonmarket or government failures (Wolf 1979a, 1979b, 1988; see also Mueller 2003). Two motivations prompted the development of this literature. One was to remind proponents of government interventions in markets that such actions are never costless. Government action comes at a cost, and that cost needs to be weighed against the cost of the perceived market imperfection. By making this point, contributors to the government failure literature sought to quell enthusiasts who believed it would be desirable to use government actions to fine-tune real market processes (Demsetz 1969; Friedman 1962). A second motivation behind the development of this literature was to highlight problems that government actions could themselves introduce into any given context, particularly the tendency for government actions to create perverse incentives for market participants (Becker 1983; Stigler 1971). Charles Wolf summed up these two motivations. Policy analysts contemplating government actions to address perceived problems should worry, said Wolf, that "the cure might be as bad as the illness" (1979b: 133).

In this chapter, we review the concept of government failure. In the process, we are reminded that instances can arise in which government actions—while at first seeming desirable—can produce results that are not better, and potentially worse, than the results produced by apparently failing markets. Often, in policy work, the available choice is between degrees and types of failure. This chapter discusses how attention to the possibility of government failure can improve the analysis and advice we produce.

At the end of chapter 10, I noted that the analysis of market failures has given us a useful language and set of metaphors that can be used in ways that extend beyond our analysis of markets and government responses to market failures. More specifically, I suggested that policy analysts can expand the scope of their interests by thinking in terms of problems created by private, decentralized decision making. Those problems could arise not just through the actions of participants in markets but also through the actions of individuals in families, in other social settings, and in their relations to the environment. We can apply the same logic in this chapter. The language of government failure can help us to think about relationships between private, decentralized decision making and public, centralized decision making. When we move beyond thinking about how governments intervene in markets, we open ourselves up to thinking more broadly about how institutional arrangements in society can be designed to most effectively allocate decision-making responsibilities between private individuals acting alone and governments acting on behalf of all members of society.

AN OVERVIEW OF GOVERNMENT FAILURE AND ITS ANALYSIS

Government failure can be technically defined, and the economic effects of government failure can be estimated. When a market is subject to market failure, the full social surplus derived from efficient market allocation goes unrealized. More specifically, a deadweight loss can result, equal to the amount of social surplus not captured as either consumer or producer surplus. Government interventions into a market subject to market failure can potentially rectify the market processes and eliminate the deadweight loss. For an efficient outcome to be realized, the costs associated with the government interventions should be outweighed by the benefits associated with eliminating the deadweight loss. From here, we can derive a conceptually precise definition of government failure. That is, government failure will be present if the costs associated with correcting a market failure are greater than the benefits captured, which can be measured as the gain in the social surplus realized by the government intervention. Clifford Winston (2006) summarized a range of specific government actions taken to address market failures that can be shown to have failed. Winston also provided estimates of the costs of those government failures, based on the logic presented here.

Policy analysts can contribute a lot to improved social outcomes by making good conceptual arguments that are informed by an understanding of the potential sources of government failure and how they might be avoided. While the technical definition of government failure is useful to bear in mind, in practice it is often very difficult to analyze government failure using this definition. Further, estimating the costs of government failure in any given instance is always going to be more difficult than estimating the costs of a market failure, an exercise that can be fraught with measurement challenges. Charles Wolf (1988) discussed those challenges at some length. Wolf noted that it is usually possible to predict whether a policy action will have a positive or negative effect, but predicting the magnitudes of those effects, and comparing them with the effects of doing nothing, can be "formidable" (p. 116). Given these observations, this chapter is intended as a general introduction to the analysis of government failure. While efforts to measure the financial implications of government failure are encouraged, such efforts can be worthwhile only when the government actions contributing to poor outcomes are well understood. The sources of costs first must be identified and ranked, starting with the most significant. Here, the focus is placed on the factors that cause government failure. As such, this chapter can assist policy analysts as they undertake all the work that would prepare the ground for estimating the costs of specific government failures.

Government and Coordination Problems

Analytical efforts to identify the sources of government failure should not be construed as "government bashing." As we think about problems of government, we should bear in mind that government is often called upon to address problems that were already in the "too-hard" basket of the market or of other social institutions. Governments, through their ability to raise revenue and to place the force of law behind their engagements with citizens, can accomplish many desirable social outcomes that could not be achieved through the voluntary cooperation of individuals. When we consider problems associated with government actions—regulation, direct service provision, provision of subsidies and social safety nets—we should be careful to think in comparative terms. Often, government actions have transformative effects on social and economic contexts. For example, in many countries, governments were the first entities that established electrical supply systems. Only after those systems had been well developed was it possible for people to begin to see how alternative systems of ownership and control could produce more efficient forms of service provision. When governments address a service gap and subsequently create conditions under which responsibility for service provision can be handed to nongovernment entities, that series of actions should be viewed in a positive light. The facilitative role of government often is not performed perfectly, but the role remains a vital one. Here, as we consider ways that government can fail, it is important to bear in mind that often the remedy to government failure will be the redesign of current systems. It is rare to find government failures being corrected through elimination of a government function. That is not because of the nature of the politics at stake but because total reliance upon coordination through decentralized, private action remains unfeasible.

Political Control

Bureaucratic structures are needed both in government and in many private organizations, simply because these offer effective ways to ensure that work gets performed. As anyone who has worked in a private company can attest, politics exist everywhere. Whether organizations are public or private, employees sometimes engage in various political maneuvers with the goal of advancing their own career interests over those of others (Reardon 2005). But there is a crucial distinction between public and private organizations, and that distinction has to do with political control. In the private sector, organizational politics is kept in check by the need for firms to compete effectively in the marketplace. Firms that become dysfunctional organizations run the risk of losing business, becoming unprofitable, and either foundering completely or being subject to an outside takeover. In the public sector, poor organizational performance can lead to concerns being raised. But there is no direct link between performance and continued existence. In government, some organizations can keep performing at mediocre levels for decades. Further, when concerns are raised about performance, the common response is that more money will be needed if those issues are to be addressed. The key reward of the marketplace—more money—can end up being dished out in the public sector most often to the worst performers.

In a discussion of the politics of structural choice, Terry Moe (1991) offered a careful explanation of the dynamics that lead to very different structures and forms of behavior between government and nongovernment organizations. Moe noted that in a world of voluntary exchange, like the private sector, organizations are structures of mutual advantage. However, politics is a world of public authority in which the driving forces of organizational design are different. Here, designs for effective organizations often become compromised. Those who design the organizations must worry that one day their political opponents will have charge over those organizations. Hence, it is typical for public organizations to be highly constrained both in the actions that they can take and in the autonomy of those who operate within them. From the standpoint of effective performance, Moe argued that public organizations "loom as structural nightmares that seem to deny all principles of reasoned judgment" (p. 127). A political logic—quite distinctive from the logic of the financial bottom-line—drives decision making in public organizations. That is why public organizations often seem like relics of another time, fixated on process, and not overly concerned about effective outcomes. Notice, though, how much people in these organizations watch out for changes in the political winds, how much they calibrate their language—but not necessarily their actions—to what they believe "the powers that be" are looking for.

Provider Capture

The notion of provider capture emerged out of studies of regulated industries and the behaviors of participants within them (see, e.g., Peltzman 1976; Stigler 1971; and Wilson 1980). Regulation of industries is often undertaken to protect consumers from harm. For example, people wishing to teach in schools, practice medicine, offer services in the construction industry, and so on must register to do so. Registration is based on prior attainment of appropriate qualifications. An argument made against this form of regulation is that members of the regulated professions exercise their political power to influence the content of those regulations and how they are enforced. When this occurs, there is a tendency for the regulations to serve a gatekeeping function, limiting the supply of relevant service providers and, hence, driving up the wages of registered practitioners above the levels that they could reasonably expect to receive in the absence of such regulation.

Similar provider capture can arise when entry of firms into industries is heavily regulated. For example, for much of the twentieth century, transportation industries were typically regulated so that operators had to be licensed to serve specific routes and pricing schedules were applied to reduce competition on those routes. While the incumbent operators did well out of these situations, the overall effect was that suppliers benefited at the expense of consumers. The deregulation efforts that began in the late 1970s in the United States and elsewhere resulted in the opening up of railroads, trucking companies, and airlines to greater competition. In most instances, the change in the regulatory regimes led to major restructuring in the relevant industries. For example, airlines adopted the hub-and-spoke system of route structures and railroad and trucking companies started engaging in far greater levels of bimodal transportation than had been the case in the past. All of this suggests that the prior regulatory regimes were primarily serving the interests of providers over consumers (Peltzman, Levine, and Noll 1989).

Perverse Incentives

Public policies introduced with the best of intentions sometimes get undermined because they create perverse incentives for relevant actors. For example, in the absence of any kind of welfare state, we worry that people who are unemployed and lack savings may find it hard to obtain food and shelter for themselves and those who depend upon them. In response, governments in most developed countries offer temporary forms of income maintenance and other benefits to those who are willing to work but who are currently unemployed. However, the presence of government assistance can create an incentive for some individuals, at the margin, to direct their efforts toward securing continued receipt of a benefit as opposed to finding long-term employment. Public policies need to be designed in ways that encourage appropriate alignment between policy goals and individual actions.

Steven Cheung (1996) has offered a classic example of government failure due to the creation of perverse incentives. Cheung's study focused on the history of a rent-control ordinance established in Hong Kong. During the twentieth century, Hong Kong experienced high levels of immigration. The entry of immigrants placed pressures on the rental housing market. To avoid sharp rental increases forcing long-established citizens out of their accommodation, the government set limits on the increases that landlords could charge. However, the government understood that the long-term solution to the housing shortage would be to have new housing built. New properties were exempted from the rent control. The result was a construction bonanza. In many cases, perfectly good apartment blocks, even fairly new ones, were demolished so that landlords could evict their low-rent current tenants and sign up high-rent new ones for their new buildings. The governor of Hong Kong observed, "I confess that where I went wrong was when I credited the landlords with having more public spirit and more refined ideas of common honesty than they appear to possess....I did not suppose that many were prepared to go to the extreme length of destroying good buildings in order merely to evade the law. I can only express my regret that I took a higher view of humanity" (quoted in Cheung 1996: 240).

Goal Displacement

When the incentives created in an organizational environment lead people to narrow the focus of their activities and devote their energies to manipulating the measurement of their performance, this is called goal displacement. John Bohte and Kenneth Meier (2000) presented an illustrative example of this practice through a study of school responses to high-stakes student testing in Texas. Bohte and Meier found evidence suggesting that schools manipulated test results by finding creative ways to exempt underperforming students from taking the high-stakes tests. Although they could not prove categorically that organizational cheating was happening, Bohte and Meier's evidence strongly suggested it. Anecdotal evidence of individual teacher practices was consistent with their evidence. Indeed, the test-taking abilities of students increased dramatically in some school districts where performance pay for teachers was influenced by student test score results. (Some teachers were caught doctoring the student responses.) The authors concluded that goal displacement is most likely to occur when much of the work being performed is hard for supervisors to observe and when the incentives for cheating are high. We see here that goal displacement is a logical consequence of establishing perverse incentives. Gary Miller (1992) has suggested that those involved in organizational design must strive to balance the use of formal, individualized incentives against efforts to create broader organizational cultures. Those broader cultures can establish informal norms of "how we do things around here" and so align individual practice with the attainment of desired organizational goals.

Institutional Inertia

In discussing the role of government in society, Milton Friedman (1962) conceded that many well-intentioned policy actions could have positive immediate effects. However, he still sounded a note of caution about adopting such policies. Friedman's concern was that government action would eliminate the incentives for innovation and system improvement characteristic of well-functioning market processes. In Friedman's words, "government would replace progress by stagnation, it would substitute uniform mediocrity for the variety essential for that experimentation which can bring tomorrow's laggards above today's mean" (p. 4). The truth underlying this observation has been demonstrated in a number of fields.

Charles Schultze (1977) noted that heavy-handed regulation of industries could curb technological progress. Regulations can specify a goal and provide incentives for its attainment. Alternately, they can stipulate practices to be followed that are expected to promote the goal. The difference matters. When emphasis is placed on ensuring specific practices are followed (perhaps to promote safety in the car industry, or reduce pollution by coal-burning electricity plants), then organizations are motivated to play by the rules; changes in practices will occur only when the regulations change. In contrast, incentives-based regulatory models encourage organizations to find innovative solutions to problems. Emissions trading schemes have been devised as a means of forcing polluters to confront the social costs associated with their activities. Under these schemes, polluters face a stark choice: either embrace new technologies that reduce pollution or purchase pollution permits, which will grow scarcer and more expensive over time.

Another classic example of institutional inertia can be found in systems of public schooling. Efforts to promote uniform standards in curriculum content and student achievement have their merits. However, system homogeneity has often resulted in school administrators, teachers, and parents becoming highly resistant to change, demonizing the introduction of new teaching technologies or approaches to school organization and pedagogy that reflect changing social conditions (Tyack and Cuban 1995).

In general, policy analysts should think hard about the longer-term effects of particular policy choices. The literature on path dependency neatly illustrates how adoption of specific technologies or policy settings can constrain progress in a range of fields of human endeavor (see, e.g., Arthur 1990; Baumgartner and Jones 2002; Greener 2002). Once people become habituated to specific forms of action and they identify their interests with those ways of being, anything more than incremental adjustments from the established norms become exceedingly difficult. Given the politics of structural choice, it can be a challenge for new government actions to be designed so that they will serve as effective platforms for ongoing policy development and adaptation in specific areas. But we do know that market processes generate information about the financial bottom line, consumer preferences, and the relative costs of inputs. As such, market processes provide incentives for innovation and change that are rarely present in government bureaucracies. This suggests that efforts to create market-like systems for the allocation and management of government resources could have long-term benefits, through allowing more innovation and efficiency in the delivery of public services. This is a useful design consideration to keep in mind.

USING GOVERNMENT FAILURE AS AN ANALYTICAL FRAMEWORK

The analysis of government failure can be usefully applied at several stages in the policy-making process. We have noted the significant roles governments play in supporting other institutional arrangements in contemporary society. Given this, many economic and social problems that become salient and lead to calls for policy action should be diagnosed with an eye to finding both elements of market failure and elements of government failure. This suggests that the analysis of government failure can be a powerful tool for helping in the definition of policy problems. A sound knowledge of the potential for government failure can also be usefully applied when policy analysts are selecting and analyzing alternative policy responses to specific policy problems. Good policy design must be informed by an awareness of the potential for government failure and how the risk of it can be lowered. Finally, the analysis of government failure can be usefully integrated into program evaluation. When efforts are being made to understand the relationship between the operations of a program and its actual impacts, concepts that emerge from discussions of government failure can prove helpful. All of this suggests that the careful analysis of government failure should be an essential part of efforts to understand the impacts of existing governmental actions and to guide reform efforts.

It is rare for explorations of government failure to be conducted in isolation from other analytical strategies. The approach should be applied in a manner that allows us to consider alternative institutional arrangements. Often, policy analysts can gain a good level of analytical traction on a problem by first asking this: In the absence of government action, what would happen here? The question leads us back to thinking about market processes or, more generally, to considering the ways that private, decentralized actions serve to reduce or exacerbate coordination problems. Given this, the analysis of government failure is often combined with the analysis of markets and market failures. It can be enhanced through careful application as a component of comparative institutional analysis. Further, efforts to combine analysis of government failure with cost-benefit analysis—even if done in a rudimentary fashion—can help decision makers appreciate the potential for dysfunctional and wasteful practices to arise due to poor policy and program design.

When engaging in the analysis of government failure, policy analysts can benefit from sharing with others their preliminary hunches. Thinking in scenario terms can be helpful. Suppose, for example, that concerns have been raised about variation in the quality of outpatient services being provided by hospitals and other medical facilities across a large metropolitan area. Among policy responses to this problem, you might consider establishing a regular ranking system that offers comparative assessments of the quality of service provision at each site. However, this should then lead you to think about the items you would use to compare across sites and how practitioners at each site could potentially manipulate their performance scores. What might the least-angelic professionals do to make their organization look good, even if actual performance is poor? Brainstorming these possibilities with others—especially people who have experience in the delivery of outpatient services—would undoubtedly help you to improve the design of the ranking system. In general, collective efforts to identify the potential for various government failures can improve your analytical work. As we develop our knowledge of public policy and learn lessons from practice—both in our own backyard and from what we learn in the literature—we can become better at anticipating design problems. After developing a list of possibilities for government failure in a given policy context, you can then discuss where you think the greatest likelihood for government failure lies. From there, efforts can be made to prioritize the elements of policy design where most attention should go to mitigation strategies.

STEPS IN THE ANALYSIS OF GOVERNMENT FAILURE

Our discussion so far has suggested actions policy analysts can take to raise their awareness of the potential for government failure. Here, a set of specific steps is introduced. By working through these steps, policy analysts can improve their ability to thoroughly and critically scrutinize a policy area for the presence of government failure. This approach is also intended to assist policy analysts design new policies and programs that are less susceptible to common types of government failure.

Step 1. Define the area of policy interest. After taking this step, you should be able to state clearly the focus of your analysis. For example, you might state, "This is a study of recent efforts to improve palliative care for victims of child cancer living in Columbus, Ohio" or "This is a study of public-private partnerships in expressway provision in Ontario." Two things are achieved by defining the area of policy interest, rather than taking a thematic approach to government failure. First, the scope of the analytical work is reduced. Good efforts to analyze government failure engage with the design features of a specific set of policies and the program or programs that emerge from them. Second, most policy problems emerge out of contexts in which combinations of centralized decision making (government actions) and decentralized decision making (market activities) have produced observed outcomes. Defining the area of policy interest ensures that we do not focus on government failure while ignoring the potential for failures from other nongovernment institutions and processes.

Step 2. Determine the objectives of government action. Public policies and the programs established to implement them are typically developed to address perceived problems. Instances of market failure or failure in other social institutions often provide grounds for policy interventions. It is helpful for policy analysts to learn the arguments made for government action in the specific policy areas of interest to them. This is a good way to gain insights into the problem or problems that government actions have been called upon to address.

Step 3. Note the nature of information and coordination problems that can arise through reliance on decentralized, private decision making. Collective action in the form of government policies and programs is usually undertaken because voluntary arrangements among individuals have not produced desired results. Reflecting on the sources of market failure, we find that information problems are often present. In the absence of adequate information, it is difficult to specify and assign property rights. Voluntary coordination among individuals also becomes difficult in such cases, because information and well-defined property rights are vital ingredients in the creation of private incentives. An appreciation of the information and coordination problems that have prompted calls for government action is an essential prerequisite for analyzing government failure. When problems have fallen into the "too hard" basket of the marketplace or other social institutions, it is often fanciful to believe that government responses will address them fully. By understanding the nature and magnitude of the initial problems, we can gain clarity into what government actions can and cannot accomplish.

Step 4. Contrast the current or favored government actions with possible alternatives. Whenever we observe institutional structures and claim that actions and outcomes associated with them represent forms of "failure," an implicit comparison is being made. It is vital that we make such comparison explicit. The best way to do this is to consider what actual possible alternative arrangements could replace the current or favored government actions. For example, concerns might have been raised that the regime of regulations for electricity production and supply in North Carolina has stifled competition. People claim that the absence of competition is creating high prices and a generation and distribution network that is outdated and prone to breakdowns. In this example, policy analysts could make useful contributions to policy discussion by looking for evidence of locations where different regulatory regimes are generating different outcomes. Suppose evidence could be found that another jurisdiction close by—say, South Carolina—has greater competition, lower electricity prices, and more reliable supply. This evidence would suggest that North Carolina has some useful things to learn from South Carolina about electricity regulation.

Step 5. Identify opportunities for undue political interference in program management. A major concern in the government failure literature is that efforts to rectify market failures can transfer too much power into the hands of a few people—elected or appointed decision makers. Policy analysts must consider the ways that a particular set of policies and programs associated with them could create opportunities for undue political interference, or have already done so. How deep into the running of a program could a politician reach? How could the program be used to advance the interests of the politician over the interests of citizens and consumers of the program? To develop answers to questions of this kind, the policy analyst will usually have to consider the historical record of a given program. When a new policy or program is being designed, the questions might be answered by observing the practices of politicians in programs with similar design elements, either within their jurisdiction or in others that offer relevant comparisons.

Step 6. Identify opportunities for provider capture.   Policy analysts should consider how powerful actors associated with service delivery in the policy area of interest have manipulated policy settings or program operations, or could do so, in order to realize benefits to the detriment of other stakeholders. For example, we know that teachers' unions are powerful and can have a lot of influence both on the design of education policies and the implementation of policies at the school district level (Moe 2006, 2009). Policy analysts seeking to explore the potential for government failure in some aspects of public schooling would be wise to consider the practices of teachers' unions. More generally, it is important to anticipate that key players in any context are likely to try to arrange things so that they benefit. Such action is rational. But policy design that allows powerful interests to benefit at the expense of weaker players is rarely beneficial to society as a whole.

Step 7. Identify perverse incentives and unintended outcomes.   Sometimes policies designed to achieve a given result produce outcomes that were unintended. Those unintended outcomes arise because the policies—perhaps through their interactions with other policy settings—establish perverse incentives for relevant actors. Knowledge of cases in which perverse incentives were created can provide useful lessons for policy analysts. Because there can be blind spots in the development of policy and program design, it is helpful for policy analysts to brainstorm with others to explore the potential for perverse incentives to be established and unintended outcomes to be realized within the policy area of interest.

Step 8. Propose changes in policy design to reduce observed government failure.   Some sources of government failure will produce more serious problems than others. It is rare to find perfect policy settings, just as it is rare to find perfectly functioning markets. This suggests that policy analysts should carefully prioritize around sources of government failure that deserve most attention. The appropriateness of prescriptions to address government failure will depend greatly on the context. Sometimes, small changes in policy design can be enough to address a significant form of government failure. At other times, much more thorough policy reform would be necessary. Indeed, there could be times when almost completely removing government actions in an area would be desirable. However, it is essential that policy analysts pay close attention to the political context when they are considering proposals to reduce government failure. When powerful interests are closely involved in the policy-making process, decision makers can find it difficult to move beyond the making of political calculations and think clearly about the longer-term consequences of their choices. Sensitivity to the political game can increase the chances that policy analysts will be able to propose policy designs that will reduce government failure and produce broad social gains. This is not to deny that the political game itself is viewed by some as the heart of government failure. Policy analysis is not about creating nirvana in one move.

Step 9. Consider ways that reliance on government action could be reduced over time. Government failure often emerges because government becomes synonymous with the delivery of goods and services in particular areas of human activity. The concentration of interests and the long-term development of ways of thinking both serve to inhibit reform efforts that could reduce the scope for government failure. As hard as it will often be, there is merit in policy analysts considering proposals for policy design that might help to loosen the grip of government on specific activities. For example, in areas where government has been closely involved in most aspects of both the funding and delivery of services, consideration might be given to creating opportunities for contracting out some aspects of service delivery. As another example, moves might be initiated to reduce government regulation in a sector and to introduce more self-regulation on the part of industry participants. Looking for ways to achieve more balance between reliance on government and the use of market-like arrangements can assist in breaking down entrenched ways of doing things. That can be a good way to reduce the prospects of government failure.

AN APPLIED EXAMPLE

This section highlights analysis contained in the following:

Martin Lodge. (2002). "The Wrong Type of Regulation? Regulatory Failure and the Railways in Britain and Germany." *Journal of Public Policy* 22: 271–297.

The development of railroad systems in the nineteenth century gave great energy to the Industrial Revolution in the old countries of Europe. The railroads were also critical to industrial development and the opening of the West in the United States. In addition, railroads became integral to colonization projects, especially those of the British Empire in India and the African continent. Today, railroads continue to be a vital part of the transportation infrastructure of all developed countries. The upgrading and expansion of railroad systems continue to be viewed as critical to the economic development of emerging economies. This is despite the emergence during the twentieth century of airlines, which eroded the passenger transportation base of railroad systems in some locations. Further, even while railroads were greatly affected by the development of trucking industries based on the expansion of highway systems, railroads have never lost their central place in the freight haulage infrastructure of both developed and developing countries.

Railroad systems involve huge amounts of infrastructure. For much of their history, this led them to be treated as natural monopolies. As a result, most railroad systems were owned and operated by governments from the outset. Those that happened to be privately owned and operated were heavily subsidized and heavily regulated by governments. Over the past few decades, governments in many countries have worried about the cost of their railroad systems. They have also sought to have them operate more effectively and efficiently. Toward this end, a variety of experimental approaches have been undertaken toward the governance, ownership, and management of railroads.

Martin Lodge (2002) carefully documented the efforts of governments in Britain and Germany to improve the performance of their railroad systems. Interestingly, Lodge showed that while the Germans were seeking to achieve greater centralization of control of their railroad systems, the British were experimenting with changes in the ownership structure of their railroads. In both instances, the governments ran into major difficulties in seeking to make their railroads work better. This led Lodge to conclude that no particular way of governing railroad systems could be said to be preferable to all others. A lot would depend upon context. In his article, Lodge explored instance of regulatory failure, which should be understood as falling within the broader umbrella of government failure. Here, Lodge's analysis of failure in the British case is used to illustrate how the analysis of government failure can generate useful insights concerning policy design.

Step 1. Define the area of policy interest. This is a study of the governance of the railroads in Britain during the 1990s. Here, the term *governance* is used to cover issues of ownership, management, subsidization by government, and the structuring of the regulatory regime under which the railroads operated. For our purposes, it is useful to think of the railroads as having two major components. One is track infrastructure. This comprises the network of tracks, the power supply, the communications systems, and train controllers that allow trains to run from place to place. The second component is train operations. This we can think of as the engines, wagons, carriages, and systems that provide an interface between trains and passengers and trains and freight. Lodge observed that, during the 1990s, "apart from a continuous stream of stories of high level spin and conspiracy involving the former Secretary of State for Transport... criticisms targeted the design of the regulatory regime, the perceived decline in safety, poor operational performance, the financial decline of train operators and the financial collapse of the privatised infrastructure operator" (2002: 271). Lodge's interest lay in explaining the design of public policies toward the railroad and the consequences of government actions. To do this, he had to consider the actions of other, nongovernment stakeholders as well as the actions of government.

Step 2. Determine the objectives of government action. Government had played a significant role in the development of the railroads in Britain and government ownership and operation of the railroads continued into the 1980s. Because of the major costs associated with creating railroads systems, it was common for governments to be heavily involved in their operations. However, in the British case, pressure for change came from two sources. First, there was a view among many analysts in Britain that selling some aspects of the railroads to private companies would lead to improved performance. Second, the European Union, which provided some subsidies for railroad systems in Europe, had called for "vertical separation" of national railroads operations, at least in accounting terms. The concern here was that too much power lay in the hands of railroad managers when they had control over all aspects of the railroad systems—that is, both track infrastructure and train operations. Potentially, so much control in a few hands could reduce incentives for making efficiency gains, while opening the possibility of train users—passengers and shippers of freight—being subjected to monopoly pricing.

Step 3. Note the nature of information and coordination problems that can arise through reliance on decentralized, private decision making. Due to the need to have multiple trains using a limited number of tracks, railroad systems are always susceptible to coordination problems. As a result, it has been common to find track infrastructure and train operations within specific regions owned and controlled by one entity—either a government-owned company or a private company. However, with improvements in communication systems, it has become technically possible to separate track infrastructure and train operations. That technological change opened the potential for track infrastructure to be owned and managed by one company and for train operations to be owned and managed by one or more other companies.

Step 4. Contrast the current or favored government actions with possible alternatives. In Britain, efforts began in the 1980s to try to reform the operations of British Rail, the government-owned and -operated monopoly. Technology opened up opportunities for multiple train operators—some focusing on passengers and others focusing on freight—to operate on the same tracks. As such, the rationale no longer existed for old systems of concentrated ownership and control. However, while greater reliance could now be placed on decentralized, private decision making in the railroads industry, powerful interests that had benefited from a monopoly-like situation did not like the idea of competition. In addition, many years of living with a government-owned monopoly served to condition many citizens to prefer that system, even if the trains ran slowly.

Martin Lodge's discussion of regulatory failure started with the British reform process of the 1990s. Several possible reform options were proposed. They included privatization of British Rail as an integrated company. This would have created a private monopoly subject to government regulation. Another alternative involved creating several private, integrated companies to own and operate all aspects of the railroads in different regions of the country. The actual approach taken was different again. Ownership and management of the track infrastructure was placed in private hands. The infrastructure monopoly was called Railtrack. Contracts, or franchises, were given to a set of companies to manage passenger service train operations. The state-owned companies that maintained the freight trains were all sold as a package to one private company. Management of track infrastructure was split between the owner, Railtrack, and another that performed maintenance on it. The Office of the Rail Regulator was established to protect user interests, to keep an eye on the actions of Railtrack, and to promote development of the railroad network. Lodge's interest lay in identifying the sources of failure that accompanied the efforts to reform the governance of the British railroads.

Step 5. Identify opportunities for undue political interference in program management. Terry Moe's (1991) observation that political organizations often "loom as structural nightmares" (p. 127) is helpful to keep in mind. Policy analysts and advisers in the British Treasury were the dominant architects of the reforms of the British railroads. They were keenly aware of the possibility that defeat of the government led by Prime Minister John Major could result in the reversal of railroad reform efforts. For that reason, the old British Rail was split up in ways that would make it hard to put back together by a new government. Note that the reforms were informed by a political logic. That logic can lead in directions distinctively different from a logic informed by the goal of maximizing system efficiency subject to known constraints.

Step 6. Identify opportunities for provider capture. Concern about provider capture also dominated the British railroad reform activities. As a result, input from British Rail into the reform plans was limited to advice on technical details. The creation of a private company, Railtrack, to manage track infrastructure was viewed as a deliberate move to further marginalize those whose interests were closely aligned with British Rail.

Step 7. Identify perverse incentives and unintended outcomes. Following the reforms, the railroads appeared to do well. Passenger travel increased by 35 percent in the decade from 1992 until 2002. Rail freight volumes increased by over 40 percent from the mid-1990s to 2002. The railroads also gained back market share that they had been steadily losing. By 2002, that market share returned to 1980s levels. However, as service usage increased, customer complaints about train operations increased. The reforms of the British railroads established in the 1990s were not completely overturned when a new political party came into power. That had been a concern of the reformers. However, greater politicization of railroads governance did occur and some structural changes were made. The Strategic Railway Authority was established and charged with providing a strategic overview of the railroad industry in Britain. Through appointments of the head of this agency, the government sought to exercise more control over railroad operations. The Strategic Railway Authority also started to compete for influence with the Office of the Rail Regulator. Railtrack, the private company that owned and managed the track infrastructure, was subjected to closer scrutiny than before. In 2001, Railtrack was taken into government administration. The company had continuously requested more subsidies for infrastructure development and had been rebuffed. In addition, while the government was prepared to increase its subsidies to various components of the railroad system, this support appeared to come with greater levels of political interference in the day-to-day operations of relevant companies.

A trade-off arose between government actions and the pursuit of an expanded railroad system. Catastrophic events like passenger train crashes were considered politically risky for the government. In response, the government sought to "manage" the railroad system to avoid recurrence of problems. However, that managerial mindset sent signals about the government's preference for interfering in railroads operations. Companies and investors that might have otherwise contributed to the growth of the reformed railroad system became nervous about further involvement in the industry. To this extent, the actions of the government could be seen as having had a detrimental effect on the railroads.

Step 8. Propose changes in policy design to reduce observed government failure. The case of the governance of the British railroads suggests several insights for would-be reformers. First, it is important to avoid policy design becoming too dominated by political calculations. The initial reforms were complicated in how they split up ownership and responsibility between governmental and nongovernmental entities. Subsequent small changes by a new government tended to exacerbate contradictions already built into the reforms. Second, there was an expectation that privatization would lead to greater private investment in the railroads. That did not occur at anticipated levels. One explanation is that the monopolist position created for Railtrack gave too few incentives for the company to engage in capital-raising efforts. Another explanation is that the threat of ongoing government involvement in the industry made investors shy. The British case does suggest that too much government interference in day-to-day operations of an industry can inhibit private sector-driven expansion.

Step 9. Consider ways that reliance on government action could be reduced over time. The reform of the British railroads offers a good case in which reliance on government action could have been reduced over time. Had privatization occurred in a manner that better reflected market realities rather than political calculations, a robust pathway could have been established toward virtual full privatization of the system. Martin Lodge argued that the reform efforts had some fundamental design flaws. He noted that "the initial regime had been designed to account for decline, minimising risks of regime collapse by safeguarding financial viability and downplaying operational risk-taking. This regime was unable to generate incentives for additional services in the light of rising passenger and freight traffic flows" (2002: 292). While the British railroad reform efforts were far from perfect, they do provide lessons that could usefully enlighten reform efforts in other countries. Even in Britain, lessons for future reforms could be usefully drawn from past mistakes.

ADVICE FOR ANALYTICAL PRACTICE

The following points are useful to bear in mind when analyzing potential sources of government failure and their effects.

- Government actions are typically predicated on assertions that other, non-government institutions cannot reliably address perceived problems. Those assertions should be carefully scrutinized.
- Due to the nature of interests in society and the difficulties of getting politicians to focus at length on specific policy issues, it is almost always easier to introduce a new government entity than it is to eliminate an old one, even if that old one is very obviously not performing at desired levels.
- People in positions of power rarely embrace change unless they are convinced that the change will make them better off.
- Sound estimates of the costs of failing systems, combined with evidence of the workability of alternative systems, can promote organizational change.
- Market and market-like processes create strong incentives for producers to innovate, either in the pursuit of production efficiencies or in the pursuit of more customers.
- Well-defined goals, clear performance indicators, and strong accountability mechanisms can encourage effective organizational practices.

ANALYSIS OF GOVERNMENT FAILURE AND OTHER ANALYTICAL STRATEGIES

Our review and discussion of analytical strategies to this point suggests an important consideration. That is, policy analysts should help people engaged in policy debates get beyond bumper sticker assertions that "government is bad—markets are good" or "government is good—markets are bad." We need to think very carefully about the full range of costs and benefits that are associated with alternative institutional arrangements. We need to see that markets rely upon government and that governments rely upon markets. At all times, it is useful to ask the following question, which places emphasis on the unique nature of specific circumstances.

From the point of view of achieving the best resource allocation, what combination of markets and government would serve us best in this instance?

It is also helpful to temper that question with another.

Would the most economically efficient outcome also be the one most desirable from the point of view of equity and human dignity?

Finally, an enormous amount of evidence now exists on the workings of markets and the workings of governments. Policy analysts should consciously draw upon that evidence to guide their thinking about policy development and the recommendations they make for policy change. Consideration of government failure reminds us that, aside from their potential to have positive effects, public policies can also generate negative effects. It is especially helpful for policy analysts to think about the dynamic nature of the effects that policies can have. That notion is captured in the following questions.

> *If we put this policy in place, what will be the immediate result? But then what might also happen as a consequence of this policy?*

Asking hard questions about the consequences of new policies is better than basing new policies on limited analysis and then blaming government in some sort of blanket way. As we work through analytical strategies available to policy analysts, we will next consider comparative institutional analysis and cost-benefit analysis. These analytical strategies can both be usefully combined with the analysis of market failure and the analysis of government failure.

Exercises

1. Markets allocate resources. Sometimes markets fail. When markets fail, government policy interventions are sometimes justified. But government actions can fail too. Together, make a list of public problems that have recently gained popular attention. Next, discuss each problem and decide whether it has been created by market failure, by government failure, by a combination of the two, or by something else.

2. Once established, government programs can be difficult to reform or eliminate, even when they are considered to no longer be performing effectively or to have outlasted their usefulness altogether. Suppose that policy makers were interested in achieving better alignment between the operating times of schools (the length of the school day, the duration of school holidays, etc.) and the workplace commitments expected of working parents. Where do you anticipate that changes could be readily made? Can you think of any changes that might be generally desirable but that would be very difficult to introduce? In discussing your answers to these questions, what insights emerge about social coordination problems and our abilities to resolve them?

The Policy Research Seminar

Organize a research-oriented seminar that will run for about ninety minutes, preferably with some light refreshments. Invite up to twelve people, and make sure you have a mixture of experienced researchers, junior researchers, and graduate students. The purpose of the discussion should be to develop ideas for the design of policy research projects that give a central place to the analysis of government failure. The project ideas should be sufficiently interesting and original that each could form the basis of a significant research paper, dissertation, or thesis. Participants should come to the seminar having read both this chapter and Martin Lodge's (2002) "The Wrong Type of Regulation? Regulatory Failure and the Railways in Britain and Germany" (*Journal of Public Policy* 22: 271–297). You might structure the discussion around the Steps in the Analysis of Government Failure presented in this chapter and applied in the overview of the Lodge study. Many other recent journal articles could have been highlighted in this chapter. Prior to the group meeting, you might have several participants locate other interesting articles that present original analyses of government failure. Discussions of this sort tend to work best when the group has a clear goal. I suggest this outcome statement: "By the end of this meeting we will have identified five possible topics for new research projects that involve analysis of government failure. We will have sketched out basic research designs for at least two of those projects." Brainstorm to get some ideas flowing. Hold the more skeptical, analytical comments until later in the seminar. Ideally, some members of the discussion group will follow up on the meeting and continue to develop, perhaps collaboratively, research designs that build from the readings and the discussion. This is a good way to promote original policy research inspired by the best contemporary applications of quantitative and qualitative research methods. For additional advice on how to run effective meetings of this kind, see (1) Michael Mintrom's (2003) "Facilitating Meetings" in *People Skills for Policy Analysts* (Washington, DC: Georgetown University Press) and (2) Tom Kelley's (2001) "The Perfect Brainstorm" in *The Art of Innovation* (New York: Currency/Doubleday).

Further Reading

Bok, Derek. (2001). "The Usual Suspects" In *The Trouble with Government*, chap. 3. Cambridge, MA: Harvard University Press.

Friedman, Milton. (1962). "The Role of Government in a Free Society." In *Capitalism and Freedom*, chap. 2. Chicago: University of Chicago Press.

Le Grand, Julian. (1991). "The Theory of Government Failure." *British Journal of Political Science* 21: 423–442.

Weimer, David L., and Aidan R. Vining. (2005). "Limits to Public Intervention: Government Failures." In *Policy Analysis: Concepts and Practice*, 4th ed., chap. 8. Upper Saddle River, NJ: Pearson Prentice Hall.

Winston, Clifford. (2006). "Policies to Correct Market Failures: Synthesis and Assessment." In *Government Failure versus Market Failure*, chap. 6. Washington, DC: AEI-Brookings Joint Center for Regulatory Studies.

Wolf, Charles, Jr. (1979). "A Theory of Non-market Failures." *Public Interest* 55: 114–133.

Comparative Institutional Analysis

The Story So Far... Society is made up of institutions that provide the rules of the game that we live by. Government systems, markets, the family, and organized religions are all instances of social institutions. Public policy can be viewed as efforts to promote better social outcomes through changing institutional structures.

Here... This chapter reviews how policy analysts can use comparative institutional analysis. Use of this technique, which compares working examples of institutional arrangements, can provide powerful evidence for supporting the development of effective public policies.

THIS CHAPTER REVIEWS

- The nature of comparative institutional analysis
- How to use comparative institutional analysis as an analytical framework in a policy project
- Steps in comparative institutional analysis
- Advice for analytical practice using this framework

Governments constantly borrow policy ideas from elsewhere when seeking to address problems in their own jurisdictions. From the perspective of saving time and effort, this can make a lot of sense. Further, when uniformity of policy approach is considered important for easing business transactions or for reducing complications in citizens' lives, taking policy cues from other governments would seem a reasonable strategy (Esping-Andersen 1990; Williamson 1994). In his classic article on the diffusion of policy innovations, Jack Walker (1969: 881) noted an instance of a fair trade law adopted by California. The law was subsequently adopted, word for word with minor variations, by twenty other states of the United States. Ten of those states even copied a couple of serious typos from the original California law. The nature of borrowing can run from this kind of straightforward copying of policies introduced elsewhere to more sophisticated responses to models developed and implemented by others (Glick and Hays 1991; Karch 2007; Volden 2006). When is it appropriate to directly copy policies from elsewhere? When would it be more appropriate to treat a policy from elsewhere as a model and then reinvent it to suit local conditions? In this chapter, we explore the nature of comparative institutional analysis. This is a general framework that can be usefully employed to advance our thinking about the identification and development of effective policy responses to specific problems.

Early in the development of policy analysis as a discipline, practitioners sometimes took the view that any given problem caused by decentralized, private decision making could be effectively remedied by government interventions. Responding to this tendency, the economist Harold Demsetz observed the following:

> The view that now pervades much public policy economics implicitly presents the relevant choice as between an ideal norm and an existing "imperfect" institutional arrangement. This nirvana approach differs considerably from a comparative institution approach in which the relevant choice is between alternative real institutional arrangements. (1969: 1)

Comparative institutional analysis is predicated on the view that effective policy responses to current problems are most likely to be struck on when policy design is closely informed by knowledge of actual working policy settings found elsewhere.

Intellectually, the roots of comparative institutional analysis can be traced back to the development of theories of the firm. As mentioned in Chapter 10, Ronald Coase (1937) asked a comparative institutional question when he wondered why, in a world of well-functioning markets, the existence of firms was necessary. Coase concluded that transaction costs associated with organizing production through markets can become so significant that it is cheaper for entrepreneurs to establish firms, create sets of labor contracts, and use hierarchical organization to direct production processes. Coase's analysis laid the groundwork for an extensive and fruitful research tradition. Major contributions that advanced comparative institutional analysis explored different organizational forms that firms can take, and how the nature of the work performed influences ownership structures and payment systems (Alchian and Demsetz 1972; Williamson 1975, 1985; Williamson and Winter 1991). Notable applications of comparative institutional analysis to understanding political organization have built on this research tradition grounded in theories of the firm. They include broad approaches to assessing the development of property rights and economic policies (North 1990; Ostrom 1990), analyses of the structure of government agencies (Horn 1995; Moe 1990), and a variety of more specific comparative studies (Alston, Eggertsson, and North 1996; Banks and Hanushek 1995; Chubb and Moe 1990; Huber and Shipan

2002). In all cases, the aim has been to identify differences in institutional design, explain the reasons for those differences, and explore the impacts of those differences on specific outcomes. For example, in their pathbreaking study of schools in America, John Chubb and Terry Moe (1990) investigated whether private schools produced better student outcomes—measured by test scores—than traditional public schools. Based on their finding that private schools tended to perform better and at lower cost, Chubb and Moe proposed a radical plan for restructuring the system of schooling in the United States.

On initial reflection, we might reasonably worry that comparative institutional analysis is conservative, that its prescription of taking our cue from existing policy settings stifles the possibility of original thought. An alternative response recognizes that the focus on actual working policy settings can promote creativity. Through playing around with evidence from elsewhere, by talking through the possibilities, we might develop breakthrough policy designs (Donahue 1999; Ingraham 2007; Levin and Sanger 1994). This is a model of discovery through induction rather than deduction. For sure, it favors evolutionary advance. But evolution can generate astonishing performance gains. Think about the advances in the development of the automobile, or in air travel. Consider the creation of handheld computing and communication devices. In all instances, thinking and design evolved through people examining real, working examples and innovating from there.

Practicing policy analysts know that a lot of policy design work involves taking cues from already existing working examples that approximate solutions to the problem at hand. Several policy scholars have recently proposed strategies for systematizing this kind of cue taking (Bardach 2008; Barzelay 2007; Rose 2005). It is important to note that the term *comparative institutional analysis* is not employed uniformly by those who have contributed relevant analytical tools. But the term is used here because it is able to encapsulate a variety of research designs. Those include efforts to learn from comparing policy settings across points in history. For example, we could compare a system of public funding for hospitals that was employed two decades ago with a system used now. We can also subsume in this analytical approach efforts made to learn from policy settings in areas that do not share substantive similarities with the focus of study, but that nonetheless offer valuable insights for policy deign. For example, we could seek to draw lessons from contemporary management of military equipment procurement processes to inform the design of contracts for the management of water purity levels in river systems.

AN OVERVIEW OF COMPARATIVE INSTITUTIONAL ANALYSIS

Comparative institutional analysis has become a popular research strategy among social scientists during the past three decades. This rise in popularity is directly linked with the emergence of what has been termed the "new institutionalism" in three fields: economics, sociology, and political science. Of course, social thinkers and social scientists have always been interested in describing different governmental structures, analyzing how structural differences influence the actions of proximate actors, and assessing overall outcomes. Classic contributions along these lines include Baron de Montesquieu's *The Spirit of Laws* ([1751]1878), Adam Smith's *The Wealth of Nations* (1776), and Alexis de Tocqueville's *Democracy in America* ([1835]2004). A common critique of institutionalist scholarship, as it was conducted in the mid-twentieth century, is that it became too fixated on description of structures. Little attention was paid to the motivations of actors within those structures, let alone the motivations of those who designed and implemented the structures in the first place (Peters 1996; Rhodes 2006). While this style of work was becoming a scholarly backwater, the behavioralist revolution in the social sciences was in full swing. Behavioralism, with its intense focus on the individual as the unit of analysis, came with its own blind spots. In particular, it gave short shrift to the ways that an individual's actions in many social settings were mediated by the formal rules and arrangements that comprise our social architecture. The new institutionalism can be viewed as a corrective both to the dry, descriptive aspects of the earlier work on institutions and to the context-free extremes of social science in the behavioralist tradition. Today, although practiced in a wide variety of ways, institutional analysis tends to share a common intention of exploring the interplay between the formal rules that structure our social, political, and economic activities, on the one hand, and the motivations and practices of intendedly rational individuals and collections of individuals, on the other (March and Olsen 2006; Morgan et al. 2010).

Institutions are typically described as the established rules of the game that constrain and guide the actions of individuals and groups in society (North 1990; Scott 2008.) Institutions provide high levels of stability in our social world. As such, they reduce the need for people to continually determine and negotiate appropriate ways to behave in a broad range of settings. Institutions formalize "norms of appropriateness" (March and Olsen 1989). While they place limits on admissible actions of individuals, the stable environments that they establish create conditions that enable high levels of creative action and human flourishing. At the broadest levels, we can think of decisions concerning choice of a common language, a common monetary currency, a system of government, property rights, a justice system, and various aspects of commercial practice as fundamental institutional structures that shape and facilitate social interactions. Of course, facilitative rules of the game must be specified across all areas of life. As a consequence, stable institutional arrangements are ubiquitous. Government actions, in the form of the development of public policies that are transformed into laws and administrative structures, represent efforts to augment and improve existing institutional arrangements.

Contemporary institutional analysis is performed by social scientists across a range of disciplines (Hall and Taylor 1996; March and Olsen 1984; Reich 2000). Typically, that analysis is curiosity-driven. It is instigated with the intention of understanding how specific institutional arrangements structure particular social, economic, or political contexts, how individuals and groups interpret those contexts, how they conduct themselves within them, and what causal links can be found among the relevant institutional arrangements and observed outcomes. Within this kind of research, comparison across institutional arrangements and contexts is crucial to improving the power of the analytical work. To make valid claims that institutions affect observed actions and outcomes, scholars need to be able to indicate variation. And variation can be observed only when a study involves two or more cases. Note, however, that a study of one case over time can allow for variation. Indeed, a lot of insightful studies incorporating institutional analysis have been produced that involve the comparison of institutional structures, the conduct of individuals and groups, and observed outcomes at discrete points in time (Carpenter 2010; Mahoney and Thelen 2010; Moe 1985; Thelen 1999). Research of this type can be valuable both for demonstrating the effects of different institutional arrangements and for offering insights into the dynamics of institutional change through time.

Policy analysts confronting policy problems in a given jurisdiction can use comparative institutional analysis to advantage. The approach lends itself to the drawing of lessons from practice to inform the design of rules and arrangements that might address the problem at hand. Given that academic research involving comparative institutional analysis is often highly detailed and can be based on months or years of in-depth work, there is a danger that work conducted over a shorter time frame might appear superficial and limited with respect to the insights it can yield. We should definitely be vigilant to the possibility that our work will lack depth. At the same time, we should not let concerns about the limits on what is feasible become immobilizing. The challenge we confront is to do the best we can with the resources and time at our disposal. There is no substitute for hard thinking. We need to think about what we can hope to gain from a comparative institutional analysis, given the problem we wish to address. We need to itemize the biggest gaps in our relevant knowledge before we can move ahead with our own institutional design work. Finally, we must find ways to increase our confidence that the lessons we hope to draw from our comparative institutional analyses will be valid.

USING COMPARATIVE INSTITUTIONAL ANALYSIS AS AN ANALYTICAL FRAMEWORK

Comparative institutional analysis is of most use to policy analysts when they are at the early stages of thinking about approaches to addressing a policy problem. Policy development work is often characterized as involving problem-directed searches for possible policy solutions. Although this is not a bad approximation of what takes place, the characterization does not capture an interesting aspect of the relationship between problems and solutions. Aaron Wildavsky (1979) argued that people wrestle with policy problems only when they sense that feasible solutions exist. In Wildavsky's view, then, problems and solutions come intertwined. This view has been supported by subsequent contributions to policy scholarship where emphasis has been placed on the social construction of problems (Cobb and Elder 1983; Schneider and Ingram 1997). John Kingdon (1984) suggested that it is commonplace to observe solutions chasing problems, which turns on its head the whole notion of problem-directed search. For our purposes, the key point is that comparative institutional analysis, when conducted early in the process of addressing a policy problem, has the potential to help us sharpen the definition of the problem and begin thinking about potential ways to address it.

To keep comparative institutional analyses manageable, it is essential for policy analysts to define the scope of their investigations. An obvious way to do this is to limit the number of cases that will be included. More subtly, the scope of any investigation can be effectively managed through careful determination of the features of an already existing institutional arrangement that are expected to be of most relevance, given the policy problem to be addressed.

Consider the following example. The school board of a medium-sized city in the United States has asked its policy analysts to explore feasible approaches to improving the quality of instruction in the city's public schools. The analysts are also told that they must come up with options for policy change that will yield observable improvements in a short space of time. Comparative institutional analysis could be usefully employed here. The scope of the investigation could be managed by sticking closely with the brief. Note two things. First, nothing has been said about improving the quality of instruction in every public school. Second, nothing has been said to imply that improvement will be measured in terms of net gains in average student scores on standardized tests. As a result, given the challenge at hand, it would be entirely reasonable for the policy analysts to focus their comparative institutional analysis on the introduction and apparent effectiveness of specific professional development programs for public school teachers. Taking this approach, they could proceed to determine what programs along these lines had been introduced in their city over the past decade, and with what results. What measures of success were employed? Were the programs deemed successful? What broader contextual factors appeared to moderate or even undermine program success? Under what circumstances might these programs have enjoyed more success? With this preliminary work in their own city completed, the policy analysts could begin to look around for efforts elsewhere that have been deemed effective in improving the quality of instruction in the local schools. Having identified candidate cases to study, they could limit the scope of their work by asking fewer questions of the programs and institutional arrangements to be studied. For instance, they could ask questions about program scope, cost, uptake, and perceived success. They could also ask questions about how broader structural arrangements appeared to support or undermine various programs. By asking a relatively small number of well-focused questions, they would be likely to gain insights into the feasibility of introducing similar programs in their own city.

It is inevitable that comparative institutional analyses of this kind will be criticized for what is left out. However, the very act of building knowledge of what has been tried elsewhere and how structural factors affected program results can be valuable for promoting intelligent conversation about effective policy design.

STEPS IN COMPARATIVE INSTITUTIONAL ANALYSIS

The details of any specific comparative institutional analysis are likely to be somewhat idiosyncratic. In all cases, analysts must adapt their approach to accommodate the nature of the policy questions motivating their work and the actual set of institutional arrangements they choose to study. Nonetheless, the following steps are offered as a general guide to conducting this kind of analysis. An applied example is presented in the section to follow. It illustrates one application of comparative institutional analysis and how it was used to generate insights for policy design.

Step 1. Select and refine the analytical questions. You need to define the policy problem you face and describe relevant current institutional settings in the jurisdiction where the problem has been observed. The relevant current institutional settings will include administrative practices, rules, structures, and governing laws. What is the view of these current arrangements? How do they serve to address the observed policy problem? How might they contribute to it? Try to describe the concerns that people have noted with the current situation. Perhaps this will result in a policy wish list, a set of things people think would be helpful for addressing the problem. From here, you can establish a short list of questions you will use to compare and contrast the situation in your jurisdiction with the situation elsewhere.

Step 2. Develop a research design, and select cases. Having identified the questions to motivate your study, you now need to develop a credible approach to answering them. Most likely, you will want to compare a set of institutional arrangements where the problem has been effectively addressed with the institutional arrangements where the problem is currently observed. The more stark the difference between the observed outcomes in your chosen institutional contexts, the more opportunities you will have for making comparisons that offer clear insights for improving policy design. However, you do not want to draw comparisons among cases in which no reasonable grounds for comparison actually exist. This suggests, then, that you should try to work with cases in which many of the broader institutional settings are similar but distinct differences can be observed in the treatment of the problem that you care about. In terms of the actual research design, you can choose to conduct detailed case study work, or some form of quantitative work, or a combination of both. A lot will depend here on the choice of the unit for analysis.

Step 3. Collect and analyze the relevant information. Once you have developed a research design and selected your cases for comparison, you will need to

Table 12.1 Setting Up a Comparative Institutional Analysis

COMPARISON CONTEXTS	RELEVANT INSTITUTIONAL DESIGN FEATURES	RELEVANT OBSERVED PRACTICES	RELEVANT OBSERVED OUTCOMES
Context A			
Context B			

gather relevant information and data. It is helpful at this stage to clarify the specific aspects of the institutional structures, the specific practices, and the specific outcomes that you will focus upon. Creating a matrix can help to guide the work, because it forces you to ensure that relevant information is being collected on each element of interest. See Table 12.1. The challenge is to find the information needed to complete the empty cells in this table. Once that information has been found, comparisons can be made across the cases. The aim is to specify the ways that differences in institutional design produce different observed practices and outcomes.

Step 4. Isolate the relationships between institutional choice and observed outcomes. A fundamental concern when we are conducting comparative institutional analysis is to ensure that any claims made about the effects of institutional design are, in fact, plausible. You do not want to conduct analysis and then have people claim that observed outcomes were driven by completely different factors that had nothing to do with the differences in institutional design. For example, suppose we were interested in exploring the effects of different systems for ensuring ongoing contact between mothers of newborn children and their general practitioners. We might also wish to know whether, across a population group, frequency of interactions between mothers and their general practitioners result in better observed health outcomes for the children after a year. The problem we confront is that differences in observed health outcomes for the children might be driven by differences in the wealth found in the jurisdictions being compared or differences in the training programs for general practitioners. These differences would not be included in our study, unless we had thought about them in advance. This is why, before we begin our study, we need to have a good sense of the institutional effects we will be looking for and possible alternative explanations that we will need to take into account, and hopefully control for in our analysis.

Step 5. Present your findings, and make recommendations. The final step in comparative institutional analysis involves drawing lessons for policy change. Good comparative work will form the basis for proposals to improve institutional design. In presenting the findings, it is necessary to offer good evidence that the comparisons made were reasonable. It is also necessary to show how institutional arrangements affect observed behaviors and outcomes.

AN APPLIED EXAMPLE

This section highlights analysis contained in the following:

Michael Mintrom. (2001). "Policy Design for Local Innovation: The Effects of Competition in Public Schooling." *State Politics and Policy Quarterly* 1: 343–363.

The charter school movement began in the United States in the early 1990s. The intention of the movement was to create schools that were publicly funded but that were able to operate independently from many of the usual administration systems found in public school districts. Although charter schools are given greater independence from traditional systems of administrative control, families are under no obligation enroll their children within them. If the schools cannot attract a sufficient number of students, they must close down. Variations of the charter school model have now been adopted in most states of the United States. Michigan was an early adopter of this approach to introducing choice for parents sending their children to publicly funded schools. Michigan also distinguished itself as a state that gave high levels of autonomy to charter schools. When these schools were being introduced, I was interested to explore the linkage between institutional arrangements and organizational innovation (Mintrom 2001). Specifically, I wanted to test a claim made by Milton Friedman (1962) that organizations operating in market contexts are more likely to be innovative than organizations operating under tight governmental control.

The large number of charter schools in Michigan and the nature of the rules they operated under offered a good context for conducting a comparative institutional analysis. I explored how innovative charter schools were compared to traditional public schools. Because charter schools were expected to introduce market like competition into the public school system, I also made a distinction between public schools subject to competition from charter schools located in their school district and those public schools not subject to such competition. This comparative institutional analysis allowed me to make several claims. First, charter schools are more innovative than traditional public schools. Second, among traditional public schools, those subject to competition from charter schools appeared to be somewhat more innovative than their counterparts that were not subject to competition. Third, although charter schools were more innovative, they were mostly working with innovations that had originally been developed in traditional public schools. Finally, the system of introducing competition among schools tended to inhibit sharing of ideas across school communities. This suggested that efforts to improve the quality of school practices would need to be based on a range of strategies, not just competition among schools for students.

Step 1. Select and refine the analytical questions. Many people care about improving public school practices and outcomes. Some of the most significant work by scholars in this area over the past two decades has focused on differences in student test scores between traditional public schools and schools of choice (including private schools that students can attend using a publicly funded voucher). My interests lay in exploring the factors that promote innovative practices within schools. My sense was that the introduction of charter schools offered a great opportunity to compare the effects of different institutional arrangements and incentives systems on the choices made by school administrators. This led me to focus on ways that schools could demonstrate innovative practices. The areas of innovation explored included curriculum design, instructional techniques, decision-making processes, and engagement with parents. The study was limited in what it considered. As well as assessing differences in student achievement across different kinds of schools, other scholars have asked questions about how parents choose schools, the financial and accountability structures that affect different kinds of schools, and the implications for democratic practice of creating choice environments. Most of those questions are best addressed using some kind of comparative institutional design. But it is important to avoid getting too ambitious with any given study. When you want to generate sound answers to your questions, you must be prepared to limit the number of questions you ask.

Step 2. Develop a research design, and select cases. The questions to be answered and the audience to be addressed both influence research design and the choice of cases. The question driving the comparative institutional analysis of charter schools and traditional public schools was this: Is the introduction of market-like competition an effective way to promote innovative practices in schools? Whenever we conduct comparative work of any kind, we need to avoid the possibility that factors beyond our control are driving differences in observed outcomes. This concern drove the decision to confine the study to schools operating within just one state. By focusing on schools in Michigan, a range of differences in institutional arrangements that tend to be found among states could be kept from affecting the results. Having said that, it is fair to say that the study would have been more impressive if the research conducted in Michigan had been replicated in another state, say, California, and if similar results had been found in both states.

Step 3. Collect and analyze the relevant information. For this study, the decision was made to survey schools to identify the kinds of innovations that they had introduced in their practices. Once the responses were received from the schools, another survey was developed. This survey contained a list of apparently innovative activities extracted from the first survey. No information was offered on where the innovations had come from. School principals were asked to rate the innovativeness of the different practices. From the set of responses, innovation scores were developed for each school across four different areas of practice. Regression analysis was used to test the effects of different institutional arrangements on the tendency of schools to use innovative practices. Table 12.2 offers a simple summary of the main findings that emerged from the study.

Table 12.2 A Comparative Institutional Analysis of Michigan Schools

COMPARISON CONTEXTS	RELEVANT INSTITUTIONAL DESIGN FEATURES	RELEVANT OBSERVED PRACTICES	RELEVANT OBSERVED OUTCOMES
Charter schools	Must attract students	School leaders made a range of efforts to adopt practices that are attractive to parents.	High scores on innovation in various areas of school practice
Urban public schools	Must operate in a specified school district but be subject to competitive pressure from charter schools for retaining students	School leaders appeared sensitive to competition and had made some efforts to adopt practices that are attractive to parents.	Moderate scores on innovation in various areas of school practice
Suburban public schools	Must operate in a specified school district and not be subject to competition from other schools, such as charter schools	School leaders appeared to be following standard operating procedures and practices with limited reflection on their attractiveness to parents.	Low scores on innovation in various areas of school practice

Step 4. Isolate the relationships between institutional choice and observed outcomes. The study took account of plausible alternative explanations for curricular and instructional innovations across all the schools, charter and traditional. To do so, information on differences in operating budgets, school size, centralized management, perceived barriers to innovation, and student performance (measured by average test scores) was included in the regression models. Even so, the results clearly demonstrated that charter schools were more innovative than the traditional schools included in the study. As well as suggesting that competition was a motivator for this, the study revealed that the inclusiveness of school decision-making processes (i.e., consulting with parents) tended to influence the degree to which the schools were innovative in their curriculums.

Step 5. Present your findings, and make recommendations. The study results indicated the effects of different institutional arrangements on the practices of schools with respect to innovation. However, as we might expect, the study also showed that competition appeared to limit sharing of good practices across schools. This led to the proposal that more effort be made at higher administrative levels to gather information about best practice in schools and disseminate it across the whole statewide school system. The results of this study were presented in two fairly simple tables. When the information was presented to policy makers in Michigan, the focus was placed on the findings and their implications for policy design. The details of the research design and regression analysis results were not highlighted in the report for policy makers. Of course, in the academic journal article, those details were given much more prominence, so that they could receive critical scrutiny and open the possibility for replication of the results.

ADVICE FOR ANALYTICAL PRACTICE

The steps in conducting comparative institutional analysis and the applied example presented here highlight several matters to keep in mind when using this approach to build knowledge for policy development. The key points can be summarized as follows.

- Focus on how differences in institutional arrangements (such as operating rules, financial mechanisms) can affect valued outcomes.
- Avoid making comparisons when extraneous variations could significantly affect observed outcomes.
- Limit the analysis to the smallest number of cases necessary to make a valid argument.
- Limit the questions you will ask of the cases. Your study of cases will always be instrumental—you are primarily interested in what the cases can tell you about the effects of different institutional arrangements.
- Present your findings in ways that highlight relevant differences in institutional arrangements and the consequences of those differences.

COMPARATIVE INSTITUTIONAL ANALYSIS AND OTHER ANALYTICAL STRATEGIES

Comparative institutional analysis is guided by the recognition that changes to public policies, be they big or small, always take place within a broader set of structural arrangements. The nature of those arrangements holds implications both for how individuals and groups interpret those policy changes and for the effectiveness of the policies themselves. Another premise of this analytical strategy is that we can always gain useful insights from considering actual, working policy arrangements, rather than relying solely on theory to guide the design of new polices.

Comparative institutional analysis is particularly useful for policy analysts who are seeking to contribute to the process of problem definition, or whose work is intended to support agenda-setting efforts. By highlighting working models of effective policy responses elsewhere, policy analysts can help solve the inevitable risk aversion that politicians show toward introducing policy approaches that have not been previously tried in their own jurisdiction. Knowledge of market and government processes, as well as the sources of market and government failures, can increase the ability of policy analysts to make effective use of comparative institutional analysis. At its best, this form of analysis clarifies the linkages between formal rules, structural arrangements, the actions of individuals and collections of individuals, and valued social and economic outcomes.

Comparative institutional analysis offers a flexible framework from which to consider alternative real institutional arrangements. There is no formal expectation concerning the number of alternative arrangements that will be included in the analysis. Nor is there any formal expectation about the kinds of concerns that might motivate a study. This flexibility makes it highly attractive. In particular, it introduces the possibility that we might effectively employ comparative institutional analysis to consider to what extent different configurations of policies, rules, and administrative procedures produce differential impacts for different groups of people. Further, comparative institutional analysis could be combined with elements of cost-benefit analysis to help us assess the relative financial merits of alternative institutional arrangements.

Exercises

1. In small groups, discuss with one another the topics of policy projects you are currently working on or know something about. From these project topics, choose one for which you think it would make sense to conduct comparative institutional analysis.

   • Make a list of the institutional arrangements that seem most relevant to the problem at the center of the policy project. Discuss what weaknesses appear to exist in those arrangements.
   • Generate a set of up to four questions that you would ask about institutional arrangements elsewhere that might have been used to address a similar problem.
   • Be prepared to give a brief report to the full group on your topic and how you propose to approach it using comparative institutional analysis.

2. The Ash Institute for Democratic Governance and Innovation at Harvard University supports a database of government programs that have won innovation awards over the past several decades.

   • Make some time to review this database and some of the cases contained there.
   • Can you find other databases that do similar things?
   • Discuss how we could make use of such databases as part of our efforts to conduct comparative institutional analysis.

3. Many studies have been conducted that make use of comparative institutional analysis. Working in small groups, locate up to five such studies. Together, choose one of these to study closely. Following the approach used in the applied example of this chapter, develop a two- to three-page summary of the study, emphasizing the ways that its author or authors employed comparative

institutional analysis. Use this summary as the basis for an in-class, group-led discussion.

Invite a Guest to Class

How do policy practitioners learn about policy developments in other jurisdictions? What kind of filtering activities occur that result in some policy developments from elsewhere receiving very close attention and others being completely ignored? Questions of this kind could serve as the basis of a class discussion with an invited guest. See my suggestions at the end of Chapter 1 for ways to involve the class members in arranging a visit by an invited guest.

The Class Project

The focus of this study could be (1) the comparison of different approaches taken in two jurisdictions to address a similar problem, (2) a before-and-after comparison of institutional arrangements associated with a specific policy in just one jurisdiction, or (3) an investigation of the potential for a policy and its accompanying set of institutional arrangements in one jurisdiction to be introduced in the students' home jurisdiction. Additional possibilities exist. Selection of the focus of the comparative institutional analysis could be done in consultation with representatives of a government agency. To promote student buy-in to the project, it would be good to offer a list of three to five possible project topics and then have a vote on which one to pursue. The challenge for the class members would be to collectively conduct a comparative institutional analysis and write it up as a policy report.

Those interested in coordinating a class project involving comparative institutional analysis should be sure to have mastered the material in Chapter 5, "Managing Policy Projects," and read my comments on the class project offered at the end of that chapter.

It is strongly suggested that the class project be conducted in a fashion that closely follows the steps in comparative institutional analysis presented in this chapter and summarized here.

Steps in Comparative Institutional Analysis

1. Select and refine the analytical questions.
2. Develop a research design, and select cases.
3. Collect and analyze the relevant information.
4. Isolate the relationships between institutional choice and observed outcomes.
5. Present your findings, and make recommendations.

Realistically, good class projects can take four to six weeks of focused effort. Students should be assigned to small groups, and each group should be assigned a clearly specified task or set of tasks to perform. To ensure transparency and accountability, everyone in the class should know what everyone else is working on. During the time that the project is running, regular class meetings should be devoted almost exclusively to discussing the project, what has been achieved recently, and what work is to be completed next. This coordination work can be demanding. To ensure that students contribute appropriately to this kind of project, it is best that no other forms of assessment be required from students while they are working on it. The risk that students will shirk their work responsibilities can be reduced by requiring students to provide brief written reports on the quality of the contributions made by their group peers during the process. The reports should be confidential, and all students should understand that the content of the reports can affect the final grade assigned to each participant. For technical details on how I have managed this, see the Appendix in Michael Mintrom (2003), *People Skills for Policy Analysts* (Washington, DC: Georgetown University Press).

A range of important pedagogical benefits can result from students working collectively on a challenging policy project. Effectively designed and executed, this kind of project can allow students to learn to engage closely with various analytical techniques, beyond those directly associated with doing comparative institutional analysis. Class projects also present amazing opportunities for students to learn the benefits of collaboration and team effort.

It is useful to remind students that they will very likely experience a U-shaped emotional journey while working on the project. That is to say, they will experience excitement near the start and a great sense of accomplishment in the end. But in the middle, things can get tough. That is why setting project milestones can be very important.

Students will find it helpful to familiarize themselves with Chapter 6, "Presenting Policy Advice." When students produce a class project, it is often very satisfying to deliver the findings and recommendations in an oral briefing for relevant practitioners.

The Policy Research Seminar

Organize a research-oriented seminar that will run for about ninety minutes, preferably with some light refreshments. Invite up to twelve people, and make sure you have a mixture of experienced researchers, junior researchers, and graduate students. The purpose of the discussion should be to develop ideas for the design of policy research projects that give a central place to comparative institutional analysis. The project ideas should be sufficiently interesting and original that each could form the basis of a significant research paper, dissertation, or thesis. Participants should come to the seminar having read both this chapter and Michael Mintrom's (2001) "Policy Design for Local Innovation: The Effects of Competition in Public Schooling" (*State Politics and Policy Quarterly* 1: 343–363). You might structure the discussion around the section "Steps in Comparative Institutional Analysis" presented in this chapter and applied in the overview of the Mintrom study. Many other recent journal articles could have been highlighted in this chapter. Prior to the group meeting, you might have several participants locate other interesting articles that present original comparative institutional analyses. Discussions of this sort tend to work best when the group has a clear goal. I suggest this outcome statement: "By the end of this meeting we will have identified five possible topics for new research projects that involve comparative institutional analysis. We will have sketched out basic research designs for at least two of those projects." Brainstorm to get some ideas flowing. Hold the more skeptical, analytical comments until later in the seminar. Ideally, some members of the discussion group will follow up on the meeting and continue to develop, perhaps collaboratively, research designs that build from the readings and the discussion. This is a good way to promote original policy research inspired by the best contemporary applications of quantitative and qualitative research methods. For additional advice on how to run effective meetings of this kind, see (1) Michael Mintrom's (2003) "Facilitating Meetings" in *People Skills for Policy Analysts* (Washington, DC: Georgetown University Press) and (2) Tom Kelley's (2001) "The Perfect Brainstorm" in *The Art of Innovation* (New York: Currency/Doubleday).

Further Reading

Barzelay, Michael. (2007). "Learning from Second-Hand Experience: Methodology for Extrapolation-Oriented Case Research." *Governance* 20: 521–543.

Casper, Steven. (2010). "The Comparative Institutional Analysis of Innovation: From Industrial Policy to the Knowledge Economy." In *The Oxford Handbook of Comparative Institutional Analysis,* ed. Glenn Morgan et al., chap. 12. New York: Oxford University Press.

Hodgson, Geoffrey M. (1998). "The Approach of Institutional Economics." *Journal of Economic Literature* 36: 166–192.

Rose, Richard. (2005). *Learning from Comparative Public Policy: A Practical Guide.* Oxon, UK: Routledge.

Scott, W. Richard. (2008). "Institutional Processes and Organizations." In *Institutions and Organizations: Ideas and Interests,* 3rd ed., chap. 7. Los Angeles: Sage.

Thelen, Kathleen. (1999). "Historical Institutionalism in Comparative Politics." *Annual Review of Political Science* 2: 369–404.

13

❧

Cost-Benefit Analysis

The Story So Far... Whenever government actions are being considered, people want to know how much they are likely to cost and what benefits they are likely to deliver.

Here... This chapter provides an overview of how cost-benefit analysis is used. Cost-benefit analysis is a vital tool for supporting informed choices concerning adoption of public policies. It can be combined with other analytical strategies, like comparative institutional analysis, to offer rich insights into the likely consequences of alternative policy proposals.

THIS CHAPTER REVIEWS

- The central place of cost-benefit analysis in policy analysis
- The identification of negative and positive effects of a policy
- Methods for estimating the costs and benefits of policy impacts
- Methods for discounting future streams of costs and benefits
- How analysts approach issues of human life and the quality of life

Cost-benefit analysis is an important tool for supporting decision making in many settings, including public policy making. On a daily basis, each of us constantly performs intuitive cost-benefit calculations. When we are contemplating decisions that involve spending a lot of money, such as buying a new car, we often make our cost-benefit calculations explicit. For example, we might list on a sheet of paper the various pros and cons associated with the different options available to us. We will also often seek advice from others, to help us make better decisions. People have also reported to me that they have used this kind of explicit weighing of pros and cons to guide decisions about graduate schools to attend and job offers to accept.

When used by policy analysts, cost-benefit analysis requires systematic definition of the potential scope and impacts of a policy or program and its likely effects. Cost-benefit analysis holds appeal because it requires analysts to transform all the likely impacts of a policy or program into monetary units. It also requires that calculation of the overall value of a program take account of expected future costs and benefits. Through this method, it is possible to make well-informed judgments about the financial wisdom of pursuing a given policy or program. Because it requires a systematic approach to identifying and weighing costs and benefits, this form of analysis is also well suited to making comparisons across alternative policy approaches or program designs. Therefore, the technique of cost-benefit analysis can be used to guide decision makers who must choose one option to pursue from a menu of several options. Cost-benefit analysis does not allow us to effectively compare all relevant attributes of a set of options. However, addressing the comparative value for money of options does help us to provide a financial backdrop against which other important considerations can be assessed.

This chapter offers an introduction to cost-benefit analysis. Because it is an analytical strategy that can require a use of complicated estimation techniques, a large body of relevant literature exists concerning how best to use it (Boardman, Greenberg, Vining, and Weimer 2005; Brent 2006). As an introductory chapter, there are limits to how much can be covered here. The goal is that, on completing this chapter, you will be able conduct rudimentary cost-benefit analyses. You will also be aware of ways that the analysis can grow complicated. Just as important, you should become informed consumers of cost-benefit analyses produced by others. You will know the kinds of questions to ask and issues to address when confronted with a task in which cost-benefit analysis would yield valuable information regarding policy options. After establishing the key elements of the technique, consideration is given to how analysts might use cost-benefit analysis to facilitate stakeholder discussions and, hence, increase the likelihood that all relevant benefits and costs of a policy or project will be identified. Emphasis is also placed on the importance of making the modeling assumptions explicit, of running different scenarios, and of taking care to be sensitive about the treatment of equity issues and the valuation of life and quality of life.

AN OVERVIEW OF COST-BENEFIT ANALYSIS

Cost-benefit analysis has long been considered a central tool for policy analysts. That is because all policy decisions involve the allocation of scarce resources. Decision makers need to know the immediate and ongoing costs associated with policy options, and how policy options differ in the benefits they can be expected to deliver. Of course, some costs and benefits cannot be easily measured, and it is the limits of cost-benefit analysis that have often caused controversy. In response, practitioners of cost-benefit analysis have developed increasingly elaborate ways to estimate the costs and benefits associated with proposed policies, programs, or projects. At the same time, alternative analytical strategies, such as social impact and environmental impact assessment, have been developed by critics of cost-benefit analysis, with the goal of broadening our understanding of policy effects beyond their financial impacts.

A criticism often made of cost-benefit analysis is that the costs of policies and programs are generally easier to measure than their benefits. Another way to put this is that, although costs can be readily identified, benefits often appear more elusive. As a result, policy debates can become dominated by disagreements between those who care mainly about value for money and financial implications of options and those who emphasize other important, but somewhat more intangible, things.

Suppose a proposal has been made to reduce pollution of a river and to clean the riverbed to restore it to good health. Such a proposal will likely impose significant costs on current polluters, which might include firms that are located along the river and who discharge waste into it, cities that allow untreated storm water and other waste water to flow into it, and farmers whose irrigation systems generate runoff of fertilizers and pesticides into the river. The costs of eliminating these types of activities could be quantified. The quantification work would not be easy, and a range of assumptions would need to be involved in making cost estimates, but it could be done. Likewise, the costs of cleaning up the riverbed could also be estimated. That would seem fairly straightforward. In contrast, a lot of the benefits of this kind of project would be harder to define and quantify. How should we value the opportunity for the river to be cleared of pollutants and able to once again sustain healthy fish stocks? How do we value the pleasures that people get from living near a clean river and taking advantage of the recreational opportunities it offers? There is a very good chance that, no matter how a cost-benefit analysis is performed in this instance, the costs will almost always come out higher than the benefits. But that is not due to the overwhelming value to society of being able to freely pollute our rivers. It is due to the ease with which we can identify costs and put dollar figures on them versus the difficulty of defining benefits and translating them into dollars.

The issues raised here are difficult. Yet even more difficulties arise when cost-benefit analyses require the analysts involved to place values on human lives.

USING COST-BENEFIT ANALYSIS AS AN
ANALYTICAL FRAMEWORK

Some analytical strategies are most useful when we are trying to understand the nature of a policy problem or devise a set of alternative approaches to addressing a problem. Others tend to become more relevant as we look ahead to considering how a policy design will be implemented and how the effectiveness of a policy or program can be evaluated. To perform effective cost-benefit analysis, we need to have a clear sense of the policy options. The more careful the design work that has been performed, the better able policy analysts will be to estimate the comparative costs and benefits of various policy options. A useful analogy here can be drawn with planning a building. Architects develop building designs, which are then scrutinized by quantity surveyors, who develop building cost estimates. Of course, experienced architects will have a good sense of ballpark costs before the quantity surveyors do their formal analysis. If nothing else, they will know that the bigger the building, the more expensive it is likely to be. If the quantity surveyors develop a cost estimate that is beyond the client's budget, it is likely the client and the architect will discuss ways to change various design features to reduce building costs. Feedback loops like this occur in the policy analysis and design process, too. By conducting cost-benefit analyses, new insights about policies emerge and these can prompt revisions and refinements of the initial development work.

All efforts to analyze policies and give advice on appropriate policy choices should incorporate at least a basic assessment of relevant costs and benefits. This will ensure answers are given to important questions about costs and value for money. Beyond that, the discipline of conducting a cost-benefit analysis can bring a further element of structure to your analytical work. In the course of doing cost-benefit analysis, we are forced to think about policies and programs as investments. Why are we making those investments? In making them, what other investment opportunities will we forfeit? We are also forced to think systematically about each component of a policy or program, the resources each requires, and the ways that each component contributes to outputs and outcomes. Finally, to communicate clearly with others about our analyses, we need to make explicit the assumptions that have been included in our work. This can help us to clarify our thinking and reduce the unexamined aspects of what we do. We are forced to consider the most central elements of the policies or programs of interest and to distinguish between core and peripheral issues. Whenever we do these things, we increase the likelihood that our analytical work will contribute powerfully to helping others understand the issues at stake and avoid making ill-informed and rash decisions.

There is always a danger that efforts at quantification of evidence about policy and program design could mask bogus assumptions and sloppy research. On this score, the better we work to take care in what we do and to document how we do it, the greater the odds that problems will be eliminated. Either we will see them for ourselves or others will point them out. When transparency becomes common practice, it gets hard for people to make inappropriate use of analytical strategies. If your good faith efforts at cost-benefit analysis provoke questions from others that lead to helpful conversations and further effort to tackle the limitations of your analysis, then this should be viewed positively.

STEPS IN COST-BENEFIT ANALYSIS

Cost-benefit analysis can be used to determine the merits of a specific action or to determine the comparative merits of several alternative actions. Typically, cost-benefit analysis is used before any action is taken, so it works as a predictive tool. The central aspect of the effort is to estimate likely outcomes of actions. The following steps indicate a general approach to conducting cost-benefit analysis. The steps could be used to guide basic attempts to undertake a cost-benefit analysis. More sophisticated cost-benefit analyses would also require the analysts to follow these steps. However, in those cases, much more attention to detail would be required at each step. As the steps are presented, brief consideration will be given to how the analytical work could be expanded and enriched to increase our confidence in the accuracy of the predictions being made. This section is followed by an applied example illustrating how these steps can inform analytical practice.

Step 1. Define the scope of the study. Cost-benefit analysis requires that all costs and benefits of an action are weighed to determine **net present value**. That is the estimated current value of taking the action. If the net present value, calculated by subtracting all estimated costs from all estimated benefits, is positive, then it is appropriate to take the action. But questions of scope arise. How far into the future should we look when estimating future streams of costs and benefits? A judgment must be made about this. Often, it is useful to develop your analysis so that it is easy to see how the net present value estimate is affected by truncating or extending the time period under consideration. Another question of scope involves its inclusiveness with respect to taking account of relevant costs and benefits. Those salient costs and benefits should always be included in an analysis. Yet one of the strengths of this kind of analysis is that it forces us to think about potential costs and benefits in a disciplined fashion, which might reveal a range of costs and benefits that were not considered when the action was initially proposed. How broadly or narrowly we define the costs and benefits to be considered in the study will have material bearings on the calculation of net present value. A related issue of scope arises when an action is to be taken in a variety of contexts, and differences in each context are expected to affect the estimation of costs and benefits as they occur there. For example, a program to alleviate child poverty would be expected to incur different types of costs when implemented in an inner city area, a suburban area, or a rural area. Because the cost-benefit estimates will differ across sites, it is helpful to take account of these differences. In such cases, analysts decide how many different cases to subject to a formal cost-benefit analysis, as part of the broader study. In sum, it is important to be clear about the scope of the study, and how decisions concerning a study's scope could affect the key study findings, which is the estimated net present value of the options under consideration.

Step 2. Identify all negative and positive effects of the policy. It is useful to think of cost-benefit analysis as an effort to move from intuitive ways of assessing the worth of an action to thorough, systematic analysis. When we rely on intuitive thinking, we run the risk that factors relevant to our decision will be overlooked. But the intention of being systematic also raises the risk that we might mask incomplete, partial thinking with the pretense of sophistication. For example, any effort to estimate the monetary costs and benefits of a policy and derive its estimated net present value will poorly serve decision makers if some significant negative or positive effects have been overlooked. Use of iterative methods, supported by both conceptual and practical insights, can greatly increase the likelihood that all negative and positive effects of a policy can be identified.

A brainstorming session among a few people who have a good understanding of the proposed action can generate initial lists of negative and positive effects. Treating negatives and positives separately at first can be a good way to promote the generation of ideas. Once initial lists of positives and negatives have been constructed, they should be discussed with stakeholders. Often, stakeholders will view proposals in blinkered ways, fixating on those issues that are salient to them. But if enough stakeholders from diverse positions are consulted, then the lists of positives and negatives will become more comprehensive. Practical insights from people on the ground can help a lot with this exercise (Forester 1999; Schön and Rein 1994). Just as important, careful conceptual thinking can help in construction of lists of negative and positive effects. For example, new insights might come from considering possible variations in effects for different groups of people, for communities in different locations, and so on. In addition, deliberately considering immediate effects then what domino effects they might have can open our awareness to new negative and positive effects. Reviewing the actual effects of similar actions adopted elsewhere is another way to increase the chances that we will identify as many as possible of the negative and positive effects of the policy of interest. From here, comprehensive lists can be completed. These will form the basis for efforts to estimate the monetary costs and benefits of the policy. Even so, it is quite likely that subsequent steps in the performance of cost-benefit analysis will lead us to rethink these lists and add or subtract items from them. So we should usually treat them as a work in progress until quite a long way into the analysis.

Step 3. Estimate the monetary costs and benefits of the policy. This is the part of cost-benefit analysis that is most likely to generate controversy. The basic problem is that valuing impacts in dollar figures is easy for some things and virtually impossible for others. By completion of this step, you should have estimated in dollar terms the costs and benefits related to the action during each year included in the time-frame of the analysis.

If an action were to have costs and benefits confined solely to the present period, then calculation of net value (NV) would be straightforward. It would involve summing the estimated dollar values of all the benefits, $Benefit_1$ to $Benefit_n$, and subtracting that sum from the sum of the estimated dollar values of all the costs, $Cost_1$ to $Cost_n$. This can be noted as follows:

$$NV = \Sigma\,(Benefit_1 + Benefit_2 + \ldots Benefit_n) - \Sigma\,(Cost_1 + Cost_2 + \ldots Cost_n).$$

We can collapse the cost and benefit terms to produce the following equation:

$$NV = (B_{1\ldots n}) - (C_{1\ldots n}).$$

Most analyses relate to actions that generate streams of costs and benefits through time. In Step 5, we will discuss how to collapse all years to the present and calculate net present value (NPV). But before we go there, it is useful to set up the

Table 13.1 Basic Template for Calculating Costs and Benefits

PERIOD	NET VALUE = (TB − TC)	TOTAL BENEFITS (TB)	TOTAL COSTS (TC)
Present			
Year 1			
Year 2			
Year 3			
Year 4			
Year 5			

basic notation. We know that in any given year, t, the net value will be equal to all benefits realized in that time period, $(B_{1...n})_t$, minus all costs incurred in that time period $(C_{1...n})_t$. We can characterize this as follows:

$$NV_t = (B_{1...n})_t - (C_{1...n})_t$$

Spreadsheets can be effectively used to support this kind of calculation work. A basic template is presented in Table 13.1. In Step 5, this basic template is developed further to allow for calculation of net present value.

The standard way to assign dollar values to costs and benefits is to observe the market values of the items involved. For example, if a local community were seeking to build a public sports center, the costs could be estimated from the market costs of that kind of construction project. Further, if the public sports center would require the employment of coaches and administrators and cleaners, then the ongoing costs of employing such people could be estimated using the prevailing wages paid to people in those occupations. The community benefits of the new sports center might be more difficult to estimate. However, willingness to pay is often used as a way to estimate benefits. For example, if it is known that some families in the community are currently prepared to pay the cost of driving each week to a facility elsewhere and to pay a user charge for their time there, then the estimated costs of those actions could be taken as a starting point for developing an indicator of the community benefits of building the sports center. The more plausible and accurate the method's use to estimate costs and benefits, the more useful the overall analysis will be. Considering the analytical work done by others can be a helpful way of gaining insights into how estimations can be made of relevant costs and benefits. A variety of techniques have been developed to produce monetary estimates of costs and benefits associated with a range of activities. For more details, readers should consult advanced textbooks on cost-benefit analysis, some of which are listed in the "Further Reading" section at the end of the chapter.

While policy analysts should seek to be comprehensive and consistent in their efforts to assign dollar values to costs and benefits, there are limits to the accuracy of estimation work. Given this, practical cost-benefit work will often require analysts to make decisions about how to prioritize their efforts. One way to do this is to make initial rough estimates of all identified major costs and benefits. Based on this work, more refined estimation work can be undertaken, focusing on those items expected to comprise the biggest components of the set of projected costs and benefits.

Step 4. Take account of opportunity costs. When any action is taken that involves expenditures, it is important to consider whether that spending represents the best use of scarce resources. Thinking back to the model of choice presented in Chapter 9, we know that it is possible for the same total expenditure on a set of goods to yield different levels of utility depending on the allocation of spending among those goods. This insight is helpful when thinking about the costs of a project, policy, or program. The opportunity cost perspective leads us to look critically upon proposed allocations of resources (e.g., time, effort, and money) and ask whether better results could be obtained from alternative allocations. At the level of the individual, the opportunity cost of an additional year spent in full-time university study is the money that could be earned based on present qualifications. At the level of public policy, other things held equal, the opportunity cost of any government activity is the best alternative use of the needed funds. When considering the costs to factor into a cost-benefit analysis, the operative question to ask is whether more social value could be obtained from spending the same amount of money elsewhere. Another way of conceptualizing this is to think of it as making expenditures at the margin, or marginal expenditures. Ask this: If we were judging how to get the best value for money from the next increment of government spending, would we be devoting it to this activity? If the answer is *no*, then an opportunity cost is being incurred. An estimate of that opportunity cost should be added to the overall costs of the activity. That will always make for a tougher test of whether the benefits would outweigh the costs. Think of it as a check on government profligacy. In the world of scarce resources, poor-quality expenditure decisions spell bad news. Policy analysts should be able to convey that point to decision makers.

Step 5. Calculate net present value. If you were offered $100 now or $100 tomorrow, it would be wise to take the $100 today. Why? Because although you could take the $100 now, you can never be certain that the $100 tomorrow will actually materialize. But we do know that if we were to raise the amount offered tomorrow by a sufficient amount above $100, then eventually you would become indifferent to having the $100 today or a greater amount tomorrow. Because you would not value $100 tomorrow as highly as you value $100 today, we can say that you discount the future value of the money. That insight is crucial for how we value future streams of costs and benefits when doing cost-benefit analysis. Cost-benefit analysts incorporate a discount rate into their work so that they can calculate the net present value today of costs and benefits to be realized in the future.

The discount rates used in cost-benefit analyses are usually set equal to a prevailing interest rate, r, in local financial markets. A crucial relationship is assumed to exist between time and the discount rate. We discount the net value of the project in a given period by $(1 + r)^t$. This means that in the present time period, when $t = 0$, the discount rate is equal to 1. However, it becomes greater than 1 with time. In Year 1, when $t = 1$, $(1 + r)^t$ becomes equal to $1 + r$. If the interest rate = 5%, or 0.05, then the discount rate would for Year 1 would be 1.05. For, Year 2, it would be 1.10, for Year 3, it would be 1.16, and so on. We see from this that costs and benefits reduce in value as dates are projected forward into the future. This logic informs the key formula that captures the essence of cost-benefit analysis. That formula is presented here.

$$\text{NPV}_{t_0 \ldots t_r} = \sum \frac{(C_{1 \ldots n} - B_{1 \ldots n})_t}{(1 + r)^t}$$

In the foregoing formula for deriving net present value (NPV), t_0 is the present time and t_x is the final future year included in the analysis. So if the analysis of costs and benefits was to have a five-year time frame, then the present time would be represented by t_0 and the last year in the analysis would be represented by t_5. Table 13.2 presents a basic template for calculating net present value. Note that although the net value in Year 1 through Year 5 is calculated to be $150 in each year in the table, the discounted value drops as time goes by. The discounted values drop more rapidly when the discount rate is set higher. Templates like this can be readily assembled in spreadsheets. Because the choice of a value for the interest rate, r, can have major effects on the results of a cost-benefit analysis, it is important that the chosen value is considered reasonable. To this end, it is helpful to follow local practices. For more discussion of discount rates and their use, see Moore and colleagues (2004). Note also that, in practice, it is very helpful to run several scenarios, changing the value of the discount rate with each. By doing so, you can determine the sensitivity of your analysis to the choice of the discount rate. If a slight change in a discount rate is all that is needed to flip the net present value from negative to positive, then this point should be clearly stated in the analysis.

Step 6. Reflect on the value of human life and quality-of-life issues. How much is a human life worth? Because this is a question that must be addressed in cost-benefit analyses, a range of estimates have been produced over the years (Sunstein 2000). Sometimes, these value estimates are made by considering people's average earning potential. Due to the use of discount rates, all cost-benefit analyses place less value on life in the future than life now. Formal efforts to value human life and the quality of human life have raised major controversies around the use of cost-benefit analyses (Ackerman and Heinzerling 2004). It is difficult to sidestep these issues. However, they can be addressed in more or less sensitive ways. Policy analysts should think carefully about how decision makers and stakeholders are likely to respond to their ways of valuing life and the quality of life. One way to reduce the potential for controversy is to work with a number of estimates,

Table 13.2 Basic Template for Calculating Net Present Value

Interest rate (*r*) :	0.05					
Total NPV:	$149					

PERIOD	t	NET PRESENT VALUE (NPV)	DISCOUNT VALUE = $(1 + r)^t$	NET VALUE = (TB – TC)	TOTAL BENEFITS (TB)	TOTAL COSTS (TC)
Present	0	-$500	1.00	-$500	$0	$500
Year 1	1	$143	1.05	$150	$200	$50
Year 2	2	$136	1.10	$150	$200	$50
Year 3	3	$130	1.16	$150	$200	$50
Year 4	4	$123	1.22	$150	$200	$50
Year 5	5	$118	1.28	$150	$200	$50

perhaps borrowing from estimates made by others. This does not eliminate the problem, but it does show you are aware that any specific effort to estimate the value of life or place values on the quality of life is necessarily subjective. Policy analysts should also consider the ways that different groups of people are differently affected by the costs and benefits of policies and programs. This can also be difficult work. However, because politicians care about fair treatment of people, incorporating this kind of work into cost-benefit analyses can make them more valuable to decision makers.

Step 7. Report study assumptions and limitations. The use of cost-benefit analysis has often prompted controversy partly because results have been developed and presented in ways that are not easily understood. Cost-benefit analysis is a technical exercise that can grow complicated. However, it is a good practice for analysts to be as open as possible about how they have gone about their work. In situations in which decisions are likely to produce winners and losers, it is important to find ways to limit the sources of controversy. Being open and clear about how you have set up your analysis is the best way to reduce suspicion about the decision-making process. Further, when analysts make the assumptions and limitations of their studies clear, they create space for productive dialogue. Decision makers should be able to ask "what if" questions and find out the results of different models that contain different assumptions. Likewise, by being explicit about the limitations of our work, it is possible that other analysts will offer advice on how to get around those limitations. Because the primary goal is to produce analytical work that supports well-informed decision making, getting constructive feedback from others should always be welcomed, even if the feedback is not complimentary. Having said these things, it is important to present the results of cost-benefit analyses in ways that account for the needs of multiple audiences. This suggests that reports will require the use of technical appendices. This is where you can include information on the methods used to estimate specific costs or benefits and explanations regarding the selection of project time frames and discount rates. In the main body of the report, tables can be used to summarize key costs and benefits, and to indicate the time periods in which different costs and benefits will be realized. More comprehensive tables might be included in appendices to the report. Increasingly, the use of websites makes it possible for a variety of technical materials to be made available, and for relevant data to be shared so that others can replicate the analytical work.

Step 8. Present results using several scenarios. When decision makers and stakeholders are trying to understand the implications of an action, a lot of useful information can be conveyed through the use of several well-chosen scenarios. A good cost-benefit analysis will identify the key drivers of change in costs incurred and benefits realized. Of course, each study will be built around unique questions, concerns, and challenges. Whenever possible, analysts should try to present a simple "dashboard" that illustrates how changes in assumptions, or changes in the values given to different costs and benefits, alter predictions of net present value. It is important that the number of scenarios presented is kept small. Three or four scenarios will usually be sufficient to give audience members a good sense of the relationship between costs and benefits. Intelligent design of cost-benefit models will make it easy for analysts to alter assumptions and other factors so that new "what if" scenarios can be quickly tested. Making it possible for decision makers to do this for themselves via a website would be helpful in many instances.

AN APPLIED EXAMPLE

This section highlights analysis contained in the following:

Sydney Rosen, Jonathon Simon, Jeffrey R. Vincent, William MacLeod, Matthew Fox, and Donald M. Thea. (2003). "AIDS Is Your Business." *Harvard Business Review* 81 (February): 80–87.

Sydney Rosen, Jeffrey R. Vincent, William MacLeod, Matthew Fox, Donald M. Thea, and Jonathon L. Simon. (2004). "The Cost of HIV/AIDS to Businesses in South Africa." *AIDS* 18: 317–324.

Acquired immune deficiency syndrome (AIDS) is a disease of the human immune system. People with AIDS experience progressive reductions in the effectiveness of their immune systems. Their bodies become increasingly vulnerable to infection and the development of tumors. AIDS is caused by the human immunodeficiency virus (HIV), which can be transmitted through, among other things, sexual contact, blood transfusion, and use of contaminated hypodermic needles. Between 1981 and 2009, the AIDS epidemic claimed an estimated twenty-five million lives worldwide, making it the most devastating epidemic in human history. At present, over thirty-three million people worldwide are living with HIV/AIDS. The suffering of victims, their loved ones, their dependent children, and those around them weighs heavily on humanity. The greatest loss of life associated with AIDS has occurred in sub-Saharan Africa. As yet, there is no known cure for it. Drug treatments can be used to retard the effects of HIV, and fortunately the costs of treatment have been falling. In many countries, information campaigns are used to educate people regarding safe sex, with the intention of preventing the spread of HIV/AIDS.

Sydney Rosen, who studies global public health issues, led a team of researchers in analyzing the impact of HIV/AIDS on public and private organizations in sub-Saharan Africa. As part of their work, they sought to identify the costs and benefits of prevention and treatment interventions. The research team started with a challenge: How can we make business leaders more aware of HIV/AIDS, and what they could do to help tackle it? Doing a cost-benefit analysis was one answer. Rosen and her colleagues treated workplace efforts to combat HIV/AIDS as the policy of interest. They construed the costs of the policy primarily as any expenditures made to reduce the risks that employees would contract HIV/AIDS. They construed the benefits of the policy primarily in terms of the avoidance of expenditures that arise when employees infected with HIV manifest the symptoms of AIDS. Although this study focused exclusively on six corporations located in South Africa and Botswana, its methodology could be generally applied to conduct cost-benefit analyses of similar organizational policies. The study illustrates several challenges that policy analysts face when they apply cost-benefit analysis, regardless of the program or policy of interest.

Step 1. Define the scope of the study. Rosen and her colleagues wanted to illustrate the costs and benefits to employers of acknowledging HIV/AIDS as a problem that they could help to address. Twenty firms in South Africa and Botswana were invited to participate in the study. For final selection, firms had to have a computerized human resources database, be willing to assist with data collection, and agree to cover some of the costs of the study. From the original twenty, six firms were selected for inclusion. The six firms differed in the size of their workforces and their industrial sectors. For example, one was a utility, one was in mining, one in agriculture, one in retail, and so on. This variation in industrial sectors held implications for the study results, because the workforces of the different firms were quite distinctive. Taken together, the six firms and their employees defined the scope of the study. The firms were treated as the units of analysis; that is, the focus was placed on firm-level costs and benefits of HIV/AIDS prevention and treatment. The study design allowed for comparisons across the six firms. The research team gathered relevant firm-level and employee-level information.

The research team commissioned voluntary, anonymous surveys of employees in each firm to determine the prevalence of HIV among the workforce. Along with taking blood samples, the surveys collected information on job level, age, sex, and racial identity. The goal was to model HIV incidence for different subgroups of the workforce. The risk of contracting HIV differs across the population. Estimates of the risks across different subgroups of the workforce assist in predicting expenditures that firms could expect to face due to the prevalence of HIV among their employees.

Step 2. Identify all negative and positive effects of the policy. The policy of interest had two goals. The first was to reduce the number of employees who will get infected by HIV. The second was to treat those who already have HIV or AIDS so that their working lives might be extended. In this study, the negative effects of the policy were identified as the costs to companies of implementing prevention and treatment programs. The positive effects of the policy were identified as the savings that companies realized due to employees not contracting HIV. Note the narrowness of this approach to identifying negative and positive effects of the policy. We could reasonably argue that saving the lives of employees would be a huge positive effect. Rosen and her colleagues obviously understood that point. However, they would have been aware of the difficulties that researchers face when seeking to place monetary values on human lives and the quality of people's lives. Their project could be viewed as an effort to help save lives. Yet, by bracketing off the consideration of weighty matters, they kept their study tightly focused. They wanted to address a business audience. Therefore, they limited their identification of negative and positive effects to those that were directly relevant to the financial bottom line of the firms in the study. Yet, as we will see, the team found it difficult

Table 13.3 The Costs of AIDS to an Employer

	DIRECT COSTS	INDIRECT COSTS
From one employee with HIV/AIDS (individual costs)	• Medical care • Benefits payments • Recruitment and training of replacement worker	• Reduced on the job productivity • Reduced productivity due to employee's absences • Supervisor's time in dealing with productivity losses • Vacancy rate until replacement is hired • Reduced productivity while replacement worker learns the job
From many employees with HIV/AIDS (organizational costs)	• Insurance premiums • Accidents due to ill workers and inexperienced replacement workers • Costs of litigation over benefits and other issues	• Senior management time • Production disruptions • Depressed morale • Loss of experienced workers • Deterioration of labor relations

Note: This table reproduces information from page 84 of Rosen et al. (2003).

to estimate even some of these effects, such as the costs to firms of depressed worker morale when colleagues become terminally ill.

In their study, Rosen and her colleagues placed most effort on identifying the costs of AIDS to an employer. Table 13.3 summarizes those costs and sets the stage for the task of estimating the monetary values of these costs.

Step 3. Estimate the monetary costs and benefits of the policy. The study focused on costs and benefits at the individual firm level. An interesting and appealing aspect of the study by Rosen and her colleagues is that monetary benefits were construed as estimated savings achieved through the avoidance of specific costs. Having identified key direct and indirect costs of AIDS to an employer, the authors then used a range of techniques to estimate those costs. For example, they used surveys of managers to help them calculate the amount of sick leave that would be taken by an AIDS victim in their final years of work. Survey estimates were also used to calculate the amount of extra time that managers needed to spend

Table 13.4 The Timing of AIDS Costs

TIME FRAME (TYPICAL)	PROGRESSION OF HIV/AIDS IN THE WORKFORCE	CURRENT COST TO FIRM	LIABILITY ACQUIRED BY FIRM
Year 0	Employee becomes infected with HIV.	Firm incurs no cost at this stage.	This is the discounted sum of all costs from years 0 through 10+.
Years 0–7	Employee feels healthy and is fully productive.	Firm incurs no cost at this stage.	
Years 7–9	Illness begins. Employee may die in the first few years or remain free of illness for years.	Sickness-related costs are incurred (leave and absenteeism, productivity loss, supervisory time, medical care, accidents).	
Years 9–10	Employee dies or leaves work due to disability.	End-of-service costs are incurred (benefit payments, funeral expenses, management time, depressed morale).	
Years 10+	Company hires replacement employee.	Turnover costs are incurred (vacancy, recruitment, training, reduced productivity while replacement learns job).	

Note: This table reproduces information from page 85 of Rosen et al. (2003).

on supervision and training as a result of losing staff. Information on retirement benefits, death and disability benefits, medical care coverage, and recruitment and training was also collected from human resources databases to support the estimation process. The costs of introducing programs to help prevent the spread of HIV in the workforce and of supporting workers who manifest AIDS symptoms were also estimated. This was done by multiplying the number of employees in each firm with the known per-person costs of such interventions.

Step 4. Take account of opportunity costs. Opportunity costs were not considered in this analysis. Had they been, the researchers would have asked the following: What would be the best alternative use of the money required to fund the firm-level AIDS prevention and treatment programs?

Step 5. Calculate net present value. For each of the six firms in their study, Rosen and her colleagues calculated the net present value of firm-funded prevention and treatment programs. To do so, they determined the timing of AIDS costs to each firm. They then applied a discount rate. They discounted each cost using the 7 percent real lending rate, which was standard in South Africa in October 2001. Taking this approach, they were then able to provide their estimates of the financial impact of the AIDS epidemic on each firm. Table 13.4 illustrates the timing of AIDS costs. This is a very clear way to portray how costs arise at different points in time.

Table 13.5 illustrates how the authors portrayed their calculation of the "tax" that AIDS imposes on individual firms. The table reveals significant variation across firms in the annual costs caused by AIDS among their employees (see row 4). This variation has two main sources. First, the firms differed by the estimated percentage of their labor force being HIV positive (see row 3). If no workers were HIV positive, then no costs would be incurred. Second, the firms had different benefit packages for employees. Those with limited benefits faced much lower costs due to AIDS than did those that offered higher benefits. Across all firms, prevention

Table 13.5 Estimated Effects of AIDS on Firms and Program Benefits

1. Firm studied	1	2	3
2. Industry	Utility	Mining	Retail
3. Estimated percentage of labor force HIV positive	7.9%	29.0%	10.5%
4. Total annual cost of AIDS as a percentage of salaries and wages	3.7%	5.9%	0.4%
5. Potential reduction in the cost of AIDS due to programs	32.5%	15.7%	0.8%

Note: This table simplifies information from page 86 of Rosen et al. (2003).

and treatment programs were calculated to reduce the cost of AIDS. The value of the prevention and treatment programs differs from firm to firm. But in all cases, introducing a program was estimated to produce positive financial effects.

Step 6. Reflect on the value of human life and quality-of-life issues. In this study, the authors did not discuss issues relating to the valuation of human lives or the quality of life. They focused on the cost of AIDS to firms and then argued that those costs could be reduced by the introduction of prevention and treatment programs. Although the focus on program costs and benefits was deliberately kept tight, the authors went to some lengths in their work to contextualize their analysis within the broader human tragedy of the AIDS epidemic. We can conclude that the authors did not need to make appeals concerning the value of human life in order to justify firm-level introduction of AIDS prevention and treatment programs. Of course, if the costs of such programs to the firms were judged to outweigh the benefits to them, then it is possible that efforts would have been made to justify program expenditures using arguments about the valuing of life and human dignity.

Step 7. Report study assumptions and limitations. In their 2004 article, Rosen and her colleagues identified and discussed a range of limitations associated with their study. For example, they noted that they studied only six firms and found considerable variations across them in terms of program benefits. Generalization from this limited set of cases would have to be done cautiously. Also, organizational effects of AIDS were calculated by considering costs per individual employee and aggregating from there. No efforts were made to measure the cumulative impact of multiple cases of AIDS in a workplace—the effects on morale and the increasing time demands on management. Perhaps one of the biggest limitations is that no consideration was given to the effects of future changes in the policies of the firms included in the study. An option for firms worried about future financial liabilities associated with employees contracting HIV would be to reduce their employment benefits. Note that Firm 3 in Table 13.5, which operated in the retail sector, offered limited benefits and so faced limited liabilities.

Step 8. Present results using several scenarios. Rosen and her team were interested in demonstrating how firms could reduce the spread of HIV and enhance their financial bottom lines in the process. To do so, they explored the potential cost savings for firms that introduced HIV prevention programs. As such, they presented several scenarios. The merit of this approach is that it leads to consideration of how differences in workforce composition and benefit programs affect the financial liabilities of firms.

ADVICE FOR ANALYTICAL PRACTICE

Several points have emerged through the foregoing discussion. These are useful to bear in mind when conducting cost-benefit analysis. By doing so, we can increase the overall quality of our analytical work and the advice based on it.

- Look for logical ways to categorize the costs and benefits associated with a proposal. For example, with respect to costs, your categories might include direct costs versus indirect costs or setup costs versus recurrent costs. This use of categories can help both with the identification of items to include in the analysis and decisions about the scope of your analysis.
- Think in terms of both the costs of a proposal and the cost savings that the proposal would generate. Cost savings can be categorized as benefits.
- Estimating dollar figures for costs and benefits can be challenging and time-consuming. Prioritize among your items to be estimated, so that you devote most effort to the biggest and most salient items. It is better to be criticized for leaving out relatively minor and difficult-to-measure costs or benefits than for leaving out those things everyone will ask about.
- People like to ask "what if" questions. Your analytical work and advice based on it will benefit from your ability to explore different scenarios around policy options. Try to develop estimation models that will allow you to easily adjust the assumptions driving your results. Also look for ways to easily include or exclude different costs and benefits in the models.
- Many proposals hold implications for saving lives and the quality of people's lives. Debates about the valuing of lives can be avoided if the costs of a proposal can be shown to be less than the value of a narrow set of benefits (or cost savings) that are relatively easy and noncontroversial to estimate.
- Because decision makers care about fairness, it is useful to indicate how costs and benefits would be distributed across different groups of people. Such an effort can open the way for informed discussions of trade-offs and of ways to compensate people for adverse effects of proposed actions.
- Always visually convey the logic of your analysis. For example, simple tables can illustrate streams of costs and benefits through time.
- Although cost-benefit analysis can become highly technical, the more user-friendly your presentation of your findings, the more productive will be discussions of those findings among decision makers.

COST-BENEFIT ANALYSIS AND OTHER ANALYTICAL STRATEGIES

Cost-benefit analysis can often serve as the central element of a policy report. However, the analysis will rarely stand alone in a study. Frequently, it will need to be preceded by a discussion of the policy problem—which might include discussions of market processes, or analyses of causes of observed problems, such as market failures, government failures, or a combination of both. Cost-benefit analysis can be effectively combined with comparative institutional analysis. It is also quite common for evaluators to incorporate elements of cost-benefit analysis into their studies of programs and their effectiveness. In sum, cost-benefit analysis is a central analytical strategy for policy analysts and it can be utilized in many ways to add value to discussions of policy options.

Exercises

1. Contemporary disagreement over the merits of using cost-benefit analysis to support decision making is captured in the opposing views expressed by Robert Hahn and Cass Sunstein (2002), who support its use, and Frank Ackerman, Lisa Heinzerling, and Rachel Massey (2005), who point to its patchy record of effective application. Nominate two teams to debate the merits of cost-benefit analysis. One team should base its argument on Hahn and Sunstein (2002), whereas the other should follow the argument of Ackerman and his colleagues (2005). Have each side make their individual cases. Use this as an introduction to a broader discussion of cost-benefit analysis and instances when it could be most effectively used.

2. It is interesting to observe how groups of people, within the space of about thirty minutes, can develop good initial plans for advancing analytical work and identify key issues at stake. In small groups, have the participants briefly describe the policy issues they are each currently working on. Together, think of ways that cost-benefit analysis could be applied to generate insights about the issue and how to address it. After this initial discussion, the group should choose one person's project to focus on. Take time to brainstorm together about how a cost-benefit analysis could be conducted for this project. Together, define the scope of the study and identify key negative and positive effects of a policy intervention. Having done this, take a few more minutes to discuss how opportunity cost considerations could be factored into the work. Also discuss the extent to which the valuing of human lives or the quality of lives could be treated in this cost-benefit analysis. Each group should be prepared to report back to the larger group on their work.

The Class Project

The focus of this study should be on determining the net present value of a new policy proposal, expected to run for a decade without major change. This presents a lot of scope for variation in the substantive focus of the project. Selection of that focus could be done in consultation with representatives of a government agency or another kind of organization, such as a not-for-profit entity or a corporation. To promote student buy-in to the project, it can be good to offer a list of three to five possible new policy proposals to be analyzed and then have a vote on which one they will investigate using cost-benefit analysis. The challenge for the class members is to collectively conduct a cost-benefit analysis and write it up as a policy report.

Those interested in coordinating a class project involving cost-benefit analysis should be sure to have mastered the material in Chapter 5, "Managing Policy Projects," and read my comments on the class project offered at the end of that chapter.

It is strongly suggested that the class project be conducted in a fashion that closely follows the steps in cost-benefit analysis presented in this chapter and summarized here.

Steps in Cost-Benefit Analysis

1. Define the scope of the study.
2. Identify all negative and positive effects of the policy.
3. Estimate the monetary costs and benefits of the policy.
4. Take account of opportunity costs.
5. Calculate net present value.
6. Reflect on the value of human life and quality-of-life issues.
7. Report study assumptions and limitations.
8. Present results using several scenarios.

Realistically, good class projects can take four to six weeks of focused effort. Students should be assigned to small groups, and each group should be assigned a clearly specified task or set of tasks to perform. To ensure transparency and accountability, everyone in the class should know what everyone else is working on. During the time that the project is running, the regular class meetings should be devoted almost exclusively to discussing the project, what has been achieved recently, and what work is to be completed next. The coordination work can be demanding. To ensure that students contribute appropriately to this kind of project, it is best that no other forms of assessment be required from students while they are working on it. The risk that students will shirk their work responsibilities can be reduced by requiring students to provide brief written reports on the quality of the contributions made by their group peers during the process. The reports should be confidential, and it should be widely understood that the content of the reports will affect the final grade assigned to each participant. For technical details on how I have managed this, see the Appendix in Michael Mintrom (2003) *People Skills for Policy Analysts* (Washington, DC: Georgetown University Press).

A range of important pedagogical benefits can result from students working collectively on a challenging policy project. Effectively designed and executed, this kind of project can allow students to learn to engage closely with various analytical techniques, beyond those directly associated with doing cost-benefit analysis. Class projects also present amazing opportunities for students to learn the benefits of collaboration and team effort.

It is useful to remind students that they will very likely experience a U-shaped emotional journey while working on the project. That is to say, they will experience excitement near the start and a great sense of accomplishment in the end. But in the middle, things can get tough. That is why setting project milestones can be very important.

Students will find it helpful to familiarize themselves with Chapter 6, "Presenting Policy Advice." When students produce a class project, it is often very satisfying to deliver the findings and recommendations in an oral briefing for relevant practitioners.

The Policy Research Seminar

Organize a research-oriented seminar that will run for about ninety minutes, preferably with some light refreshments. Invite up to twelve people, and make sure you have a mixture of experienced researchers, junior researchers, and graduate students. The purpose of the discussion should be to develop ideas for the design of policy research projects that give a central place to cost-benefit analysis. The project ideas should be sufficiently interesting and original that each could form the basis of a significant research paper, dissertation, or thesis. Participants should come to the seminar having read both this chapter and the two articles by Sydney Rosen and her colleagues discussed in the text. See (1) Sydney Rosen, Jonathon Simon, Jeffrey R. Vincent, William MacLeod, Matthew Fox, and Donald M. Thea (2003), "AIDS Is Your Business" (*Harvard Business Review* 81 [February]: 80–87), and (2) Sydney Rosen, Jeffrey R. Vincent, William MacLeod, Matthew Fox, Donald M. Thea, and Jonathon L. Simon (2004), "The Cost of HIV/AIDS to Businesses in South Africa" (*AIDS* 18: 317–324). You might structure the discussion around the section "Steps in Cost-Benefit Analysis" presented in this chapter and applied in the overview of the Rosen et al. study. Many other recent journal articles could have been highlighted in this chapter. Prior to the group meeting, you might have several participants locate other interesting articles that present original cost-benefit analysis. Discussions of this sort tend to work best when the group has a clear goal. I suggest this outcome statement: "By the end of this meeting we will have identified five possible topics for new research projects that involve cost-benefit analysis. We will have sketched out basic research designs for at least two of those projects." Brainstorm to get some ideas flowing. Hold the more skeptical, analytical comments until later in the seminar. Ideally, some members of the discussion group will follow up on the meeting and continue to develop, perhaps collaboratively, research designs that build from the readings and the discussion. This is a good way to promote original policy research inspired by the best contemporary applications of quantitative and qualitative research methods. For additional advice on how to run effective meetings of this kind, see (1) Michael Mintrom's (2003) "Facilitating Meetings" in *People Skills for Policy Analysts* (Washington, DC: Georgetown University Press) and (2) Tom Kelley's (2001) "The Perfect Brainstorm" in *The Art of Innovation* (New York: Currency/Doubleday).

Further Reading

Ackerman, Frank, Lisa Heinzerling, and Rachel Massey. (2005). "Applying Cost-Benefit Analysis to Past Decisions: Was Environmental Protection Ever a Good Idea?" *Administrative Law Review* 57: 155–192.

Boardman, Anthony E., David H. Greenberg, Aidan R. Vining, and David L. Weimer. (2005). "Introduction to Cost-Benefit Analysis." In *Cost-Benefit Analysis: Concepts and Practice,* 3rd ed., chap 1. Upper Saddle River, NJ: Prentice Hall.

Brent, Robert J. (2006). "Introduction to CBA." In *Applied Cost-Benefit Analysis,* 2nd ed., part I. Northampton, MA: Edward Elgar.

Hahn, Robert W., and Cass R. Sunstein. (2002). "A New Executive Order for Improving Federal Regulation? Deeper and Wider Cost-Benefit Analysis." *University of Pennsylvania Law Review* 150: 1489–1552.

Stokey, Edith, and Richard Zeckhauser. (1978). "Project Evaluation: Benefit-Cost Analysis" and "The Valuation of Future Consequences: Discounting." In *A Primer for Policy Analysis,* chaps. 9 and 10. New York: Norton.

Sunstein, Cass R. (2000). "Cognition and Cost-Benefit Analysis." *Journal of Legal Studies* 29: 1059–1103.

14

✦○

Gender Analysis

The Story So Far... We can gain insights into the operational effective-ness of policies through conducting comparative institutional analy-ses. Cost-benefit analysis can offer insights into the financial merits of policy proposals.

Here... We review how to improve our knowledge of policy effects by employing gender analysis. Feminist scholars and policy analysts have long recognized how the gendered nature of society can pro-duce unequal opportunities and outcomes for men and women. Policy analysts should be vigilant to avoid the perpetuation of social discrimination and seek ways to eliminate it.

THIS CHAPTER REVIEWS

- Why gender analysis matters
- Approaches to gender analysis
- Analysis of organizational decisions through a gender lens
- Integrating gender analysis into all policy analysis

The concepts and analytical strategies traditionally associated with policy analysis can be applied in many ways to gain insights into policy problems and effective ways to address them. However, as their usage has spread, criticisms have emerged. Among other things, representatives of groups who have sometimes had limited access to decision making have worked to make explicit the nature of biases contained in a lot of policy design and policy implementation.

I am indebted to Jacqui True for her many useful suggestions concerning the content of this chapter.

Consider, for example, a compensation test that is commonly discussed in welfare economics and has informed how many policy analysts have thought about policy-driven change. This is called the Kaldor-Hicks compensation test, noted also in Chapter 4.[1] It states that if a change from the status quo generates sufficient gains for some people that they could compensate those who lose from the change and yet still be better off, then the change should be considered socially valuable. Yet, a proviso included within the test is that the compensation from those who gain to those who lose need not actually happen. From a strict utilitarian perspective, this is a reasonable test. From the standpoint of those who could lose and not be compensated for their losses, it is a rather unsatisfying test. It assumes away any issues of power and politics. But issues of power and politics stand at the very heart of public policy decision making. We cannot wish them away.

GENDER AND RACE ANALYSIS

Today, gender and race analysis are tools commonly used to trace the processes, decisions, and practices that can generate unequal outcomes for members of different social groups. This chapter on gender analysis and the one to follow on race analysis review how these newer analytical strategies are being used. Suggestions are made for how policy analysts might routinely integrate sensitivity to gender and race issues into their analytical and advisory work. Importantly, once we begin to disaggregate society into distinctive groups of people, we come to see that good policy analysis and policy design work should be informed by considerations of social differences. When this occurs, policy analysts can do a lot to promote well-informed conversations about the pursuit of social justice, human rights, the rights of children, and more inclusive democratic practice. Application of gender analysis and race analysis really can serve to promote positive change in the world, change that supports government objectives such as human flourishing, advancing human rights, and social equity. Indirectly, efforts to address gender and racial biases can also contribute to government objectives such as efficiency and effective institutions.

Sexism and racism represent two of the most prevalent forms of discrimination found in contemporary societies. Many other forms of discrimination also exist. Gary Becker (1957) pioneered economic analysis of discrimination. In the model he developed, he included a variable to capture individual taste for discrimination. When employers have a taste for discrimination, that taste can lead to decision making that is driven less by the desire to maximize profits. If such discrimination is common among employers, then it can be expected that individuals from favored groups will cost more to employ and those from groups that are routinely the object of discrimination will cost less to employ. Given these assumptions, Becker predicted that market dynamics would serve to curb discrimination

---

[1] Most textbooks on intermediate microeconomics will discuss this compensation text. See Hicks (1939) and Kaldor (1939).

over time. That is because those firms with a taste for discrimination would not be as profitable as those without it.

Unfortunately, evidence suggests that labor market discrimination can often remain, even in the face of the dynamics Becker noted. There are two reasons. First, in sectors in which profits are high, perhaps due to lack of competition, the incentives not to discriminate can be weak. Second, markets represent significant institutions in society, but others matter too. Practices and attitudes developed in one historical period can carry over into subsequent periods. This typically occurs through everyday interactions in many social settings. Always, those interactions are subject to formal and informal assumptions and norms that can have strong effects in shaping individual perceptions and behaviors. Actions by governments have proved most effective for eliminating discrimination and the disadvantage that stems from it. Even so, the power of governments is never pervasive, just as the power of markets is never pervasive. Consequently, government actions have sometimes met with success and sometimes those actions to eliminate discrimination have been subject to strong and effective resistance.

Policy Motives

As an entry point to our review of gender and race analysis, I begin by considering an argument made by Nancy Fraser (1998). Fraser contended that contemporary disputes surrounding issues of gender and race justice, among other things, are motivated by two broad concerns. One of these is redistribution. As different groups in society become aware of uneven distribution of resources, calls are often made for governments to engage in forms of redistribution. Such calls, made on behalf of people with limited means to support themselves or their families, led to the development of the welfare state in its various forms. But Fraser also noted concern for recognition among groups that have been subject to marginalization and discrimination. So-called identity politics often involves groups seeking to gain recognition in the broader social discourse. When such recognition occurs, it serves to break down forms of *cultural domination*. Cultural domination can be said to exist when the practices and assumptions of a given social group are almost unconsciously treated as benchmarks against which the practices and assumptions of all other groups are viewed as deviations.

Governments can use a range of policy approaches to promote redistribution of resources and to broaden the recognition and respect accorded to different social groups. Nancy Fraser observed that the pursuit of redistribution and the pursuit of recognition can counteract one another. Redistribution is deliberately done to reduce material differences among different groups of people. Meanwhile, recognition serves to make salient and even celebrate differences among groups. To the extent that the cultural identity of a marginalized group is closely tied to material status, then redistribution could be viewed as inadvertently eroding some significant forms of group identity. For example, government policies that reduce barriers for girls and women to be educated and that eliminate overt forms of discrimination in the workplace can greatly improve the material status of women in society. At the same time, those policies serve to undermine traditionally gendered forms of identity. In a more equal material context, it becomes harder for women to achieve social status through the embrace of unpaid female roles, such as managing the household, raising children, performing voluntary work, and organizing the social life of the family. Yet the goals of redistribution and recognition need not be mutually exclusive. Sometimes, they will be complementary.

Policy Actions

To advance her discussion of redistribution and recognition, Nancy Fraser proposed that government policies toward those who have been subjected to discrimination and marginalization be classified as either affirmative or transformative. *Affirmative policies* are designed to promote the interests of a group, while keeping the basic institutional arrangements of society in place. Consider, for example, the case of universities and their employment practices toward women. Historically, many university departments have been male dominated. In response to calls for change, university hiring committees have increasingly been required to include women on their short lists of job candidates for tenure-track positions. This move has had significant results. It has been an affirmative move, because it has affirmed the right of women who are equally qualified as men to be given equal treatment in hiring processes. But this move is not transformative. *Transformative policies* seek to change institutional structures and organizational operating procedures. Within universities, a transformative policy regarding the employment of women as faculty members would scrutinize the tenure-track system itself. For a start, it would recognize that the rigid time frames and stretching expectations of productivity imposed on junior faculty can have harsher implications for women than for men. To the extent that most junior faculty must run the gauntlet of the tenure track during their thirties means that academic women often must defer childbearing until after they have attained tenure. Among tenured academics in their forties, childless academic women are more common than childless academic men. A transformative policy move would seek to address the processes that generate such an outcome. Not surprisingly, it is usually more difficult to have transformative policies adopted and implemented than affirmative ones. Neither can be adopted and implemented easily. Both affirmative and transformative changes typically happen only after significant, concerted political effort. That means political battles around such change are more the norm than the exception.

Utilizing Nancy Fraser's concepts, Jacqui True has developed a simple typology for assessing policy motives and policy actions. It is reproduced here as Table 14.1, and I have elaborated on it by providing an example concerning universities and the employment of women faculty members. The typology suggests that affirmative policy actions are better than nothing, but the best policy actions are transformative. It also suggests that policies motivated by redistribution or by recognition can each have positive effects. However, the best outcomes, in terms of significantly reducing discrimination and disadvantage, can be achieved when policies are motivated by both.

Table 14.1 A Typology of Policy Motives and Policy Actions

POLICY ACTION: POLICY MOTIVE:	AFFIRMATIVE	TRANSFORMATIVE
Redistributive	Improves material conditions of a group but does not change institutional arrangements. ***Example:*** *Changes in hiring processes lead to more women appointed as junior faculty in universities.*	Improves material conditions of a group and changes institutional arrangements. ***Example:*** *Changes in hiring processes and tenure processes lead to more women being hired, retained, and promoted in universities.*
Recognition-based	Recognizes a group but does not change institutional arrangements. ***Example:*** *University publicizes the accomplishments of its women faculty members.*	Recognizes a group and changes institutional arrangements. ***Example:*** *University works with women faculty members to establish a campus environment in which women feel as equally welcome, respected, and appreciated as their male colleagues.*

AN OVERVIEW OF GENDER ANALYSIS

When applied by people interested in public policy, gender analysis has typically been motivated by a desire to improve the status of women in society, relative to that of men. Gender analysis has been used to advance women's economic and social emancipation. As such, contributions in this area of policy analysis have placed the focus on women's experiences in specific contexts and outcomes associated with those experiences. This makes a lot of sense. Yet, there is a danger that the almost exclusive focus on women will lead us to overlook relevant aspects of gender relations. In turn, that can lead to the development of partial policy responses. More thorough gender analysis could lead to more effective policy development. The key here is to use gender analysis in ways that involve thinking hard about men and their practices as well. Jeff Hearn and Linda McKie (2008) have made this point effectively in their essay on gender analysis and domestic violence. They start with the question, "What is the problem here?" That question forces us to think in terms of naming, defining, and recording. What is domestic violence? Mostly, it is violence perpetrated against women by men in private settings. In the past, gender analysis of domestic violence has typically focused on the effects of violence on women and how women might be protected from it. Only limited attention has been paid to men's violent behavior. Hearn and McKie observed, "Gendering men's violence entails linking abuse to practices, values and assumptions that are widely accepted as normal, i.e. challenging the construction of men in ways that include power over and violence towards women" (p. 79).

Effective gender analysis should illuminate how gender dynamics operate in specific contexts. When we think only in terms of problems for women, we implicitly promote that form of cultural domination that normalizes—and almost renders invisible—the practices of men that can contribute to those problems. Effective gender analysis, therefore, should closely scrutinize how people are defining problems. Usually, gender analysis begins with observations of differences in specific outcomes for men and women. Observed differences then prompt questions about the processes that generate those outcomes. This can lead to consideration of actions that could serve to change those processes in ways that reduce observed differences in outcomes for men and women. Those actions might include developing new government policies. They might also include reforming current policies that are found to be contributing in unintended ways to undesirable outcomes. Here, we consider three commonly used approaches to conducting gender analysis. These are the analysis of aggregate statistics (that can tell us about differences in outcomes of interest), process tracing (that can tell us how differences in outcomes are generated), and tests for discriminatory practice (that can help in the design of policy actions).

Analysis of Aggregate Statistics

Good, conceptually based arguments can do a lot to clarify the issues at stake in discussions concerning gender discrimination and resulting disadvantage for women. But careful presentation of findings from the analysis of appropriate statistical information can prove highly persuasive. In a classic article on giving policy advice, James Verdier (1984) said that much can be gained from emphasizing a few crucial and striking numbers. These numbers can often be difficult to accumulate or calculate, but they are usually worth the effort. Many good examples could be offered of studies in which researchers have performed careful analysis of aggregate statistics to generate significant insights regarding gender differences. In the best work, the initial effort involves illustrating the existence of a gap in outcomes between men and women. Often, people will display skepticism about the numbers and they will want reassurance that what is being observed represents social reality. The worry is that some apparent differences result from the processes by which data was collected or of particular interpretations being placed upon the data. That is why analysts will often take a lot of care to test for the possibility that observed gaps would disappear if data were collected or interpreted differently. Analysis of aggregate statistics will usually go from portrayal of gender gaps to the development and testing of causal explanations for why those gaps exists.

Doris Weichselbaumer and Rudolf Winter-Ebmer (2007) used the analysis of aggregate statistics to document international gender wage gaps. They then tested for country-level variables that tended to be associated with wider or narrower gaps. To begin their analysis, the authors noted that in industrialized countries in the 1960s, on average, men in paid employment received wages that were 65 percent higher than those for women. This statistic was based on an aggregation of men's earned incomes and women's earned incomes. Within specific industry sectors and job types, the gap would be expected to be much smaller. By the 1990s, this gap had closed to an average of 30 percent across the same set of countries. The authors suggested that this closing of the overall gap could be explained by several "productivity-relevant developments" (p. 238). These included women accumulating more experience in their paid work, with fewer interruptions in their labor market engagements. Smaller family size is a major explanation for that change. Further, women's education has become increasingly labor market oriented. Meanwhile, technological change and industrial restructuring have both contributed to a relative devaluation of physical strength and an increased demand for white-collar workers.

In their study, Weichselbaumer and Winter-Ebmer were especially interested to explore factors that might have reduced gender discrimination in the workplace. First, they tested Gary Becker's claim that it is harder for employers to indulge their taste for discrimination in highly competitive markets. Second, they tested for the effects of international conventions, such as the Convention for the Elimination of Discrimination Against Women (CEDAW), which was adopted by the General Assembly of the United Nations in 1979. The authors used the Economic Freedom Index as a measure of market competitiveness in each of the countries included in their study. Consistent with Becker's theory, they found that the gender wage gap was smaller in countries where there was greater economic competitiveness. The authors also found that the gender wage gap was smaller in countries that had ratified international conventions supporting equal treatment of men and women. They were careful to point out that ratification of a convention in itself should not be viewed as a crucial impetus for change. Rather, when countries sign onto such conventions, this typically triggers new national policies to be adopted that foster integration of women into the paid workforce, such as national equal treatment laws, measures that facilitate compatibility of work and family duties, and so on.[2]

Process Tracing

Analysis of aggregate statistics often involves efforts to identify the causes of observed outcomes. To that extent, analytical work takes account of both outcomes and processes. However, use of aggregate statistics can have its limits. In particular, it rarely allows us to subject social and organizational processes to close scrutiny. The qualitative method of process tracing can be of significant value here. Process-tracing techniques were developed through studies of individual decision-making processes (Svenson 1979) and studies of decision making in organizations (Cyert and March 1963; March and Olsen 1989).

When mapping decision-making processes, it is necessary to know what content or information is processed and how it is processed. When applied to organizational decision making, the method has much in common with aspects of comparative institutional analysis, introduced in Chapter 12. That is because it

---

[2] Readers interested in further exploration of gender gaps in labor markets should consult International Labour Office (2010).

is concerned with carefully identifying sequences of decision-making steps and how decisions are made. By tracing out processes and scrutinizing decision-making processes, it becomes possible for policy analysts to identify precisely where systematic forms of discrimination are taking place and how they contribute to the disadvantage of women. A study on the status of women scientists at the Massachusetts Institute of Technology offers a useful example of how people used process tracing as part of a gender analysis.

In 1994, three senior women faculty in the School of Science at the Massachusetts Institute of Technology (MIT) started discussing the quality of their professional lives.[3] The women realized that gender differences had probably caused their professional lives to differ significantly from those of their male colleagues. Interestingly, they had never previously discussed the issue with one another. They were uncertain whether their experiences were unique and whether their perceptions were accurate. To address their knowledge gaps, they collaborated with administrators in the school. They formed the Committee on Women Faculty. They also made a list of all tenured women faculty in the School of Science and started to systematically document the experiences of those women as professional scientists and how they perceived their departmental status relative to their male colleagues. Because there were actually very few women faculty in the school, this became an issue for analysis too. Data for both men and women faculty in the school were collected and studied concerning salary, office and laboratory space, resources for research, named chairs, prizes, awards, amount of salary paid from individual grants, teaching obligations and assignments, committee assignments—departmental, institute, and outside professional activities and committees. Pipeline data was collected to show changes in the numbers of women and men students and faculty over time. Most data were obtained from the dean's office in the school or from the central administration at MIT.

Data reviews revealed that in some departments, men and women faculty appeared to share equally in material resources and rewards; in others, they did not. Inequitable distributions were found involving space, amount of nine-month salary paid from individual research grants, teaching assignments, awards and distinctions, and inclusion on important committees and assignments within the department. Although primary salary data were confidential and were not provided to the committee, it was known that a case of serious underpayment of senior women faculty in one department had already been discovered and corrected two years before the committee formed. Other possible inequities in salary were identified by the committee from the limited data made available to it.

The committee sought data to try to determine whether the number of women faculty was increasing. The data revealed that there were very significant numbers of women students in the sciences at MIT but that the pipeline leaked at every

---

[3] The following narrative is based on material contained in two reports obtained from the following websites in March 2010. The 1999 report: http://web.mit.edu/fnl/women/women.html. An update for 2002, and additional relevant reports: http://web.mit.edu/faculty/reports/.

career stage. Fewer women than men went on to do PhDs in the sciences. When it came to making appointments of junior faculty members, fewer women were found in the applicant pools than men. As a result, fewer women were appointed than men. Further, records of tenure and promotion decisions again revealed that male colleagues faced better odds than their women colleagues of continuing in their positions. It was also apparent that overall, the percent of women faculty had not changed for at least ten years—probably closer to twenty years—and there was no indication that there would be any change in the foreseeable future.

Having conducted this process-tracing study, in 1999, the Committee on Women Faculty reported its work, along with recommendations, including the following:

- Giving the committee permanent status
- Reviewing the school's compensation system and how salary adjustments were made
- Ensuring annual collection of relevant statistics
- Working to raise consciousness of gender discrimination in the school
- Placing women in influential positions, including as heads and as members and chairs of key committees
- Replacing administrators who knowingly practiced or permitted discriminatory practices against women faculty
- Watching for, and intervening to prevent, the isolation and gradual marginalization of women faculty that frequently occurred, particularly after tenure
- Promoting integration, and preventing isolation, of junior women faculty
- Addressing the childbearing issue for junior women faculty
- Making the policy on maternity leave and tenure clock uniform throughout the institute, and make the policies widely known so that they become routine
- Taking steps to change the presumption that women who have children cannot achieve equally with men or with women who do not have children
- Addressing the family-work conflict realistically and openly, relying on advice from appropriate women faculty, in order to make MIT more attractive to a larger pool of junior women faculty, and to encourage more women students and postdoctoral fellows to continue in academic science

The 1999 report of the Women Faculty in the School of Science was a "wake-up call" to the MIT faculty and had a number of positive effects. Once the problems were recognized and data presented, the dean of science was able to effect changes mitigating most of the problems. However, the issue of marginalization, experienced by almost every woman faculty member, remained more difficult to address.

Tests for Discriminatory Practices

So far, we have reviewed how statistical analysis and process tracing can be used to conduct gender analysis. Here, we review tests for discrimination. These tests fall into two categories. Some can be performed in instances in which a "natural experiment" is presented. This means that the presence of discrimination can be observed using available information. At other times, information about discrimination must be generated. However, people are good at changing their behaviors when they know they are being observed. This can corrupt any study findings. As a result, a range of efforts have been made to test for discrimination using covert research techniques.

We will first consider a test for discriminatory practice that made use of available information. Until the 1970s, the great symphony orchestras in the United States consisted of members who were largely handpicked by the music director. Although virtually all had auditioned for the position, most of the contenders would have been the students of a select group of music teachers. To overcome this seeming bias in the hiring of musicians, most major orchestras in the United States changed their audition policies in the 1970s and 1980s. As part of this move toward impartiality, emphasis was placed on the quality of musicianship above all else. This was done by asking players to audition behind a screen. Their playing was judged by a jury who knew nothing about the identity of the players. Although most orchestras now use this "blind" audition system, some adopted it earlier than others. This created an opportunity in which researchers could carefully assess the effects of the move from auditions in which candidate identity was known to blind auditions.

Claudia Goldin and Ceclia Rouse (2000) took advantage of this opportunity to test for discrimination in orchestra auditioning processes. They tested whether female players had been subject to discrimination. If orchestras tended to employ more women musicians after adoption of screened auditions, then this would suggest that discrimination had occurred under the old system. By testing for this effect across a range of orchestras that adopted the new auditioning practice at different times, Goldin and Rouse were able to rule out the possibility that observed results were being driven by other dynamics. For example, the argument could be made that more women were appointed to orchestras because more women began auditioning, not because of actions that reduced the ability of juries to discriminate. But the research design took account of that possibility. Goldin and Rouse found that use of the screen increased the probability of women being advanced from preliminary rounds of auditions and the probability that a woman contestant would be a winner in the final round. They estimated that the switch to blind auditions could explain one-third of the increase in the proportion of women among new hires in orchestras. Another third was explained by increases in the pool of women candidates. It is quite possible that when women knew that they would not be subjected to discrimination in the auditioning process, more decided to try out for the orchestras. This study suggests that elimination of a process that allowed for sex discrimination had two positive effects. First, it opened opportunities for women that had not previously existed. Second, it raised the overall quality of the musicianship in the orchestras.

Covert research designs have also be used to test for discriminatory practices. Ian Ayres and Peter Siegelman (1995) conducted a study testing for race and gender discrimination in bargaining for a new car. The authors noted that the prices listed for new cars are often open to negotiation. The dealers selling the cars have discretion as to how much of a discount off the listed price they will offer potential buyers. The outcomes of negotiations of this kind could be driven by a range of factors that would not necessarily suggest discrimination on the part of the sellers. For example, in their book *Women Don't Ask,* Linda Babcock and Sara Laschever (2003) noted the tendency for women to be less aggressive than men in a range of negotiation contexts. For their study of discrimination in bargaining for a new car, Ayres and Siegelman selected pairs of testers to resemble each other as closely as possible on every indicator other than sex or race. For example, they trained all the testers to bargain uniformly and gave them bargaining scripts to follow. They also had them bargain for the same model of car at the same dealership. All testers were aged between twenty-eight and thirty-two years old, they all had three to four years of postsecondary education, and all were subjectively chosen to have average attractiveness. They were carefully scripted to display similar indicators of social class. For example, they all went to the dealerships in similar rented cars, wore similar "yuppie" sportswear, and volunteered at the beginning of the bargaining that they could provide their own financing for the car. In all, over 300 bargaining episodes were initiated at over 150 dealerships in the Chicago area. Ayers and Siegelman found that, on average, dealers offered African American and female testers significantly higher prices than the white males they were paired with, even though all testers used identical bargaining strategies. The authors concluded that the car dealers appeared to offer higher prices to African American and women testers because they figured that they could do so profitably and get away with it, not because the dealers harbored any particular animus toward African Americans and women. Nonetheless, this study clearly showed that discrimination can persist, even in competitive markets.

USING GENDER ANALYSIS AS AN ANALYTICAL FRAMEWORK

Gender analysis can be used to illuminate policy discussions at several of the stages in the policy-making process. It can usefully inform problem definition and agenda setting efforts. It can also be used to good effect at the policy adoption stage, when careful policy design work must be performed. Finally, there are many instances at the program evaluation stage when gender analysis can cast light on the ways that current public policies and programs associated with them serve to reduce or, in some cases, exacerbate gender gaps.

In the past, feminist scholars and policy practitioners have raised concern that gender analysis should not itself become marginalized in governmental advice-giving systems. For example, establishing a Ministry of Women's Affairs creates a temptation for analysts in other advice-giving agencies to ignore gender issues in their own policy work, assuming that, if they exist, they will be addressed elsewhere by the gender experts. This concern has led to gender mainstreaming: an effort to have gender issues routinely incorporated into policy analysis produced in all parts of government (True and Mintrom 2001). Often, it will make sense for policy analysts who have a specific interest in gender issues to focus their attention on the analysis of gender differences. However, in terms of having policy influence, it is crucial that those who do this kind of work engage in productive dialogue with others who do not. Here I suggest ways that sensitivity to gender differences can inform policy analysis. The approach is similar to that used in Chapter 7, on doing ethical policy analysis.

Gender Analysis and Problem Definition

When people are discussing a problem, it is useful to consider how that problem might affect women and men differently. From here, consideration can be given to why any differences exist. Sometimes, the differences might occur unintentionally, or as the result of historically embedded practices. At other times, institutional arrangements, daily practices, and decision-making processes might be deliberately intended to have different impacts on men and women. When thinking in terms of problem definition, it is important to recognize that a lot of biologically and historically based differences in gender roles in households and broader society have been pervasive in their influence on policies and practices elsewhere (i.e., schools, workplaces, policing, the military, and health service provision). Close scrutiny should be given to instances in which the legacies of past practices, either formal or informal, could be said to undermine contemporary efforts to promote key objectives of government: human flourishing, effective institutions, efficiency, sustainability, advancing human rights, and social equity.

Gender Analysis and Construction of Alternatives

Policy alternatives, by definition, place emphasis on the things that governments can do to address a specific problem. However, alternative policy approaches often implicitly—if not explicitly—contain different notions of responsibility for a problem and who should address it. Often, issues of gender become salient when high levels of reliance are placed on individuals and families for making policies work. Being sensitive to the balance of responsibility among government, market participants, and families is a good starting point for considering how different policy alternatives might affect men and women differently, and the desirability of those differences.

Gender Analysis and Selection of Criteria

Including gender impacts in the criteria used to judge policy alternatives opens the opportunity for explicit consideration to be given to different effects of policies on men and women. Gender analysis can also inform other criteria used to assess policy alternatives. For example, when a policy is expected to have different impacts on men and women, those impacts might be discussed with reference to economic efficiency, social equity, and where the burden will lie for compliance with the policy.

Gender Analysis and Prediction of Outcomes

Inclusion of gender impacts as a criterion for selecting among policy alternatives ensures that gender analysis will inform the prediction of outcomes. Consideration could be given here to differences that might arise between short-term and long-term outcomes. For example, changes to labor laws that facilitated more compatibility of work and family duties could be expected to have relatively minor short-term effects. Longer term, they could have major positive effects on the economic productivity of women—and, potentially, men as well. Such positive effects could then raise overall measures of a nation's economic performance. Another example of differential impacts over time could arise with a policy that directly addresses discrimination against women in a workplace. Such a policy could result in short-term negative consequences for men. (Think of the case of introducing blind auditions for orchestras; some men would have been miffed.) However, longer term, the policy would promote more efficient allocation of people to positions. That would have positive economic consequences overall.

Reporting Gender Analysis

In reporting gender analysis, it is important that trade-offs be discussed among potential policy alternatives, given the selection criteria employed. Efforts to address discrimination against women could be comprehensive or more piece-meal. The merits of each approach should be explicitly addressed. In general, it is useful when conducting gender analysis to acknowledge the broader societal context in which policy occurs. Many issues associated with gender differences, discrimination, and disadvantages for women arise out of institutional arrangements that historically have had little to do with explicit government actions. Although government actions can sometimes have dramatic effects in terms of reducing discrimination and disadvantage, at other times those effects can be muted because of strong countervailing social forces. It can be especially helpful in such instances for policy analysts to manage expectations of decision makers and stakeholders. This can be done, for example, by explaining what is known about the introduction of such policies in other contexts and the extent to which impacts appear to stay constant, increase, or diminish with time.

STEPS IN GENDER ANALYSIS

The foregoing discussion of how to use gender analysis as an analytical framework was deliberately general in approach. Now we turn to more specific steps. These are intended to be applicable for most studies that involve assessing differences in experiences and outcomes for men and women in specific context and how differences caused by discriminatory policies and practices might be addressed. The six steps introduced here are applied in the section to follow, which introduces an applied example.

Step 1. Select a specific context in which women appear significantly disadvantaged relative to men. By narrowing the focus of a study, available resources can be used to gain depth of knowledge about a particular manifestation of disadvantage. Often, deep investigations generate insights that can subsequently be generalized. For example, a detailed study that reveals disadvantage and discrimination in a particular school, hospital, accounting firm, or police department can alert people to circumstances and practices that are common to all such institutions. One good study can have powerful effects. That is the kind of study worth doing.

Step 2. Assemble evidence allowing you to illustrate differences in men's and women's experiences in similar contexts. The better the evidence you collect within a specific context, the stronger the claims you will be able to make about women's disadvantage relative to men. Sometimes, available statistics will provide the information you need. All that will be required is for you to bring those statistics together and analyze them in ways that have not been previously considered. At other times, original data collection will be required. If quantitative data collection is not an option, it is important to remember that case study work relying on interviews, observation, and narrative can do a lot to draw attention to a problem. When carefully performed, work of this kind can prompt others to collect the data that will be necessary to facilitate more rigorous analysis.

Step 3. Develop a process-tracing method to show how specific institutional arrangements, social practices, or decision making are discriminatory. When evidence shows that women are significantly disadvantaged relative to men in a specific context, then causal explanations need to be developed. At this step, effort should be made to answer the following kind of questions.

- Before they enter this context, on what relevant criteria could men and women be said to be most equal?
- On what relevant criteria could they be said to be most unequal?
- What factors in this context tend to support equal treatment of women and men?
- When does equal treatment of women and men produce equivalent outcomes for both groups?
- When does equal treatment serve to further disadvantage women?
- What specific decision points in this context can allow people to engage in discrimination?
- What evidence suggests that discrimination is occurring at those decision points?
- What daily, normalized practices in this context could be viewed as discriminatory?
- What stories do men in this context tell about the decision points and practices you have identified?

- What stories do women in this context tell about those same decision points and practices?
- Where do the stories converge, and where do they diverge?

Answers to questions of this kind could be collected using a range of observational techniques. Preliminary or pilot work will usually allow you to refine the set of questions you want to address. Systematic collection of data through surveys of people in the context can allow you to engage in subsequent statistical tests to explore the relationship between specific features of the context and the outcomes it generates. Focusing only on women can usually generate some useful insights. But efforts should be made to study the situation of both women and men in the context. This will allow for direct comparison across the groups. It can also reveal information that is counterintuitive but valuable for generating insights about effective ways to address and eliminate discrimination.

Step 4. Highlight discriminatory policies or practices, and show how they disadvantage women compared with men. Often, studies will reveal multiple forms of disadvantage and discrimination within given contexts. It is important to prioritize among these and choose those that you intend to focus upon. In general, your focus should be on the most systematic and serious forms of discrimination.

Step 5. Propose policy actions to rectify the discrimination and disadvantage. It can be helpful at this step to consider the extent to which the observed discrimination and disadvantage can be addressed. Government actions can make huge differences in terms of forcing people to change their practices. But sometimes, government actions can also have limited effects. Policy analysts must consider what policy actions would be likely to have the most powerful effects. They also must consider how feasible specific policy actions might be, given the context and the range of factors—social, institutional, economic, and current government policy settings—that serve to shape the practices of women and men within that context.

Step 6. Address the view that gains for women spell losses for men. For people who view their lives as a series of zero-sum games, every encounter that results in a good outcome for someone else can be viewed as a personal loss. At a narrow, competitive level, it is easy to find instances in which one person's gain is another person's loss, at least in the short term. When actions are being proposed to rectify discrimination against women and the disadvantages that flow from it, attention must be paid to the actual or perceived losses for men. Discriminatory practices are perpetrated by people who figure that they can get away with them. They figure they can get away with them because they have been in positions of privilege and power. People usually do not give up such positions without a fight. Workable solutions to discrimination and disadvantage usually need to have powerful supporters who can use their power to enforce compliance with policy changes.

Careful, strategic thinking is required to determine the most effective ways to change power dynamics in specific contexts.[4] If losses for men can be minimized and everyone can see the potential for gains, then change is more likely to happen. Indeed, many changes that have been introduced primarily to improve the situation of women have had benefits for men. These include giving women and men equal access to education, moves toward more flexible work hours, interventions to eliminate domestic violence, and efforts to broaden and objectify definitions of merit for the purposes of employment and promotion.

AN APPLIED EXAMPLE

This section highlights analysis contained in the following:

Savita Kumra and Susan Vinnicombe. (2008). "A Study of the Promotion to Partner Process in a Professional Services Firm: How Women Are Disadvantaged." *British Journal of Management* 19: 65–74.

Broad social changes in industrialized countries during the past few decades have enabled women to enter many industries and professions that were once heavily male dominated. However, a body of literature has indicated that women often experience difficulty reaching senior positions in their chosen fields of work. That is despite women increasingly having similar educational levels, years of service, and levels of job performance as their male peers. This phenomenon is referred to as the *glass ceiling*. It occurs when barriers to advancement are subtle, almost unseen, but still strong. Concrete ceilings also exist. They tend to occur in professions in which being an in-your-face tough guy is considered essential to career advancement.

Savita Kumra and Susan Vinnicombe (2008) observed that women often appear to have difficulty making it to partner in professions such as law, accounting, management consulting, and investment banking. To understand the dynamics at stake, and to test for the presence of discrimination, the two researchers conducted a study of a global management consulting firm. Within this study, they interviewed both male and female consultants about their perceptions of the promotion to partner process within their firm. Here, I use Kumra and Vinnicombe's study as a practical illustration of how to apply the steps in gender analysis noted earlier.

Step 1. Select a specific context in which women appear significantly disadvantaged relative to men. The authors focus on a category of organizations termed

---

[4] Gail Collins (2009), Jane Mansbridge (1986), and Sheila Rowbotham (2010) have offered insightful analyses and reflections upon coalition building and mobilization strategies employed by leaders in women's movements in the United States and the United Kingdom during the twentieth century.

professional service firms. Available statistics reveal that firms in this category often employ entry-level women and men at the in numbers approaching gender parity. However, among the ranks of partners—that is, the most senior members of these firms—men far outnumber women. This does not appear to be an artifact of history. That is, the evidence suggests that waiting sufficiently long enough will not result in major changes in the gender composition of partners in firms of this kind. The authors wanted to find out why that is so.

Step 2. Assemble evidence allowing you to illustrate differences in men's and women's experiences in similar contexts. The authors were aware of quantitative studies exploring why fewer women made it to partner in law firms than men, and the explanations given. However, Kumra and Vinnicombe were especially interested in process tracing, and exploring perceptions of women and men concerning the process of promotion to partner in professional service firms. To this end, they focused their study on the United Kingdom practice of a single international consulting firm. They obtained a list of consultants in the firm and then drew a sample from it to reflect a range of views on the promotion process. The sample consisted of both female and male consultants, representing a variety of ages and employment levels, all below partner. A total of thirty-four interviews were conducted with nineteen women and fifteen men.

Step 3. Develop a process-tracing method to show how specific institutional arrangements, social practices, or decision making are discriminatory. Kumra and Vinnicombe conducted semistructured interviews with each of the participants in their study. Because promotion was deemed a sensitive topic, the authors did not ask their subjects to provide information or examples in relation to the course their own careers had taken, or to disclose actions that they had adopted personally to advance their careers. Rather, they were asked to advise an ambitious friend on how to gain promotion to partner within the firm. In adopting an advisory role, the authors anticipated that interviewees would be willing to give their advice on how to advance within the firm without feeling the need to hold anything back. Interviewees were also asked if there were things they would specifically advise their friend not to do (actions that could inhibit their chances of promotion). The interviewees were also asked whether they felt that the promotion process in the firm was fair. All the interviews were recorded and transcribed. The authors then coded the results.

Step 4. Highlight discriminatory policies or practices, and show how they disadvantage women compared with men. The respondents each provided detailed accounts of their perceptions of the promotion to partner process within their firm. Across all the interviews, two main areas of potential disadvantage for women emerged. The first issue was the self-managed nature of the career advancement process within the firm. All but one of the interviewees mentioned this. The interviewees noted the need for individuals to be effective networkers in the firm and to be self-promoting about their achievements. The men interviewees appeared generally more comfortable with this than the women interviewees. The authors noted that women may avoid self-promotion, believing those who behave "out of role" risk social censure for behaving outside their gender stereotype norms.

The second issue to emerge was the need for people to fit a mold in order to succeed within the firm. Three-quarters of the interviewees discussed this issue. There was general agreement about what the mold was and its gendered nature. The authors provided comments to illustrate the point. Example 1: "One of the qualities you want to see in partners is that when you walk into a room people stop and take notice that you're there...which is why there are so many big tall male partners." Example 2: "I think a lot of the partners like what I call a 'good bloke.' Someone who will go out drinking, play snooker, and I can spot a mile off the type of person who's going to appeal." (See Kumra and Vinnicombe 2008: 70–80.) The authors said male and female interviewees agreed that to advance within the firm, it was necessary to understand and emulate the prevailing model of success. In essence, this meant that people who made partners were those who looked and acted like existing partners, a predominantly male group.

Step 5. Propose policy actions to rectify the discrimination and disadvantage. Kumra and Vinnicombe observed that the disadvantages women face in relation to the promotion to partner process arise from a combination of firm-based and societal factors. Women who have been socialized more to cooperate than to compete found it difficult to get ahead in the context of the self-managed career. The authors did not propose any policy actions in light of their findings. That is primarily because they saw the study as small and difficult to generalize from. Their primary goal was to prompt further research on the potential for discrimination in professional service firms. However, government efforts to facilitate more awareness of discriminatory practices in professional workplaces could help to change corporate cultures. In addition, efforts could be made to establish best-practice cultures in public sector agencies.

Step 6. Address the view that gains for women spell losses for men. This matter was not addressed in the study. However, it was obvious that some serious cultural domination was at work in the firm being studied. That cultural domination involved a certain form of masculinity, not shared by all professional men. So a question worth considering would be how professional women in this industry could collaborate with male colleagues who do not fit the tall, drinking, snooker-playing stereotype and develop more hospitable workplaces.

ADVICE FOR ANALYTICAL PRACTICE

Gender analysis can be improved by incorporating the following suggestions.

- People can be subject to discrimination and not be fully aware of it. Others can perpetuate it and not realize they are doing so. Treat gender analysis as a way of raising awareness about problems rather than an exercise in allocating blame.

- Develop simple but striking ways to illustrate how women are disadvantaged in specific contexts.
- Having identified problems, suggest appropriate remedial actions. It is even better if you can offer examples of working solutions.
- Treat public policies and government actions as tools among a broader set of remedies, which might include forms of nongovernmental action. In general, it is best to use government solutions as a last resort.
- Sort your proposed solutions into categories. Some will be hard to introduce; others will be easier. Some will make big differences; others will make minor differences. You might suggest sequencing changes, starting with those that will be easier but that will make big differences. This will build momentum for tackling the hard things.
- Any actions to reduce discrimination can be costly. Try to estimate those costs. But also estimate the costs of the discrimination itself, and of not addressing it.

GENDER ANALYSIS AND OTHER ANALYTICAL STRATEGIES

As policy analysts, we need to be aware of the ways—both explicit and subtle—that gendered assumptions can influence policy design and organizational practices. The analyses of gender discussed in this chapter suggest that acquiring good data disaggregated by gender is vital. Sometimes, this data can be acquired from existing sources. Other times, it needs to be generated through carefully designed studies. The studies highlighted here mostly focused on situations that involved women holding relatively privileged social positions. The studies revealed that even for such women—who have a lot of efficacy in their lives—gender bias can be pervasive and detrimental to their well-being and their career development. We should expect to find gender bias playing out in a range of ways in other situations. Gendered assumptions about who performs care work in the family or what kind of work is suitable for paid employment significantly influence people's lives. Once we start looking for the ways that gender differences and gendered assumptions are embedded in society, we can find many instances in which better design of policies, rules, and organizational activities could produce better and more equal outcomes for all members of society.

Gender analysis can be effectively combined with several other analytical strategies. For example, the approach is highly compatible with the analysis of markets, market failure, and government failure. It can be combined with comparative institutional analysis. Further, aspects of cost-benefit analysis can be incorporated into gender analyses, and sensitivity to the gendered impacts of programs and policies can be incorporated into cost-benefit analyses. The focus in this chapter has been on gender discrimination and the disadvantage that can stem from that. However, discrimination and disadvantage can be experienced for a variety of reasons. Often people find themselves being discriminated against on multiple grounds. That is why, for example, gender analysis can be combined to good effect with race analysis, which is covered in the next chapter.

Exercises

1. Often, people hold quite strong views about what forms of work in society and the household comprise "men's work" and what forms comprise "women's work." Questions arise as to how much these views shape policy design. How much should public policies conform to current social expectations? How much should public policies consciously seek to break down gendered assumptions that significantly disadvantage women compared with men? We cannot hope to resolve these questions here. But we should at least be able to identify the broad areas of public policy in which such questions are most likely to be highly salient. In small groups, make a list of social and policy areas where men and women are most likely to be treated differently.

2. In small groups, reflect on some of the policy reports or policy studies that you have read. Note any instances in which gender analysis was included in the analytical work. In general, discuss ways that gender analysis could be used to enhance the analysis of policies and their impacts in your fields of policy work.

The Policy Research Seminar

Organize a research-oriented seminar that will run for about ninety minutes, preferably with some light refreshments. Invite up to twelve people, and make sure you have a mixture of experienced researchers, junior researchers, and graduate students. The purpose of the discussion should be to develop ideas for the design of policy research projects that give a central place to gender analysis. The project ideas should be sufficiently interesting and original that each could form the basis of a significant research paper, dissertation, or thesis. Participants should come to the seminar having read both this chapter and Savita Kumla and Susan Vinnicombe's (2008) "A Study of the Promotion to Partner Process in a Professional Services Firm: How Women Are Disadvantaged" (*British Journal of Management* 19: 65–74). You might structure the discussion around the section "Steps in Gender Analysis" presented in this chapter and applied in the overview of the Kumra and Vinnicombe study. Many other recent journal articles could have been highlighted in this chapter. Prior to the group meeting, you might have several participants locate other interesting articles that present original gender analyses. Discussions of this sort tend to work best when the group has a clear goal. I suggest this outcome statement: "By the end of this meeting, we will have identified five possible topics for new research projects that involve gender analysis. We will have sketched out basic research designs for at least two of those projects." Brainstorm to get some ideas flowing. Hold the more skeptical, analytical comments until later in the seminar. Ideally, some members of the discussion group will follow up on the meeting and continue to develop, perhaps collaboratively, research designs that build from the readings and the discussion. This is a good way to promote original policy research inspired by the best contemporary applications of quantitative and qualitative research methods. For additional advice on how to run effective meetings of this kind, see (1) Michael Mintrom's (2003) "Facilitating Meetings" in *People Skills for Policy Analysts* (Washington, DC: Georgetown University Press) and (2) Tom Kelley's (2001) "The Perfect Brainstorm" in *The Art of Innovation* (New York: Currency/Doubleday).

Further Reading

Ayres, Ian, and Peter Siegelman. (1995). "Race and Gender Discrimination in Bargaining for a New Car." *American Economic Review* 85: 304–321.

Fraser, Nancy. (1998). "From Redistribution to Recognition: Dilemmas of Justice in a Post-Socialist Age." In *Feminism and Politics: Oxford Readings in Feminism,* Chapter 20, ed. Anne Phillips. New York: Oxford University Press.

Hearn, Jeff, and Linda McKie. (2008). "Gendered Policy and Policy on Gender: The Case of 'Domestic Violence.'" *Policy and Politics* 36: 75–91.

Pager, Devah. (2007). "The Use of Field Experiments for Studies of Employment Discrimination: Contributions, Critiques, and Directions for the Future." *Annals of the American Academy of Political and Social Science* 609: 104–133.

Weichselbaumer, Doris, and Rudolf Winter-Ebmer. (2007). "The Effects of Competition and Equal Treatment Laws on Gender Wage Differentials." *Economic Policy* 22 (April): 235–287.

15

Race Analysis

The Story So Far... Different analytical strategies can be used to assess the actual or the anticipated effects of policies against relevant criteria. We have considered several.

Here... We review ways to study social and economic disadvantage associated with race, and how such disadvantage gets perpetuated. We consider how policy analysts can contribute to better social and economic outcomes for all. The analytical steps proposed here for doing race analysis are similar to those proposed for doing gender analysis.

THIS CHAPTER REVIEWS
- The place of race analysis in public policy analysis
- Approaches used to test for discriminatory practices
- Approaches to studying gaps among groups in the attainments of valued outcomes
- How public policy choices can affect racial differences

Cultural, ethnic, and racial differences have created enormous conflicts in many societies. Policy analysts need to be highly attuned to the social contexts in which they work, and be aware that different policy designs might be interpreted in quite different ways by different groups in society (Kymlicka 2001). Just as people who have different kinds of professional training view problems and situations differently, it is common to find people from different race and ethnic groups in society holding contrasting views about problems and appropriate solutions.

Aggregate statistics often reveal stark differences across racial and ethnic groups with respect to the attainment of desired social and economic outcomes.

Several concerns are raised when some groups in society appear systematically disadvantaged. From the perspectives of social equity and the promotion of human rights, all people should be able to enjoy equality of opportunity and be free from discriminatory practices. From the perspective of effective institutions and economic efficiency, it is preferable for society that arbitrary forms of disadvantage and discrimination are eliminated.

As the usage of mainstream methods of policy analysis has spread, such as the use of cost-benefit analysis, there has been a degree of criticism of those methods. Among other things, representatives of groups who have sometimes had limited access to decision making have led efforts to make explicit the biases contained in policy design and policy implementation. Today, race analysis and gender analysis are tools commonly used to study the decisions, practices, and processes that can generate unequal outcomes for members of different social groups. Using examples from the United States, this chapter reviews how policy analysts can use race analysis. It shows how such work can support efforts to advance a range of goals, including human rights, social justice, the rights of children, and more inclusive democratic practice.

AN OVERVIEW OF RACE ANALYSIS

In the United States, a lot of consideration has been given to the ways that differences and tensions between racial groups manifest themselves in social and economic disparities and everyday discrimination. Laws are in place to counter overt discrimination. Yet, evidence indicates that some people still view others around them in discriminatory ways. In this overview, several contemporary problems and analytical approaches to exploring them are highlighted. All of them take their starting point from observed differences in outcomes for African Americans and whites. Two fundamental questions have driven these analyses: What explains these different outcomes? What can be done to eliminate them?

Three analytical approaches are discussed. The first considers the circumstances under which race-based discrimination could be justified. Testing for statistical discrimination versus racial prejudice allows analysts to isolate incidents in which discrimination has occurred and racial prejudice appears the most plausible explanation. Later in this chapter, in an applied example, we will further consider use of this type of test. It can illustrate the pernicious effects of "racial profiling"—or stereotyping—as an administrative practice used by government agents and corporate decision makers. The second analytical approach involves confronting misattribution problems. Race is frequently employed as a marker category, but its meaning can actually be vague. Further, when people place too much reliance on race as an explanation of behavioral differences, interpretation mistakes can be made. Those mistakes can perpetuate racial prejudice and have a range of undesirable behavioral effects. We discuss how race analysis can address this problem. The final analytical approach discussed involves tracing complex processes. Observed outcome gaps among racial groups have prompted careful analytical work. Frequently, as that analytical work has proceeded, it has become clear that differences that manifest themselves as race-based are driven by complex processes, whereby interactions among disadvantage, social structures, and institutional arrangements cannot be separated. Here, process tracing becomes a grail quest: A search for those places where specific policy interventions could have powerful, transformative effects on outcomes.

Testing for Statistical Discrimination versus Racial Prejudice

Tests for discriminatory practices were introduced in Chapter 14, "Gender Analysis." Two common kinds were discussed. The first involves collecting available statistical information and analyzing it to find evidence of discrimination. Claudia Goldin and Ceclia Rouse's (2000) study of the move to blind auditions of musicians for orchestras served as an example. The authors found that, controlling for other possible explanations, more women were selected as orchestra players once judges could no longer see the players and could only hear their playing. By implication, gender discrimination had occurred in the past. The second kind of test involves covert collection of new data for analysis. Situations are created in which the actions of people suspected to engage in discriminatory practices can be directly observed. Ian Ayres and Peter Siegelman's (1995) study of race and gender discrimination in bargaining for a new car illustrated the approach. There, evidence of discrimination was generated by comparing car dealers' price quotes for new cars. The investigators used matched pairs of shoppers and maintained the same conditions in all cases, except that they varied the race and gender of the new car buyers in the pairs. Ayres and Siegelman found evidence of systematic discrimination, so that all people who were not white men tended to be quoted higher new car prices than their white male counterparts. Building on methods like those employed by Ayres and Siegelman (1995) and Goldin and Rouse (2000), tests for racial discrimination have become highly sophisticated.

In the United States during the 1990s, significant controversy arose concerning how police officers on highway patrol selected the cars they would pull over to stop and search. The claim was commonly made that police officers were engaging in "racial profiling." In practice, this meant that officers were more likely to stop and search cars driven by African Americans than they were to stop and search cars driven by whites. Similar concerns have been raised about treatment of Hispanic drivers versus white drivers. To date, there have been over 200 court cases involving allegations of racial profiling on the part of law enforcement agencies in the United States. In defense of apparent racism, the argument has been made that it is legitimate because, given specific contexts, nonwhite people are more likely to break the law than white people. The controversy over racial profiling led to the development of new statistical tests allowing researchers to assess whether the actions of police officers were fair or discriminatory.

Kate Antonovics and Brian G. Knight (2009) noted that courts in the United States have consistently ruled against what appear to be racist policing practices regarding traffic stops and automobile searches. However, it is not easy to empirically distinguish between fair and racist actions. The authors noted that "statistical discrimination" arises when police officers are uncertain about whether a suspect has committed a particular crime. If there are racial differences in the propensity to commit that crime, then the police may rationally treat individuals from different racial groups differently. In contrast, racial prejudice is manifested when police unfairly target particular groups.

In their study of policing in Boston, Antonovics and Knight explored the reasons for observed racial differences in the rate at which the vehicles of African American, Hispanic, and white motorists were searched during traffic stops. Rather than focus exclusively on the race of each driver being stopped, the authors also considered the race of each of the officers initiating a stop. They argued that if statistical discrimination alone explained differences in the rate at which drivers from different racial groups were stopped, then stop-and-search decisions should also be independent of the race of the police officer initiating the stop. They also argued that if stops and searches were more likely to occur when the race of the officer differed from the race of the driver, then this would show racial prejudice. They tested these arguments on a data set they constructed that matched the race of the officer to the race of the driver for every traffic stop made by officers in the Boston Police Department for a two-year period. In addition to being able to discern differences in the likelihood that motorists from different racial groups were subject to stops and searches, they were also able to determine whether those patterns differed depending on the race of the officers involved.

Antonovics and Knight found that if the race of the officer differed from the race of the motorist, then the officer was more likely to conduct a search of a stopped vehicle than otherwise. The authors argued that their results could not be explained by standard models of statistical discrimination and, instead, were consistent with racial prejudice. In addition, the authors ruled out the possibility that their findings were driven by differences in the ease or difficulty officers confronted when seeking to search members of their own racial group versus members of other racial groups. They also showed that the manner by which officers were assigned to neighborhoods within the city did not account for their findings. Rather, their results suggested that racial prejudice played a substantial role in explaining differences in the rate at which motorists from different racial groups were searched during traffic stops. The study was important for the way that it distinguished empirically between statistical discrimination and racial prejudice. Further, because it showed that racial prejudice is not the preserve of white police officers, the study suggested the need for exploration of how broader social relations, policy design, and institutional structures might encourage acts of race-based hostility on the part of authority figures. Policy implications arise from these findings. They suggest that law enforcement agencies should take care to introduce training and routines that make officers aware of their potential to appear discriminatory in their practices, and the consequences of taking discriminatory actions. Further, careful monitoring of practices should be routinized so that actions by officers that are motivated by racial prejudice can be identified and eliminated.

Confronting Misattribution Problems

The foregoing discussion illustrated how policy analysts can gain insights into racial discrimination and disadvantage by noting the behaviors and experiences of people falling into different racial categories. In the United States, it is common to find studies that categorize individuals into specific racial or ethnic groups—for example, white, African American, Hispanic, Asian, Native American. In his discussion of race analysis and policy analysis, Samuel L. Myers Jr. (2002) called for more scrutiny of the merits of using race as a category. The basic problem is that mistakes can arise in how we interpret situations and the causal stories that we tell about what we see (Stone 2002). Grounded in studies of cognitive psychology, many scholars have noted the tendency for people to use mental shortcuts or heuristics as the basis for social judgments. Mostly, these heuristics serve us well. However, sometimes they can lead us to make mistakes (Fiske and Taylor 2008; Nisbett and Ross 1980; Thaler and Sunstein 2008). For example, stereotyping is a common strategy used to ascribe attributes to people in the presence of limited information. We use stereotyping to make quick judgments about likability, intelligence, social status, and trustworthiness. But sometimes our stereotyping leads us to make wrong decisions. When a lot of people employing the same stereotype make wrong decisions, poor social outcomes can result. Myers (2002) suggested that race analysis can be used to challenge inappropriate stereotyping. In his own scholarship, he has shown how this kind of race analysis can be performed effectively. Here, I draw on his work with Sheila Ards to illustrate how race analysis can confront misattribution problems.

In 1992, a study published by the Federal Reserve Bank of Boston suggested that African Americans and Hispanics faced discrimination when seeking mortgages to buy homes (Munnell, Browne, McEneaney, and Tootell 1992). The evidence suggested that an unexplained racial gap existed in who received home loans. During the subsequent debate a key question arose: "If lenders do discriminate, then why?" (Myers 2002: 172). In 1999, the United States Federal Home Loan Mortgage Corporation, known as Freddie Mac, released a report that suggested that African Americans had worse creditworthiness than whites. Freddie Mac proposed that efforts be made by lenders to educate African Americans about financial planning and management to improve their creditworthiness. Notice here the implication that race itself can be taken as a marker of creditworthiness. The report created a major controversy, with members of Congress weighing in.[1] Prompted by the release of this report and the controversy that ensued, Sheila Ards and Samuel Myers conducted a race analysis exploring linkages between bad credit, wealth, and race. The study was published in the *American Behavioral Scientist* in 2001.

Ards and Myers proposed to examine "the myth of bad credit in the Black community" (p. 224). They began by noting that African Americans historically have had higher savings rates than whites. Up until the 1940s, many African Americans

---

[1] See D'Vera Cohn (1999).

simply saved to purchase consumer items and never sought loans at all. This was a result of discrimination in lending. Prevailing institutional structures promoted distinctive behaviors among people of different races because those prevailing institutions were themselves racist. Ards and Myers noted that neither the historically high savings rate nor the lower use of credit shielded even good African American credit risks from the emerging stereotype that all blacks are bad risks. Using contemporary data from several sources, the authors compared African Americans and whites as credit risks within three wealth levels: high, medium, and low. They concluded that some African Americans are poor credit risks, but many are not. The authors found no statistically significant difference in bad credit rates between black and white households at the lowest and highest wealth levels. In the middle levels they did find differences, but they explained these as resulting mainly from the tendency for African Americans to have to spend a higher proportion of their income on rental housing than do whites. This results in lower assets and lower net worth, leading to poorer creditworthiness. But this is also a legacy of structural circumstances; it does not imply any inherent lack of creditworthiness of African Americans compared with whites. Significantly, the authors found misattribution problems among African Americans themselves.

The race analysis produced by Ards and Myers can be summarized as follows.

1. Past wealth inequality and the credit institutions supporting it have contributed to bad credit in the present.
2. Lenders believe that African Americans have bad credit, so they are more likely to deny loans to African Americans than to whites.
3. African Americans with good credit, observing that African Americans are denied credit in disproportionate numbers, begin to believe that they, too, would be turned down for loans and assume that they, too, have bad credit.
4. African Americans with bad credit apply for loans and, like whites with bad credit, are turned down.
5. Those African Americans who are turned down for loans (and who have bad credit) serve to stigmatize the entire population of potential African American borrowers as having bad credit.
6. In contrast, whites with bad credit, who represent a relatively small portion of the white population, do not generate a bad stereotype for the entire white population.
7. The credit gap continues because African Americans with good credit believe that they have bad credit and African Americans with bad credit continue to signal to the market that all African Americans are like them. Note that the problem here is conceptually identical to information asymmetry problems in the market for used cars, discussed in Chapter 10, "Market Failure." When bad credit risks drive good credit risks from the market, the possibility arises that the market will collapse.

8. Policies supporting education of African American loan applicants about planning and financial management could risk further marking African Americans as a group and closing off profitable opportunities to bring good credit risks into the credit market (pp. 224–225).

9. An appropriate public policy response in this instance would be to support strategies that encourage African Americans who are good credit risks to easily signal their good credit risk and, hence, face no discrimination. The goal is to have people's creditworthiness judged by financially relevant criteria, not by race. Lenders could profit from developing more relevant and accurate measures of creditworthiness.

In sum, race analysis can be effectively used to confront misattribution problems. Such work is consistent with the whole point of policy analysis, as noted in Chapter 2. There, I suggested that policy analysis, as a practice, embodies the belief that if we can break free from instinctual reactions, assess the situation, and think hard about it, then we will increase the odds that good outcomes will result. The good policy analyst enjoins us to take a deep breath, take time to think, talk to others, collect more information, reflect upon it, and only after that choose a course of action. That is precisely the approach to race analysis adopted by Ards and Myers (2001) and that Myers (2002) proposed be more widely employed by policy analysts.

Tracing Complex Processes

Many indicators of gaps among racial groups in the attainment of desired outcomes can be found in contemporary societies. Sadly, gaps commonly exist in relation to average household income, wealth accumulation, educational attainment, and health status. The causes of these gaps are complex. Yet, efforts to address them are often accorded urgency among advocacy groups, opinion leaders, and politicians. Well-intentioned people desire to see those gaps close, and they look to policy analysts for advice on how that can be achieved. Here I discuss what is commonly referred to in the United States as the "black-white test score gap." According to Christopher Jencks and Meredith Phillips (1998), this gap refers to the lower average scores that African Americans attain on vocabulary, reading, and mathematics tests, as well as on tests that claim to measure scholastic aptitude and intelligence. The gap has been observed among children prior to their entry into kindergarten, and it persists into adulthood. Across all such tests for which accurate data has been amassed, the average African American test score tends to be below 75 percent of the average white American test score. In a book on the topic, former United States Secretary of Education Rod Paige has referred to this gap as "the greatest civil rights challenge of our time" (Paige and Witty 2010).

It is well understood that aggregate differences in test scores are subject to change. Indeed, gaps among men and women closed during the twentieth century, and, on some measures, gaps between African Americans and whites also closed to some degree. Eliminating the present gap would open new educational opportunities for African Americans. That would likely have significant labor market effects and could serve to close gaps in the average incomes of African Americans and whites. In turn, that could have major implications for health outcomes. Overall, closing black-white test score gaps represents a goal for which attainment would undoubtedly have huge and positive transformative effects on American society. Although a small minority of people might mistakenly believe that closing the gap would erode some level of privilege currently enjoyed by whites, the bigger picture is a highly positive one. Historically, plenty of evidence exists of broad economic development benefiting all in society (Helpman 2004; North 1981).

Policy makers need to know the factors that have caused the test score gap. They also need to know which of those factors could be influenced by changes in government policy. From there, a prioritization exercise could occur. That is to say, efforts could be made to order policy changes by their expected impacts, from most influential to least influential. Among the policy changes expected to have the greatest impacts, consideration could then be given to which ones could be introduced most easily and which would be the hardest. Economists and social scientists have produced excellent studies of the test score gap. (For recent examples, see, e.g., Card and Rothstein 2007; Fryer and Levitt 2004; and Stiefel, Schwartz, and Ellen 2006.) Their combined efforts have offered insights into family effects, school effects, and peer effects on student achievement. As more convergence occurs in the results of these studies, policy makers will be able to promote change with more certainty that their efforts will have positive payoffs. However, the politics of such change efforts are highly complex. Knowledge of what changes are needed is a prerequisite for decisive action. So is political consensus and leadership.

USING RACE ANALYSIS AS AN ANALYTICAL STRATEGY

Policy analysts can make effective use of race analysis in two distinctive ways. First, race analysis can be performed as stand-alone work, in which the focus in placed on a specific problem known to be generating racial disparities. Our overview has highlighted several studies of that kind. The following applied example highlights another. Second, concerns about racial differences can be made salient at each step in the process of doing policy analysis. When this approach is taken to race analysis, the most important goal is to raise awareness of race issues among the participants in the policy-making process.

In the past, policy analysts often assumed that all citizens had common interests and concerns. The emphasis was placed on attaining policy outcomes judged as good for society overall; the effects on specific groups or individuals were given much less attention. For example, it is well known that the creation of the Cross-Bronx Expressway, which began in 1948, had significant benefits for traffic flow in the New York region but that it had devastating social consequences for the section of the Bronx that it went through. In that instance, sound use of race analysis might have resulted in much more sensitivity to the communities directly affected by the project. Robert Moses, who authorized the work, was sensitive to race issues, but closing gaps was not part of his agenda (Caro 1974).

Race Analysis and Problem Definition

When any policy problem is being defined, policy analysts should consider how people from different race and ethnic groups might define it. We should not assume that some problems lend themselves to race analysis and others do not. Ask this question: How does race matter here? If the problem under consideration involves policies that are already in place, it is useful to consider whether any race bias associated with those policies was intentional or if it emerged through the ways people interpreted those policies. It is always useful to discuss problem definition broadly. Sensitivity to race issues can lead to more consultation. That is a good thing.

Race Analysis and Construction of Alternatives

As a first step to addressing policy problems, analysts need to gather information and explore what possible policy approaches could be effective. By acknowledging from the outset that policies can have differential impacts on people from different racial or ethnic groups, alternatives that could have negative effects for specific groups are more likely to be dropped from consideration. That allows attention to be focused on policy alternatives that can potentially benefit all social groups and not perpetuate disadvantage.

Race Analysis and Selection of Criteria

When we adopt a race perspective, we explicitly make impacts on people of different races a criterion for judging the relative merits of different policy alternatives. However, there is value in thinking carefully about interactions between race impacts and the other criteria used to evaluate the merits of policies. For example, sensitivity to race means that we are likely to consider the equity effects of a policy in a manner that involves more disaggregation across social groups than would normally be the case.

Race Analysis and Prediction of Outcomes

When we are doing policy analysis, we predict policy outcomes by comparing each policy alternative against our selected evaluative criteria. Following this method, we are then able to determine the relative merits of each policy alternative and the trade-offs that we would face in choosing one over others. By highlighting differential race impacts in our analysis, we reduce the potential for policies to have adverse consequences for specific racial groups.

Reporting Race Analysis

The impacts of social structures, existing institutional arrangements, and entrenched forms of racial prejudice can present formidable barriers to policy efforts designed to achieve greater racial equality in society. When race analysis is being reported, policy analysts should be clear about the size and nature of the challenges to be faced. They should also indicate their estimates of the effectiveness of any new policies being proposed, when they expect positive results to be observed, and where problems could arise.

STEPS IN RACE ANALYSIS

As noted earlier, race analyses can be undertaken for a variety of reasons and they can be focused on a variety of contexts. Drawing on insights emerging from the discussion in this chapter, several general steps are now proposed for performing race analysis. Readers familiar with Chapter 14, "Gender Analysis," will notice some close similarities between the analytical steps proposed there and those proposed here. That is because both analytical approaches are concerned with the exploration of differences among groups, the impact of those differences, the factors that support those differences, and how socially undesirable differences can be reduced through policy actions.

Step 1. Select a specific context in which significant racial disparities are known or expected to exist. There is good reason to believe that racial disadvantage is driven by discrimination and that discriminatory practice is widespread. However, considerable effort is required to collect evidence of discrimination and make convincing causal connections between it and the perpetuation of disadvantage. For that reason, race analysis is typically performed with reference to specific contexts. The need to keep a narrow focus can feel frustrating to those who would like to promote transformative social change. However, it is important to note that convincing analysis of well-chosen cases can be persuasive and influential.

Step 2. Assemble evidence allowing you to confirm the existence of racial disparities. This evidence can be assembled from existing sources, or original data collection can be undertaken. Given the resources required to conduct original data collection, it usually makes sense to begin a study by assembling relevant existing evidence. Often, working with such evidence will be sufficient to make the case for more resources to be devoted to supporting original data collection. Whenever data is gathered and presented to illustrate a gap or a difference among racial groups, it is essential that care be given to considering all plausible explanations for why they are observed. Good race analysis always involves careful efforts to test competing explanations for gaps and differences.

Step 3. Develop a process-tracing method to show how specific institutional arrangements, social practices, or decision making are discriminatory. Process-tracing methods can take a variety of forms. For example, a study of discrimination in police enforcement efforts would seek to explore decision-making processes that increase the likelihood of specific encounters occurring.

Relevant questions become these: What are the demographics of a given police force? How do recruitment strategies affect those demographics? What are the demographics of various districts in which the police force operates? How are officers assigned to specific districts? In what ways might decision-making routines influence the likelihood that police officers will target members of one race over another? In general, the set of questions that prompt process tracing will be unique to each context being studied. By reviewing prior studies—both in similar contexts and in different contexts—it is possible to improve your ability to develop sound process-tracing methods.

Step 4. Highlight discriminatory policies or practices, and show how they disadvantage specific racial groups. Often, studies will generate evidence of discrimination occurring in a variety of ways. If this is the case, then decisions need to be made about the specific forms of discrimination that will be highlighted. It will usually make sense to focus on those that have the most significant impact in terms of perpetuating disadvantage. Careful process-tracing work will lay the foundations for this step.

Step 5. Propose policy actions to rectify the discrimination and disadvantage. Identifying and interpreting discriminatory policies and practices is the first step. The point, of course, is to eliminate them. Often, rectifying discrimination and disadvantage can be difficult, because it emerges out of institutional arrangements and social practices that have been long established. Learning from what has worked in other contexts can be particularly useful for building knowledge about what might work in the present case. In general, the search for policy solutions should seek to achieve maximum impact with the least effort. There is little point in proposing that significant resources be devoted to actions that will yield only incremental changes.

Step 6. Scrutinize the proposed policy actions to avoid unintended negative effects. Given that discrimination and disadvantage are often perpetuated through practices and structures that are not easily changed, it is vital that efforts be made to create new policies that will actually be effective. People resist change. Sometimes, they will face incentives to undermine policy changes. That can have detrimental effects. When policy changes designed to eliminate discrimination do not have the intended effect, they can promote cynicism on the part of both those who would have benefited from effective policy and those who were required to implement it. Efforts to gain deep appreciation of organizational contexts and how new policies will be interpreted within them can generate major payoffs. Such efforts can be especially important when the policy goal is significant behavioral change.

Step 7. Estimate the gains for all groups that would result from effective policy change. The elimination of discriminatory practices clearly benefits those who were previously the object of discrimination. However, eliminating discrimination usually brings with it many positive consequences that can be shared by all. Proposals for change based on careful race analysis can become more convincing when they are supported by some assessment of their costs and benefits. As with any cost-benefit analyses, good faith attempts to estimate the net present value of policy changes usually serve to advance discussions around the value of a change. In turn, such discussions can lead to incremental improvements in estimation methods. Policy makers are much more likely to support and promote change efforts when they have received clear information about the size and distribution of gains and losses.

AN APPLIED EXAMPLE

This section highlights analysis contained in the following:

Paul M. Ong and Michael A. Stoll. (2007). "Redlining or Risk? A Spatial Analysis of Auto Insurance Rates in Los Angeles." *Journal of Policy Analysis and Management* 26: 811–829.

For most people, possession of an automobile is crucial for economic and social participation. Among other things, we drive to get to work, to get our children to school, to shop, and to engage in sports, entertainment, and social events. But for many people, automobile ownership is expensive. Aside from the outlays required to purchase an automobile, there are also ongoing costs. When people cannot afford to cover those costs, they may need to rely on public transport. Yet even when public transport systems are very good, lack of access to an automobile can be restrictive.

It is well known that automobile insurance rates differ dramatically from place to place. Usually, the variation is explained based on different levels of risk associated with driving in particular locations. However, anecdotal evidence has suggested that automobile insurance rates are often much higher for people who live in poor neighborhoods with high concentrations of racial minorities, such as African Americans and Hispanics. For people living in such neighborhoods, expenses associated with automobile ownership would already comprise a higher share of household expenses than would be the case for more affluent people. An unjustified premium on automobile insurance would therefore be pernicious. At the margin, it could force people to go without an automobile, thereby making it harder for them to participate in many forms of economic and social activity.

Paul Ong and Michael Stoll were curious to explore whether some of the variation in automobile insurance rates could be due to racial discrimination. They found that both risk and discrimination factors were associated with spatial variations in insurance costs. They found that African American, Hispanic, and poor neighborhoods were adversely affected. In short, the authors found evidence of race discrimination. Using the steps in race analysis presented earlier, I here discuss how Ong and Stoll conducted their study.

Step 1. Select a specific context in which significant racial disparities are known or expected to exist. In California, there has been considerable debate about the setting of car insurance premiums. Discrimination, known as *redlining*, occurs when individuals face higher rates because they live in places with a disproportionately large number of people who are poor and either African American or Hispanic. Civil rights and drivers' interest groups in California have advocated for legislation eliminating the use of place in setting car insurance premiums. They claim that the practice lends itself to redlining, especially when oversight of insurance company practices is limited. For their part, the insurance companies say that they need to cover costs. Their concern has been to protect themselves from place-based risks that are not fully revealed in an individual's driving record but that may affect insurance costs.

Step 2. Assemble evidence allowing you to confirm the existence of racial disparities. The authors constructed a unique data set to examine the relative influence of place-based socioeconomic characteristics (or redlining) and place-based risk factors on the place-based component of automobile insurance premiums. They combined census data and car insurance rate quotes from multiple companies for subareas within the city of Los Angeles. The quotes were collected over the Internet for the year 2000 from multiple insurance companies for each postal zip code area in the city of Los Angeles. To capture the geographic variation of insurance rates, the authors held the characteristics of the "applicant" constant by using the same demographic profile for every zip code. The "applicant" was a twenty-five-year-old, employed single mother, who among other things, had been driving for seven years, and had taken a driver training course. She owned a 1990 Ford Escort LX two-door hatchback with no antitheft device and parked it on the street. She carried only the minimum insurance required. Note that the race of the "applicant" was not specified. That is because the authors sought to test whether insurance companies charged higher premiums to anyone residing in neighborhoods known to have high concentrations of African Americans or Hispanics. The insurance premium entered in the data set for each zip code was the average of quotes from at least six companies. The authors used 2000 census data to assign percentages of the population in each zip code area that was African American or Hispanic and the percentage of the population that was below the poverty line. Information about car accidents and car crime was gathered from other data sets and included in the authors' unique data set. Multivariate regression models were then used to estimate the independent contributions of these risk and redlining factors to the value of the place-based component of the car insurance premium.

Step 3. Develop a process-tracing method to show how specific institutional arrangements, social practices, or decision making are discriminatory. The authors found that both risk and redlining factors were associated with variations in insurance costs. Even when risk factors were taken into account, they found that a premium was charged for car insurance in predominantly African American and Hispanic neighborhoods. The authors could not use their statistical analysis to determine the exact practices that insurance companies use to set rates. For their part, the insurance companies refused to provide this information. The authors stated that the redlining hypothesis did not dispute the role of risk in setting insurance premiums, but it did suggest that discriminatory practices influenced premium values. If insurance companies set higher rates because they assumed that living and driving in African American and Hispanic neighborhoods carries more risk, then this can be described as statistical discrimination. It takes facts about risk into account. However, problems arise when the premium rate is set well above the level that would truly compensate for those risks. That is when statistical discrimination turns into redlining, which is a form of racial prejudice. Ong and Stoll (2007) noted that insurance companies stand to profit from redlining. "At the same time, such an approach would also taint low-income minority neighborhoods that are in fact not risky" (p. 827).

Step 4. Highlight discriminatory policies or practices, and show how they disadvantage specific racial groups. The authors could not prove that redlining was occurring, but their evidence strongly suggested it.

> Regardless of how the insurance rates are set, residents in disadvantaged neighborhoods suffer direct and indirect impacts of a higher insurance premium. The direct cost is the higher out-of-pocket expense for auto premiums, which can equal $1,000 per year for basic coverage, an extremely high amount for those with low-incomes.... There are also indirect effects because higher premiums can be a barrier to automobile ownership, which in turn limits access to social activities, services, and economic opportunities. (p. 827)

Step 5. Propose policy actions to rectify the discrimination and disadvantage. The authors suggested that the impacts of spatial inequality of insurance premiums is a matter of public policy. Insurance companies have fought hard to avoid public disclosure of their rate-setting methods (p. 816). In light of this, the authors did not discuss specific remedies.

Step 6. Scrutinize the proposed policy actions to avoid unintended negative effects. The authors did not propose a specific policy change, and so this step was not taken. Suppose, however, that a policy change was proposed that would compel insurance companies to be explicit about risk calculation and prove that their pricing practices are not discriminatory. Effort would then need to be made to ensure that the companies would not devise new methods to profit from discriminatory pricing practices.

Step 7. Estimate the gains for all groups that would result from effective policy change. The authors did not do this in their study. It would have been appropriate had they been explicit about the kind of policy change they would like to see. (Of course, they could not do that because they were denied access to information on the rate-setting practices of insurance companies.) Estimation work of this kind could involve determining the size of the reductions in insurance rates that would be faced by people in poor neighborhoods if premiums were based purely on assessment of observed risk factors. It could also involve estimating changes in car ownership levels as a result of the reduction in the cost of insurance. This, in turn, could be a starting point for considering the potential for the policy change to result in more integration of people in poor neighborhoods into social and economic activities that are predicated on access to a car.

ADVICE FOR ANALYTICAL PRACTICE

Here are some observations concerning race analysis for public policy.

- Race analysis frequently calls for application of highly sophisticated econometric tests on specially collected data. This can prove a formidable challenge for many policy analysts. However, efforts to achieve more clarity about an issue are always necessary before rigorous analysis can be performed. There are many ways that people can make significant contributions to race analysis without doing high-level data analysis. Clarifying that the right questions are being asked is a good starting point.
- Reports containing race analysis often promote debates and disagreement. Given this, policy analysts must strive to avoid making mistakes or obvious omissions in their work. If you are going to create debates and disagreements, it is best to have them focus on the implications of your work, not on the accuracy or merits of the work itself.
- Nobody should feel uncomfortable doing race analysis, so long as they are respectful of others and how they might respond to their work. People who contend that only representatives of a specific race or ethnic group should study that race or ethnic group tend to miss the bigger picture. Effective knowledge creation has never occurred in a vacuum. All of society gains when smart people crowd around pressing problems and seek to understand them.

RACE ANALYSIS AND OTHER ANALYTICAL STRATEGIES

Racial categorization of people attracts frequent controversy. Historically, it has been the basis for egregious war crimes and acts of systematic and massive oppression. We live with the legacies. Even as disputes have raged about appropriate terms to use to describe and distinguish among people, perceived racial differences have served as powerful markers of social status and social disadvantage. In all societies, racial differences get closely tied to explanations of social disparity—education gaps, income gaps, health gaps, and differences in how people experience social and governmental systems of control. If we aspire to make the world more peaceful and prosperous, then we must think seriously about how to reduce racism and race-based disadvantage.

This chapter has focused on race and race analysis in the context of the United States of America. The focus could have been placed on other countries, where the histories of racial differences and their legacies likewise contain their share of state-sanctioned violence, social oppression, human indifference, sadness, and shame. I chose to highlight race analysis in the United States because of the extensiveness of the analytical work conducted there, which continues to generate concepts and methods that can be adapted and applied in many other places in the world. The chapter has reviewed approaches policy analysts use to explore inequality and discrimination. Many people hope that knowledge generated from such explorations will be put to good effect. People of different races can experience life very differently, even while in close proximity to one another. The accretion of knowledge about those differences can form the basis for public policies designed to reduce race-based inequality and eliminate practices driven by racial prejudice.

Race analysis has the potential to inform each step in policy analysis, from problem definition to policy implementation and program evaluation. Conscious integration of race analysis into policy analysis offers a powerful way to make public policies more effective. It increases the possibility that government actions will promote the objectives of human flourishing, social equity, and the advancement of human rights. At the same time, it can contribute to the development of effective institutions and greater economic efficiency. Race analysis is compatible with other analytical strategies introduced in this book. It can be strengthened by linking it to concepts most closely associated with the analysis of market failure and government failure. Because institutions can serve both to perpetuate and to reduce racism and social disadvantage, rich insights can come from efforts to combine comparative institutional analysis with race analysis. The social costs of racial disparities can be huge. Given this, race analysis can be strengthened by efforts to calculate the costs and benefits of current arrangements and to estimate the economic gains that could accompany change. Because people often experience discrimination in multiple ways, policy analysts can generate new insights into problems and potential solutions by combining race analysis with gender analysis. Finally, racial prejudice and, hence, disadvantage are often perpetuated in situations in which laws and formal rules prohibit it. Clearly, implementation problems exist. This suggests efforts to improve social outcomes could benefit from analytical work that combines race analysis with implementation analysis.

Exercises

1. Consider Table 15.1, reported by the Office of Minority Health, in the United States Department of Health and Human Services. The table shows that in 2006, African American men and women were 30 percent more likely to die from heart disease, as compared to non-Hispanic white men and women.

   Suppose that a foundation that funds health policy research has asked you to devise a strategy for reducing the 30 percent higher rate of heart disease deaths among African Americans compared with non-Hispanic whites. The foundation wants you to consider policy efforts that focus on improving health outcomes for African Americans.

   Samuel L. Myers Jr. (2002) has observed that policy studies often do little more than include race as a variable to explain differences in observed outcomes. The social processes that serve to construct characteristics or behaviors ascribed to race are ignored. Hence, little or no effort is given to interpreting the meaning of race as a category, or how meanings of race might change across time and space. Policy analysis informed by race analysis closely investigates the social construction and interpretation of race.

   You are keen to respond to the foundation in a fashion that employs race analysis as proposed by Samuel L. Myers Jr. In groups, make a list of bullet points capturing the analytical approaches you might take in your study. In the full group, discuss your lists.

2. Douglas Massey and Robert Sampson (2009) recalled a controversial episode in American politics that was prompted by a policy report. In 1965, Daniel Patrick Moynihan proposed that the United States government should urgently act to develop a well-funded employment program to promote greater entry of African American men into the paid workforce. Because the report was leaked and it created a political storm, President Lyndon B. Johnson decided not to act upon its recommendations. Many subsequently saw this as a missed opportunity for American society.

   Assign a small group of people to read the article by Massey and Sampson and summarize the major race-based differences that the authors identify as

Table 15.1 Age-Adjusted Heart Disease Death Rates per 100,000 (2006)

	AFRICAN AMERICAN	NON-HISPANIC WHITE	AFRICAN AMERICAN/ NON-HISPANIC WHITE RATIO
Men	326.5	250.0	1.3
Women	216.1	160.9	1.3
Total	262.3	200.3	1.3

Source: Centers for Disease Control and Prevention (2009), *National Vital Statistic Report 57*(14), Table 17.

existing in contemporary American society. The group should note suggestions made to address those differences, especially those that involve public policy. After the group presents its findings, discuss how policy analysts could help to support constructive public conversations of ways to reduce racial disparities.

3. In small groups, discuss situations in which you think racial discrimination could produce different outcomes for different groups of people.

   • Together, make a list of up to three such situations.
   • Try to formulate a hypothesis that could be tested. For example, "White police officers are more likely to target African American drivers to ticket than they are to target white drivers." Or "Covertly, insurance companies tend to charge nonwhite people more than white people for car insurance."
   • Explain the public policy implication of your hypothesis. That is, if you suspect that discriminatory action is occurring, consider what kind of public policy actions could be taken to reduce or eliminate that action.
   • Together, discuss a research strategy that you could use to test your discrimination hypothesis.
   • Finally, discuss how you could conduct policy analysis like this while minimizing the chances that it would fuel racial tensions.

Further Reading

Antonovics, Kate, and Brian G. Knight. (2009). "A New Look at Racial Profiling: Evidence from the Boston Police Department." *Review of Economics and Statistics* 91: 163–177.

Ards, Sheila D., and Samuel L. Myers, Jr. (2001). "The Color of Money: Bad Credit, Wealth and Race." *American Behavioral Scientist* 45: 223–239.

Ayres, Ian, and Peter Siegelman. (1995). "Race and Gender Discrimination in Bargaining for a New Car." *American Economic Review* 85: 304–321.

Massey, Douglas S., and Robert J. Sampson. (2009). "Moynihan Redux: Legacies and Lessons." *Annals of the American Academy of Political and Social Science* 621: 6–27.

Myers, Samuel L., Jr. (2002). "Presidential Address—Analysis of Race as Policy Analysis." *Journal of Policy Analysis and Management* 21: 169–190.

Stiefel, Leanna, Amy Ellen Schwartz, and Ingrid Gould Ellen. (2006). "Disentangling the Racial Test Score Gap: Probing the Evidence in a Large Urban School District." *Journal of Policy Analysis and Management* 26: 7–30.

Teasley, Martell, and David Ikard. (2010). "Barack Obama and the Politics of Race: The Myth of Postracism in America." *Journal of Black Studies* 40: 411–425.

16

Implementation Analysis

The Story So Far... A primary goal of policy analysis is to develop public policies that effectively address perceived problems without creating new ones. That is why policy analysts consider a range of likely effects of new policies.

Here... We review the use of implementation analysis. This work can increase the chances that new policies will perform as intended, that they will not create unintended negative consequences, and that they will not be undermined by opponents. Some form of implementation analysis should be included in all policy projects.

THIS CHAPTER REVIEWS
- The importance of successful policy implementation
- The distinction between theory failure and implementation failure
- The merits of sequence mapping and scenario writing
- How to assess and manage possible barriers to effective implementation
- How individuals and organizations interpret and reinterpret policy

Implementation is the step in the policy-making process in which ideas are transformed into actions. The creation of public policies involves both policy design work and policy implementation. Yet policy analysts commonly pay more attention to policy design than to implementation. In 2004, the prime minister of Australia observed, "I think one of the things we lack in the public service both at a Commonwealth and a State level is a consolidated focus on the efficient and timely and sympathetic delivery of services. We tend to look at service delivery as an afterthought rather than as a policy priority."[1] A policy initiative is more likely to achieve the best possible outcomes when the question of how the policy is to be implemented has been an integral part of policy design. This point was made long ago by Jeffrey L. Pressman and Aaron Wildavsky (1973). In the preface to their classic text on implementation, these authors observed, "The separation of policy design from implementation is fatal" (xxv). Evaluation scholars have long made the distinction between theory failure and implementation failure (Chen 1990). The distinction is useful. When a new public policy is established, the policy's success will depend on the quality of the initial design work and the effectiveness of implementation. A poorly designed policy that is carefully implemented will still produce poor outcomes. However, there are times when a policy exhibiting very good design can run into problems because of bungled implementation. This chapter offers an overview of policy implementation, with the goal of indicating how attention to implementation within the policy design phase can increase the ability of governments to deliver highly effective public policies.

If we think in terms of concepts and their application, then we see that people in many settings, not just people in and around government, face implementation challenges. Indeed, scholars of business processes have devoted a huge amount of attention over the past few decades to understanding how organizations engage in change processes. As well as drawing on insights from the public policy literature on implementation, in this chapter I utilize insights from the business literature. Many new programs and strategies introduced in the corporate world, accompanied by plenty of hoopla, have ended up failing due to poor implementation. Policy analysts can learn a lot from studies of how businesses have struggled with implementation. Jeffrey J. Fox (1998) observed that in business, "the concept doesn't have to be perfect, but the execution of it does" (p. 131). On reflection, it is rare for any idea to be perfect. We can think of many instances in which a new public policy has been introduced that has required extensive later refinement. Such refinement need not imply that the original policy idea was wrong. Knowledge constraints, funding constraints, and political constraints often result in new policies starting life in somewhat modest or awkward forms. Poor implementation could result in premature policy failure. In contrast, when such new policies are effectively implemented, they can serve as the platforms for subsequent major advances and improvements. Examples could be found in many areas, including the development of income maintenance programs, aspects of criminal justice, the evolution of public education, and strategies to promote environmental sustainability.

AN OVERVIEW OF IMPLEMENTATION ANALYSIS

Effective implementation analysis makes use of techniques commonly employed in project management. Some of those techniques were discussed in Chapter 5, "Managing Policy Projects." Because implementation requires coordination of the

---

[1] Australian National Audit Office (2006: 5).

actions of a range of stakeholders, it is an inherently political process. Various insights from the political science literature are also relevant to implementation analysis. The possibility that bureaucrats will act to maximize their own interests during implementation has long been acknowledged (Niskanen 1971). A rich body of work grounded in principal-agent models and informed by insights from game theory used empirical evidence to explore the degree to which elected politicians could maintain control over bureaucrats (Calvert, McCubbins, and Weingast 1989; McCubbins and Schwartz 1984; Miller and Moe 1983). In turn, contributions to this literature and the literature on government failure (reviewed in Chapter 10) have informed efforts to improve the accountability of bureaucrats to their political masters. Early efforts of that sort conducted in the 1980s and 1990s were termed "the new public management" and were chronicled in a range of studies (Aucoin 1996; Boston et al. 1996; Hood 1991; Kettl 2000). Scholarly attention has also been given to how behavioral norms, coupled with appropriate incentives structures, can reduce the distance between the preferences of political decision makers and bureaucratic behavior (Brehm and Gates 1997; Miller 1992). Contributions to the political science literature on collective action, coalition building, and policy change also contain many insights relevant to implementation analysis (Mintrom and Norman 2009; Olson 1965; Sabatier 1993).

Envisioning Policy Success

When Martin Luther King Jr. gave his "I Have a Dream" speech in August 1963, he noted, "There are those who are asking the devotees of civil rights, 'When will you be satisfied?'" In response, King enumerated several concrete examples of what the achievement of civil rights for African Americans would look like. They included the following: the ending of police brutality, voting rights for African Americans in Mississippi, the banishment of signs stating "For Whites Only," and the elimination of everyday discrimination (such as African Americans being declined motel or hotel rooms). Proposals for policy change should always include clear indicators of policy success for three reasons. First, when people have clear visions of their goals, they are much more likely to put energy into their attainment. Second, it is especially important in the midst of change, when commitments can easily lag, that concrete images of success are available to motivate people in their efforts. Third, through continual reference to the vision, people can attain a sense of their progress—what has been accomplished so far and what is yet to be achieved. Keeping track of successes, even small ones, can be hugely important for building confidence that the broader goals can be attained (Canfield 2005; Kotter 1996).

Brainstorming techniques can prove helpful when policy analysts are seeking to envision policy success. For example, a meeting could be called with stakeholders, in which they are asked to offer success indicators. After some initial brainstorming, a more systematic, analytical approach should be taken to stating the key success indicators for the policy. Richard F. Elmore (1979) proposed that policy analysts engage in the process of "backward mapping" as part of implementation analysis. Taking this approach, policy analysts should start by considering the specific changes that they anticipate the policy will produce. They should then work backward from that point, figuring out at each step what other changes will be necessary to facilitate that change. Elmore developed this method for implementation analysis by reflecting on policy change in the field of education. If the goal of a policy change is to promote improved reading outcomes for children at each grade level, then backward mapping would suggest that we start in the classroom. We should specify the desired behavioral changes in the children and their approaches to reading. Having done that, we should consider what teachers would need to do differently and what resources and forms of support they would need to change their own practices. Those considerations would lead to reflection on what school administrators could do to support their teachers and what school boards could do to support their schools. From here, clear ideas can be developed about what kind of provisions should be made in the new policy to ensure that organizational arrangements, procedural rules, and resources are all appropriately aligned to support the desired changes.

In general, it is helpful for policy analysts to engage in some form of scenario writing that links the proposed policy to specific actions conducted by the change targets (Bardach 1977; Weimer and Vining 2005). Such work need not be elaborate. But, wherever possible, it should be collaborative in nature. Scenario writing works best when it is informed by input from the people whose behaviors will need to change to make the policy a success. Therefore, a short statement setting out how the policy is expected to work can serve as the starting point for eliciting comments and concerns.

The process of envisioning policy success should culminate with completion of two documents.

- A list of the primary policy goals, and indicators of policy success. The indicators should be measurable.
- A narrative of behavioral changes that must accompany introduction of the policy and the organizational arrangements, procedural rules, and resources that will be required to support those behavioral changes.

Identifying Tasks and Task Dependencies
Successful policy implementation involves establishing new organizational arrangements and procedural rules. It also involves securing resources to support desired new behaviors. Establishing these new conditions should be treated as a policy project. That is because it is nonroutine work, it has a clear start and a clear finish, and the products are unique. It is crucial to notice the difference here between delivery of the policy (which will be ongoing) and creation of the system that facilitates policy delivery (the implementation project). Within project management, a key discipline involves establishing a *work breakdown structure*. As noted in Chapter 5, this requires breaking an activity into all its component tasks and identifying task dependencies. Task dependencies arise whenever it makes logical sense to complete one task before completing another. Depending on the

scope of the new policy, it is possible that implementation will require several projects to occur, some in parallel, and some only after preliminary work has been conducted.

Although all implementation projects will be unique and a lot of details will need to be worked out as the project proceeds, there are some important actions that policy analysts can take to ensure that these projects run smoothly. For example, they can break implementation into several large tasks and suggest an appropriate sequencing for completion of those tasks. Having a sense of the scope of the work and the kinds of skills required to complete it is also helpful for guiding the development of governance arrangements for the implementation project. When the implementation work is expected to require major commitments from personnel in several government agencies and from stakeholder groups, it will often make sense to create a project steering committee. Members of that committee would then provide oversight for all the project work and establish lines of accountability.

The process of identifying tasks and task dependencies can become highly complicated and will continue into the actual implementation work. It is unrealistic to expect that all relevant tasks and task dependencies will be worked out before implementation starts. However, policy analysts should strive to support effective implementation by thinking about the work breakdown structure. Efforts to envision policy success and what is needed to attain it should culminate in a document identifying the following:

1. The major tasks associated with the implementation project
2. An initial cost estimate for the project
3. A realistic time frame for completion of the project
4. What agencies and stakeholders will contribute to the project
5. An appropriate governance structure for the project and lines of accountability

Identifying Threats to Successful Implementation

Decision makers never appreciate new policies that, subsequent to adoption, blow up in their faces. That explains why many politicians who are able to control policy agendas tend to reduce new policy work to a trickle in the period leading up to an election. New policies can be politically risky (Althaus 2008; Lindblom 1959). Policy analysts can increase the likelihood of a new policy being adopted if they have taken care to document and address all significant risks associated with it. Although risk analysis can become complex, the basic approach is straightforward (Barton 2004). It involves first working with others to generate a list of all possible risks associated with policy implementation. This is another case in which brainstorming around a few key categories is a good way to start the process. Here are some suggested categories:

- Risk that implementation will be more complex, will take longer, and will be more expensive than originally estimated.

- Risk that political opponents will try to frustrate the change process.
- Risk that some stakeholders will seek to have undue influence on the process and shape the process to their advantage.
- Risk that unanticipated equity concerns or forms of discrimination will emerge during implementation.

Through efforts to identify relevant risks associated with implementation of a new policy, a list of risks—or a risk schedule—can be created. Once this set of potential risks has been established, some useful analysis can be performed. Effective risk assessment requires that we determine the probability of an adverse event and the impact that such an event would cause (Heldman 2005). When insufficient information is available to make judgments of this kind, effort should be made to acquire it.

Although it is impossible to manage all implementation risks, some useful actions can be taken. First, in instances in which preparation work could reduce the risk of an adverse event occurring, careful consideration should be given to doing that work. Such effort is called *risk mitigation*. Second, there will be times when the likelihood of an adverse event cannot be controlled. In such cases, it is helpful to consider contingencies. These are actions that will be taken should the event occur. Third, when key risks are being assessed, it is useful to think about what warnings would indicate that an adverse event is about to happen. Adopting a risk management mind-set can be helpful for supporting effective implementation. A good effort to perform a preliminary risk assessment will generate a risk dashboard that can be continuously consulted by those who are subsequently charged with policy implementation. Nothing can ever be made certain through this kind of exercise. However, advanced preparation can greatly improve the ability of an implementation team to perform their work effectively.

Closing Knowing-Doing Gaps

Resistance to change is not always politically motivated. Generally, people become set in their ways of doing things and find change difficult. They know that they should change their practices, but old habits die hard (Pfeffer and Sutton 2000). From the perspective of valuing a stable society, human inertia can often be a good thing. However, when change is strongly desired, that tendency to maintain the status quo can become a problem. Policy analysts can improve the likelihood of successful implementation by paying attention to contextual factors. It is useful to understand how people make sense of their current contexts and how they are likely to interpret policy change.

Sometimes people yearn for change, and when it comes, they embrace it. They do not need incentives to change. Sometimes, people are open to change, but they do need some prompting. Having people see what is in it for them to change can be helpful. In addition, taking actions that can help people to transition from old ways to new ways can ease implementation. Sometimes, this can be as simple as offering information to people in language that is easy for them to understand.

Working with a small group of opinion leaders can be a way to have people learn about and gain appreciation for the positive aspects of change from their peers. At other times, it can be helpful to offer training programs that give people the skills they will need to perform well in the new context. Cash payments, rewards, or bonuses can sometimes serve as appropriate tools for prompting people to change (Rogers 1995).

Sometimes people struggle with change. Rather than sharing the predispositions of those promoting change, people view changes from the perspective of what is most familiar to them. Taking their current context as the default position, they tend to interpret changes in their own ways. The key question, although not necessarily articulated as such, becomes this: How can we accommodate this change with the least disruption to what we currently do? Unsurprisingly, the response typically involves incremental adjustments. Adoption of change occurs against a backdrop of the old ways of doing things, which hardly change (Tyack and Cuban 1995; Weick 1995). It is easy to look around and find evidence of this kind of incremental adaptive process. People like to do things in ways that they are familiar with and comfortable with. As a result, changes tend to get added onto current arrangements; they do not substitute for them. That is why, for example, most university lecture theaters and seminar rooms could be mistaken for museums of teaching technology—some still with their enduring blackboards and sticks of chalk, even as (almost) everyone is using the latest presentational devices.

Implementation can be more effective when it is preceded by an assessment of people's appetite for change. Observing what people do in their current context and talking with them about proposed changes can yield useful information.[2] Such engagements with people's practices need not be systematic, but careful observation is likely to generate more accurate assessments. Policy analysts should consider developing a document that indicates potential resistance to change and effective ways to address it. In the process, the conclusion might be reached that some aspects of the change agenda were too ambitious. It is better to learn that before implementation begins than during it. Development of a variation on the conflict analysis matrix presented in Figure 16.1 could serve this purpose well. This matrix was devised to support better management of public disputes (Carpenter and Kennedy 1988).

Planning for Evaluation

The efforts of policy and program evaluators are vital for generating information on the success of government actions. Surprisingly, the development of policy analysis and program evaluation as disciplines has occurred with somewhat limited engagement between them. Fortunately, as policy analysts are coming to

---

[2] This view is informed by Ronald A. Heifetz's (1994) emphasis on leadership as "identifying the adaptive challenge" (ch. 4) and Robert E. Quinn's (2000) proposal that change leaders engage in honest dialogue with the change target, so as to mutually learn ways to win-win solutions (p. 11).

Party	Issues	Interests	Importance of issues (high, medium, low)	Sources of power and Influence	Positions taken, or options proposed	Interested in working with others?	Comments
A							
B							
C							

Figure 16.1 Conflict Analysis Matrix
Source: Carpenter and Kennedy (1988: 87).

realize the importance of evidence for guiding policy choice, more convergence is happening. Policy analysts can do a lot to increase the likelihood of effective future evaluation of a new policy and its delivery systems. The key to good evaluation is good information (Rossi, Lipsey, and Freeman 2004; Weiss 1998). Knowledge of conditions before a new policy has been introduced is essential for allowing evaluators to measure how much contribution a new policy has made to the attainment of desired goals. Creative action at the implementation stage can lay the foundations for effective evaluation. Indeed, as Schultz (2004) has documented, systematic, sequential implementation of a new policy opens possibilities for evaluators to perform high-quality tests of program effectiveness. It is good practice for policy analysts to think hard about ways to support future evaluation work.

USING IMPLEMENTATION ANALYSIS AS AN ANALYTICAL FRAMEWORK

So far in this chapter, implementation analysis has been presented as work to be performed prior to when a policy is put in place. It is good practice to make implementation analysis a standard part of the policy analytic work that is done to support proposals for policy change. By working through the set of actions noted in the overview of implementation analysis, policy analysts will often gain new insights into the context in which the policy will be introduced and the kinds of issues that might arise when the policy is transformed from a set of ideas into a set of government actions. Conducting a thorough implementation analysis would involve a lot of work. This would be worthwhile work when the policy change being proposed is major and is expected to affect a lot of people in significant ways. In such circumstances, a policy report focused exclusively on anticipated implementation concerns would be merited. Often, policy analysts simply do not have the time or resources to do extensive implementation analysis prior to a policy being adopted. In those cases, making at least some effort to think hard about implementation will pay off. Even including a short discussion highlighting key concerns can be helpful for alerting others to the kinds of issues that might emerge during the implementation stage.

Beyond analysis intended to support effective policy implementation, implementation analysis is often performed after a new policy or program has been established. This is called *post hoc* analysis (literally meaning analysis performed after implementation of an intervention), which is quite distinctive from *a priori* analysis (literally meaning analysis performed before implementation of an intervention). As we have seen in previous chapters, we commonly find various analytical strategies, such as the analysis of government failure, comparative institutional analysis, gender analysis and race analysis being used to assess existing programs in a post hoc fashion. Policy analysts engage in implementation analysis after the policies and programs have been established to draw lessons for future practice. Helpful lessons can be drawn both from cases of successful implementation and cases of implementation failure. Lessons can also be drawn from the many cases of implementation exhibiting elements of both success and failure. Sometimes, implementation analyses of this kind are performed as part of broader program evaluations. However, as interest in implementation itself has grown, more studies have been produced as stand-alone forms of policy analysis.

STEPS IN IMPLEMENTATION ANALYSIS

The following steps have been developed to guide implementation analysis. Of course, implementation analysis will always need to be tailored to the specific circumstances under which a new policy is being introduced or—in the case of post hoc studies—has been introduced. Further, there will be times when comprehensive analysis is called for. At other times, an initial implementation analysis might be contained within just a couple of pages of a broader report. In all cases, careful judgments will be required to determine how much depth will be devoted to each of the steps set forth here.

Step 1. Identify the overall purpose of the new policy, where it will be implemented, and how success has been defined. Usually, this will be a straightforward step. If it is not, then this suggests that insufficient work has been done during the policy design phase. It is useful in this step to note the problem or problems that the policy is intended to address. It can be useful to record here how problems of this kind have been addressed previously, either in this particular jurisdiction or elsewhere.

Step 2. Identify who will be responsible for policy implementation and the behavioral changes that implementation is expected to produce. Many new policies are introduced with the expectation that the related programs or systems of service delivery will be the responsibility of an existing governmental agency. Sometimes, that responsibility might be shared or new agencies might be created.

It is important to document where responsibility is to lie. It is also important to state the behavioral changes the new policy is intended to promote.

Step 3. Specify the institutional, organizational, and procedural changes required to support the new policy. Desired behavioral changes must be encouraged. Usually, this will require changes to be made to existing institutional arrangements. New organizational structures might be developed, and new operating procedures will certainly be required. By documenting these, it is possible to gain clarity around the magnitude of the change effort that is required, and where the most significant effort will need to be focused.

Step 4. Treating implementation as a project, note the key tasks required to establish the new policy context. The implementation project involves taking the ideas embodied in the new policy and transforming them into governmental routines. A focus on the scope of the implementation project, the governance of it, and lines of responsibility can bring clarity to the complexity of the work involved, how long it will take, and the resource requirements.

Step 5. Identify any significant threats to successful implementation and how they can be addressed. Risk management is a central element of project management. Identifying the likely sources of threats to the viability of the implementation project offers a starting point for assessing how adverse events might be avoided, what could be done if they did arise, and what kind of early indicators might suggest they are emerging. Often implementation is subject to risks created by politics. Conflicts that have not been resolved when the policy was being designed and adopted can emerge again here. Stakeholders can do a lot to make implementation difficult. It is useful to understand in advance the likely sources of problems and how they might be addressed. Note that when a new policy is introduced sequentially across a set of distinctive sites, knowledge gained from early successes and failures can inform subsequent implementation efforts.

Step 6. Consider how institutional inertia might hinder change and how it can be overcome. There are good reasons that people in established institutional and organizational structures resist change. Implementation analysis should include consideration of where, how, and why resistance could emerge and hinder the change process. Not all resistance is driven by hostility. Often, people resist change simply because they have not been consulted about it and no effort has been made to explain how it could benefit them. By assessing people's appetite for change, it is possible to develop effective ways to secure desired outcomes.

Step 7. Ensure provisions have been made for evaluation of the new policy and associated programs. Evaluation should be treated as an integral component of the policy-making process, not as an afterthought. Therefore, before a new policy is implemented it is vital that baseline information is collected on all the actions and outcomes that the policy is expected to influence. Knowing from the outset how success will be defined greatly eases the future challenges for evaluators. By explicitly looking ahead to evaluation while conducting the implementation analysis, it is possible that wise actions can be taken to support subsequent evaluation.

AN APPLIED EXAMPLE

This section highlights analysis contained in the following:

Suna Bayrakal. (2006). "The U.S. Pollution Prevention Act: A Policy Implementation Analysis." *Social Science Journal* 43: 127–145.

Many governments worldwide have engaged in efforts over the past few decades to protect the environment and reduce industrial pollution. In Chapter 10, "Analysis of Market Failure," we discussed possible government actions in response to negative externalities, such as pollution generated through the production process. Those government actions can include prescriptions of what polluters must do to address the problem. Sometimes, such action is referred to as "heavy-handed" or as exhibiting a "command-and-control" mentality. We also noted in Chapter 11, "Analysis of Government Failure," that highly prescriptive regulations can impede technological progress. Those subject to regulation often direct their energies toward compliance with established rules and do not explore effective ways to reduce production of the negative externality. However, in response to calls by economists to establish incentives-based approaches to reducing negative externalities, governments everywhere have recently begun experimenting with alternatives to command-and-control regulatory approaches.

In this applied example, we consider a case in which the U.S. government introduced a voluntary, incentives-based policy to further promote environmental protection. This was the Pollution Prevention Act, passed by the Congress in 1990. Suna Bayrakal (2006) conducted an implementation analysis to assess the process that transformed the policy into government actions. In so doing, she effectively applied theoretical insights derived from the policy literature on implementation (Bardach 1977; Goggin et al. 1990; Najam 1995; Pressman and Wildavsky 1973; Sabatier and Mazmanian 1981). Bayrakal judged that the Pollution Prevention Act had mixed success, and that its limitations could be blamed on key features of the implementation process. This is a useful case to consider because it identifies several problems that emerged when a new approach to practice was expected to be taken, even as the dominant standard operating procedures remained in place. Bayrakal's analysis neatly highlights the institutional inertia problem.

Step 1. Identify the overall purpose of the new policy, where it will be implemented, and how success has been defined. The purpose of the Pollution

Prevention Act was to prevent or reduce pollution at the source. Until this act, the other legislation adopted by the U.S. Congress had focused on addressing pollution at the tailpipe. That involved waste treatment and disposal. It did not tackle the source of the problem. In contrast to previous legislation, the Pollution Prevention Act construed pollution broadly to include any form that affected water, air, and land. This was intended to prevent transfer of pollution among media (such as solid waste being incinerated resulting in air pollution). Most important, industry compliance with the Pollution Prevention Act was to be voluntary. Rather than impose regulations and assign fines for noncompliance, this law proposed the use of information exchange, training, technical assistance, award programs, and use of the federal procurement selection processes to promote desired practices by businesses. Provision was also made for grants to states to support their pollution prevention programs. Some of those programs offered subsidies to businesses seeking to reduce pollution at the source.

The law was to be implemented locally, which meant in practice that the states would be involved, at least to some degree, in making the law work. At the time the law was adopted, a number of states had already adopted their own pollution prevention laws. Many were to do so following the passage of the Pollution Prevention Act in Congress.

Policy success was not formally defined in the act. The act directed the United States Environmental Protection Agency to establish standard pollution prevention measurement methods and goals. This did not happen.

Step 2. Identify who will be responsible for policy implementation and the behavioral changes that implementation is expected to produce. The United States Environmental Protection Agency was responsible for policy implementation. The view was taken that regulatory obstacles and lack of information and assistance to industry had resulted in excessive pollution and cost. The Pollution Prevention Act was nonprescriptive. It was expected to encourage firms to adjust their production processes in ways that would reduce their reliance on pollution-producing inputs. This would involve firms switching their attention from managing compliance with environmental regulations to process innovation.

Step 3. Specify the institutional, organizational, and procedural changes required to support the new policy. First, the Pollution Prevention Act had implications for the activities of the United States Environmental Protection Agency. Second, it also had implications for industry. Third, it had implications for how the Environmental Protection Agency would engage with industry. We will discuss each set of implications in turn.

The United States Environmental Protection Agency was required to set up a new internal unit, to be called the Office of Pollution Prevention and Toxics. The office was to establish an advisory panel comprising of industry, state, and public interest group representatives. It was to build on prior data collection efforts to support information exchange. It was also required to establish systems to measure pollution prevention and to set goals for improvements over time. It was to administer industrial training and technical assistance programs, and provide funding for state programs. The staff members in the office were directed to "advise and coordinate" with other agency staff. They had no ability to require behavioral changes on the part of anyone elsewhere in the agency.

For industry, the Pollution Prevention Act signaled a shift in how concerns about environmental impacts would be addressed. Up to this point, firms tended to concentrate their concerns about pollution within a single office dedicated to ensuring compliance with various state and federal laws. Firms faced strong incentives to carefully manage compliance issues, because to be found in breach of relevant laws could result in heavy penalties. The Pollution Prevention Act, being voluntary, placed no new compliance requirements on firms. However, to respond to the spirit of the act, firms would have to encourage staff across many areas of work to become more environmentally conscious and change their behaviors accordingly. The act held implications for aspects of manufacturing, design, operations, production, purchasing, and product and process development. In other words, making a serious attempt to prevent pollution as the law envisaged would require radical changes at the firm level.

Step 4. Treating implementation as a project, note the key tasks required to establish the new policy context. At a formal level, establishing the procedures to support the Pollution Prevention Act seemed straightforward. Bayrakal (2006: 131) described them as involving "a minor organizational change." Although a lot of effort did appear to go into creating systems within the Environmental Protection Agency that would support effective implementation, there were problems. Failure to establish standard pollution prevention measurement methods created a serious implementation gap. Without clear measures of success, realistic goals could not be set. In the absence of realistic goals, agency staff would have little incentive to engage in productive, problem-solving interactions with industry representatives. Within a context in which agency staff and industry often acted as adversaries, and only the most limited incentives were created for behavioral changes, implementation failure was almost assured. As it turns out, program successes emerged mainly in instances in which implementation efforts were greatly assisted by actors in state-level environmental protection agencies.

Step 5. Identify any significant threats to successful implementation and how they can be addressed. The voluntary, incentives-based nature of the Pollution Prevention Act immediately reduced the potential for it to generate hostile responses from industry. But it also meant that it represented a way of doing things that was inconsistent with standard operating procedures and habits of mind established within the Environmental Protection Agency. The compliance culture of the agency and the adversarial nature of its relationships with industry served as significant threats to successful implementation. These threats were not considered prior to implementation. Had they been, more funds would have been allocated to the implementation task and the Office of Pollution Prevention and Toxics would have been given more power and influence within the broader structure of the agency.

Step 6. Consider how institutional inertia might hinder change and how it can be overcome. Institutional inertia posed serious challenges for effective implementation of the Pollution Prevention Act. Bayrakal (2006: 137) suggested that because of the requirements of earlier state and federal laws concerning pollution, the Environmental Protection Agency and state agencies had all been developed around compliance enforcement structures. This meant that a move to cooperation with industry would require a change both in mind-sets and practices. Meanwhile, firms had also developed internal industry systems that mirrored the governmental compliance regime. Previous regulations and the ways that government agencies and firms had adapted to them did not produce a context conducive to voluntary government-industry engagements and collaborations. In Bayrakal's words, "Entrenched regulatory compliance programs and investment in expensive pollution control systems and expertise...restrict[ed] more widespread industry acceptance and implementation" (2006: 133).

Could a solution be found to institutional inertia? Interestingly, the provisions in the Pollution Prevention Act 1990 allowed for federal government matching grants to support state-level pollution prevention initiatives. Many states took advantage of this opportunity and used the matching grants to support expansion in the operations of their own environmental protection agencies. Bayrakal mentions two cases in which state actions appear to have sidestepped institutional inertia. In New Jersey and Minnesota, innovative actions were taken, supported by federal funds, to promote greater cooperation between regulators and industry in pollution prevention. This evidence is consistent with Robert E. Quinn's suggestion that agents of change usually achieve little when they try to work within established structures. According to Quinn, "changing the structure seldom leads to increased performance and...such changes are highly resisted" (2000: 52). Success tends to come when change agents make use of informal, ad hoc networks and find ways to cross functional boundaries and hierarchical levels by focusing on action flows and objectives, not on functions and positions. This appears to be exactly what happened in the states where implementation of the Pollution Prevention Act met with success. (For a range of insights regarding the virtues of networks in supporting implementation, see Agranoff 2007.)

Step 7. Ensure provisions have been made for evaluation of the new policy and associated programs. Bayrakal (2006: 135) noted that provision was made in the legislation for program evaluation. The Environmental Protection Agency was expected to report to Congress on the success or otherwise of the policy. However, Bayrakal raised the possibility that a conflict of interest was established by charging the Environmental Protection Agency with both implementation and evaluation. The worry would be that only good news would be reported. Bayrakal was aware of earlier criticisms suggesting that the Environmental Protection Agency had a poor track record of evaluating its own programs. The comment suggests the importance of ensuring that evaluation is performed by independent actors. In this case, awareness that an independent and high-stakes evaluation would be conducted in the future might have prompted the Environmental Protection Agency to put more energy into developing measures of program performance and use them to guide program management.

ADVICE FOR ANALYTICAL PRACTICE

When policy analysts are considering implementation issues, it is useful to remember the following points.

- The politics of policy making does not end with passage of the enabling laws. Implementation offers another site for political action. Implementation analysis should be informed by an awareness of power and how specific actors can use their power either to support or undermine implementation efforts.
- Priority should be given to establishing specific, measurable, agreed, realistic, and time-bound policy goals to be achieved through implementation. These SMART goals can focus the attention of those charged with making the policy work. They can also be used to establish milestones marking accomplishments on the way to full implementation.
- When behavioral changes are desired, it is useful to consider what new structures and incentives will be needed to support those changes.
- Current policy settings, standard operating procedures, and habits of mind can inadvertently undermine new policies, especially when the guiding assumptions contained in those new polices represent a break from the past.
- People often need explicit support in changing their practices. Creating visual and tactile objects (maps, diagrams) that help people understand the vision for change can ease implementation processes. So can regular updates on progress and efforts to highlight success stories.
- Encouraging the creation of new networks and partnerships that stretch across and around traditional organizational structures can greatly facilitate change efforts.
- Policy implementation requires policy champions. Without their dedicated efforts, it is possible that policies launched with great expectations will result in ruined hopes.

IMPLEMENTATION ANALYSIS AND OTHER ANALYTICAL STRATEGIES

Policy analysts can do many things to ensure that governments respond in effective ways to policy problems. Helping others to define problems and develop sound ways to address them are crucial tasks for policy analysts. This chapter has highlighted the importance of thinking beyond policy design to consider policy implementation. By augmenting their proposals for change with implementation analysis, policy analysts can reduce the possibility of both theory failure and implementation failure. Theory failure arises when policy proposals contain unrealistic assumptions. But as we have seen, looking ahead to implementation can force us to revisit our policy design work. Sometimes, people discount the possibility of contextual factors to undermine policy designs. Other times, they overestimate the strength of the policy idea. This can lead them to forget that other people—who hold different but quite legitimate views—might respond to the new policy in unhelpful ways. The more we think about implementation in advance, and the more time we take to listen to stakeholders reactions, criticisms, and suggestions for improvement, the greater the likelihood that we will devise effective policy. Implementation failure arises when a policy that is sound in its design is inadequately translated into government actions. Inadequate translation can occur for many reasons. However, by treating implementation as a project, it is possible to identify in advance potential threats to the project and how they might be managed.

Our ability to effectively apply implementation analysis can be supported by awareness of how government failure can arise and how it can be avoided. Comparative institutional analysis was developed initially out of concerns that too many public policies were guided by theory rather than observation of practical ways to address policy problems. Implementation analysis, like comparative institutional analysis, is intended to bring more realism to policy design work. Much can be gained by considering cases of implementation success and failure in other contexts and using the insights gained to inform policy design work back home. Comparative institutional analysis and implementation analysis can be highly complementary. By integrating insights from cost-benefit analysis into implementation analysis, costly mistakes can be avoided. When gender analysis and race analysis inform implementation analysis, issues of discrimination and disadvantage can be highlighted. In turn, this can lead us to consider how policy implementation can serve to promote desirable social outcomes.

Exercises

1. As a group, select an idea for policy change that you are familiar with but that has not been implemented. In smaller groups, use bullet points to list key implementation steps you think would be required to make this change happen successfully. Have some groups inform their work with the notion of "backward mapping." Have others try "forward mapping." Compare and contrast the lists created by the different groups.

2. In considering why efforts to change various managerial and teaching practices within public schools have often proved difficult, scholars working out of different disciplines have offered divergent answers. Those influenced by economic

analysis argue that the incentives for change have not been strong enough.[3] Educational sociologists argue that administrators, teachers, and parents have shared notions of what constitutes a "real school" and that reforms are often resisted and adjusted at the local level.[4] How might thinking in terms of institutions and how they shape people's actions and beliefs help us understand these divergent interpretations of schools and reform efforts? In turn, what lessons could we draw from this that would help us to improve the chances that policy changes will be effectively implemented?

3. In 2002, the *New York Times* published an article highlighting research on a poverty alleviation program established in Mexico (Krueger, 2002). Locate this article and read it. What does it tell us about the connection between implementation and evaluation? Can you think of other instances, closer to home, in which this kind of approach could be used to support effective program evaluation? (A longer article on this work, by T. Paul Schultz, is noted in the "Further Reading" section at the end of the chapter.)

Invite a Guest to Class

Implementation represents an area of public policy development with myriad war stories. What is an example of a big policy screwup you are familiar with? What did you learn from it? How sure are you that a similar situation couldn't happen again? Questions like this—*posed lightly and respectfully!*—could prompt a very interesting meeting between a guest speaker and the class. See my suggestions at the end of Chapter 1 for ways to involve the class members in arranging a visit by an invited guest.

The Class Project

The focus of this study could either be a policy that has recently been adopted and is just beginning to be implemented or a policy that has been implemented. Selection of the focus of the implementation analysis could be done in consultation with representatives of a government agency. To promote student buy-in to the project, it can be good to offer a list of three to five possible project topics and then have a vote on which one to pursue. The challenge for the class members is to collectively conduct an implementation analysis and write it up as a policy report.

Those interested in coordinating a class project involving implementation analysis should be sure to have mastered the material in Chapter 5, "Managing Policy Projects," and read my comments on the class project offered at the end of that chapter.

---

[3] See, for example, Chubb and Moe (1990); Hanushek (1994).
[4] See, for example, Fullan (2007); Tyack and Cuban (1995).

It is strongly suggested that the class project be conducted in a fashion that closely follows the steps in implementation analysis presented in this chapter and summarized below.

Steps in Implementation Analysis

1. Identify the overall purpose of the new policy, where it will be implemented, and how success has been defined.
2. Identify who will be responsible for policy implementation and the behavioral changes that implementation is expected to produce.
3. Specify the institutional, organizational, and procedural changes required to support the new policy.
4. Treating implementation as a project, note the key tasks required to establish the new policy context.
5. Identify any significant threats to successful implementation and how they can be addressed.
6. Consider how institutional inertia might hinder change and how it can be overcome.
7. Ensure provisions have been made for evaluation of the new policy and associated programs.

Realistically, good class projects can take four to six weeks of focused effort. Students should be assigned to small groups, and each group should be assigned a clearly specified task or set of tasks to perform. To ensure transparency and accountability, everyone in the class should know what everyone else is working on. During the time that the project is running, the regular class meetings should be devoted almost exclusively to discussing the project, what has been achieved recently, and what work is to be completed next. The coordination work can be demanding. To ensure students contribute appropriately to this kind of project, it is best that no other forms of assessment be required from students while they are working on it. The risk that students will shirk their work responsibilities can be reduced by requiring students to provide brief written reports on the quality of the contributions made by their group peers during the process. The reports should be confidential, and it should be widely understood that the content of the reports can affect the final grade assigned to each participant. For technical details on how I have managed this, see the Appendix in Michael Mintrom (2003), *People Skills for Policy Analysts* (Washington, DC: Georgetown University Press).

A range of important pedagogical benefits can result from students working collectively on a challenging policy project. Effectively designed and executed, this kind of project can become a space where students learn to engage closely with a range of analytical techniques, beyond those directly associated with doing implementation analysis. Class projects also present amazing opportunities for students to learn the benefits of collaboration and team effort.

It is useful to remind students that they will very likely experience a U-shaped emotional journey while working on the project. That is to say, they will experience excitement near the start and a great sense of accomplishment in the end. But in the middle, things can get tough. That is why setting project milestones can be very important.

Students will find it helpful to familiarize themselves with Chapter 6, "Presenting Policy Advice." When students produce a class project, it is often very satisfying to deliver the findings and recommendations in an oral briefing for relevant practitioners.

The Policy Research Seminar

Organize a research-oriented seminar that will run for about ninety minutes, preferably with some light refreshments. Invite up to twelve people and make sure you have a mixture of experienced researchers, junior researchers, and graduate students. The purpose of the discussion should be to develop ideas for the design of policy research projects that give a central place to implementation analysis. The project ideas should be sufficiently interesting and original that each could form the basis of a significant research paper, dissertation, or thesis. Participants should come to the seminar having read both this chapter and Suna Bayrakal's (2006) "The U.S. Pollution Prevention Act: A Policy Implementation Analysis" (*Social Science Journal* 43: 127–145). You might structure the discussion around the section "Steps in Implementation Analysis" presented in this chapter and applied in the overview of the Bayrakal study. Many other recent journal articles could have been highlighted in this chapter. Prior to the group meeting, you might have several participants locate other interesting articles that present original implementation analyses. Discussions of this sort tend to work best when the group has a clear goal. I suggest this outcome statement: "By the end of this meeting we will have identified five possible topics for new research projects that involve implementation analysis. We will have sketched out basic research designs for at least two of those projects." Brainstorm to get some ideas flowing. Hold the more skeptical, analytical comments until later in the seminar. Ideally, some members of the discussion group will follow up on the meeting and continue to develop, perhaps collaboratively, research designs that build from the readings and the discussion. This is a good way to promote original policy research inspired by the best contemporary applications of quantitative and qualitative research methods. For additional advice on how to run effective meetings of this kind, see (1) Michael Mintrom's (2003) "Facilitating Meetings" in *People Skills for Policy Analysts* (Washington, DC: Georgetown University Press) and (2) Tom Kelley's (2001) "The Perfect Brainstorm" in *The Art of Innovation* (New York: Currency/Doubleday).

Further Reading

Australian National Audit Office. (2006). *Implementation of Programme and Policy Initiatives: Making Implementation Matter.* Canberra: Australian National Audit Office. Available online.

Bossidy, Larry, and Ram Charan. (2002). "The Execution Difference." In *Execution: The Discipline of Getting Things Done,* chap. 2. New York: Crown Business.

Elmore, Richard F. (1979). "Backward Mapping: Implementation Research and Policy Decisions." *Political Science Quarterly* 94: 601–616.

Heldman, Kim. (2005). "What Is Risk Management?" In *Project Manager's Spotlight on Risk Management,* chap. 1. San Francisco: Harbor Light Press.

Kotter, John P. (1996). "Successful Change and the Force That Drives It." Chapter 2 in *Leading Change.* Boston, MA: Harvard Business School Press.

Pfeffer, Jeffrey, and Robert I. Sutton. (2000). "Knowing 'What' to Do Is Not Enough." In *The Knowing-Doing Gap: How Smart Companies Turn Knowledge into Action,* chap. 1. Boston, MA: Harvard Business School Press.

Schultz, T. Paul. (2004). "School Subsidies for the Poor: Evaluating the Mexican Progresa Poverty Program." *Journal of Development Economics* 74: 199–250.

Weimer, David L., and Aidan R. Vining. (2005). "Adoption and Implementation." In *Policy Analysis: Concepts and Practice,* 4th ed., chap. 11. Upper Saddle River, NJ: Pearson Prentice Hall.

PART III

Improving Your Practice

17

◆◯

Developing as a Policy Analyst and Advisor

The Story Ends... Appropriately applied, the conceptual tools, management techniques, and analytical strategies presented in this book will help you to make solid contributions to policy discussions and debate. But policy analysis is an art, and improvement is always possible. Further, new challenges keep arising that require creative analytical responses.

Here... Suggestions are offered for how you can continue to improve your practice and become a highly accomplished analyst and advisor.

THIS CHAPTER REVIEWS
- The importance of staying positive
- Approaches to promoting creativity
- Ways to improve through deliberate practice
- An effective approach to change leadership

This book has introduced the general knowledge and skills required to perform effectively as a policy analyst. Throughout, exercises and further readings have been suggested to deepen knowledge and skills on each of the chapter topics. This fits with the intention that the book serves both to build general analytical capabilities and as an invitation to closer engagement with more specialist contributions to the field of policy analysis. This chapter discusses ways to keep developing as policy analysts and advisors. Always, people's evolving substantive interests will dictate the specific pathways they follow for knowledge acquisition. So my purpose here is not to offer signposts toward additional analytical strategies. Rather, I highlight several mutually compatible things we can do to become top performers within our chosen fields. These suggestions derive from reflection on my own practice. That practice has been influenced by contributions made by others from a range of fields, some of which intersect barely at all with the discipline of policy analysis.

Policy analysts can gain a lot from being positive in their approach to life. As positive thinking becomes our default position, we also tend to become more open to others. When we are open to others, when we relax our fixed views of situations and problems, we can unleash creative energy. That energy is a crucial ingredient to addressing conceptual and practical challenges. Following the insights of people who have studied the development of star performers across many fields, I offer practical suggestions for how policy analysts can use deliberate practice to build their skills.

People develop their interests in public policy and policy advising because, at some level, they want to change the world. We can all list ways that the world could become a better place. But then what? My interest in how people move from ideas to actions has been the impetus for ongoing research on policy entrepreneurship, political leadership, and the dynamics of policy change (Miller and Mintrom 2006; Mintrom 2000; Mintrom and Norman 2009). I end this book with suggestions for developing as change leaders.

THE POWER OF POSITIVE THINKING

Doing policy analysis is usually difficult. Problems can be complex and effective solutions hard to find. Then there is the political context—and the tendency for people to get heavily invested in particular outcomes and be prepared to play tough and dirty to realize them. The demands placed on policy analysts and advisors can be extreme at times. But I am reminded of a statement by Alva Myrdal, one of Sweden's most significant political figures of the twentieth century, a campaigner for nuclear disarmament, and a winner of the Nobel Peace Prize. "We gain nothing by walking around the difficulties and merely indulging in wishful thinking.... [I]t is not worthy of human beings to give up.... The greatness of being human ... lies in not giving up, in not accepting one's own limitations" (quoted in Edelman 1992: 58). This observation holds appeal because it places tenacity and creative endeavor at the heart of what it means to live well. When I reflect on the power of positive thinking, I see it as the power to transform apparent impossibilities into unambiguous accomplishments. It is the belief and commitment that has propelled people to make major conceptual and technical breakthroughs across vast areas of human activity.

Positive thinking has been touted frequently as a way to improve our lives and the lives of those around us. Early proponents, like Norman Vincent Peale (1954) were taken to task for the anecdotal and selective evidence they used to support their claims. Barbara Ehrenreich (2009) offers a trenchant critique of what she terms the "self-improvement industry," arguing that proponents of positive thinking too often gloss over the structural, societal dimensions of problems and individualize the attribution of success and failure. However, Barbara Frederickson (2009), through path-breaking contributions to the field of positive psychology, has amassed a raft of well-produced evidence to support her claims for the powerful and transformative role that positive thinking can play in our lives. Positive thinking, believing in ourselves, reaching out to others, defining and working toward common goals are not hokum. And positive thinking is not necessarily individualistic.

When we adopt positive attitudes toward others, it is much easier for everyone to get along and for good outcomes to be realized. When we move beyond considering what everything means for us and take actions that are intended primarily to benefit others, we can open many possibilities for achievement. None of this is easy. It requires us to look for the good in people, to appeal to it, and to ignore the more trying aspects of people's personalities and actions. Reflecting on my own experiences, I know that I have felt most energized and driven to attain results when a friend, colleague, or manager has been encouraging and shown their faith in my talents. As I have systematically adopted a positive and encouraging stance toward students and colleagues, I have observed incredible outcomes. My actions in this regard have been closely informed by my reading of Robert E. Quinn (2000) and Marianne Williamson (2004). But as both those authors have taken pains to emphasize, being positive, looking for the good in difficult people, and trying to move things forward in the face of major organizational obstacles is challenging. We need to find ways to put aside the instinct to be defensive, to assign blame, to attack. Frederickson's (2009) suggestions for how to do this include developing a propensity to kindness and generosity, identifying and playing up the positives in a situation, and temporarily removing ourselves from situations to have quiet time, to connect with the world around us, and to gain perspective. Trying hard to appreciate how other people feel and showing respect for those feelings is important too. When we do, we clear the air, and we open possibilities for collective action. We change ourselves, and in so doing we change how others see us and how they respond to us. In the world of policy making, this is how we can break through conflicts and keep conversations moving forward (Forester 1999; Schön and Rein 1994).

DEVELOPING OPENNESS AND CREATIVITY

The novelist F. Scott Fitzgerald famously observed, "The test of a first-rate intelligence is the ability to hold two opposing ideas in mind at the same time and still retain the ability to function."[1] Policy analysts need such intelligence. The good news is that this kind of intelligence can be consciously developed. Smart, creative professionals are the product of training and context. Howard Gardner's work on multiple forms of intelligence and the support that creative geniuses derive from

---

[1] The observation was made at the opening of *The Crack-Up* (1936). See Edmund Wilson (1945).

their broader cultural milieus confirm this point (Gardner 1993a, 1993b). So, too, does Daniel Goleman's work on emotional intelligence (Goleman 1995, 1998). Many contributions have explored approaches individuals can use to develop their creative problem solving skills (Buzan 2002; De Bono 1970; Tharp 2003). Others have begun to explore how creativity can be integrated into the practices of organizations that make money from generating ideas (Carlson and Wilmot 2006; Kelley 2001). Here, I suggest ways that policy analysts can develop openness and creativity. In doing so, I draw on Roger Martin's (2007) discussion of what he terms "integrative thinking."

Training for policy analysis, like training for many other professions, tends to promote effort directed toward simplification of complexity. We develop models of problem situations and attempt to specify a set of distinct alternative solutions. Usually, the list of alternative solutions is shaped, at least to some degree, by an assessment of what is politically feasible or popular at the time. When we begin to work on problems and think about solutions, we typically confront a lot of divergent information. A key task is to find convergence in this information. The proposal that we strive to be more open and creative does not imply significant deviation from standard processes. Importantly, however, we are asked to stick a while longer in that uncomfortable space populated by discrepant evidence and opposing ideas. Why? According to Roger Martin (2007), by allowing ourselves to play with the evidence and ideas confronting us, we are more likely to develop original solutions that take us to whole new ways of thinking about our context and the processes generating the problems we face. Martin urges that we resist assuming that the best solution will be found among existing, known solutions. We should keep our options open and allow for the possibility that we can get beyond "either/or" thinking and consider "both/and" possibilities.

Concretely, there are several things we can do to become more open and creative policy analysts. First, we should seek to generate a range of views on problems and solutions, going beyond obvious interpretations and options. For this, we can invite others into discussions with us, where we listen closely to how they think about the relevant situation and broader context. We might initiate a brainstorming session—or series of such sessions—where ideas can be proposed and others can build on them, and where skeptical, analytical thinking is avoided until the session is over. Second, we might look for ways to draw unusual connections and comparisons, looking to draw lessons for the present case from apparently unrelated policy cases. Third, we might develop a set of favored attributes of a policy solution. Even if we might recognize that such attributes are presently associated with mutually incompatible solutions, we should do this. The act of thinking in terms of desired outcomes and discussing them with others can open the possibility for breakthrough solutions—that is, solutions that function more effectively than any that are currently available. Pursuing actions along these lines will often take courage. After all, it means abandoning common wisdom and also asking others for help, and such actions make us vulnerable to criticism. Without courage, we are likely to stick close to what has worked in the past. We can always do better than that.

SKILL BUILDING THROUGH DELIBERATE PRACTICE

Inside and outside of government, there is high demand for top-performing policy analysts and advisors. Within the profession, individuals have a lot of opportunities to develop their skills and knowledge in policy areas of most interest to them. As people acquire experiences and make the most of new opportunities, they also build reputations for their good efforts. Although this line of work is challenging, a lot of rewards can come to those who take their work seriously and who continually strive to add value. In considering the pathways ahead, we might wonder how it is that some people have such success in their careers and others seem to drift. The differences are sometimes attributed to three things: talent, hard work, and luck. Reflecting on these ingredients for success, we see that hard work is the one we have most control over. But if we put in the effort, then we can also do things that add to our talent and luck. As we engage in policy projects, we often gain new experiences and we get to work with others who we can learn from. So hard work can help people build their talents. Further, when we work hard and others get to see our commitment, new opportunities tend to open up for us. The harder people work, the luckier they get!

K. Anders Ericsson and others have conducted close studies of how people become experts across a range of fields (see Ericsson, Prietula, and Cokely 2007). Ericsson defines real experts in any field as those who can consistently perform better than their peers, who generate successful outcomes, and who can replicate their expertise in laboratory-type situations. Although the work of policy analysts has not been subjected to this kind of investigation, it is clear that it approximates other professions that have been studied, such as decision making and software design. According to Ericsson, developing expertise requires great struggle and a lot of honest self-assessment. It normally takes people at least a decade of deliberate practice to achieve expertise in a field. This deliberate practice is defined as practice that focuses on tasks beyond your current level of competence and comfort, the ones that require you to stretch yourself. Only by working at the things you cannot currently do are you able to turn yourself into the expert you wish to become. It is also important to have good teachers or mentors. This means people who are able to give constructive feedback, and the feedback might be difficult to take at times. Often, as people develop their abilities, they outgrow particular mentors. Shifting from one mentor to another can be painful at times, but it is part of the struggle.

Ericsson and his colleagues have proposed that the case method, as used in many professional training situations including policy schools, can be particularly helpful for promoting deliberate practice. In these situations, students are given a real-life situation to address. After they have completed the exercise, they can compare what they did with what the people in the real-life case actually did. Through intensive case method teaching, it is possible for us to gain a lot of practice and a lot of useful feedback in a concentrated span of time. We can also set challenges for ourselves that are designed to build our expertise. For example, if you know of a new policy project that is being worked on by a team of senior colleagues, you might take the time to think about the issues at stake and how you would attempt to address them. Doing this homework and then comparing your answers with the answers that the team produced represents a good opportunity for learning and for analyzing areas where your own ideas came up short. Difficult as it can be, focusing closely on mistakes, how they arose, and how they could be avoided in the future can be hugely important for developing your expertise. But it is also helpful to remember that hitting success is great for building your confidence. Through our successes we can learn and grow, and get new insights into our work. So celebrating successes and building upon them is also a good way to learn, and one that counterbalances the soul-destroying aspect of revisiting mistakes.

BECOMING A CHANGE LEADER

Promoting change is hard work. Yet, we often pursue our work as policy analysts precisely because we believe that we have important things to offer and that our actions can make a difference. Exploring this in depth would take us into whole new literatures. For now, I wish to offer insights from a model presented by Robert E. Quinn (1996). Quinn proposed that leaders need to simultaneously promote stability in some things and change in others. Further, they need to attend simultaneously to internal organizational dynamics and external pressures. This way of considering the world of the change leader generates four key questions. First, where should we be heading as an organization? Second, how can we bring others in the organization along with us? Third, what do our current customers want and how can we improve what we give them? Fourth, looking at our internal processes, what things can we do to improve on our current operating procedures? Asking questions like this can be helpful in many settings.

As you would expect, our training as policy analysts can be helpful for supporting our work as change leaders. One thing good policy analysts do is take stock of their current context and the antecedents of problems before they jump into developing solutions. In a useful study of the successes and failures of new CEOs in business settings, Larry Greiner and his colleagues (2003) discovered that the relatively small group of CEOs in their study who were able to affect significant changes during their terms in office shared a common practice. That is, they tended to make only incremental changes in their first few months in office. Mainly, they spent this time getting to understand their context and the people they were working with. Only after this period did they launch significant change efforts. When they did, they knew how to achieve a good fit between people and positions in the changed structures. They also knew appropriate ways to mobilize and empower employees to pursue desired outcomes. There are important lessons here for people aspiring to affect significant change.

I wish to end with an inspiration for all policy analysts. I believe we each have an endless capacity to bring new meanings to our shared existence. We perform at our best when we undertake actions intended to promote the well-being of others. By building new knowledge, by applying what we already know, and by showing kindness of spirit (even when unappreciated by others), we can do great things. We can make our world a better place. As we build our unique careers and strive to perform at our best, we can come to see more clearly our connections to those around us, and those who have come before. We can attain new understandings of what is possible for the future and how we might create effective pathways to that future, pathways that others will follow.

Further Reading

Bennis, Warren. (2003). "Deploying Yourself: Strike Hard, Try Everything." In *On Becoming a Leader,* rev. ed., chap. 6. New York: Basic Books.

Ericsson, K. Anders, Michael J. Prietula, and Edward T. Cokely. (2007). "The Making of an Expert." *Harvard Business Review* 85 (July–August): 115–121.

Fredrickson, Barbara. (2009). "A New Toolkit" In *Positivity: Groundbreaking Research Reveals How to Embrace the Hidden Strength of Positive Emotions, Overcome Negativity, and Thrive,* chap. 11. New York: Crown.

Martin, Roger L. (2007). "Choices, Conflict, and the Creative Spark" In *The Opposable Mind: How Successful Leaders Win through Integrative Thinking,* chap. 1. Boston: Harvard Business School Press.

Quinn, Robert E. (2000). "An Invitation to Transformation." In *Change the World: How Ordinary People Can Accomplish Extraordinary Results,* chap. 1. San Francisco: Jossey-Bass.

Bibliography

Ackerman, Frank, and Lisa Heinzerling. (2004). *Priceless: On Knowing the Price of Everything and the Value of Nothing*. New York: New Press.

Ackerman, Frank, Lisa Heinzerling, and Rachel Massey. (2005). "Applying Cost-Benefit Analysis to Past Decisions: Was Environmental Protection Ever a Good Idea?" *Administrative Law Review* 57: 155–192.

Agranoff, Robert. (2007). *Managing within Networks: Adding Value to Public Organizations*. Washington, DC: Georgetown University Press.

Akerlof, George A. (1970). "The Market for 'Lemons': Quality Uncertainty and the Market Mechanism." *Quarterly Journal of Economics* 84: 488–500.

Alchian, Armen A., and Harold Demsetz. (1972). "Production, Information Costs, and Economic Organization." *The American Economic Review* 62: 777–795.

Alston, Lee J., Thráinn Eggertsson, and Douglass C. North (Eds.). (1996). *Empirical Studies in Institutional Change*. New York: Cambridge University Press.

Althaus, Catherine. (2008). *Calculating Political Risk*. Sterling, VA: Earthscan.

Amy, Douglas J. (1984). "Why Policy Analysis and Ethics Are Incompatible." *Journal of Policy Analysis and Management* 3(4): 573–591.

Anderson, James. (1975). *Public Policy-Making*. New York: Praeger.

Antonovics, Kate, and Brian G. Knight. (2009). "A New Look at Racial Profiling: Evidence from the Boston Police Department." *Review of Economics and Statistics* 91: 163–177.

Ards, Sheila D., and Samuel L. Myers, Jr. (2001). "The Color of Money: Bad Credit, Wealth and Race." *American Behavioral Scientist* 45: 223–239.

Arthur, W. Brian. (1990). "Positive Feedbacks in the Economy." *Scientific American* 262 (February): 92–99.

Aucoin, Peter. (1996). *The New Public Management Canada in Comparative Perspective*. Kingston, Ontario: McGill-Queen's University Press.

Austin, Robert D. (2004). *Managing Projects Large and Small*. Boston, MA: Harvard Business School Press.

Australian National Audit Office. (2006). *Implementation of Programme and Policy Initiatives: Making Implementation Matter*. Canberra: Australian National Audit Office. Available online.

Axelrod, Robert. (1984). *The Evolution of Cooperation*. New York: Basic Books.

Ayres, Ian, and Peter Siegelman. (1995). "Race and Gender Discrimination in Bargaining for a New Car." *American Economic Review* 85: 304–321.

Babcock, Linda, and Sara Laschever. (2003). *Women Don't Ask*. Princeton, NJ: Princeton University Press.

Bachrach, Peter, and Morton S. Baratz. (1962). "Two Faces of Power." *American Political Science Review* 56: 947–952.

Banks, Jeffrey S., and Eric A. Hanushek. (1995). *Modern Political Economy: Old Topics, New Directions*. New York: Cambridge University Press.

Bardach, Eugene. (1977). *The Implementation Game: What Happens after a Bill Becomes a Law*. Cambridge, MA: MIT Press.

Bardach, Eugene. (1998). *Getting Agencies to Work Together: The Practice and Theory of Managerial Craftsmanship*. Washington, DC: Brookings Institution Press.

Bardach, Eugene. (2008). *A Practical Guide for Policy Analysis: The Eightfold Path to More Effective Problem Solving*. 3rd ed. Washington, DC: CQ Press.

Bardach, Eugene, and Robert A. Kagan. (2002). *Going by the Book: The Problem of Regulatory Unreasonableness*. With a new introduction by the authors. New Brunswick, NJ: Transaction.

Barrow, C. J. (2000). *Social Impact Assessment: An Introduction*. New York: Oxford University Press.

Barton, Larry. (2004). *Crisis Management: Master the Skills to Prevent Disasters*. Boston: Harvard Business School Press.

Barzel, Yoram. (1989). *Economic Analysis of Property Rights*. New York: Cambridge University Press.

Barzelay, Michael. (2007). "Learning from Second-Hand Experience: Methodology for Extrapolation-Oriented Case Research." *Governance* 20: 521–543.

Bates, Robert H. (2001). *Prosperity and Violence: The Political Economy of Development*. New York: W. W. Norton.

Baumol, William J., John C. Panzar, and Robert D. Willig. (1982). *Contestable Markets and the Theory of Industry Structure*. New York: Harcourt Brace Jovanovich.

Bayrakal, Suna. (2006). "The U.S. Pollution Prevention Act: A Policy Implementation Analysis." *Social Science Journal* 43: 127–145.

Baumgartner, Frank R., and Bryan D. Jones. (Eds.). (2002). *Policy Dynamics*. Chicago: University of Chicago Press.

Becker, Gary S. (1957). *The Economics of Discrimination*. Chicago: University of Chicago Press.

Becker, Gary S. (1983). "A Theory of Competition among Pressure Groups for Political Influence." *Quarterly Journal of Economics* 98: 371–400.

Bennis, Warren (2003). *On Becoming a Leader*. Rev. ed. New York: Basic Books.

Benveniste, Guy. (1984). "On a Code of Ethics for Policy Experts." *Journal of Policy Analysis and Management* 3(4): 561–572.

Bernanke, Benjamin S. (2005). Remarks at "Panel Discussion: The Transition from Academic to Policymaker." Annual Meeting of the American Economic Association, Philadelphia, Pennsylvania, January 7. Retrieved from http://www.federalreserve.gov/newsevents/speech/2005speech.htm.

Bikhchandani, Sushil, David Hirshleifer, and Ivo Welch. (1992). "A Theory of Fads, Fashion, Custom, and Cultural Change as Informational Cascades." *Journal of Political Economy* 100: 992–1026.

Bish, Robert L., and Vincent Ostrom. (1973). *Understanding Urban Government: Metropolitan Reform Reconsidered.* Washington, DC: American Enterprise Institute for Public Policy Research.

Black, Ron. (2004). *The Complete Idiot's Guide to Project Management with Microsoft Project 2003.* New York: Alpha.

Blinder, Alan S. (1987). *Hard Heads, Soft Hearts: Tough-Minded Economics for a Just Society.* Reading, MA: Addison-Wesley.

Boardman, Anthony E., David H. Greenberg, Aidan R. Vining, and David L. Weimer. (2005). *Cost-Benefit Analysis: Concepts and Practice.* 3rd ed. Upper Saddle River, NJ: Prentice Hall.

Bohte, John, and Kenneth J. Meier. (2000). "Goal Displacement: Assessing the Motivation for Organizational Cheating." *Public Administration Review* 60: 173–182.

Bok, Derek. (1996). *The State of the Nation: Government and the Quest for a Better Society.* Cambridge, MA: Harvard University Press.

Boston, Jonathan, et al. (1996). *Public Management: The New Zealand Model.* Auckland: Oxford University Press.

Brehm, John, and Scott Gates. (1997). *Working, Shirking, and Sabotage: Bureaucratic Response to a Democratic Public.* Ann Arbor, MI: University of Michigan Press.

Brent, Robert J. (2006). *Applied Cost-Benefit Analysis.* 2nd ed. Northampton, MA: Edward Elgar.

Buzan, Tony. (2002). *How to Mind Map.* London: Thorsons.

Cabral, Luis M. B. (2000). *Introduction to Industrial Organization.* Cambridge, MA: MIT Press.

Cahn, Steven M. (Ed.). (2010). *Political Philosophy: The Essential Texts.* 2nd ed. New York: Oxford University Press.

Calvert, Randall L., Mathew D. McCubbins, and Barry R. Weingast. (1989). "A Theory of Political Control and Agency Discretion." *American Journal of Political Science* 33: 588–611.

Campbell, Donald E. (2006). *Incentives: Motivation and the Economics of Information.* 2nd ed. New York: Cambridge University Press.

Canfield, Jack. (2005). *The Success Principles: How to Get From Where You Are to Where You Want to Be.* New York: Harper Resource Books.

Card, David, and Jesse Rothstein. (2007). "Racial Segregation and the Black-White Test Score Gap." *Journal of Public Economics* 91: 2158–2184.

Carlson, Curtis R., and William W. Wilmot. (2006). *Innovation: The Five Disciplines for Creating What Customers Want.* New York: Crown Business.

Caro, Robert A. (1974). *The Power Broker: Robert Moses and the Fall of New York.* New York: Knopf.

Carpenter, Daniel. (2010). *Reputation and Power: Organizational Image and Pharmaceutical Regulation at the FDA.* Princeton, NJ: Princeton University Press.

Carpenter, Susan L., and W. J. D. Kennedy. (1988). *Managing Public Disputes: A Practical Guide to Handling Conflict and Reaching Agreement.* San Francisco: Jossey-Bass.

Chen, Huey-tsyh. (1990). *Theory-Driven Evaluations.* Newbury Park, CA: Sage Publications.

Cheung, Steven N. S. (1996). "Roofs or Stars: The Stated Intents and Actual Effects of a Rents Ordinance." In *Empirical Studies in Institutional Change,* ed. Lee J. Alston, Thráinn Eggertson, and Douglass C. North, chap. 6. New York: Cambridge University Press.

Chubb, John E., and Terry M. Moe. (1990). *Politics, Markets, and America's Schools*, Washington, DC: Brookings Institution.

Coase, R. H. (1937). "The Nature of the Firm." *Economica* 4: 386–405.

Coase, R. H. (1960). "The Problem of Social Cost." *Journal of Law and Economics* 3: 1–44.

Cobb, Roger W., and Charles W. Elder. (1983). *Participation in American Politics: The Dynamics of Agenda-Building*. 2nd ed. Boston, MA: Allyn and Bacon.

Cohn, D'Vera. (1999). "Credit Study Attacked: Freddie Mac Data Called Incomplete." *Washington Post*, October 5, B1.

Collins, Gail. (2009). *When Everything Changed: The Amazing Journey of American Women from 1960 to the Present*. New York: Little, Brown.

Collins, Jim. (2001). *Good to Great*. New York: HarperBusiness.

Cook, Curtis R. (2005). *Just Enough Project Management*. New York: McGraw-Hill.

Cook, Thomas D., and Donald T. Campbell. (1979). *Quasi-Experimentation: Design and Analysis Issues for Field Settings*. Boston, MA: Houghton Mifflin.

Cooper, Phillip J. (2003). *Governing by Contract: Challenges and Opportunities for Public Managers*. Washington, DC: CQ Press.

Covey, Stephen M. R. (2006). *The Speed of Trust: The One Thing That Changes Everything*. New York: Simon and Schuster.

Covey, Stephen R. (1989). *The Seven Habits of Highly Effective People*. New York: Simon and Schuster.

Covey, Stephen R. (1991). *Principle-Centered Leadership*. New York: Free Press.

Cyert, Richard M., and James G. March. (1963). *A Behavioral Theory of the Firm*. Englewood Cliffs, NJ: Prentice-Hall.

Dahl, Robert A. (1998). *On Democracy*. New Haven, CT: Yale University Press.

Dales, J. H. (1968). *Pollution, Property and Prices: An Essay in Policy-making and Economics*. Toronto: University of Toronto Press.

David, Paul A. (1994). "Why Are Institutions the 'Carriers of History'?: Path Dependence and the Evolution of Conventions, Organizations and Institutions." *Structural Change and Economic Dynamics* 5: 205–220.

De Bono, Edward. (1970). *Lateral Thinking*. London: Penguin Books.

Demsetz, Harold. (1969). "Information and Efficiency: Another Viewpoint." *Journal of Law and Economics* 12: 1–22.

Derthick, Martha. (1979). *Policymaking for Social Security*. Washington, DC: Brookings Institution.

Dixit, Avinash K., and Barry J. Nalebuff. (2008). *The Art of Strategy: A Game Theorist's Guide to Success in Business and Life*. New York: W.W. Norton.

Donahue, John D. (1989). *The Privatization Decision: Public Ends, Private Means*. New York: Basic Books.

Donahue, John D. (Ed.). (1999). *Making Washington Work: Tales of Innovation in the Federal Government*. Washington, DC: Brookings Institution Press.

Edelman, Marian Wright. (1992). *The Measure of Our Success*. New York: HarperCollins.

Ehrenreich, Barbara. (2009). *Bright-Sided: How the Relentless Promotion of Positive Thinking Has Undermined America*. New York: Metropolitan Books.

Elmore, Richard F. (1979). "Backward Mapping: Implementation Research and Policy Decisions." *Political Science Quarterly* 94: 601–616.

Epictetus. ([circa 55–135 AD] 1994). *The Art of Living: The Classic Manual on Virtue, Happiness, and Effectiveness, A New Interpretation by Sharon Lebell*. New York: HarperCollins.

Epstein, Paul D., et al. (2006). *Results That Matter: Improving Communities by Engaging Citizens, Measuring Performance, and Getting Things Done*. San Francisco: Jossey-Bass.

Ericsson, K. Anders, Michael J. Prietula, and Edward T. Cokely. (2007). "The Making of an Expert." *Harvard Business Review* 85 (July–August): 115–121.

Esping-Andersen, Gøsta. (1990). *The Three Worlds of Welfare Capitalism*. Cambridge, UK: Polity Press.

Esty, Daniel C., and Andrew S. Winston. (2006). *Green to Gold: How Smart Companies Use Environmental Strategy to Innovate, Create Value, and Build Competitive Advantage*. New Haven, CT: Yale University Press.

Eyestone, Robert. (1978). *From Social Issues to Public Policy*. New York: John Wiley and Sons.

Fiske, Susan T., and Shelley E. Taylor. (2008). *Social Cognition: From Brains to Culture*. Boston: McGraw-Hill Higher Education.

Florida, Richard. (2005). *Cities and the Creative Class*. New York: Routledge.

Forester, John. (1999). *The Deliberative Practitioner: Encouraging Participatory Planning Processes*. Cambridge, MA: MIT Press.

Fox, Jeffrey J. (1998). *How to Become CEO*. New York: Hyperion.

Fox, Jeffrey J. (2002). *How to Become a Great Boss*. New York: Hyperion.

Frankfort-Nachmias, Chava, and David Nachmias. (1996). *Research Methods in the Social Sciences*. 5th ed. New York: St. Martin's Press.

Fraser, Nancy. (1998). "From Redistribution to Recognition: Dilemmas of Justice in a Post-Socialist Age." In *Feminism and Politics: Oxford Readings in Feminism*, ed. Anne Phillips, 430–460. New York: Oxford University Press.

Fredrickson, Barbara. (2009). *Positivity: Groundbreaking Research Reveals How to Embrace the Hidden Strength of Positive Emotions, Overcome Negativity, and Thrive*. New York: Crown.

Friedman, Benjamin M. (1995). "Principles of Economics." *American Economist* 39: 28–36.

Friedman, Milton. (1953). "The Methodology of Positive Economics." In *Essays in Positive Economics*. Chicago: University of Chicago Press.

Friedman, Milton. (1962). *Capitalism and Freedom*. Chicago: University of Chicago Press.

Fryer, Roland G., Jr., and Steven D. Levitt. (2004). "Understanding the Black-White Test Score Gap in the First Two Years of School." *Review of Economics and Statistics* 86: 447–464.

Fullan, Michael. (2007). *The New Meaning of Educational Change*. 4th ed. New York: Teachers College Press

Gardner, Howard. (1993a). *Creating Minds*. New York: Basic Books.

Gardner, Howard. (1993b). *Multiple Intelligences: The Theory in Practice*. New York: Basic Books.

Geiger, Roger L. (1993). *Research and Relevant Knowledge: American Research Universities since World War II*. New York: Oxford University Press.

Glick, Henry R., and Scott P. Hays. (1991). "Innovation and Reinvention in State Policymaking: Theory and the Evolution of Living Will Laws." *Journal of Politics* 53: 835–850.

Goggin, Malcolm L., Ann O'M. Bowman, James P. Lester, and Laurence J. O'Toole, Jr. (1990). *Implementation Theory and Practice: Toward a Third Generation*. Glenview, IL: Scott, Foresman.

Goldin, Claudia, and Cecilia Rouse. (2000). "Orchestrating Impartiality: The Impact of 'Blind' Auditions on Female Musicians." *American Economic Review* 90: 715–741.

Goldsmith, Marshall. (2007). *What Got You Here Will Not Get You There*. New York: Hyperion.

Goldsmith, Stephen, and William D. Eggers. (2004). *Governing by Network: The New Shape of the Public Sector*. Washington, DC: Brookings Institution Press.

Goleman, Daniel. (1995). *Emotional Intelligence*. New York; Bantam Books.

Goleman, Daniel. (1998). *Working with Emotional Intelligence*. New York: Bantam Books.

Gormley, William T. (1995). *Everybody's Children: Child Care as a Public Problem*. Washington, DC: Brookings Institution.

Gormley, William T., Jr., and David L. Weimer. (1999). *Organizational Report Cards*. Cambridge, MA: Harvard University Press.

Greener, Ian. (2002). "Theorising Path-Dependency: How Does History Come to Matter in Organisations? *Management Decision* 40: 614–619.

Greiner, Larry, Thomas Cummings, and Arvind Bhambri. (2003). "When New CEOs Succeed and Fail: 4-D Theory of Strategic Transformation." *Organizational Dynamics* 32: 1–16.

Gunningham, Neil, and Joseph Rees. (1997). "Industry Self-Regulation: An Institutional Perspective." *Law and Policy* 19: 363–414.

Gutmann, Amy. (Ed.). (1994). *Multiculturalism: Examining the Politics of Recognition*. Princeton, NJ: Princeton University Press.

Hahn, Robert W. (1989). "Economic Prescriptions for Environmental Problems: How the Patient Followed the Doctor's Orders." *The Journal of Economic Perspectives* 3: 95–114.

Hahn, Robert W. (2009). "Greenhouse Gas Auctions and Taxes: Some Political Economy Considerations." *Review of Environmental Economics and Policy* 3: 167–188.

Hahn, Robert W., and Cass R. Sunstein. (2002). "A New Executive Order for Improving Federal Regulation? Deeper and Wider Cost-Benefit Analysis." *University of Pennsylvania Law Review* 150: 1489–1552.

Hall, Peter, and Rosemary C. R. Taylor. (1996). "Political Science and the Three New Institutionalisms." *Political Studies* 44: 936–957.

Hanushek, Eric. (1994). *Making Schools Work: Improving Performance and Controlling Costs*. Washington, DC: Brookings Institution.

Hardin, Garrett. (1968). "The Tragedy of the Commons." *Science* 162: 1243–1248.

Hay, Colin, Michael Lister, and David Marsh. (Eds.). (2006). *The State: Theories and Issues*. New York: Palgrave Macmillan.

Hayek, F. A. (1945). "The Use of Knowledge in Society." *American Economic Review* 35: 519–530.

Hearn, Jeff, and Linda McKie. (2008). "Gendered Policy and Policy on Gender: The Case of 'Domestic Violence.'" *Policy and Politics* 36: 75–91.

Heckelman, Jac C. (Ed.). (2004). *Readings in Public Choice Economics*. Ann Arbor: University of Michigan Press.

Heerkens, Gary R. (2002). *Project Management*. New York: McGraw-Hill.

Heifetz, Ronald A. (1994). *Leadership without Easy Answers*. Cambridge, MA: Belknap Press of Harvard University Press.

Heldman, Kim. (2005). *Project Manager's Spotlight on Risk Management*. Alameda, CA: Harbor Light Press.

Helpman, Elhanan. (2004). *The Mystery of Economic Growth*. Cambridge, MA: Harvard University Press.

Hicks, John R. (1939). "Foundations of Welfare Economics." *Economic Journal* 49: 696–712.

Hobbes, Thomas. ([1651] 1996). *Leviathan*, ed. J. C. A Gaskin. Oxford: Oxford University Press.

Hochschild, Jennifer L. (1981). *What's Fair? American Beliefs About Distributive Justice.* Cambridge, MA: Harvard University Press.

Hodgson, Geoffrey M. (1998). "The Approach of Institutional Economics." *Journal of Economic Literature* 36: 166–192.

Hood, Christopher. (1991). "A Public Management for All Seasons?" *Public Administration* 69: 3–19.

Horn, Murray J. (1995). *The Political Economy of Public Administration: Institutional Choice in the Public Sector.* New York: Cambridge University Press.

Huber, John D., and Charles R. Shipan. (2002). *Deliberate Discretion: The Institutional Foundations of Bureaucratic Autonomy.* New York: Cambridge University Press.

Ingraham, Patricia W. (Ed.). (2007). *In Pursuit of Performance: Management Systems in State and Local Government.* Baltimore, MD: Johns Hopkins University Press.

International Labour Office. (2010). *Women in Labour Markets: Measuring Progress and Identifying Challenges.* Geneva: ILO.

Jenkins-Smith, Hank C., and Paul A. Sabatier. (Eds.). (1993). *Policy Change and Learning: An Advocacy Coalition Approach.* Boulder, CO: Westview Press.

Jensen, Robert. (2007). "The Digital Provide: Information (Technology), Market Performance, and Welfare in the South Indian Fisheries Sector." *Quarterly Journal of Economics* 122: 879–924.

Jones, Bryan D. (2001). *Politics and the Architecture of Choice: Bounded Rationality and Governance.* Chicago: University of Chicago Press.

Jones, Charles. (1970). *An Introduction to the Study of Public Policy.* Belmont, CA: Wadsworth.

Jones, Laurie Beth. (1995). *Jesus, CEO: Using Ancient Wisdom for Visionary Leadership.* New York: Hyperion.

Kaldor, Nicholas. (1939). "Welfare Propositions of Economics and Interpersonal Comparisons of Utility." *Economic Journal* 49: 549–552.

Kalt, Joseph P. (1983). "The Creation, Growth, and Entrenchment of Special Interests in Oil Price Policy." In *The Political Economy of Deregulation*, ed. Roger Noll and Bruce M. Owen. Washington, DC: American Enterprise Institute.

Kant, Immanuel. ([1785] 1997). *Groundwork of the Metaphysics of Morals*, ed. Mary Gregor. Cambridge: Cambridge University Press.

Karch, Andrew. (2007). *Democratic Laboratories: Policy Diffusion Among the American States.* Ann Arbor: University of Michigan Press.

Kelley, Tom. (2001). *The Art of Innovation.* New York: Currency/Doubleday.

Kelman, Steven. (1988). *Making Public Policy: A Hopeful View of American Government.* New York: Basic Books.

Kettl, Donald F. (2000). *The Global Public Management Revolution: A Report on the Transformation of Governance.* Washington, DC: Brookings Institution Press.

Kettl, Donald F., and John J. DiIulio, Jr. (Eds.). (1995). *Inside the Reinvention Machine: Appraising Governmental Reform.* Washington, DC: Brookings Institution.

Kingdon, John. ([1984] 1995). *Agendas, Alternatives, and Public Policies.* 2nd ed. Boston, MA: Little, Brown.

Klyza, Christopher McGrory, and David J. Sousa. (2008). *American Environmental Policy, 1990–2006: Beyond Gridlock.* Cambridge, MA: MIT Press.

Kotter, John P. (1996). *Leading Change*. Boston, MA: Harvard Business School Press.

Kraft, Michael E., and Scott R. Furlong. (2007). *Public Policy: Politics, Analysis, and Alternatives*. 2nd ed. Washington, DC: CQ Press.

Kramer, Roderick M. (1999). "Trust and Distrust in Organizations: Emerging Perspectives, Enduring Questions." *Annual Review of Psychology* 50: 569–598.

Krugman, Paul. (1993). "How I Work." *American Economist* 37: 25–32.

Krueger, Alan B. (2002). "Economic Scene: A Model for Evaluating the Use of Development Dollars, South of the Border." *New York Times*, May 2, 2002, p. C2

Kumla, Savita, and Susan Vinnicombe. (2008). "A Study of the Promotion to Partner Process in a Professional Services Firm: How Women Are Disadvantaged." *British Journal of Management* 19: 65–74.

Kymlicka, Will. (2001). *Politics in the Vernacular: Nationalism, Multiculturalism, and Citizenship*. New York: Oxford University Press.

Kymlicka, Will. (2007). *Multicultural Odysseys: Navigating the New International Politics of Diversity*. New York: Oxford University Press.

Laffont, Jean-Jacques, and David Martimort. (2002). *The Theory of Incentives: The Principal-Agent Model*. Princeton, NJ: Princeton University Press.

Le Grand, Julian. (2003). *Motivation, Agency, and Public Policy: Of Knights and Knaves, Pawns and Queens*. Oxford: Oxford University Press.

Levin, Martin A., and Mary Bryna Sanger. (1994). *Making Government Work: How Entrepreneurial Executives Turn Bright Ideas into Real Results*. San Francisco: Jossey-Bass.

Lindblom, Charles E. (1959). "The Science of 'Muddling Through.'" *Public Administration Review* 19: 79–88.

Lindblom, Charles E. (1968). *The Policymaking Process*. Englewood Cliffs, NJ: Prentice-Hall.

Locke, John, ([1690] 2004). *Second Treatise of Government*. With an introduction by Joseph Carrig. New York: Barnes & Noble Books.

Lodge, Martin. (2002). "The Wrong Type of Regulation? Regulatory Failure and the Railways in Britain and Germany." *Journal of Public Policy* 22: 271–297.

Lynn, Laurence E. (2006). *Public Management: Old and New*. New York: Routledge.

Machiavelli, Niccolò. ([1517] 1975). *The Discourses*. Translated from the Italian, with an introduction and notes by Leslie J. Walker; with a new introduction and appendices by Cecil H. Clough. London: Routledge and Paul.

Mahoney, James, and Kathleen Thelen. (Eds.). (2010). *Explaining Institutional Change: Ambiguity, Agency, and Power*. New York: Cambridge University Press.

Majone, Giandomenico. (1989). *Evidence, Argument, and Persuasion in the Policy Process*. New Haven: Yale University Press.

Mansbridge, Jane J. (1986). *Why We Lost the ERA*. Chicago: University of Chicago Press.

March, James G., and Johan P. Olsen. (1984). "The New Institutionalism: Organizational Factors in Political Life." *American Political Science Review* 78: 734–749.

March, James G., and Johan P. Olsen. (1989). *Rediscovering Institutions: The Organizational Basis of Politics*. New York: Free Press.

March, James G., and Johan P. Olsen. (2006). "Elaborating the 'New Institutionalism.'" In *The Oxford Handbook of Political Institutions*, ed. R. A. W. Rhodes, Sarah A. Binder, and Bert A. Rockman, chap. 1. New York: Oxford University Press.

Martin, Roger L. (2007). *The Opposable Mind: How Successful Leaders Win through Integrative Thinking*. Boston: Harvard Business School Press.

Massey, Douglas S., and Robert J. Sampson. (2009). "Moynihan Redux: Legacies and Lessons." *Annals of the American Academy of Political and Social Science* 621: 6–27.

Maxwell, John C. (1999). *The 21 Indispensable Qualities of a Leader.* Nashville, TN: Thomas Nelson.

Mayhew, David R. (1974). *Congress: The Electoral Connection.* New Haven, CT: Yale University Press.

McCraw, Thomas K. (1984). *Prophets of Regulation.* Cambridge, MA: Belknap Press.

McCubbins, Mathew D., and Thomas Schwartz. (1984). "Congressional Oversight Overlooked: Police Patrols versus Fire Alarms." *American Journal of Political Science* 28: 165–179.

Meyerson, Debra, Karl E. Weick, and Roderick M. Kramer. (1996). "Swift Trust and Temporary Groups." In *Trust in Organizations: Frontiers of Theory and Research*, ed. Roderick M. Kramer and Tom R. Tyler, 166–195. Thousand Oaks, CA: Sage.

Mill, John Stuart. (2003). Utilitarianism and On Liberty *including Mill's "Essay on Bentham" and Selections from the Writings of Jeremy Bentham and John Austin*, 2nd ed., ed. Mary Warnock. Malden, MA: Blackwell.

Miller, Gary J. (1992). *Managerial Dilemmas: The Political Economy of Hierarchy.* New York: Cambridge University Press.

Miller, Gary J., and Terry M. Moe. (1983). "Bureaucrats, Legislators, and the Size of Government." *American Political Science Review* 77: 297–322.

Miller, Raymond, and Michael Mintrom. (Eds.). (2006). *Political Leadership in New Zealand.* Auckland: Auckland University Press.

Mintrom, Michael. (1997). "Policy Entrepreneurs and the Diffusion of Innovation." *American Journal of Political Science* 41: 738–770.

Mintrom, Michael. (2000). *Policy Entrepreneurs and School Choice.* Washington, DC: Georgetown University Press.

Mintrom, Michael. (2001). "Policy Design for Local Innovation: The Effects of Competition in Public Schooling." *State Politics and Policy Quarterly* 1: 343–363.

Mintrom, Michael. (2003). *People Skills for Policy Analysts.* Washington, DC: Georgetown University Press.

Mintrom, Michael, and Phillipa Norman. (2009). "Policy Entrepreneurship and Policy Change." *Policy Studies Journal* 37(4): 649–667.

Mintrom, Michael, and John Wanna. (2006). "Innovative State Strategies in the Antipodes: Enhancing the Ability of Governments to Govern in the Global Context." *Australian Journal of Political Science* 41: 161–176.

Mocan, Naci. (2007). "Can Consumers Detect Lemons? An Empirical Analysis of Information Asymmetry in the Market for Child Care." *Journal of Population Economics* 20: 743–780.

Moe, Terry M. (1979). "On the Scientific Status of Rational Models." *American Journal of Political Science* 23: 215–243.

Moe, Terry M. (1985). "Control and Feedback in Economic Regulation: The Case of the NLRB." *American Political Science Review* 79: 1094–1116.

Moe, Terry M. (1990). "Political Institutions: The Neglected Side of the Story." *Journal of Law, Economics, and Organization* 6 (Special Issue): 213–253.

Moe, Terry M. (1991). "Politics and the Theory of Organization." *Journal of Law, Economics, and Organization* 7 (Special Issue): 106–129.

Moe, Terry M. (2001). *Schools, Vouchers, and the American Public.* Washington, DC: Brookings Institution Press.

Moe, Terry M. (2006). "Political Control and the Power of the Agent." *Journal of Law, Economics, and Organization* 22: 1–29.

Moe, Terry M. (2009). "Collective Bargaining and the Performance of the Public Schools." *American Journal of Political Science* 53: 156–174.

Montesquieu, M. de Secondat. ([1751] 1878). *The Spirit of the Laws*. Translated from French, by Thomas Nugent. New ed., rev., by J. V. Prichard. London: G. Bell and Sons.

Moore, Mark A., Anthony E. Boardman, Aidan R. Vining, David L. Weimer, and David H. Greenberg. (2004). "Just Give Me a Number! Practical Values for the Social Discount Rate." *Journal of Policy Analysis and Management* 23: 789–812.

Morgan, Glenn, et al. (Eds.). (2010). *The Oxford Handbook of Comparative Institutional Analysis*. New York: Oxford University Press.

Mueller, Dennis C. (Ed.). (1997). *Perspectives on Public Choice: A Handbook*. New York: Cambridge University Press.

Mueller, Dennis C. (2003). *Public Choice III*. New York: Cambridge University Press.

Munnell, Alicia H., Lynn E. Browne, James McEneaney, and Geoffrey M. B. Tootell. (1992). "Mortgage Lending in Boston: Interpreting HMDA Data." (Working Paper Series No. 92-7). Boston: Federal Reserve Bank of Boston.

Myers, Samuel L., Jr. (2002). "Presidential Address—Analysis of Race as Policy Analysis." *Journal of Policy Analysis and Management* 21: 169–190.

Najam, Adil. (1995). *Learning from the Literature on Policy Implementation: A Synthesis Perspective*. WP-95-61. Laxenburg, Austria: International Institute for Applied Systems Analysis. Available at http://www.iiasa.ac.at/Admin/PUB/Documents/WP-95-061.pdf.

Nisbett, Richard, and Lee Ross. (1980). *Human Inference: Strategies and Shortcomings of Social Judgment*. Englewood Cliffs, NJ: Prentice Hall.

Niskanen, William A., Jr. (1971). *Bureaucracy and Representative Government*. Chicago: Aldine, Atherton.

North, Douglass C. (1981). *Structure and Change in Economic History*. New York: Norton.

North, Douglass C. (1990). *Institutions, Institutional Change, and Economic Performance*. New York: Cambridge University Press.

Oehler, Andreas, and Daniel Kohlert. (2009). "Financial Advice Giving and Taking—Where Are the Market's Self-Healing Powers and a Functioning Legal Framework When We Need Them?" *Journal of Consumer Policy* 32: 91–116.

Okun, Arthur M. (1975). *Equality and Efficiency: The Big Tradeoff*. Washington, DC: Brookings Institution.

Oliver, Paula. (2008). "State Staff Promised More Say if Key Wins." *New Zealand Herald*, September 25.

Olson, Mancur, Jr. (1965). *The Logic of Collective Action: Public Goods and the Theory of Groups*. Cambridge, MA: Harvard University Press.

Ong, Paul M., and Michael A. Stoll. (2007). "Redlining or Risk? A Spatial Analysis of Auto Insurance Rates in Los Angeles." *Journal of Policy Analysis and Management* 26: 811–829.

Osborne, David, and Ted Gaebler. (1992). *Reinventing Government: How the Entrepreneurial Spirit Is Transforming the Public Sector*. Reading, MA: Addison-Wesley.

Ostrom, Elinor. (1990). *Governing the Commons: The Evolution of Institutions for Collective Action*. New York: Cambridge University Press.

Ostrom, Elinor. (1999). "Coping with Tragedies of the Commons." *Annual Review of Political Science* 2: 493–535.

Ostrom, Elinor, Roy Gardner, and James Walker. (1994). *Rules, Games, and Common-Pool Resources*. Ann Arbor: University of Michigan Press.

Page, Scott E. (2007). *The Difference: How the Power of Diversity Creates Better Groups, Firms, Schools, and Societies*. Princeton, NJ: Princeton University Press.

Paige, Rod, and Elaine Witty. (2010). *The Black-White Achievement Gap: Why Closing it is the Greatest Civil Rights Issue of our Time*. New York: AMACOM, American Management Association.

Peale, Norman Vincent. ([1954] 2007). *The Power of Positive Thinking*. New York: Fireside/ Simon & Schuster.

Peltzman, Sam. (1976). "Toward a More General Theory of Regulation." *Journal of Law and Economics* 19: 211–240.

Peltzman, Sam, Michael E. Levine, and Roger G. Noll. (1989). "The Economic Theory of Regulation after a Decade of Deregulation." *Brookings Papers on Economic Activity. Microeconomics* 1989: 1–59.

Pepall, Lynne, Dan Richards, and George Norman. (2008). *Industrial Organization: Contemporary Theory and Empirical Applications*. 4th ed. Malden, MA: Blackwell.

Peters, B. Guy. (1986). *American Public Policy: Promise and Performance*. 2nd ed. Chatham, NJ: Chatham House.

Peters, B. Guy. (1996). "Political Institutions: Old and New." In *A New Handbook of Political Science*, ed. Robert E. Goodin and Hans-Dieter Klingemann, chap. 7. New York: Oxford University Press.

Pfeffer, Jeffrey, and Robert I. Sutton. (2000). *The Knowing-Doing Gap: How Smart Companies Turn Knowledge into Action*. Boston, MA: Harvard Business School Press.

Pierson, Paul. (2000). "Increasing Returns, Path Dependence, and the Study of Politics." *American Political Science Review* 94: 251–267.

Plante, Thomas G. (2004). *Doing the Right Thing: Living Ethically in an Unethical World*. Oakland, CA: New Harbinger .

Popovich, Mark G. (Ed.). (1998). *Creating High-Performance Government Organizations: A Practical Guide for Public Managers*. San Francisco: Jossey-Bass.

Pratt, John W., and Richard J. Zeckhauser. (Eds.) (1985). *Principals and Agents: The Structure of Business*. Boston, MA: Harvard Business School Press.

Pressman, Jeffrey L., and Aaron Wildavsky. (1973). *Implementation: How Great Expectations in Washington Are Dashed in Oakland*. Berkeley: University of California Press.

Quinn, Robert E. (1996). *Deep Change: Discovering the Leader Within*. San Francisco: Jossey-Bass.

Quinn, Robert E. (2000). *Change the World: How Ordinary People Can Accomplish Extraordinary Results*. San Francisco: Jossey-Bass.

Quinn, Ryan W., and Robert E. Quinn. (2009). *Lift: Becoming a Positive Force in Any Situation*. San Francisco: Berrett-Koehler.

Rabe, Barry G. (2004). *Statehouse and Greenhouse: The Stealth Politics of American Climate Change Policy*. Washington, DC: Brookings Institution Press.

Radin, Beryl A. (2000). *Beyond Machiavelli: Policy Analysis Comes of Age*. Washington, DC: Georgetown University Press.

Rawls, John. (1971). *A Theory of Justice*. Cambridge, MA: Belknap Press of Harvard University Press.

Reardon, Kathleen Kelley. (2005). *It's All Politics: Winning in a World Where Hard Work and Talent Aren't Enough*. New York: Currency/Doubleday.

Reich, Simon. (2000). "The Four Faces of Institutionalism: Public Policy and a Pluralistic Perspective." *Governance* 13: 501–522.

Reynolds, Paul D. (1979). *Ethical Dilemmas and Social Science Research.* San Francisco: Jossey-Bass.

Rhodes, R. A. W. (2006). "Old Institutionalism." In *The Oxford Handbook of Political Institutions,* ed. R. A. W. Rhodes, Sarah A. Binder, and Bert A. Rockman, chap. 6. New York: Oxford University Press.

Riker, William H. (1986). *The Art of Political Manipulation.* New Haven, CT: Yale University Press.

Rochefort, David A., and Roger W. Cobb. (Eds.) (1994). *The Politics of Problem Definition: Shaping the Policy Agenda.* Lawrence: University Press of Kansas.

Rogers, Everett M. (1995). *Diffusion of Innovations.* 4th ed. New York: Free Press.

Roosa, Stephen A. (2008). *Sustainable Development Handbook.* Lilburn, GA: Fairmont Press.

Rose, Richard. (2005). *Learning from Comparative Public Policy: A Practical Guide.* Oxon, UK: Routledge.

Rosen, Sydney, Jonathon Simon, Jeffrey R. Vincent, William MacLeod, Matthew Fox, and Donald M. Thea. (2003). "AIDS Is Your Business." *Harvard Business Review* 81 (February): 80–87.

Rosen, Sydney, Jeffrey R. Vincent, William MacLeod, Matthew Fox, Donald M. Thea, and Jonathon L. Simon. (2004). "The Cost of HIV/AIDS to Businesses in South Africa." *AIDS* 18: 317–324.

Rosen, Harvey S. (2007). *Public Finance.* 8th ed. New York: McGraw-Hill/Irwin.

Rosenau, Pauline Vaillancourt. (Ed.). (2000). *Public-Private Policy Partnerships.* Cambridge, MA: MIT Press.

Rossi, Peter H., Mark W. Lipsey, and Howard E. Freeman. (2004). *Evaluation: A Systematic Approach.* 7th ed. Thousand Oaks, CA: Sage.

Rowbotham, Sheila. (2010). *Dreamers of a New Day: Women Who Invented the Twentieth Century.* New York: Verso.

Sabatier, Paul A. (1991). "Toward Better Theories of the Policy Process." *PS: Political Science and Politics* 24: 147–156.

Sabatier, Paul A. (1993). "Policy Change and Learning: An Advocacy Coalition Approach." In *Theories of the Policy Process,* ed. Paul. A. Sabatier. Boulder, CO: Westview Press.

Sabatier, Paul A., and Daniel A. Mazmanian. (1981). "The Implementation of Public Policy: A Framework for Analysis." In *Effective Policy Implementation,* ed. Daniel A. Mazmanian and Paul A. Sabatier. Lexington, MA: Lexington Books.

Sample, Steven B. (2002). *The Contrarian's Guide to Leadership.* San Francisco: Jossey-Bass.

Samuelson, Paul A. (1954). "The Pure Theory of Public Expenditures." *Review of Economics and Statistics* 36: 387–389.

Sanders, James R., et al. (1994). *The Program Evaluation Standards.* 2nd ed. Thousand Oaks, CA: Sage.

Sandler, Todd. (1992). *Collective Action: Theory and Applications.* Ann Arbor: University of Michigan Press.

Sandler, Todd. (2004). *Global Collective Action.* New York: Cambridge University Press.

Savas, E. S. (1987). *Privatization: The Key to Better Government.* Chatham, NJ: Chatham House.

Schneider, Anne Larason, and Helen Ingram. (1997). *Policy Design for Democracy.* Lawrence, KS: University Press of Kansas.

Schneider, Mark, Paul Teske, and Melissa Marschall. (2000). *Choosing Schools: Consumer Choice and the Quality of American Schools.* Princeton, NJ: Princeton University Press.

Schön, Donald A., and Martin Rein. (1994). *Frame Reflection: Toward the Resolution of Intractable Policy Controversies.* New York: Basic Books.

Schultz, T. Paul. (2004). "School Subsidies for the Poor: Evaluating the Mexican Progresa Poverty Program." *Journal of Development Economics* 74: 199–250.

Schultze, Charles L. (1977). *The Public Use of Private Interest.* Washington, DC: Brookings Institution.

Scott, W. Richard. (2008). *Institutions and Organizations: Ideas and Interests.* 3rd ed. Los Angeles: Sage.

Self, Peter. (1977). *Econocrats and the Policy Process: The Politics and Philosophy of Cost-Benefit Analysis.* Boulder, CO: Westview Press.

Sen, Amartya. (2001). *Development as Freedom.* New York: Oxford University Press.

Shonkoff, Jack P., and Deborah A. Phillips. (Eds.). (2000). *From Neurons to Neighborhoods: The Science of Early Child Development.* Washington, DC: National Academy Press.

Simon, Herbert A. (1955). "A Behavioral Model of Rational Choice." *Quarterly Journal of Economics* 69: 99–118.

Simon, Herbert A. (1991). "Bounded Rationality and Organizational Learning." *Organization Science* 2 (Special Issue: Organizational Learning: Papers in Honor of (and by) James G. March): 125–134.

Singleton, Sara. (1998). *Constructing Cooperation: The Evolution of Institutions of Co-management in Pacific Northwest Salmon Fisheries.* Ann Arbor: University of Michigan Press.

Smith, Adam. (1776). *An Inquiry into the Nature and Causes of the Wealth of Nations.* London: W. Strahan and T. Cadell.

Smith, James A. (1991). *The Idea Brokers: Think Tanks and the Rise of the New Policy Elite.* New York: Free Press.

Stavins, Robert N. (1997). "Policy Instruments for Climate Change: How Can National Governments Address a Global Problem?" Discussion Papers dp-97–11, Resources for the Future.

Stevens, Joe B. (1993). *The Economics of Collective Choice.* Boulder, CO: Westview Press.

Stiefel, Leanna, Amy Ellen Schwartz, and Ingrid Gould Ellen. (2006). "Disentangling the Racial Test Score Gap: Probing the Evidence in a Large Urban School District." *Journal of Policy Analysis and Management* 26: 7–30.

Stigler, George. (1971). "The Theory of Economic Regulation." *Bell Journal of Economics and Management Science* 2: 3–21.

Stokes, Donald E. (1997). *Pasteur's Quadrant: Basic Science and Technological Innovation.* Washington, DC: Brookings Institution Press.

Stokey, Edith, and Richard Zeckhauser. (1978). *A Primer for Policy Analysis.* New York: W. W. Norton.

Stone, Deborah. (2002). *Policy Paradox: The Art of Political Decision Making.* Rev. ed. New York: W. W. Norton.

Sunstein, Cass R. (2000). "Cognition and Cost-Benefit Analysis." *Journal of Legal Studies* 29: 1059–1103.

Svenson, Ola. (1979). "Process Descriptions of Decision Making." *Organizational Behavior and Human Performance* 23: 86–112.

Tabb, William K. (2004). *Economic Governance in the Age of Globalization.* New York: Columbia University Press.

Teske, Paul, Mark Schneider, Michael Mintrom, and Sam Best (1993.) "Establishing the Micro Foundations of a Macro-Level Theory: Information, Movers, and the Competitive Local Market for Public Goods." *American Political Science Review* 87 (September): 702–713.

Thaler, Richard H., and Cass R. Sunstein. (2008). *Nudge: Improving Decisions about Health, Wealth, and Happiness.* New Haven, CT: Yale University Press.

Tharp, Twyla. (2003). *The Creative Habit: Learn It and Use It for Life.* New York: Simon & Schuster.

The Federalist papers ([1787–1788] 1961) (Authors: Alexander Hamilton, James Madison, John Jay.) With an introduction, table of contents, and index of ideas by Clinton Rossiter. New York: New American Library.

Thelen, Kathleen. (1999). "Historical Institutionalism in Comparative Politics." *Annual Review of Political Science* 2: 369–404.

Tiebout, Charles M. (1956). "A Pure Theory of Local Expenditures." *Journal of Political Economy* 64: 416–424.

Tocqueville, Alexis de. ([1835] 2004). *Democracy in America.* Trans. Arthur Goldhammer. New York: Library of America

True, Jacqui, and Michael Mintrom. (2001). "Transnational Networks and Policy Diffusion: The Case of Gender Mainstreaming." *International Studies Quarterly* 45(1): 27–57.

Tyack, David B. (1974). *The One Best System: A History of American Urban Education.* Cambridge, MA: Harvard University Press.

Tyack, David B., and Larry Cuban. (1995). *Tinkering toward Utopia: A Century of Public School Reform.* Cambridge, MA: Harvard University Press.

Verdier, James M. (1984). "Advising Congressional Decision-Makers: Guidelines for Economists." *Journal of Policy Analysis and Management* 3(3): 421–438.

Volden, Craig. (2006). "States as Policy Laboratories: Emulating Success in the Children's Health Insurance Program." *American Journal of Political Science* 50: 294–312.

Wade, Robert. (1990). *Governing the Market: Economic Theory and the Role of Government in East Asian Industrialization.* Princeton, NJ: Princeton University Press.

Walker, Jack L. (1969). "The Diffusion of Innovations Among the American States." *American Political Science Review* 63: 880–899.

Weichselbaumer, Doris, and Rudolf Winter-Ebmer. (2007). "The Effects of Competition and Equal Treatment Laws on Gender Wage Differentials." *Economic Policy* 22 (April): 235–287.

Weick, Karl E. (1995). *Sensemaking in Organizations.* Thousand Oaks, CA: Sage.

Weimer, David L., and Aidan R. Vining. (2005). *Policy Analysis: Concepts and Practice.* Upper Saddle River, NJ: Pearson Prentice Hall.

Weiss, Carol H. (1980). "Knowledge Creep and Decision Accretion." *Science Communication* 1: 381–404.

Weiss, Carol H. (1992). *Organizations for Policy Analysis: Helping Government Think.* Newbury Park: Sage.

Weiss, Carol H. (1998). *Evaluation.* 2nd ed. Upper Saddle River, NJ: Prentice Hall.

Weiss, Janet A., and Mary Tschirhart. (1994). "Public Information Campaigns as Policy Instruments." *Journal of Policy Analysis and Management* 13: 82–119.

Weiss, Linda. (1998). *The Myth of the Powerless State: Governing the Economy in a Global Era.* Cambridge, UK: Polity Press.

Wildavsky, Aaron. (1979). *Speaking Truth to Power: The Art and Craft of Policy Analysis.* Boston, MA: Little-Brown.

Wildavsky, Aaron. (1992). *The New Politics of the Budgetary Process*. 2nd ed. New York, NY: HarperCollins.

Williamson, John. (Ed.). (1994). *The Political Economy of Policy Reform*. Washington, DC: Institute for International Economics.

Williamson, Marianne. (2004). *The Gift of Change: Spiritual Guidance for Living Your Best Life*. New York: HarperCollins.

Williamson, Oliver E. (1975). *Markets and Hierarchies, Analysis and Antitrust Implications: A Study in the Economics of Internal Organization*. New York: Free Press.

Williamson, Oliver E. (1985). *The Economic Institutions of Capitalism: Firms, Markets, Relational Contracting*. New York: Free Press.

Williamson, Oliver E., and Sidney G. Winter (Eds.). (1991). *The Nature of the Firm: Origins, Evolution, and Development*. New York: Oxford University Press.

Wilson, Edmund. (Ed.). (1945). *The Crack-Up: With Other Uncollected Pieces, Notebooks and Unpublished Letters to Fitzgerald from Gertrude Stein and Essays and Poems*. New York: New Directions.

Wilson, James Q. (Ed.). (1980). *The Politics of Regulation*. New York: Basic Books.

Winston, Clifford. (2006). *Government Failure versus Market Failure*. Washington, DC: AEI-Brookings Joint Center for Regulatory Studies.

Wolf, Charles, Jr. (1979a). "A Theory of Non-market Failures." *Public Interest* 55: 114–133.

Wolf, Charles, Jr. (1979b). "A Theory of Nonmarket Failure: Framework for Implementation Analysis." *Journal of Law and Economics*. 22: 107–139.

Wolf, Charles, Jr. (1988). *Markets and Governments: Choosing between Imperfect Alternatives*. Cambridge, MA: The MIT Press.

Wood, Christopher. (1995). *Environmental Impact Assessment: A Comparative Review*. Burnt Mill, UK: Longman Scientific & Technical.

Index

Page numbers followed by *f* denote figures; those followed by *t* denote tables.

CPSIA information can be obtained at www.ICGtesting.com
Printed in the USA
BVOW08s0142220814

363522BV00006B/7/P

9 780199 730964